MICROCHAKRAS
InnerTuning for Psychological Well-being

Sri Shyamji Bhatnagar
and David Isaacs, Ph.D.

Illustrations by Pieter Weltevrede

Inner Traditions
Rochester, Vermont • Toronto, Canada

Inner Traditions
One Park Street
Rochester, Vermont 05767
www.InnerTraditions.com

InnerTuning® is a registered trademark of Shyamji Bhatnagar

Library of Congress Cataloging-in-Publication Data
Bhatnagar, Sri Shyamji.
    Microchakras : innertuning for psychological well-being / Sri Shyamji Bhatnagar and David Isaacs ; color illustrations by Pieter Weltevrede.
        p. cm.
    Includes bibliographical references and index.
    ISBN 978-1-59477-213-9 (pbk.)
    1. Chakras. 2. Psychology—Miscellanea. I. Isaacs, David, Ph. D. II. Title.
    BF1442.C53B43 2009
    131—dc22

                                                                2009017427

Printed and bound in the United States by P. A. Hutchison Company

10 9 8 7 6 5 4 3 2 1

Text design and layout by Virginia Scott Bowman
This book was typeset in Garamond Premier Pro with Avant Garde Gothic and Gil Sans as display typefaces

Consciousness is, was, and shall ever be.

To the fulfillment of our species.

NOTE TO THE READER
ON THE PRESENTATION OF
SANSKRIT WORDS

This book introduces the InnerTuning method of transliterating Sᵃmskretᵃ (Sanskrit), which utilizes the small capital and superscript fonts of a standard word processor. The advantages and significance of the system are discussed in chapter 1, where a detailed pronunciation guide is also provided. The Sᵃmskretᵃ sounds and words used in this book may also be heard at www.innertuning.com.

Contents

Acknowledgments

The senior author wishes to give special thanks to Alisa Rose for her inspiration and dedication during the writing of this book.

The senior author also wishes to thank Mary Howard and Gale Smith for organizing the original writings of Chakra Psychology and the following for promoting his work in various ways: Yvette Meijer Barbas, Armelle Denolle, Claire Dewerchin, Enrique Gallego, Gary Gewant, Mavis Gewant, Claude Goodman, Kathy Graveraux, George Herrington, Marjorie Holcomb, Tom McManus, Marcia Miller, Elaine Minto, Loré Mitra, John Myers, Kamal Sharma (his sister), Robert Tuschak, Dirk Uittenbogaard, Constantin van Hiel, Barbara Waaben, and Saskia Wiegerinck.

The authors wish to thank Jack Begg for applying his considerable talent to improve the precision and flow of the text.

They also wish to thank Dr. Deepa Awal and Dr. Dev Ketu for their assistance in constructing the Glossary and the following for their helpful suggestions: Nancy Chang, Suhas Joshi, and Barbara Stacy.

For their superb professionalism, the authors extend thanks to Nancy Yeilding, Laura Schlivek, and other members of the editorial staff at Inner Traditions.

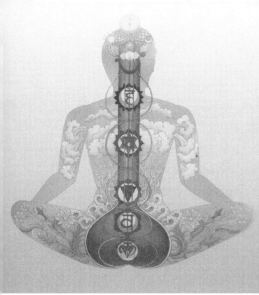

Discovery of the Microchakras

Sri Shyamji Bhatnagar

I was born during the intense heat of the summer of 1936 in northwest India. My entrance into the world was nearly fatal—caused by double pneumonia. Since my father was a prominent eye surgeon who ran his own hospital and was a physician to the royal Sultan of Mardan, he was able to arrange the intensive care necessary for my survival. However, my early years were filled with continuous pain due to my weakened lungs.

Members of my family were followers of Swami Dayananda, who in 1875 had founded the Hindu reform movement known as Arya Samaj. These teachings are a modified form of VAdaant. I learned many mantra-s and practices from the VAd-s at home. My mother was a devotee of Gayatri and we often participated in sacred ceremonies.

My mother was an extraordinary woman in many ways. I remember, for example, a time when she stopped the funeral arrangements for a baby born four months too soon. She held the dying baby in her hand and chanted the powerful Gayatri mantra for five hours while feeding her water. Strength gradually returned to the baby and she opened her eyes. Today, this baby is a mother of three children. I was amazed at the concentration and faith of my mother in spite of the disbelief of all around her.

In 1947, British rule of the subcontinent terminated and a bloody war broke out between India and newly partitioned Pakistan. As my family was Hindu, we could no longer live freely in the new Muslim nation of Pakistan. We became exiles from the land of our ancestors and settled in the bustling Indian city of Dehra Dun, a railroad terminus in the foothills of the Himalayas.

When I was nearly thirteen years old, I took a train with a group of boys to a nearby village, a favorite pastime of ours. We planned to spend a few hours picking lichee nuts in the countryside and afterward to jump on a slowly moving train to return home. The idea held much excitement for us. On this particular trip, however, because I had picked a few extra lichees, I missed the train. The other boys got on the train and laughed at me. I returned to the orchard to wait for the next train.

While eating my lichees, I heard an extraordinary sound. It seemed to be coming from every direction in which I turned, yet I could not determine the source. Then, a few moments later, I noticed something I had not seen before. Seated before me, on a mound of rock, was an extraordinary yogi—in full lotus posture—chanting the sacred syllable AUM. He looked liked someone from another era. Despite his obvious dexterity, he seemed to be well over one hundred years of age, or in some sense ageless.

I walked toward the mound where he was sitting. He had soft glittering eyes and, to my astonishment, called me by my first name. He also told me the name of my father, my father's father, and so on for six generations. He said that I had been his disciple in my previous life and asked me to meet him at a ShEvᵃ temple in Dehra Dun to continue our work.

When I returned home, I asked my father to verify the names of our ancestors. He remembered all but two. He got in touch with my grandfather who remembered one more name. The sixth name remains a mystery.

My guru imparted a rare oral tradition of sacred sounds (naadᵃ yogᵃ) coupled with the science of breath (svᵃrᵃ yogᵃ). This enabled me to chant with microtones. The brilliance and effectiveness of his teachings were transformative, both spiritually and physically. The pain in my chest gradually disappeared. The grace of the guru and the spiritual practices he imparted are the basis for my life's work and teachings.

After I had studied with him for four years, our family moved to another town where I went to college and studied philosophy, comparative religion, and history. In college I met Harish Johari, who was three years my senior. We became best friends and he tutored me in writing poetry and in the study of philosophy. I had the wonderful opportunity of living with him and his family for a full year.

In 1960 I migrated to the United States and eventually became a citizen. Initially I lived in California; it was there I began my work on the relation of sound and consciousness.

In 1966, I returned to India for a year to see my family and friends. Harish introduced me to his teacher, Pandit R. Panday, an Ayurvedic physician with whom we studied together for seven months. Among other things, he taught us mᵃntrᵃ-s used for various medicinal preparations. The three of us decided to create an organization—Satyam, Shivam, Sundaram (Truth, Goodness, and Beauty)—in Bareilly, India. It was dedicated to the purpose of researching the interrelationships of sound, Ayurveda, mᵃntrᵃ, and Western healing modalities. Upon my return from

India, I established a branch of this organization in New York City. In 1970, the name was changed to SRI Centre International.

While still in India, on a pilgrimage with Harish in the high Himalayas, I sat outside a temple to meditate. During this meditation, I had an extraordinary vision of my own chᵃkrᵃ-s. Vortices of light emanated throughout my subtle body and illuminated three channels, which fed into the two hemispheres and the lower portion of my brain. I could see photons of various hues radiating from my hands. I felt euphoric. This experience was a prelude to another dramatic occurrence in January of 1967 in my West Village apartment in New York City.

Sri Shyamji with Harish Johari (right) near Amarnath, Himalayas
(circa 1977)

What took place at that time was a form of automatic writing. For more than five hours I was in an unusual state of awareness and wrote continuously. Then I fell asleep on the writing pad. When I awoke and read what I had written, it was a description of 147 microchakras within the classical seven chªkrª-s. It baffled me. As far as I knew, these subdivisions had never been revealed before. I have spent the rest of my life refining my knowledge of the microchakras and using this knowledge to help others.

Once I became aware of the microchakras, I noticed that whenever I chanted in microtones I could feel their pulsation within me. Apparently the years of chanting had prepared me to receive the knowledge revealed in the automatic writing.

In addition to chanting, I discovered that I could activate the microchakras by playing the tambura. This is an ancient stringed instrument that is usually used in India only for the purpose of assisting vocalists and instrumentalists. I developed a way to use it as a solo instrument.

At the time I discovered the microchakras I was living in a fifth-floor walk-up. My next door neighbor was an elderly lady who suffered from arthritis. I carried her groceries upstairs. One day she told me that she used to lean against the wall between our apartments at times when I was chanting and playing the tambura. She found that the vibrations through the wall relieved the pain of her spinal arthritis.

I invited her into my apartment to sit alongside me while I played and chanted. We did this for many sessions. Then I experimented in order to see if the energy could travel directly through my hands to the affected area of her spine. When I touched her spine, I could transfer most of the sound energy through my hands, which brought her greater relief. She was my first client.

As I worked with others, I realized that people found relief from emotional issues as well. Students who regularly received InnerTuning demonstrated that their sound sensitivity expanded to the skin level. They could feel the vibrations with their entire body. The benefits of the sound were greatly enhanced. Gradually I noticed that their egos were becoming more refined and they started to have higher chªkrª experiences. Their stress levels dramatically reduced. I concluded that I had discovered a system that could help people at the psychospiritual level. I continue to travel throughout the United States and Europe teaching this system. Along the way, I have frequently taught at Esalen and other growth centers as well as at various universities.

Two well-known parapsychologists, Professor Ten Hoff and Professor Henry van Praag, heard a series of five lectures I delivered at the Royal Tropical museum in Amsterdam. Professor van Praag had me teach in his newly founded University of

Lugano. After twelve years of teaching in the department of Chakra Studies, I was awarded a title of Honorary Professor.

Kindred Spirit, a prestigious magazine in London, awarded my *Heart Chakra* CD, which is included inside the back cover of this book, the title of "The Most Inspirational Musical Album of 2001."

Today, many people are interested in exploring the inner world and transforming their awareness. Advanced thinkers in physics are keen to understand the relation between quantum reality and the true nature of Reality. Many physicians and psychologists are interested in the relationship between subtle energies and health. It is my hope that this book will offer a new perspective that will help them to progress toward their goals.

Swami Ātmanandendra Saraswati

I am grateful to all my students who have given me the opportunity to serve them and thereby develop my system. I am also grateful to my family for their patient help to finish this book. A particular thanks is offered to those volunteers who have given their selfless service—making it possible for my organizations to flourish at home and abroad.

I wish to express a special gratitude to Swami Ātmanandendra Saraswati who refined my knowledge of Vᴀdaantᵃ, both through his brilliant discourse and through the purity of his lifestyle.

It is my hope that this book will propel many to engage in the greatest adventure ever—spiritual epiphany and Self-discovery.

The Science of Microchakra Psychology

David Isaacs, Ph.D.

Like Shyamji, I was born in 1936 but on the other side of the world—in Saint John, New Brunswick, Canada. This was in a land of peace and freedom, far from the war that raged in other parts of the globe at that time.

My family enabled me to spend many happy summer seasons along the beautiful Saint John river. It was there that I developed a feeling of deep connection to nature and a predisposition to the fundamentals of Shyamji's teaching.

My academic career began at McGill University in Montreal, where I earned a Bachelor of Arts degree. My introductory psychology professor was D. O. Hebb, whom I later learned had international stature in his profession as a physiological psychologist. He was the first person I had ever met who was a real scientist. He impressed me greatly and I told myself that I wanted to be like him when I grew up. The years at McGill were very happy as I learned from a psychology faculty whom I felt were genuinely dedicated to a search for truth.

In 1959, I graduated from McGill, having decided that I wanted to become a professor of psychology specializing in the topic of thinking. This was just before the "cognitive revolution" of the 1960s in psychology. Behaviorism was still a dominant force in academic psychology. With its emphasis on overt behavior, it had little use for unobservable thoughts, which it wrote off as "sub-vocal" speech. Northwestern University in Illinois had one of the few graduate programs that even mentioned the topic of thinking.

I went to Northwestern and was steeped in what they proudly called "dust bin" psychology (after the 1930s drought in the American Midwest). It was a form of psychology deeply committed to behaviorism and was indeed as dry as dust. In this tradition, I did a Master's degree on a "hot topic" of the time. It was subsequently published in the *Journal of Experimental Psychology* and reprinted in a book of readings by Oxford University Press.

I believe that it was Bertrand Russell who said, "There is nothing more difficult than the effort to believe that which each day becomes more unbelievable." The idea that behaviorism was the way to search for truth in psychology had become unbelievable to me (and to many others as well). I swore to myself that I would not continue for a doctorate unless I could work with someone whose approach I respected.

I decided that the probabilities of meeting such a person would be greater in the New York City area. Accordingly I accepted a teaching position that was available in the psychology department at the University of Bridgeport, Connecticut, which was within commuting distance of Manhattan.

A few years after I began my work at Bridgeport, Jerome L. Singer published his groundbreaking book on daydreaming. I had found my man. He was at the City University of New York at the time and I commuted there to complete a doctorate in their Personality program while continuing to teach at Bridgeport. My doctoral dissertation was on *Daydreaming and Mindwandering.*

After finishing at CUNY, I had the feeling that there was something very important missing from my education and that it concerned music. A few years later, in the spring of 1979, I received an announcement in the mail for a workshop in Manhattan to be conducted by Shyamji on the topic of sound and psychology. I thought that this might be the missing element and decided to go. I was totally amazed by what I learned and experienced at this workshop. Shyamji offered regular classes in Manhattan on Wednesday evenings. There was no doubt that I would attend.

At the initial workshop I met Dr. Harry Brown, a psychiatrist who made a presentation in support of Shyamji's work. Harry and I discovered that we both lived in the same town in Connecticut. For many years thereafter, we commuted together to Shyamji's Wednesday night class. For approximately the first year, on the ride home, I would mutter to Harry, "I don't believe this. Nobody can know these things." We agreed that Shyamji's work was better than anything either of us had encountered in psychology or psychiatry. At one point Harry exclaimed "After Shyamji, nobody will ever fool us again!"

I remained at Bridgeport for twenty-nine years before retiring. During this time, I taught a variety of graduate and undergraduate courses and seminars. These included: History and Systems of Psychology, Personality, Cognitive Processes, Altered States of Consciousness, Statistics, and Computer Applications in Psychology. I programmed a minicomputer (in the days before the laptop computer) and ran several courses from it in order to provide self-paced testing for my own students and those of a few other faculty.

Shyamji's influence upon me, both personally and professionally, has been profound. At the center of this influence is his teaching that a) much is to be discovered by directing our attention inward and b) it is extremely important to balance the activity of our tripartite brain: subcortical brain, right cerebral hemisphere, and left cerebral hemisphere. These are the areas dedicated to intuition, feeling, and reasoning respectively.

In following the methods he has provided, I have acquired a new perspective on myself, on the human species, and on the cosmos itself. This book is intended to help you do the same.

For the past four hundred years, science has been the force that has most influenced change on this planet. Yet science has been hobbled by a willful commitment to a materialistic worldview and one that has claimed to be "value free."

In recent decades this viewpoint has been questioned by many, particularly in light of the discovery in quantum physics that the fundamental nature of the universe is indeterminate. Much of manifestation is dependent upon a human observer acting as cocreator with a Cosmic Intelligence. This Intelligence only reveals itself to those who turn their attention inward and search for it. In order for the human species to evolve, more and more people must feel and intuit the presence of the Cosmic Mind. Reason alone cannot do this.

The subjective science of Microchakra Psychology is offered as a contribution to science in general as it makes a midcourse correction and expands to discover the nonmaterial universe that pervades all. Then science can demonstrate that it is indeed a self-correcting system and play an essential role in moving our species to an age of wisdom and peace.

1

Preparation for the InnerTuning Adventure

AN OVERVIEW OF THE SYSTEM

The theory and practices presented in this book are intended to aid those who wish to actively pursue their personal development as psychospiritual beings. They are also intended to assist the courageous pioneers who wish to expand science beyond the limitations of a purely materialistic view. In this system, the theory is called Microchakra Psychology and the practices, InnerTuning. Working with the theory of Microchakra Psychology helps to select and focus the InnerTuning practices; conversely, working with the practices makes the theory come alive. Both theory and practice are extensions of spiritual traditions emanating from ancient India.

The material part of the universe is explored by directing our attention and senses outward; the nonmaterial (spiritual) part can be investigated by directing them inward. When this is done, with appropriate preparation, many interesting discoveries may be made. Among the reports from the sages of ancient India were:

- ✦ The universe is created from extremely subtle sound.
- ✦ The human body is pervaded by a nonmaterial subtle body. This body has a correspondence with the physical body and influences all of its cells. The subtle body is the locus of feeling.
- ✦ Both the physical body and the subtle body are pervaded and influenced by a causal body. This body is the locus of thought.
- ✦ All human experience proceeds from the casual body through the subtle body to the physical body.
- ✦ In the center of the subtle body, occupying an area much less than the diameter of a hair, lie three major channels that run the length of the spine. The right channel carries solar energy downward from the left hemisphere of the brain to the base of the spine. The left channel carries lunar energy upward

from the base of the spine to the right hemisphere. The central channel is filled with the red energy of fire. It is the fire of desire and carries memories of our unfulfilled desires from all previous lives, human and prehuman.

✦ Radiating from the area of the three channels are seven major chᵃkrᵃ-s (vortices of spinning subtle energy). They vibrate in proximity to distinct segments of the spine, running from its base to the top of the skull. Each influences one or more specific organs of the body. For example, the fourth chᵃkrᵃ influences the heart and the lungs.

✦ Each chᵃkrᵃ may be represented as a lotus flower with a unique number of petals. Each petal is responsive to a distinct sound vibration. In this way the activity of the chᵃkrᵃ may be influenced by sound, mᵃntrᵃ (a sonic release of innate patterns of energy), and suggestion.

Major features of the cosmos, and of the humans within it, are highlighted in chapter 2, and the operation of the channels and chᵃkrᵃ-s is presented in chapter 3.

Microchakra Psychology

As mentioned in his preface, the senior author was able to verify these descriptions of the three bodies through personal experience. Within a year thereafter, he had another experience that revealed to him that each of the classical chᵃkrᵃ-s appeared as a subdivision of every other chᵃkrᵃ. These subdivisions are called microchakras. Each chᵃkrᵃ has seven microchakras in contact with each of the three channels—for a total of twenty-one microchakras. Hence the seven major chᵃkrᵃ-s have a combined total of 147 microchakras. These form the base of Microchakra Psychology, which is detailed in chapters 4 through 9.

Microchakra Notation

Microchakra Psychology uses the following notation to indicate the relation of a microchakra to its chᵃkrᵃ.

chᵃkrᵃ:microchakra

For example, 5:4 refers to the fourth microchakra of the fifth chᵃkrᵃ. If it is also important to emphasize the channel with which the microchakra is associated, the prefixes "L," "R," and "C" are used to indicate the left, right, and central channels respectively. Hence L2:1 indicates the first microchakra of the second chᵃkrᵃ in the left channel.

The chᵃkrᵃ-s are also related to fundamental motivational principles, which are referred to in Sᵃmskretᵃ as lɛŋgᵃ-s. The first three chᵃkrᵃ-s and their microchakras have goals that are directed solely toward basic personal satisfaction. They constitute the first motivational principle. The goals of most people are limited to the first three chᵃkrᵃ-s. The fourth and fifth chᵃkrᵃ-s have goals that include selfless service to others or to a deity as well as to our own unique creativity. Eventually they lead to discovery of an inner spiritual guru. These objectives constitute the second motivational principle. The third motivational principle is based on the sixth and seventh chᵃkrᵃ-s. Its goals are transcendence of the usual human condition and realization of the Self.

The microchakras enable each chᵃkrᵃ to process information from both the internal and external environments in order to meet its goals. Hence each chᵃkrᵃ functions as a mind. It may operate independently or in conjunction with other chᵃkrᵃ minds. As one proceeds from the first to seventh chᵃkrᵃ-s, the energies required to operate the chᵃkrᵃ mind become more subtle and refined.

Each chᵃkrᵃ mind is capable of employing four types of mentation: observation, reasoning, feeling, and intuition. Psychospiritual growth requires the development of all four—in contrast to the overemphasis of reasoning found in many school systems.

Microchakra Psychology places particular emphasis upon the first three years of a girl's life and the first three and a half years of a boy's life. This is the amount of time that it takes for energy to slowly descend within the right channel from the seventh chᵃkrᵃ to the first chᵃkrᵃ. It then establishes in the child a sense of being grounded and connected to the earth plane. Microchakra Psychology terms this period of time the "right-channel age."

During the right-channel age, as the solar energy slowly descends in the right channel, it enhances the connection between the physical body and the corresponding microchakras of the right channel. Good parenting practices will facilitate a connection and contribute to an "opening" to the microchakra. On the other hand, poor parenting practices contribute to a "block." The effect of blocks on the operation of a chᵃkrᵃ mind is negative. They make it more difficult for the chᵃkrᵃ to attain its goals. For example, a parent who habitually ignores or disparages a young child's attempts at drawing or building something contributes to a block in the third microchakra of the third chᵃkrᵃ. This reduces the effectiveness of the third chᵃkrᵃ mind. In contrast, a parent who praises these efforts of the child contributes to an opening and a more effective mind.

In this example, the memory of the disparaging incidents is stored in "apaanic pods" connected to the microchakra. These are toxic memory banks. Memories of the incidents of praise are stored in "praanic pods." These are reservoirs of memory that generate vital or positive energy.

The deleterious effect of blocks and their related apaanic pods that are established in the right-channel age will often last a lifetime. There is no known way to remove them. Their effect may, however, be overcome by developing an opening in the corresponding left-channel microchakra. This often takes considerable effort.

InnerTuning

InnerTuning consists of a variety of practices designed to a) decrease the toxicity of the apaanic pods and permit the chᵃkrᵃ minds to function more clearly, b) alleviate emotional problems based on blocked microchakras, c) integrate the functioning of the causal, subtle, and physical bodies, d) permit the use of higher chᵃkrᵃ-s. These practices—which are described in detail in chapter 10—include:

Purification. Purifications involve fasting combined with the ingestion of bodily cleansers and nutrients. They are designed to remove toxins from all three bodies. They may be done individually or with a group. In the latter case, one benefits from the presence of like-minded caring people when painful emotions are released by the purification process.

Dawn rising. The ancient sages called the 90 minutes before sunrise the "time of the gods." They understood that the most pure energy of the day was available at that time and they availed themselves of it. InnerTuning encourages that meditation commence 24 minutes before sunrise. Synchronization of the breath with the hemispheres of the brain is also encouraged at dawn or at sunset (see chapter 10).

Chanting. Chanting oneself or listening to specific InnerTuning recordings is an important means to energize and balance the chᵃkrᵃ-s.

Silence. The ancient sages appreciated the value of speech fasts. They would remain silent (mownᵃ) for extended periods of time. Today, there are many practical barriers to obtaining long periods of silence. Nevertheless, InnerTuning advises dwelling in silence as much as possible. It is in silence that our attention may penetrate most deeply within and reveal aspects of ourselves we had not suspected. It is in silence that the three bodies have the greatest opportunity for integration.

Devotion. Devotion is the primary means to raise energy from the first motivational principle to the second. Devotion may be directed toward a personal deity (of any faith) or toward a cause that betters humanity and in which we firmly believe.

Observation. The practice of gaining distance from our thoughts, feelings, and bodily sensations is called "observation." It helps us to gain control over them.

Observation (often called "nonattachment") has been used by various spiritual and psychological approaches to human development. InnerTuning also recommends it, as well as a more advanced version associated with the third motivational principle.

THE IMPORTANCE OF THE SᴬMSKRETᴬ (SANSKRIT) LANGUAGE

According to the spiritual tradition of ancient India, basic truths of the universe reverberate subtly, eternally, and everywhere. It is said that in the current epoch, before recorded history, they were first heard by unusually gifted intuitives. The language in which these truths were received was Sᵃmskretᵃ, popularly known as Sanskrit.

Tradition teaches that the sounds of Sᵃmskretᵃ were used to create the universe and all objects within it. The fifty-two sounds of the Sᵃmskretᵃ alphabet encompass most of the sounds found in the major languages of the world since ancient times. The creative potential of Sᵃmskretᵃ is at the root of the mysterious power of mᵃntrᵃ.

In addition to mᵃntrᵃ, the tradition provides a sophisticated Sᵃmskretᵃ vocabulary with which to describe the fundamental laws of the universe and the spiritual nature of human beings. In order to benefit from this wisdom, accumulated over a vast span of time, Microchakra Psychology emphasizes the central importance of a number of Sᵃmskretᵃ terms.

For millennia, Sᵃmskretᵃ was passed from generation to generation through an oral tradition, which employed very strict methods of recitation designed to preserve the purity of the language. It had no associated written script. Eventually it came to be expressed in a number of different scripts. The one most widely used today is DᴀvᵃnaagᵃrEE (commonly spelled Devanagari).

The effect of mᵃntrᵃ-s upon the causal, subtle, and physical bodies is influenced by five factors. The first factor is precision of articulation. Precise articulation stimulates the petals of the lotus associated with each chᵃkrᵃ, thereby maintaining the optimum rotation of the chᵃkrᵃ. Accordingly, every effort is made to teach correct pronunciation.

The second factor is intensity of devotion. Intense devotion while chanting a mᵃntrᵃ may shift attention beyond an egocentric state toward a deity or higher cause.

The third factor is traditional meter. Each mᵃntrᵃ has a prescribed meter.

The fourth factor is melody. Personal creativity of the chanter may add to the efficacy of the mᵃntrᵃ.

The fifth factor is sentiment. Depth of feeling enhances the effect of the mᵃntrᵃ.

These five factors serve to open blocked microchakras through the medium of sooryᵃ *aakaashᵃ* (see page 30).

Systems of Transliteration

Each of the letters of the Sᵃmskretᵃ alphabet (written in the Dᴀvᵃnaagᵃᴛᴇᴇ script) is pronounced in only one way. Hence there is an unambiguous match between the distinct shape of the Sᵃmskretᵃ character and its sound. This is not the case in English, where a given letter of the alphabet may be pronounced in different ways that vary with the context. For example, the letter "i" is pronounced differently in the words "fin," "fine," and "machine." Similarly, the letter "e" is pronounced differently in "be," "bend," and "plaster." Such cases lead to problems when attempting an unambiguous transliteration from Dᴀvᵃnaagᵃᴛᴇᴇ to the Roman script. Several systems have been proposed to handle these difficulties.

The IAST System

The system most widely used in academic circles was developed in 1912 at a meeting of the Congress of Orientalists in Athens. This system, called the IAST (International Alphabet of Sanskrit Transliteration), has been widely used since that time to establish a very large body of important scholarly material. Various criticisms have led to the development of alternative systems such as Harvard-Kyoto and ITRANS. So far, none has met with universal acceptance.

The IAST system has received at least two major criticisms:

1. It uses diacritical marks to indicate pronunciation of some characters. These marks are not available to those who use the standard English keyboard for the Roman script.
2. The use of the letter "a" at the end of many words is misleading. It causes the English reader to fully pronounce the letter rather than to emit only a tiny exhalation, which is the correct pronunciation.

The senior author's criticisms of the IAST are based on his extensive experience in developing sound sensitivity and language awareness. As a young child he learned two distinct dialects of Punjabi and also spoke Pashto and Urdu. Following this, he met his guru and practiced the yoga of sound (naadᵃ yogᵃ) including the oral tradition of mᵃntrᵃ. In subsequent years, he learned to speak Hindi and English, then to read Persian and mᵃntrᵃ-s in Sᵃmskretᵃ. In his opinion, the IAST transliteration reflects insufficient appreciation of the psychospiritual force of precisely articulated Sᵃmskretᵃ based mᵃntrᵃ-s.

Sᵃmskretᵃ and the Petal Sounds. In the Tantric tradition, each chᵃkrᵃ is represented by a lotus flower with petals (the number of petals is different for each chᵃkrᵃ). Each petal is a receiver for a specific sound. Almost all letters of the Sᵃmskretᵃ alphabet provide one specific sound that stimulates one matching petal when it is pronounced. Its effect is greatly enhanced when combined with the nasal sound "m." Hence the sound represented by a Sᵃmskretᵃ character is called a "petal sound."

In order for a petal sound to be effective in providing energy to a chᵃkrᵃ, it must be made with precision and purity. Unfortunately, the various regional dialects of Sᵃmskretᵃ within India have contributed imprecision to the use of the language. Some examples of how pronunciation varies from province to province are: a) "Vedanta" is pronounced "Vedant" in the north and "Vedantaa" in the south; b) "Valmiki," the author of the epic *Ramayana*, is called "Balmiki" in Bengal, where "Va" becomes "Ba," "Vishnu" becomes "Bishnu," and "Vali" becomes "Bali;" c) elsewhere, "sh" may be mispronounced; for example "santoshi" as "santosi." This regionalism has undoubtedly influenced the IAST system and contributed to its inadequacies.

Vocalization Awareness. Proper pronunciation of a Sᵃmskretᵃ consonant requires attention to breath (aspirated or not aspirated), lips (degree and shape of opening), and position of the tongue within the mouth. There are five major positions:

Guttural: Back of tongue raises toward the soft palate.
Palatal: Front of tongue raises to touch the hard palate.
Cerebral: Tip of tongue assumes a retroflex position.
Dental: Tip of tongue placed behind teeth.
Labial: Lips are a) pressed together, b) vibrated, c) opened.

InnerTuning Transliteration

This book employs its own system of transliteration, which is intended to help the English reader develop as precise a pronunciation as possible—even though there are significant obstacles in the path. These include the fact that there are only twenty-six characters in the English alphabet, in contrast to the fifty-two characters of Sᵃmskretᵃ. In order to deal with this discrepancy, InnerTuning uses some special characters, which are formed by using the superscript and small capital options of standard fonts. These special characters and their pronunciations are:

ᵃ (superscript a)—a short exhale breath, one-half the duration of a normal "a."
(There is no equivalent for this in the Dᴀvᵃnaagᵃrᴇᴇ script.)

ᴀ (small capital)—as in "a**te**"

ᴇ (small capital)—as in "**be**"

ᴇᴇ (small capitals)—as in "**bee**"

ɪ (small capital)—as in "h**eight**"

ᴅ (small capital)—as in "**dug**"

ɴ (small capital)—no example in English

sʜ (small capital)—as in "**sharp**"

ᴛ (small capital)—as in "**tea**"

Table 1.1 lists the fifty characters based on the petal sounds and gives examples of English words that contain similar sounds. Necessarily, some of these examples are better than others. All sounds, particularly the "r" sound, will be more accurate if pronounced while half-smiling. Most of the transliterations in this book are from InnerTuning and are based on Table 1.1. However, the IAST system of transliteration has been maintained in quotations that have employed it and in some proper names and book titles that have also used it. The IAST system is listed in column 3 of Table 1.1.

It is suggested that the reader go through Table 1.1 at least once before proceeding. On the first reading of the book, do not be overly concerned about pronunciation. Most Sᵃmskretᵃ words appear in parentheses after the English translation and may be skipped on first reading. Those Sᵃmskretᵃ words that are not in parentheses have no translation or are basic to comprehension of Microchakra Psychology. The important words are repeated a number of times in the text and should gradually be acquired.

A glossary of all Sᵃmskretᵃ words used in the book is found in appendix B. The InnerTuning transliteration of each word is followed by the Dᴀvᵃnaagᵃrᴇᴇ script upon which it is based. The senior author's pronunciation of the words in the glossary and the sounds in Table 1.1 may be heard at www.innertuning.com.

TABLE 1.1. INNERTUNING TRANSLITERATION
AND PRONUNCIATION OF SᴬMSKRETᴬ ALPHABET

English character(s) used in InnerTuning transliteration (in alphabetical order)	English word or word combination containing approximate petal sound	IAST transliteration of Sᵃmskretᵃ character	Sᵃmskretᵃ character	Vowel abbreviation (for combination with other characters)	Type of sound
ᵃ	**a**wry	(a)	अ॒		vowel
a	**a**tone	(a)	अ		vowel
aa	**a**rm	(ā)	आ	ा	vowel
A	**a**te	(e)	ए	े	vowel
ah	**ah**	(ah)	अः	ः	vowel
b	**b**un	(b)	ब		labial
bh	a**bh**or	(bh)	भ		labial
ch	**ch**arm	(c)	च		palatal
chh	Fren**ch h**orn	(chh)	छ		palatal
D	**d**ug	(ḍ)	ड		cerebral
d	**the**	(d)	द		dental
DH	a**dh**ere	(ḍh)	ढ		cerebral
dh	**the h**en	(dh)	ध		dental
E	b**e**	(i)	इ	ि	vowel
EE	b**ee**	(ī)	ई	ी	vowel
g	**g**ut	(g)	ग		guttural
gh	bi**g h**ost	(gh)	घ		guttural
ha	**ha**lt	(ha)	ह		guttural
I	h**ei**ght	(ai)	ऐ	ै	vowel
j	**j**ut	(j)	ज		palatal
jh	he**dge h**og	(jh)	झ		palatal

English character(s) used in InnerTuning transliteration (in alphabetical order)	English word or word combination containing approximate petal sound	IAST transliteration of Sᵃmskretᵃ character	Sᵃmskretᵃ character	Vowel abbreviation (for combination with other characters)	Type of sound
k	lark	(k)	क		gutteral
kh	khaki	(kh)	ख		gutteral
l	large	(l)	ल		dental
lrEE	pull ream	(ḹ)	ॡ		vowel
lri	pull ring	(!)	ऌ		vowel
m	must	(m)	म		labial
n	nut	(n)	न		dental
N	no example	(ṇ)	ण		cerebral
ng	ring	(ṅ)	ंड		gutteral
nj	conjunct	(ñ)	ञ		palatal
o	oat	(o)	ओ	ो	vowel
oo	oodles	(ū)	ऊ	ॆ	vowel
ow	owl	(au)	औ	ौ	vowel
p	pup	(p)	प		labial
ph	put	(ph)	फ		labial
r	run	(r)	र	ॆ	cerebral
re	repeat	(ṛ)	ऋ	ॄ	vowel
rrEE	hurry	(ṝ)	ॠ	ॄ	vowel
s	sun	(s)	स		dental
SH	sharp	(ṣ)	ष		cerebral
sh	sure	(ś)	श		palatal
T	tea	(ṭ)	ट		cerebral

English character(s) used in InnerTuning transliteration (in alphabetical order)	English word or word combination containing approximate petal sound	IAST transliteration of Sᵃmskretᵃ character	Sᵃmskretᵃ character	Vowel abbreviation (for combination with other characters)	Type of sound
t	**t**housand	(t)	त		dental
TH	**t**oy	(ṭh)	ठ		cerebral
th	**th**under	(th)	थ		dental
u	b**oo**k	(u)	उ	ৃ	vowel
ung	s**ung**	(an)	अं	़	vowel
v	**v**ine	(v)	व		labial
y	**y**arn	(y)	य		palatal

Note: The 49 distinct Sᵃmskretᵃ characters listed above (beginning with अ) all represent petal sounds. The fiftieth petal sound is ksa (क्ष, tac**k sh**arp). Two non-petal sounds (tra त्र and gya ज्ञ) complete the 52 character Sᵃmskretᵃ alphabet.

Plurals in Sᵃmskretᵃ are formed according to complex rules. The common scholarly practice of transliterating plurality into English by the symbol "-s" is followed in this book.

THE TRADITIONS OF TᴬNTRᴬ AND VᴅDAANTᴬ

The Laws of the Universe

The ancient way of life taught on the Indian subcontinent for millennia was based on the "eternal laws" (Sᵃnaatanᵃ Dhᵃrmᵃ), which were regarded as laws of the universe. It was thought that appreciation of the laws would enable a person to lead a life in harmony with the universe. No distinction was made between physical and spiritual laws.

In this tradition, there was absolutely no concept or word for "religion" until the idea was introduced by other cultures—Greek, Muslim, French, and British—that invaded the country. These cultures misinterpreted the essential idea of dhᵃrmᵃ as "religion" in order to proselytize their own views of life. Gradually the term "Hinduism" came to refer to the extremely varied spiritual practices of the native inhabitants of the Indian subcontinent. Prior to these invasions there was no "religion" known as Hinduism.

It is in the original spirit of the eternal laws (Sᵃnaatanᵃ Dhᵃrmᵃ) that Microchakra Psychology and InnerTuning are offered as a contribution to an emerging psycho-spiritual science. They draw freely from both modern science and two main traditions of ancient Indian wisdom, Tᵃntrᵃ and VAdaantᵃ.

The scope of these traditions is vast. Microchakra Psychology makes most use of the aspect of the tantric tradition devoted to the principle represented by the god ShEvᵃ (Shaivism) and the Advɪtᵃ, nondual, form of VAdaantᵃ. It also suggests that, ages ago, these might have been just one tradition, Tᵃntrᵃ-Advɪtᵃ, which later diverged. In the balance of this book the term *tradition* alone is sometimes used when no distinction needs to be made between Tᵃntrᵃ and Advɪtᵃ VAdaantᵃ.

The Tantric Tradition

The term tᵃntrᵃ refers to the expansion of awareness, which it accomplishes by a variety of methods. These are chiefly mᵃntrᵃ (sound), yᵃntrᵃ (diagram), and mudraa (gesture or posture). In addition, certain fasts and other procedures designed to cleanse and purify are called tᵃntrᵃ-s. Tᵃntrᵃ also includes a large set of ideas and belief systems designed to facilitate inner exploration and alignment with the subtle energies of the universe.

Chief among the beliefs of Tᵃntrᵃ is the existence of gods (dAvᵃ-s) and goddesses (dAvEE-s). These are patterns of energy that may be invoked to help the functioning of the chᵃkrᵃ-s. For example, the energy that is the god GᵃNAshᵃ may be summoned by chanting an appropriate mᵃntrᵃ. This can strengthen the body-mind patterns with which GᵃNAshᵃ is associated, namely, the first chᵃkrᵃ and first microchakras.

In the Tantric tradition a deity is both a principle and a being. That is, it functions as an abstract idea (mediated by the left hemisphere of the brain) and a felt presence (mediated by the right hemisphere of the brain). Thinking about the deity and feeling its quality of energy may bring a similar energy to a person's own being because both hemispheres are involved.

There is a similarity between this understanding of deities and the concept of "archetypes" proposed by the psychologist Carl Jung. Jung believed that the "collective unconscious" of humankind contained various archetypes or prototypical patterns that could influence individual minds. Examples include the Great Mother and the Cosmic Man. Both the Tantric deities and Jung's archetypes reflect the view that there are enduring nonmaterial patterns of energy and information in the universe that can aid the expansion of the mind.

Microchakra Psychology often uses the term *archetype* to refer to all gods, goddesses, demons, and demonesses. In this way, emphasis is placed on the quality of energy (positive or negative) that these terms represent and not on a variety of other connotations that are more appropriate to a purely religious interpretation.

In the Shaivite aspect of the Tantric tradition, the manifest universe is regarded as having two poles, one dynamic and the other static. The static pole is represented by the god Shɛvᵃ, the male principle. Shᵃktɛ, the female principle is the dynamic pole. It is Shᵃktɛ who creates the universe and is worshipped as the Mother Goddess. Additional information about Shɛvᵃ and Shᵃktɛ will be presented below.

Advɪtᵃ Vᴀdaantᵃ

The original truths heard for millennia by the intuitive sages (rɛsHɛ-s) were eventually written down in sacred books of Sᵃmskretᵃ (Vᴀdᵃ-s). The spiritual teaching of Vᴀdaantᵃ is the "end" or culmination of this tradition. There are several versions of Vᴀdaantᵃ. Of sole concern to Microchakra Psychology is the teaching of the nondual version: Advɪtᵃ Vᴀdaantᵃ. Whenever the term Vᴀdaantᵃ is used by itself in this book, it may be assumed that the reference is to Advɪtᵃ Vᴀdaantᵃ. (Other aspects of Advɪtᵃ Vᴀdaantᵃ are discussed in appendix A.)

The term "nondual" refers to the ancient belief that at the level of absolute reality only one Being exists, as expressed by this quote from one of the ten principal UpᵃnɛsHᵃd-s (commonly spelled "Upanishads"), one of the foundational texts of Advɪtᵃ Vᴀdaantᵃ. The UpᵃnɛsHᵃd-s teach about Consciousness, which they call Sᵃt. The Chaandogyᵃ UpᵃnɛsHᵃd (6.2.1) says:

Before [creation] my dear, this world was just Being (*Sat*), one only, without a second.[1]

This belief is central to Advɪtᵃ Vᴀdaantᵃ and to those nondual forms of Tantric Shaivism that Microchakra Psychology has utilized. It is important to note that the reference is to a living "Being," not to unconscious matter: Consciousness precedes creation. Sᵃt is subtler than the subtlest in nature (prᵃkretɛ) and pervades all. It is the substratum to which the manifest world owes its appearance.

Sᵃt is forever changeless and indivisible—the One without a second. As the witnessing principle in all, Sᵃt provides the unchanging foundation that permits change to be perceived. This principle is frequently referred to as the Witness (saak-sHɛɛ). Both nondual Shaivism as well as Vᴀdaantᵃ teach that Divinity is internal and all-pervading—it is our essence or Self (Aatmaa). This is in contrast to some religious teachings that Divinity is external. Sᵃt is not an object and cannot be apprehended as such. Rather, it is the Cosmic Subject and can be "known" only by cosmic intuition. The Brhᵃdᵃrᵃnyᵃkᵃ UpᵃnɛsHᵃd (3.4.2) states:

You cannot see the seer of seeing, you cannot hear the hearer of hearing, you cannot think the thinker of thinking, you cannot know the knower of knowing. He [It] is your Self, present within All.[2]

The Upᵃnᴇsʜᵃd-s teach that Sᵃt is beyond words and often use the pronoun That (Tᵃt) to point toward the indescribable Sᵃt. "That Thou Art" (Tᵃt tvᵃm asᴇᴇ) is the unique message of the Upᵃnᴇsʜᵃd-s. To be totally in harmony with this truth is to be liberated—a rare occurrence in human history. It is not even possible to approach this truth without transcending the mind. An essential step in this direction is to perceive the difference between the Self and the ego. This advanced and subtle process is called discernment (vᴇchaarᵃ); it is a practice for those working with the third motivational principle.

Advɪtᵃ Vᴀdaantᵃ refers to the absence of discernment as avᴇdyaa, or ignorance. It is the normal state of affairs. The Brhᵃdᵃrᵃnyᵃkᵃ Upᵃnᴇsʜᵃd (2.4.14) says:

For where duality appears to be, there one sees another, there one smells another, there one hears another, there one speaks to another, there one thinks of another, there one knows another. Where, verily, for him everything has become his own Self,

Then whereby would one smell what?

Then whereby would one see what?

Then whereby would one hear what?

Then whereby would one speak to what?

Then whereby would one think of what?

Then whereby would one know what?

By whom all this is known, by what means can he be known? Ah! By what means can (one) know the knower?[3]

When ignorance has sufficiently faded, one refers to the universe as an "apparent" universe and to creation as "apparent" creation.[4]

The Self can never be an object to us; it is Consciousness, the One without a second. Microchakra Psychology teaches that the spiritual journey requires continuous refinement of the ego until it can finally merge with the Self. The journey toward the Self begins by internalizing the senses (prᵃtyaahaarᵃ). This requires special effort as, most of the time, awareness is captured by the five senses (hearing, seeing, smelling, touching, and tasting)—as they play endlessly with the outer world. With some care and instruction, these senses can be redirected inward. Spiritual seekers of diverse traditions have done this throughout the ages.

Consciousness is, was, and shall ever be.
Universes come and go.

Synonyms for Consciousness

Sᵃt	(Truth or Being)
Tᵃt	(That)
Pᵃrᵃmaatmaa	(Supreme Being, Absolute)
Pᵃrᵃmᵃ SHEvᵃ	(Supreme Being, Absolute)
Aatmaa	(Supreme Being within individuals)
Divinity	
Self	
Stasis	

Consciousness and Awareness

Upon the unchanging substratum that is Consciousness, the objective and constantly changing world of nature makes its appearance. This is a world of name (naamᵃ) and form (roopᵃ). The objects in it have no independent existence apart from Consciousness. It is this limitless Consciousness that underlies limited human awareness.

Nondual Consciousness is devoid of the subject and object relationship. The manifestation of the objective world brings a distinction between subject and object. The subject is aware of the object and feels different from it. Hence awareness belongs to the domain of duality.

The authors wish to thank Sri Ātmanandendra Saraswati for drawing our attention to this distinction. They have subsequently learned that the ancient tradition of Saamkhyᵃ also refers to it.[5] The importance of the distinction between Consciousness and awareness cannot be overestimated. Failure to comprehend it accounts for much of the confusion in contemporary discussions of "consciousness."

THE NEED FOR KNOWLEDGE OF THE SELF

"Know Thyself!" urged Socrates and other wise men of ancient India and Greece. Those who have accepted this challenge have never found it easy, regardless of where or when they lived.

The twentieth century has been the bloodiest in human history and there is the distinct possibility that the twenty-first century will exceed it. As a global society now forms, evolution demands that increasingly more people take Socrates' message seriously. To commence to know ourselves, we must recognize one basic fact: Human beings are immortal spirits (jEEvᵃ-s) temporarily encapsulated in both material and nonmaterial fields.

We need to know as much as we possibly can about this mystical relationship. Vast amounts of literature already exist on the subject. It has been developed through the centuries by courageous individual explorers as well as philosophical and esoteric groups. Their teachings, for many different reasons, have not found universal application and acceptance in the same way as established discoveries in the modern sciences. However, as the twenty-first century commences, a major rapprochement has begun between the mystical and scientific traditions.

THE SCIENTIFIC PARADIGM

Modern science began in the sixteenth century with Galileo's systematic study of the movement of the sun, moon, and planets. In the next century, Newton articulated the basic laws of motion, which enabled scientists to predict the trajectory of all bodies, including heavenly ones, with great accuracy. The universe itself was described as a giant machine, like a clock whose gears moved with utmost precision. As science achieved more and more success in the following centuries, the definition of what science itself was (and was not) received considerable attention. A majority position emerged that defined science as the objective search for the laws of nature. This objectivity placed the scientist at a respectful distance from the objects studied. Viewpoints that were tainted by subjectivity (such as metaphysics, religion, and vitalism) were deemed irrelevant to the scientific enterprise. Science, which had originally been a pursuit for the truth about nature, became a pursuit for the truth about matter, which became the only reality. Science became materialistic science.

Most scientists were content with this emphasis on materialism until the early twentieth century and the rise of quantum physics. Classical physics had studied the world of large objects down to the level of the atom. It assumed that atoms were the building blocks from which the natural world was constructed. Quantum physics continued the investigation of nature at the subatomic level, beginning with the electron. What was discovered was startling and is still not fully understood. However, there was no doubt that the laws of classical physics did not apply at the quantum level. In a sense, matter disappeared. Among other things, quantum physics discovered that:

1. Electrons, under some measuring conditions, showed the characteristics of a wave; under other measuring conditions, the electron appeared to be a par-

ticle. This phenomenon is called wave/particle duality. The solid building block changed to an ambiguous entity.

2. The ambiguity is resolved only when an observer measures with the intention of finding a wave or finding a particle. Human intention determines the experimental outcome. This places subjectivity at the heart of experimental science, at least at the very minute level.

3. Nonlocality is a fundamental fact of the universe. The assumption of locality states:

. . . a measurement at one point in space cannot influence what occurs at another point in space if the distance between the points is large enough so that no signal can travel between them at light speed in the time allowed for measurement. . . . Quantum physics, however, allows for what Einstein disparagingly termed "spooky actions at a distance." When particles originate under certain conditions, quantum theory predicts that a measurement of one particle will correlate with the state of another particle even if the distance between particles is millions of light years. And the theory also indicates that even though no signal can travel faster than light, the correlations will travel instantaneously, or in "no time."[6]

Experimental evidence confirms that "spooky actions at a distance" do occur and that the universe is fundamentally nonlocal.

The above findings have moved some physicists to a newfound interest in the topic of consciousness. For example:

Quite apart from the issue of whether consciousness needs quantum theory, there are good reasons for believing that quantum theory needs consciousness. Hence any hope of being able to explain consciousness in terms of physics is likely to be frustrated by the fact that we cannot understand physics without consciousness.[7]

Contemplation of the implications of quantum theory has led a number of scientists, beginning with David Bohm, to advocate a holonomic model of the universe. In the holonomic model, each part of the universe contains the whole universe within it. This is in contrast to the view of classical physics that the universe consists of discrete and interacting parts.

The neuropsychologist Karl Pribram provides data to show that neuronal firing in the brain occurs in a manner compatible with quantum mechanics. In agreement with Bohm, he suggests that we have a quantum brain interpreting a quantum universe.

These developments and others have contributed to the call for a new definition of science that includes the subjective, such as in R. G. Jahn and B. J. Dunne[8] and B. A. Wallace.[9] Microchakra Psychology and InnerTuning are offered as a contribution to this new science, with specifics given in chapter 11.

Knowing and Feeling the Same Hologram

The holonomic interpretation of the universe reminds us of the immense interrelatedness among all that exists. Francis Thompson, a nineteenth-century poet, expressed this intuition in his famous lines from *The Mistress of Vision:*

> That thou canst not stir a flower
> Without the trembling of a star

InnerTuning suggests that the universe vibrates as "one song" that whispers of the same vitality in all existence.

2
The Cosmic Play

Microchakra Psychology is based upon a specific cosmology derived from classical sources, which we call the "LEElaa model." Unlike current scientific cosmologies that pertain solely to the physical field, the LEElaa model demands that we use not only our reason but also our feelings and intuition in order to comprehend its significance.

THE THREE FIELDS
AND THE THREE BODIES

Tᵃntrᵃ describes the universe as composed of three fields of energy. In addition to the material physical field (sthoolᵃ shᵃrEErᵃ), there are two nonmaterial fields. The first field beyond the material field is called the subtle field (sookshmᵃ shᵃrEErᵃ). It operates at a faster vibratory rate than does the physical field and completely pervades it. The second nonmaterial field is called the causal field (kaarᵃNᵃ sharEErᵃ). It vibrates even faster than the subtle field and pervades both the subtle and physical field. The existence of these three fields is a basic assumption of Microchakra Psychology and InnerTuning.

Before anything manifests in the physical field, it first appears in the causal field and then in the subtle field. The planets, stars, and other heavenly bodies that we see in the sky have their counterparts in both nonmaterial fields. Similarly, the human body has a causal body and a subtle body (see plate 1).

The causal field is the locus of cosmic wisdom. This wisdom is called Mᵃhᵃt—a contraction of Mᵃhaa tᵃtvᵃ (the Great Principle, the primal aspect of ShᵃktE). Mᵃhᵃt is the Cosmic Intelligence of the cosmos and the source of its design. The causal field is also the source of the personal causal body with its thoughts (vrettE) and intentions.

Within the subtle field is the subtle body, which consists of a network of information pathways and the vortices of spinning energy called chᵃkrᵃ-s. Feelings are formed in the subtle body.

The physical body belongs to the physical field where instincts, sensations, and emotions are experienced. The thoughts and feelings that originate in the subtler fields are enacted here.

The following chapters will present numerous details regarding the functioning of the three bodies as vehicles for psychospiritual growth.

THE COSMIC CYCLES

The Tantric and Vedic traditions teach that the universe is created and dissolved again and again in endless cycles and subcycles. The largest cycles last billions of years. In an interview regarding his documentary *Cosmos* the astronomer Carl Sagan discussed this time scale:

> But the main reason that we oriented this episode of *Cosmos* toward India is because of that wonderful aspect of Hindu cosmology which first of all gives a time-scale for the Earth and the universe—a time-scale which is consonant with that of modern scientific cosmology. We know that the Earth is about 4.6 billion years old, and the cosmos, or at least its present incarnation, is something like 10 or 20 billion years old. The Hindu tradition has a day and night of Brahma in this range, somewhere in the region of 8.4 billion years.
>
> As far as I know, it is the only ancient religious tradition on the Earth which talks about the right time-scale. We want to get across the concept of the right time-scale and to show that it is not unnatural. In the West, people have the sense that what is natural is for the universe to be a few thousand years old, and that billions is indwelling [an article of faith only], and no one can understand it. The Hindu concept is very clear. Here is a great world culture which has always talked about billions of years.
>
> Finally, the many billion year time-scale of Hindu cosmology is not the entire history of the universe, but just the day and night of Brahma and there is the idea of an infinite cycle of births and deaths and an infinite number of universes, each with its own gods.
>
> And this is a very grand idea. Whether it is true or not, is not yet clear. But it makes the pulse quicken . . .[1]

The subcycle of most relevance consists of four ages (yuga-s). These are Satya yuga (1,728,000 years), Trataa yuga (1,296,000 years), Dvaapr yuga (864,000 years), and Kale yuga (432,000 years). The four ages have different properties, particularly varying manifestations of satva, the universal quality of light, purity, or truth, and of dharma, or the principle of duty. In Satya yuga, tendencies toward satva dominate and people are aware that essentially they are divine. The bull of dhᵃrmᵃ (sense of duty) stands on all four feet. Most people have a strong intuition regarding dhᵃrmᵃ. In succeeding yugᵃ-s fewer people are able to use sᵃtvᵃ and awareness of Divinity devolves. In TrAtaa yugᵃ the bull of dhᵃrmᵃ stands on three feet, meaning that approximately 75 percent of the people still have a strong sense of dhᵃrmᵃ. In Dvaaprᵃ yugᵃ, the bull of dhᵃrmᵃ stands on two feet; only 50 percent of the people respond to dhᵃrmᵃ. In Kᵃlᴇ yugᵃ, the use of sᵃtvᵃ reaches its lowest point. The word kᵃlᴇ means "dark" and in darkness human life is filled with suffering (dukhᵃ) and conflict. The bull of dhᵃrmᵃ stands on one foot only. Three-quarters of the population is confused and lacks a sense of moral direction. The remaining 25 percent struggle to uphold dhᵃrmᵃ and enliven the seeds of the Sᵃtyᵃ yugᵃ of the next cycle. It is commonly believed that we have been in Kᵃlᴇ yugᵃ since 3,102 B.C.E.[2]

Lᴇᴇ LAA: A MODEL OF THE PLAY OF
COSMIC INTELLIGENCE

In his discussion of time scale noted above, Sagan observed that the teachings of ancient India require us to stretch our concept of "time;" similarly, the Lᴇᴇlaa model requires us to stretch our concept of "mind" in a manner that some will regard as incredible. For many, it will require reversing long held habits of thought, including the belief that the universe is fundamentally matter and that consciousness somehow emerges from it.

In the traditions of both VAdaantᵃ and Tᵃntrᵃ the universe is not born of matter but of mind. In verse 10:6 of the Bhᵃgvat GEEtaa (commonly spelled Bhagavad Gita), Sri Krishna as representative of Consciousness states that all creatures are born of his mind. Likewise, the Tantric tradition teaches:

> *As it is here, so it is there.*
> *Yᵃthaa PᴇndA Tᵃthaa BrᵃhmaandA*
> (transliteration of Sᵃmskretᵃ original)

From this teaching, it follows that the human mind is a reflection of the Divine mind. Such an understanding seems to be in agreement with both the holonomic theory of the universe and the Biblical view that God created man in his own image (Genesis 1:27). Objective science has specifically rejected this view—calling it "anthropomorphism." Tᵃntrᵃ, on the other hand, makes extensive use of this relationship. Observation of the human mind is assumed to provide a path toward understanding of the greater cosmic mind: the human capacity for play is a reflection of a universal capacity.

According to Tᵃntrᵃ the universe is a play (lᴇᴇlaa) emerging from the Cosmic Potentiality (Mᵃhaakuɴdᵃlᴇɴᴇᴇ), which lies beyond spacetime. During the quiescent periods of the vast cosmic cycles of time, Cosmic Potentiality is in union with Stasis (Pᵃrᵃmᵃ Shᴇvᵃ); the entire ego of the universe is in a state of surrender, submerged in a black hole.* Quiescence terminates when Cosmic Potentiality (Mᵃhaakuɴdᵃlᴇɴᴇᴇ) wills to manifest more of her endless unfulfilled potential and thereby experience more of her own autonomy. In order to do this she must leave her embrace with Stasis (Pᵃrᵃmᵃ Shᴇvᵃ). As Vibrancy (Shᵃktᴇ), she moves as far away as possible from Stasis (Pᵃrᵃmᵃ Shᴇvᵃ). Once at the farthest distance, expressed in matter as hard as diamond, she turns and ascends back to Stasis (Pᵃrᵃmᵃ Shᴇvᵃ). This pattern of departure from Stasis and return to it is acted out on both the cosmic and personal levels. The design of the play originates outside spacetime, but the play itself occurs within spacetime. At the cosmic level, stars are born and stars are dissolved; universes are born and universes are dissolved. At the human level, Vibrancy (Shᵃktᴇ) establishes a game of hide and seek, so that all mortals may also participate in the play.

The perception of life as a play is transcultural:

> *All the world's a stage*
> *And all the men and women merely players:*
> *They have their exits, and their entrances;*
> Sʜᴀᴋᴇsᴘᴇᴀʀᴇ, *As You Like It,* Aᴄᴛ II, Sᴄᴇɴᴇ VII

Every entity that evolves across countless cycles of birth, death, and rebirth (samsaarᵃ-s) is termed a jᴇᴇvᵃ. The ultimate goal of the jᴇᴇvᵃ is to gain liberation (mokshᵃ) from these cycles and return to the source of all—the Self (Aatmaa). This is possible only through a human body. Until the mind of each of the seven chᵃkrᵃ-s attains contentment, it is mandatory for the jᴇᴇvᵃ to be reborn and to continue the play for another act. The cycle of birth, death, and rebirth continues until awareness finally identifies with Consciousness (Tᵃt) and the jᴇᴇvᵃ is liberated from the play. Awareness of the inevitability of this cycle may help to overcome the fear of death.

Consciousness is ever present, infinite, and eternal; it is the reality that every form, animate or inanimate, must eventually realize. Human birth is a rare opportunity to not only understand the principles of creation but also practice some time-tested techniques to bring our awareness through the seven chᵃkrᵃ minds to the

---

*The capacity of a black hole to annihilate the material world was foreshadowed in the tradition by the destructive power of Rudrᵃ Shᴇvᵃ, discussed in chapter 3.

ultimate unity with the Self (adhyaatmᵃ yogᵃ—the unity discussed in the Bhᵃgvat GEEtaa). If we treat life as anything more or anything less than a cosmic play, we set ourselves up for great suffering.

The principle that the microcosm reflects the macrocosm has been most extensively applied in the Shaivite model of the universe known as the thirty-six tᵃtvᵃ-s. This term is derived from the word Tᵃt, which means "that." The tᵃtvᵃ-s are "that which is." In most instances, they may be thought of as principles whereby the universe functions. The thirty-six tᵃtvᵃ model was built on an earlier twenty-four tᵃtvᵃ model developed by the ancient system of Saamkhyᵃ. It describes a universe that is fundamentally subjective. The model, in turn, shows how such a subjective universe can generate an objective one. The Shaivite literature contains several variations of the basic model.

The LEElaa model presented here is a hybrid model. Among other things, it replaces some of the usual thirty-six tᵃtvᵃ-s with a description of the classical stages of sound. These are static sound, luminous sound, illuminated sound, and audible sound. The LEElaa model has only one purpose—to help people understand and play their role in the cosmic game. Most components of the model were developed by ancient sages and have been used for countless centuries by those who wished to participate in the game with enhanced awareness of its chief features. It forms a background against which the activities of the chᵃkrᵃ-s and microchakras are viewed. It takes place in seven phases.

Phase 1: A Cycle of Manifestation Emerges from a Cycle of Rest

Before a cycle of manifestation commences, Cosmic Potentiality (MᵃhaakuNdᵃlEnEE) is in the total embrace of Stasis (Pᵃrᵃmᵃ ShEvᵃ)—Consciousness. They are one and infinite. Latent within Cosmic Potentiality (MᵃhaakuNdᵃlEnEE) are the following:

- ✦ An awareness of its omniscience, omnipotence, and omnipresence
- ✦ A desire to separate from Stasis in order to manifest its potential and experience its autonomy
- ✦ Impressions stored from its last separation
- ✦ An awareness of the three fields in which its autonomy will be played out

Static Sound (Pᵃraa)

In the initial phase of manifestation, sound has no vibration. It is static (unstruck) sound, the pᵃraa (beyond) state of sound. Cosmic Potentiality (MᵃhaakuNdᵃlEnEE) is coiled with fifty coils around an infinitesimal point (bEndu), which represents Consciousness or Stasis. The fifty coils are the silent version of the fifty sounds represented in Table 1.1; they are the building blocks of the universe in seed form.

In the process of creation Cosmic Potentiality uncoils, and each uncoiling activates a silent sound. The first sixteen silent sounds are tools for the energy of cognition (gyaanᵃ shᵃktE), the next sixteen are used by the energy of will (EchhaÆ shᵃktE), and the following sixteen belong to the energy of action (kreyaa shᵃktE). Two additional sounds are left, which activate the final blueprint of creation.

Cosmic Potentiality (MᵃhaakuNdᵃlEnEE) realizes "I have the ability to create, to preserve and to transform." It then makes the decision to manifest. Initially, the thought of separation from Stasis is very subtle and discreet. It starts with a faint stir, which is called prᵃNᵃvᵃ. PrᵃNᵃvᵃ is the silent (unstruck) sound frequency of the movement of Cosmic Potentiality (MᵃhaakuNdᵃlEnEE) as it starts to disengage from the embrace of Stasis. This disengagement is the origin of luminous sound.

Luminous Sound (PᵃshyᵃntE)

In the next stage, silent sound creates light (prᵃkaashᵃ) and illumines itself. In this light, Cosmic Potentiality (MᵃhaakuNdᵃlEnEE) focuses upon itself and its infinite possibilities. As the Great Principle (Mᵃhaa tᵃtvᵃ) or Cosmic Intelligence, it designs the manifestation that is to unfold in spacetime.

Illuminated Sound (Mᵃdhyᵃmaa)

Luminous sound condenses to form illuminated sound. It is slightly audible—very soft and less than a whisper. At this point, Cosmic Potentiality (MᵃhaakuNdᵃlEnEE) has manifested in the subtle field. It then commences to generate audible sound.

Audible Sound (VIkhᵃrEE)

About to experience her true form, Cosmic Potentiality (MᵃhaakuNdᵃlEnEE) changes to the Great Vibrancy (MᵃhaashᵃktE) who separates from Stasis with a series of cosmic blasts (vEsphoTᵃ).

At this point the four stages of sound have emerged. Pratyāgātmānanda includes the following passage in his discussion of the sonic basis of the universe as it progresses from static sound to audible sound:

> In this view of sound, the whole universe is luminous, and it has degrees of luminos-
> ity. . . . Modern physics gives the hint how sound produces light by a small experi-
> ment. If a glass rod is made to vibrate vigorously at ultra-sonic frequencies and then
> is held between the finger and the thumb, it burns the skin. The reason is that sound
> is producing fire and light. This, again, is not the whole story of the creation of the
> universe by sound. As the sound concentrates and condenses, it creates geometric
> figures. This explains not only the origin of dimensions, curves, figures, shapes, and

sizes, but also the fact that as the process of condensation goes on, sound produces solid, liquid, and gas. The straight lines of visionary sound (*paśyantī*) create atmosphere and the climate. The illuminated sound of middle stage (*madhyamā*) produces in its train, liquid that can adapt its size and shape to any container. Finally disintegrated (*vaikharī*) sound produces the solid with all its curves, cubes upon cubes, parallelograms and endless concentric circles. In other words, all matter, whether solid, liquid or gaseous, is the result of coagulation of sound. As blood coagulates whenever it becomes manifest on the surface outside its inner container, so does sound coagulate into matter whenever it comes out of its earlier stages of *parā, paśyantī,* and *madhyamā*. The paradox therefore is that the quality of sound is silence. In silence it is omnipotent, omniscient, and omnipresent. It is in that view the universe is conceived in sound. It is born in sound. It grows and lives in sound. The universe is the result of an idea. Every idea is the result of a sound. As no creation of any kind is possible without an idea behind it, so every creation is the result of a non-vibratory sound or the "sphota", the unseen, the unheard, and uncognised focal or foetal tension. Sound creates air, atmosphere, and climate, and then only it reaches the stage of vibration. When it reaches the stage of vibration, sound creates light. Light is nothing but sound of a particular frequency. Every vibratory sound has a shape and a size. According to the density of the sound, the shape is either solid, liquid, or gas. The three dimensions that the biological senses apprehend are not the only dimensions. There are many other dimensions.[3]

Phase II: The Primary Principle to Govern the Universe Is Established

The Great Vibrancy (Mᵃhaashᵃktᴇ) establishes the primary principle (tᵃtvᵃ) that will govern the universe *within* spacetime. It is the principle of Vibrancy (Shᵃktᴇ tᵃtvᵃ). As a deity, this principle is worshipped as the Mother Goddess who appears in many forms.

Vibrancy is also called the goddess of speech (Vaagᵃdᴀᴠᴇᴇ). All manifestation is the result of sound as it travels through the four levels from static to audible. Vibrancy's creation through the sound of speech (vaak) is comparable to the use of the Word in the Biblical account of creation. Vibrancy expresses her powers of knowledge, will, and action through the petal sounds of the chᵃkrᵃ-s.

Even though Vibrancy has separated from Stasis, she still carries its essence within her. Vibrancy manifests this essence as the principle of Stillness (Shᴇᴠᵃ tᵃtvᵃ). When worshipped as a deity, this principle is called "Lord Shᴇᴠᵃ"—the consort of the Mother Goddess.

Any time we attempt to meditate we are trying to locate the Shᴇᴠᵃ tᵃtvᵃ within ourselves—the point of Stillness, the axle upon which Vibrancy rotates.

Phase III: The Tripartite Principles Are Established

Vibrancy (Sh^aktE) establishes the three principles that will govern the manifest universe, thereby making patent the potency within her.

+ The principle of transformation-dissolution—associated with her omniscience and ruled by MahAshvar^a
+ The principle of preservation—associated with her omnipresence and ruled by VESHNu
+ The principle of creation—associated with her omnipotence and ruled by Br^ahmaa

Br^ahmaa is reflected in the fact of ongoing and continuous creation. The creations of Br^ahmaa are preserved by VESHNu.

Phase IV: Vibrancy Establishes the Principles of Limitation

Principle of Concealment (Maayaa T^atv^a)

In order for the cosmic game to proceed, the essential truth that we are Consciousness has to be hidden from us. This is the task of the general principle of concealment or illusion (Maayaa t^atv^a), which employs the following five specific principles (t^atv^a-s) of limitation (p^anch^a k^anchuka-s) to create the illusion. The same Vibrancy (Sh^aktE) who created Stillness (ShEv^a) now conceals him.

Principle of Time (Kaal^a T^atv^a)

The immortality of Consciousness is limited by the principle of time (kaal^a), which produces mortal time-bound creatures. Our concept of mortality stops us from realizing that which is behind all mortals. We need to transcend time in order to reveal the Consciousness that we already are.

Principle of Partition (K^alaa T^atv^a)

The omnipresence of Consciousness is limited by partition or division (k^alaa), which produces objects and beings that appear separate from each other.

The principle of partition is a very clever aesthetic aspect of Vibrancy. It disguises or veils the infinite reality behind its forms. It is the division (k^alaa)— the art and the variety in nature—which we see. These include the beauty of the flowers, the patterns of the clouds, the ripples in the water and the glory of the sunrise. Nature uses horrifying varieties as well, such as lightning, tornadoes, and earthquakes. All these different divisions of nature (k^alaa-s) hide the reality of the nondual Consciousness behind all creation.

Principle of Blemished Knowledge (Vɛdyaa Tᵃtvᵃ)

The omniscience of Consciousness is limited by imperfect or blemished knowledge (vɛdyaa), which arises either as thoughts in the left hemisphere or as feelings in the right hemisphere.

The left hemisphere may develop a network of useful conceptual knowledge and may solve many practical problems. This very success can be an obstacle to be overcome on the return to Consciousness. It is popularly said that we have to go out of our minds to realize who we really are. This means that blemished knowledge, like the other limitations, must be transcended on the path to Self-discovery. To do so requires considerable skill. The rational mind must be used as an aid to go out of the rational mind. This is a particular challenge for those scientists who pride themselves on their empirically based rationality.

On the other hand, the feelings of those who are dominated by the right hemisphere may be less inhibiting but still provide significant barriers to transcendence.

Principle of Attachment (Raagᵃ Tᵃtvᵃ)

The bliss of Consciousness is limited by interest, desire, and pleasure. Pleasure is a state that arises when a mind momentarily rests in the union with an object of desire.

Many of life's activities are engaged in purely for the pleasure they provide. We become attached to these activities and engage in them repeatedly. By providing this small measure of bliss, the principle of attachment exerts control over us. Transcendence of this attachment is required to discover that our essential nature is bliss without limit.

Principle of Cause and Effect (Nɛyᵃtɛ Tᵃtvᵃ)

The omnipotence of Consciousness is limited by karmic laws of cause and effect (nɛyᵃtɛ). Kᵃrmᵃ is the strategy that Vibrancy uses to keep us involved in time—through a chain of action and reaction. The creation of good kᵃrmᵃ and bad kᵃrmᵃ ties us to a cycle of birth—death—rebirth (sᵃmsaarᵃ). Rebirth occurs to enable us to pay for bad deeds or to be rewarded for good ones. In this way, we are kept part of the tapestry of creation continuously woven by the Mother Goddess. In some lifetime or another, everyone must come to understand this game and seek to return to Consciousness. This will happen either through the help of an outer guru or our own intuitive inner guru located in the sixth microchakra of the fifth chᵃkrᵃ. This awareness will help us to direct our energies upward toward the higher chᵃkrᵃ-s and to eventually gain liberation from the cycle of successive lives. As a step in this process, we learn to create neutral karmᵃ and thwart the strategy that binds us to rebirth. Neutral karmᵃ is free from the desire for reward.

Phase V: Vibrancy Establishes the Players in the Game

Principle of Free Will (Purushᵃ Tᵃtvᵃ)

The spirit of free will (purushᵃ tᵃtvᵃ) is "I," the immortal subject. This is the awareness that Self is distinct from Nature (prᵃkretᴇ) including ego. Many people have yet to attain the epiphany of free will as it is concealed by the five limitations (pᵃnchᵃ kᵃnchuka-s).

Principle of Nature (Prᵃkretᴇ Tᵃtvᵃ)

At this point, the limitations imposed by the principle of concealment (maayaa tᵃtvᵃ) and the five principles of limitation (pᵃnchᵃ kᵃnchuka-s) have divided each being into two parts: free spirit (purushᵃ tᵃtvᵃ) and empirical nature (prᵃkretᴇ tᵃtvᵃ). Prᵃkretᴇ tᵃtvᵃ attempts to hold us in its grip, while purushᵃ tᵃtvᵃ draws us upward toward transcendence of prᵃkretᴇ.

Phase VI: Vibrancy Creates an Individual with a Psychic Organ (antahᵃkᵃrᵃnᵃ)

The psychic organ has four main aspects: ego (ahᵃmkaarᵃ tᵃtvᵃ), intelligence (buddhᴇ tᵃtvᵃ), sensory mind (mᵃnᵃsᵃ tᵃtvᵃ), and awareness (chᴇttᵃ tᵃtvᵃ).

Principle of Ego (Ahᵃmkaarᵃ Tᵃtvᵃ)

Ahᵃmkaarᵃ is a sense of personal identity or ego. The term is derived from ahᵃm = "I am" + kaarᵃ = "repetition." The ego is constructed through repetition. Hence it is convenient to think of ahᵃmkaarᵃ as the "Me-maker." Ahᵃmkaarᵃ begins with neutral energy that has no identity of its own and creates a meaningful personal identity by attaching to various objects (such as the body), feelings, and thoughts that are our most cherished possessions. These attachments constitute the "Me." There is only one "I," the eternal indivisible Self.

Principle of Intelligence (Buddhᴇ Tᵃtvᵃ)

Buddhᴇ (intelligence) is the process of evaluating information and making decisions. Buddhᴇ may be perceived as having different degrees of discernment. When buddhᴇ operates wisely it is called su buddhᴇ (beautiful buddhᴇ). Its opposite is ku buddhᴇ (ugly buddhᴇ). Su buddhᴇ bestows decisions that are in keeping with dhᵃrmᵃ; the decisions of ku buddhᴇ tend to go against dhᵃrmᵃ.

Principle of Sensory Mind (Mᵃnᵃsᵃ Tᵃtvᵃ)

Mᵃnᵃsᵃ (sensory mind) is the most basic level of mental functioning. It organizes the data coming from the five senses into meaningful perceptions. The significance of these perceptions is determined by ah^{a}mkaar^a and buddh$\text{E}$. M^{a}n^{a}s^a may also be thought of as a locus of desires.

Principle of Awareness (ChEtt^a T^{a}tv^a)

ChEtt^a refers to the screen of awareness upon which our experiences appear and thought waves ripple. It also refers to memory.

Phase VII: The Sensory-Motor System and the Elements Are Established

Vibrancy, working in the subtle field, next creates each of the five subtle sense organs (gyaan$\text{A}$ndr$\text{E}$y^a) and organs of action (k^{a}rm$\text{A}$ndr$\text{E}$y^a), in association with the first five ch^{a}kr^a-s.

TABLE 2.1. THE SUBTLE ORGANS

Ch^{a}kr^a	Sense Organ	Action/Organ
5	Auditory	Speech/Mouth
4	Tactile	Grasping/Hands
3	Visual	Moving/Feet
2	Gustatory	Procreation/Genitals
1	Olfactory	Defecation/Anus

The sense organs of the subtle field, in turn, generate corresponding subtle sensations (t^{a}nmaatraa-s), which are precursors of the gross elements. These stages are detailed in Table 2.2.

TABLE 2.2. THE PRECURSORS
AND CONSTITUENTS OF THE ELEMENTS

Subtle Organ	Subtle Sensation (t^{a}nmaatraa)	Gross Element	Constituents of Gross Element
Auditory	Sound	*aakaash^a*	*aakaash^a*
Tactile	Touch	*air*	½ *air* + ½ *aakaash^a*
Visual	Form	*fire*	½ *fire* + ¼ *air* + ¼ *aakaash^a*
Gustatory	Taste	*water*	½ *water* + ⅙ *fire* + ⅙ *air* + ⅙ *aakaash^a*
Olfactory	Smell	*earth*	½ *earth* + ⅛ *water* + ⅛ *fire* + ⅛ *air* + ⅛ *aakaash^a*

The five elements are *aakaash*, *air* (vaayu), *fire* (agnE), *water* (aapah), and *earth* (prethvEE). The Sᵃmskretᵃ word is used for the first element, *aakaash*, since no satisfactory translation has been found. The common translations of "space" or "ether" are both inadequate. The term *elements* in this context has a very different meaning from the use of the term in modern chemistry. Whereas the elements in chemistry are units of physical analysis only, the elements of this model permeate or pervade all three fields: causal, subtle, and physical. On the causal plane, they contribute to the archetypes of the universe; on the subtle plane they are the basis for feeling and qualitative experience (anubhᵃvᵃ); on the physical plane they influence sensation and molecular activity.

The five permeating elements are called tᵃtvᵃ-s. (Note that this meaning of tᵃtvᵃ differs from the meaning, "principle," that was given above. Context determines which meaning is implied.) The elements, tᵃtvᵃ-s, are representatives of Tᵃt in the manifest world. In order to emphasize their difference from modern chemistry's Periodic Table of Elements (e.g., helium, iron, phosphorus, etc.) as well as their difference from dictionary meanings, the five elements are italicized in this book.

In Table 2.2, note that the gross elements are listed from least dense (*aakaash*) to most dense (*earth*). As a denser element appears, it incorporates the elements that preceded it. This is shown in column 4. It is also important to note that all other elements may ultimately dissolve back into *aakaash*.

The physical body, including the physical senses, consists of the five gross elements. Bone and other solids are produced from *earth;* bodily fluids from *water;* metabolism from *fire;* breathing and locomotion from *air;* space between tissues from *aakaash*. After death, the elements of the body return to the universal elements.

AAKAASH^A

Aakaash is the subtlest and purest of the five elements. It is the element of the fifth chᵃkrᵃ that is named "Ultra Pure" (VEshuddhᵃ). All sound brings forth *aakaash*. Depending upon the quality of the sound, *aakaash* will vary from gross to highly refined. Consider, for example, the different effects created in each of the following cases: dynamite explosion, thunder, screeching brakes, a cry of pain, screams of an angry parent, folk music, symphony, gentle rain, the song of a bird, classical singing, or ethereal chanting.

What we experience and absorb in the silence, as sound fades, is *aakaash*. Gross and frightening sounds produce dark blue or black *aakaash*. As *aakaash* becomes more refined, its color changes to gray, red, purple, violet, and finally gold. The latter is among the finest *aakaash* and is called sooryᵃ *aakaash* (effulgent golden *aakaash*).

It is produced by ethereal chanting and other methods. Absorbing soory^a *aakaash^a* purifies apaan^a and has a healing effect on the immune system; it also aids the integration of the subtle and physical fields. Soory^a *aakaash^a* can significantly contribute to the civilizing of the early brain. The use of refined sound is a major spiritual tool.

When spiritual practice (saadh^anaa) is focused on improving the hearing faculty, one can become extremely sensitive to significant nuances. This sensitivity, from here on, will be referred to as *sound sensitivity*. InnerTuning is particularly helpful in developing sound sensitivity. It is important to understand that sound sensitivity is independent of musical sensitivity. A person may be musically sensitive but not sound sensitive and vice versa.

Working with the subtle sounds of InnerTuning increases the capacity to identify and appreciate *aakaash^a,* which helps us to appreciate the highest ch^akr^a-s and feelings never sensed before.

EIGHTFOLD NATURE

In addition to being pervaded by the five elements (t^atv^a-s), the three fields of energy in the universe are also pervaded by three qualities (guN^a-s). Together they compose eightfold nature. The three qualities (guN^a-s) are t^am^as, r^aj^as, and s^atv^a. T^am^as is the quality of inertia or solidity. It is felt in such instances as darkness, heaviness, lethargy, sleep, and ignorance. The guN^a of t^am^as is associated with the principle of transformation and the deity MahAshvar^a. The English adjectival form of t^am^as is "tamsic." R^aj^as is the quality of action, either constructive or destructive. Any physical or mental act utilizes r^aj^as. The qualities of impulsivity and restlessness are also r^aj^as. The guN^a of r^aj^as is associated with the principle of creation and the deity Br^ahmaa. The English adjectival form of r^aj^as is "rajsic." S^atv^a is the quality of light or purity or truth. It is associated with the principle of preservation and the deity VESHNu. The English adjectival form of s^atv^a is "satvic." Life's purpose requires a balance of t^am^as, r^aj^as, and s^atv^a.

R^aj^as may be used to transform t^am^as into s^atv^a. A common example is that of a burning candle. The wax (t^am^as) is transformed into light (s^atv^a) by the burning (r^aj^as). Once the candle is lit, this process is automatic. In the human, on the other hand, the relationships among the guN^a-s may be influenced by free will. The body is t^am^as and the energy it produces is r^aj^as. Depending upon one's purpose, this energy may be used to produce more r^aj^as or converted to either t^am^as or s^atv^a.

Foods are also tamsic, rajsic, satvic, and any combination thereof. Large four-legged animals are tamsic. Small animals (including fish and fowl) are rajsic-tamsic. Vegetables (including onions and garlic) are rajsic; so also are most grains, seeds, and nuts. Fruits, sprouts, and tender leaves are satvic. (Any food that could ordinarily walk away from your plate is not satvic.) There are tamsic, rajsic, and satvic habits. Bringing outside shoes inside the house is a tamsic habit. Having an excessive sense of accomplishment is a rajsic habit. Cleanliness, rising before dawn, and meditating are satvic habits. Postures are also tamsic, rajsic, and satvic: reclining is tamsic; walking is rajsic; sitting with the spine erect is satvic.

This ancient description of nature in terms of the five elements and three guɴ^a-s clearly emphasizes quality and personal experience over quantity and measurement. Both the words t^atv^a (that which is) and guɴ^a (quality) may be captured by the English word *quiddity*—"the essence that makes something the kind of thing it is and makes it different from any other."[4]

These time-tested quiddities of eightfold nature (asht^adhaa pr^akretᴇ) can form the building blocks of a subjective science, thereby bridging understanding between the material and nonmaterial aspects of nature (see plate 2). Among the reasons for this is that these eight quiddities pervade all three fields and may be influenced by a number of variables, including sound.

Whether the term *qualities* is used to refer to all of eightfold nature or limited to the guɴ^a-s, it emphasizes the right hemispheric (feeling) interpretation of eightfold nature and ignores the fact that each aspect is also a principle—the left hemispheric interpretation. Each quiddity is, in essence, both feeling and principle.

TRIPARTITE BRAIN STRUCTURE
AND SPIRITUAL EVOLUTION

In his extensive cross species analysis of brain evolution, P. D. MacLean elaborated on his concept of the "triune" brain in humans.[5] According to him, the core of the human brain is the "reptilian" brain, which is connected with the most primitive behavior patterns. This is surrounded by the "paleomammalian" brain or limbic system, which has an important function in emotional expression. The outermost layer of the triune brain is the "neomammalian" brain. This is the location of the neocortex with its left and right hemispheres. MacLean uses the term "directional" to refer to the progressive changes that occurred as the brain evolved.

With MacLean and others, Microchakra Psychology asserts that the human brain evolved from that of simpler creatures over a vast span of time. However, instead of the "triune" distinction emphasized by MacLean, Microchakra Psychology emphasizes a different "tripartite" distinction. It combines the "reptilian" and "paleomammalian" brains into the "early" brain and emphasizes the differences between the right and left portions of the neocortex (see plate 3).

The Shaivite tradition teaches that when ShᵃktE, the dynamic force of the universe, realized her ability to create, preserve, and transform, she created three main deities to govern the manifest world: the principle of creation (Brᵃhmaa), the principle of preservation (VᴇsʜNu), and the principle of transformation (Mahᴀshvarᵃ). Microchakra Psychology suggests that the principle of creation is primarily represented in the left cerebral hemisphere (rational mind) and the principle of preservation in the right cerebral hemisphere (feeling mind). The principle of transformation has its foremost representation in the (phylogenetically) early brain.

The potential for harmonizing the tripartite brain gives the human a unique opportunity for spiritual evolution. It is the senior author's hypothesis that the two cerebral hemispheres appeared during human evolution to support the refinement of the early brain. This refinement literally involves modification of the brain's neurochemical circuits. Among other practices, properly intoned sounds and mᵃntrᵃ-s must be used to accomplish this refinement and balance the energies in the tripartite brain.

The early brain is often referred to as the "primitive" or "animal" brain. Spiritual evolution requires that the early brain be refined. Once this has been accomplished it would be a misnomer to refer to it as "primitive" or "animal-like." The layer of the early brain that influences the physical field by directing the autonomic nervous system already functions under universal law (retᵃ, see below). Complete harmonizing of the tripartite brain requires that the layers of the early brain that connect to the subtle and causal fields also function perfectly according to retᵃ—then liberation (mokshᵃ) is attained.

The early brain is pervaded by the central of the three major channels that run the length of the spine. In this channel abstract information about all previous lives is stored and all parapsychological potentials are seeded. Refinement of the early brain requires weakening or removing the false identifications with the transitory physical, subtle, and causal fields. This is facilitated through an understanding of the relationship between subtle aspects of the breathing process and brain functioning. Basic to this understanding is the awareness that lunar energy flows through the left nostril and activates the right hemisphere. This energy flow allows one to be more relaxed and sensitive to feelings. Similarly, solar energy flows through the right nostril and activates the left hemisphere, facilitating sequential thinking and rationality. When breath flows evenly through both nostrils (sushumnaa breath) the tripartite brain is in balance. At this time, there is an increased capacity for intuition and meditation.

The Principle of Cortical Representation

Parts of the physical human body are represented within the cortex. This is most strikingly illustrated by the "phantom limb" phenomenon wherein pain may be felt "in" a limb that has been amputated. In fact, it is the limb's representation in the cortex (which has escaped amputation) that contributes to the feeling.

The cortex is divided into six layers of distinctly different anatomical structure. Microchakra Psychology suggests that each of the first six chᵃkrᵃ-s is represented in a corresponding layer of the brain. The seventh chᵃkrᵃ lies outside eightfold nature and is represented differently in the brain.

THE THREE LᴇNGᴬ-S

All human understanding proceeds from three possible perspectives. Tᵃntrᵃ refers to these as the three lᴇngᵃ-s or motivational principles. The first lᴇngᵃ (Svᵃyambhoo lᴇngᵃ) refers to an egocentric perspective. Care for one's personal interests is the primary motivation. When the second lᴇngᵃ (Baaɴᵃ lᴇngᵃ) is active, energy is focused on helping others. The third lᴇngᵃ (ᴇtᵃrᵃ lᴇngᵃ) is cosmic centered and energy is aimed at transcending the ordinary world of sense dominated experience. It is helpful to consider these different lᴇngᵃ-s in addressing many philosophical and psychological issues. Prᵃkretᴇ tᵃtvᵃ operates most strongly in the first lᴇngᵃ. Purushᵃ tᵃtvᵃ operates primarily in the second and third lᴇngᵃ-s.

The First Lᴇngᵃ

The egocentric desires of the first lᴇngᵃ are based in the first three chᵃkrᵃ-s. Ego-centered desires include: 1) the desire for physical security; 2) the desire for inter-personal relationships based on exchange; 3) the desire for personal power. These are located in the first, second, and third chᵃkrᵃ-s respectively. Ego-centered desires are our most basic desires and have much in common with other mammals. They emerge from the phylogenetically older structures of the brain, particularly the limbic system. The personal desires of the first lᴇngᵃ tend to seek instant gratification regardless of others—"Me first!"

The ego-centered attitude is "I am the doer and I am the owner of all I possess including my abilities and potentials." The ego likes to believe that it is always in control. It has no feeling of the existence of Self (Aatmaa) even if it has heard or read about it.

In exchanges with others, the ego seeks to be the "winner" of the transaction. The first lᴇngᵃ ego feels soothed when it is treated as royalty and made the center of attention. If it becomes addicted to this treatment, it becomes difficult to share anything, including attention, possessions, and love. There is a tendency to believe "I am special" and to feel superior to others.

In fact, the third chᵃkrᵃ ego *is* special. It is solar and sends light to the other chᵃkrᵃ-s just as the sun (sooryᵃ) sends light to the other planets. This transmission is by means of the third microchakra in each chᵃkrᵃ. The energy that it sends to the two chᵃkrᵃ-s beneath it is represented by a downward-pointing triangle. Solar energy, however, is harsh and intoxicating. It must be refined and the ego softened. When this refinement occurs, the downward-pointing triangle will reverse and the energy will flow upward to stimulate the second lᴇngᵃ. Refinement may be aided by a principled lifestyle that includes the considerate use of money, sexuality, and personal power.

When the first lᴇngᵃ is dominant, the senses are only directed outward. Sharp distinctions between perceiver, perceiving, and object perceived are experienced. The first lᴇngᵃ emphasizes our separateness. We make judgments about others in terms of our own set of values. In this way, we construct a map of the world with our ego at the center and everyone and everything else categorized in terms of our own personal likes and dislikes. This is an egocentric existence.

When the first lᴇngᵃ is active we are most vulnerable to being conditioned by authorities and to adopting stereotypical beliefs and patterns of reasoning. The ego initially develops in order to focus intelligence on meeting the needs and wishes of the first lᴇngᵃ. In early childhood, the development of the ego is completely dependent upon concerned adults. The initial form of learning is mainly by imitation and later by instruction. By the time adulthood is reached, the ego has usually amassed a network of beliefs, attitudes, and strategies for fulfilling the needs of the first lᴇngᵃ in a way similar to others in the same social group.

In the first lᴇngᵃ, it is most difficult for the ego to observe itself. It prefers to express its strengths and hide its weaknesses. Psychological growth requires that we first develop a healthy ego—where self-esteem is neither too low nor too high. If this is achieved, then first lᴇngᵃ desires may be fulfilled and contentment achieved in a smooth fashion. This is not easy. It is at the level of the first lᴇngᵃ that our childish attitudes and expectations are initially formed. They must eventually yield to an adult view, entailing a capacity for objective self-reflection and a sense of personal responsibility. In later chapters, we shall see the crucial role of intuition in the third chᵃkrᵃ (3:6) in aiding this shift. Unless this shift to adulthood occurs, the ego remains weak or inflated. From the standpoint of the guɴᵃ-s, this is a situation where tᵃmᵃs and rᵃjᵃs dominate and sᵃtvᵃ has little opportunity to make an appearance.

The Second Lᴇngᵃ

As the microchakras related to the first lᴇngᵃ experience contentment, energy naturally rises to the second lᴇngᵃ. This is the realm of the fourth and fifth chᵃkrᵃ-s. The ego is sufficiently refined that we experience a reduction in the influence of the first lɛngᵃ upon our life. This is accompanied by a refinement of the early brain. These changes are facilitated by drawing closer to the natural world of plants and animals—the evolutionary home of the early brain. Those raised in urban competitive environments may benefit greatly from time spent in a rural setting.

The shift of energy to the second lɛngᵃ marks a major change in a person's being. The fourth chᵃkrᵃ contains an enormous reservoir of unconditional love. Through sharing love unconditionally, the ego is able to free itself from the selfishness associated with the first lɛngᵃ. The unconditional love may be directed toward another human, a cause, or a personal deity. In the epic *Ramayana,* Hᵃnumaanᵃ loves the Divine couple Sɛɛtaa and Raamᵃ unconditionally. In the Old Testament, Job loves the Lord unconditionally despite the afflictions poured upon him. Throughout history, martyrs have died willingly for their deity. Many people have lived quiet lives completely dedicated to a cause that they have felt to be much greater than themselves. Policemen, firemen, and soldiers give their lives every day.

It is important to appreciate the distinction between conditional and unconditional love. Conditional love always contains some element of compensation even if it is only a thought. The loving parents may have some hope that their child will respond to them in a similar manner when they are old. On the other hand, unconditional love has no expectation whatsoever.

Unconditional love first needs to be directed toward oneself. This will help remove remaining first lɛngᵃ fears and defenses; then the devotional self of the second lɛngᵃ may be released. It is this devotional self that has the inner strength to move away from the selfish aspects of the conditioned self. Hence the ego no longer believes itself to be the doer; it is an ego in name only. It is this ego that can offer unconditional love and say with conviction "Not my will but Thy will!"

From the perspective of the first lɛngᵃ, those giving unconditional love may seem to sacrifice a lot. For the person who *is* unconditional, there is no sense of sacrifice. It is simply a natural outpouring from second lɛngᵃ awareness.

As energy reaches the fifth chᵃkrᵃ, our capacity for communication becomes clearer and more in line with dhᵃrmᵃ. We are not careless with words and promises made are not taken lightly. Creativity flows more freely. If the sixth microchakras of the fifth chᵃkrᵃ (5:6) of all three channels (L, C, R) are open, the subtle promptings of the inner guru may emerge to help raise the energy even higher. When the second lɛngᵃ is dominant, the senses are not only directed outward but also at times directed inward. The sharp distinction between perceiver, perceiving, and percept lessens.

In the first lɛngᵃ, the ego was encased in a powerful sense of separateness from other people or deities with whom it had negotiations and dealings. Now, in the second lɛngᵃ, there emerges a sense of the underlying commonality of all existence.

Accordingly, some dissolution of the sense of separateness takes place. The more the dissolution occurs, the stronger the feeling that the ego and the object it is perceiving are essentially one. For example, the earth is perceived as a living organism. Thus naturally the earth's longevity becomes as important as our own. A relationship based on the second lɛngᵃ is very different from one based on the first. Compassion, tolerance, patience, and forbearance are some of the outstanding qualities of the second lɛngᵃ.

We embrace the attitude of "reverence for life." When a fly, mouse, or other creature enters our home, we prefer to capture it carefully and release it rather than kill it. Such a visit is not regarded as an affront to the ego punishable by death.

When the second lɛngᵃ is dominant, it becomes easier for the ego to observe itself. The external orientation of the first lɛngᵃ contributed to deep attachments between the ego and those people or objects that satisfied its desires. It is usually very difficult to distance ourselves and look objectively at such attachments. However, when the second lɛngᵃ becomes dominant and the ego more refined, looking at those attachments objectively becomes less of a challenge. When detachment is successful, there always remains the possibility of a shadow side to the refined ego as long as it remains self-conscious of its accomplishment. As long as we are aware of our saintliness, unsaintliness is still there, no matter how discrete.

The Third Lɛngᵃ

The third lɛngᵃ is the desire to transcend the empirical world of duality (vyᵃvᵃhaarᵃ) and to return to the Self. It is associated with the sixth and seventh chᵃkrᵃ-s. As a result of the refinement of the ego in the second lɛngᵃ, service to others was willingly undertaken and karmic debts repaid (see below). In the third lɛngᵃ, the ego has only one major goal: to raise its vibrational level even further and to discover the Self (Aatmaa). The ego now has a one-pointed focus on activities that will help to achieve this goal: penetration to finer layers of thought and intuition, deeper meditation, and practice of discernment (vɛchaarᵃ). All else is of little interest. Through vɛchaarᵃ it becomes clear that anything that one can be aware of has to be outside of oneself.[6] Thus the clear distinction between the eternal Self and the temporary ego gradually arises.

Third lɛngᵃ motivation includes the transcendence of nature, which requires breaking our identifications with the physical field (represented by our body), the subtle field (represented by our feelings), and the causal field (represented by our thoughts). Only then are we free to be our Self and to realize that we are not our body, not our feelings and not our thoughts. The latter point is particularly important for the development of a psychospiritual science. It reveals that the belief of

Descartes that "I think, therefore, I am" was an error and has served as a barrier for scientific appreciation of Consciousness.

By following appropriate methods, the third lɛngᵃ aspirant discovers an inner sanctuary where there is a Self that is just perfect as it is. It has to do nothing to be Divine, it just is Divine. We are the carriers of that Self. Once awareness enters into that inner sanctuary, then we realize it is the most perfect place, the most perfect Being. It has always been here and it will always be here, even as our bodies come and our bodies go.

The ancients did not want to use a word for this Beingness, so they referred to it as Tᵃt (That). Later on, other schools used the word Aatmaa, which is also employed by Microchakra Psychology. The word *soul* should not be used as a synonym for Aatmaa, as it has a wide variety of connotations. These often include the idea that the soul can be punished and go to hell or rewarded and go to heaven. Aatmaa, on the other hand, is perfect and unchanging, beyond reward and punishment.

Dominance of the third lɛngᵃ is rare. Many cultures do not recognize the third lɛngᵃ. The statement "I am God," accompanied by an unusual lifestyle, may—in the minds of many—automatically qualify one for institutionalization. Yet, it may sometimes reflect a legitimate third lɛngᵃ awareness on the part of a deeply sensitive person who is not interested in the everyday world. The Tantric and Vedic traditions have developed an extensive terminology to describe the third lɛngᵃ. These traditions give great respect and reverence to individuals who are dominated by cosmic centered motivation.

Balance of the Three Lɛngᵃ-s
The majority of people live their lives primarily in the first lɛngᵃ with some input from the second. Most religions encourage people to raise their energy to the second lɛngᵃ by praying to a nonmaterial power and caring for other people. When any such care is absent, life is totally dominated by the first lɛngᵃ. It may be a completely selfish life or include acts of altruism based on principle rather than feeling.

A significant minority of people live their lives primarily in the second lɛngᵃ. These are people whose first lɛngᵃ desires are simple and who derive their greatest satisfaction from service to others or to a larger cause. They alleviate the pain of the world for many.

In this Kᵃlɛ yugᵃ very few people live their lives in the third lɛngᵃ. There are not many who are ready for sustained focus on the cosmic, and competent teachers are rare.

Some people are born with more than one lɛngᵃ active. If the first and second are active, usually the first is dominant during the initial 18 to 21 years; then the second lɛngᵃ takes over. If the third lɛngᵃ is not active, they will not be interested in the question, "Who am I?" On the other hand, if the third lɛngᵃ is also active, they will start to do their spiritual practices early in life when the first lᴇng^a is not even mature. They will go to school with regular boys and girls, and they will marry, but they will still follow practices that keep the third lᴇng^a nurtured. In the later years of life, if the first and second lᴇng^a-s are content, they may live in a forest or cave.

For most people, InnerTuning recommends devoting appropriate time to each lᴇng^a. As cosmic awareness evolves through focus on the third lᴇng^a, its energy may be directed downward to refine the egos of the other two lᴇng^a-s.

Transcendence of the Lᴇng^a-s

Transcendence of all three lᴇng^a-s is called liberation (moksh^a). Upon liberation all duality is dissolved. The distinction between knower, known, and knowledge is erased. All ignorance is washed away. As a snake loses its old skin, so the non-Self falls off a person who simply remains as the Self; such a being is termed a gyaanᴇᴇ (one who knows) by Advɪt^a Vᴀdaant^a. The Tantric tradition also describes a temporary state of merging. Such a state is called a s^amaadhᴇ. In this condition, breathing is suspended and energy is concentrated in the seventh ch^akr^a; duality and the world of spacetime do not exist. The distinction between a perceiver and a percept does not arise. When the s^amaadhᴇ is over, however, all aspects of daily life return—with increased third lᴇng^a motivation.

Microchakra Psychology suggests that liberation occurs when a) all microchakras in both the left channel and the central channel are open and b) the effects of all right-channel blocks have been mentally overcome. At this point the jᴇᴇv^a is established in the Self (sv^at^antry^a).

RET^A, DH^ARM^A, AND K^ARM^A

Ret^a

Ret^a is fabulous

it just is

Ret^a is autonomous

it just is

Ret^a is continuous

it just is

Ret^a is miraculous

it just is

It is because it

just is

S. BHATNAGAR

Retª can be translated as "inherent universal law"—it has the connotation of Truth. The planets circulate around the sun in conformity to retª. Animals naturally function according to retª. The autonomic nervous system obeys retª. Very spiritually advanced humans have a life style in accord with retª. In all of these cases the natural law is followed without deliberate effort. It just happens.

The stronger the ego (ahªmkaarª), the more difficult it is to follow retª. For this reason, the principle of dhªrmª (duty) is necessary in order to teach each person how to advance spiritually. If you support dhªrmª, then dhªrmª will support you.

Some people in the first lɛngª may have difficulty giving their support to dhªrmª. They may be confused and not recognize their duty or they may be strongly attached to nondharmic pursuits. When the second lɛngª becomes active, there is an eagerness to discern and follow dhªrmª. In the third lɛngª, dhªrmª may be transcended as it merges into retª.

Human free will allows either choices that are in accord with Cosmic Intelligence (dharmic) or are blemished and go against it (adharmic). Dhªrmª can be placed into three categories: personal, group, and cosmic. Sometimes there is conflict between dhªrmª-s within a category or between categories. The general rule is that the lesser dhªrmª should yield to the greater dhªrmª. The need to set this priority may produce considerable struggle within a person's conscience.

The Law of Kªrmª

Tradition indicates that all human pursuit is for one or more of four basic goals: 1) economic prosperity, 2) pleasure, 3) moral attainment, and 4) liberation. When we are completely content with our physical, subtle, and causal bodies, we are perfect candidates for liberation (mokshª). If, on the other hand, we have lived a life of righteousness but, for example, are not content and wish to have a more beautiful physical body, we will be reborn to have one.

Along its path of evolution, each jɛɛvª is presented with opportunities to exercise its free will and make dharmic or adharmic choices. These choices are expressed as actions (kªrmª), which may be physical acts, speech, or simply thoughts. Acts of merit contribute toward happiness (sukhª); blemished acts (paapª) contribute toward suffering (dukhª). Neutral acts do not contribute to karmic bondage. This is the *law of kªrmª*. Through it, the universe expresses moral law as precisely as it expresses physical law.

There are no accidents. Apparently "random" events are simply those whose karmic reasons lie beyond our usual understanding—with an intelligence far greater than our own. In the Tantric tradition, this is what is known as Mªhªt, the Cosmic Intelligence. Each jɛɛvª carries a record of its kªrmª within its central channel.

This may be thought of as a karmic credit card. Blemished or adharmic acts form the debits; dharmic acts form the credits. Neutral acts do not appear on the card. Microchakra Psychology hypothesizes that credits are manifested through openings in the microchakras, either in this birth or a subsequent one. Similarly debits are manifested through blocks.

For liberation (mokshᵃ), the balance must equal zero. An excess of either debits or credits will cause rebirth. Blemished kᵃrmᵃ must be corrected through suffering or joyful spiritual practice (saadhᵃnaa); actions in accord with Cosmic Intelligence must be rewarded. Both necessitate another birth. In each birth, the results of both positive and negative kᵃrmᵃ are experienced, consciously or unconsciously.

An example of the law of kᵃrmᵃ concerns an old lady standing at a street corner and hesitant to cross. If you help her cross the street while thinking "this is the right thing to do," some karmic credit is accrued. If you do not think of anything other than the natural act of helping her across the street, the karmic effect is neutral. If you ignore her, a karmic debt is incurred.

Unfortunately, an increasingly contentious society sometimes interferes with fulfilling dharmic obligations. Once, while standing at a street corner in New York City, the senior author saw a man fall to the ground with half of his body in the path of oncoming traffic. As he pulled him to safety, he asked the person standing next to him to call for emergency service. The man did so but then admonished: "You should not get involved; you could be sued."

As each act is committed, its memory traces (sᵃmskaarᵃ-s, literally: "completely made") register in the subtle and causal fields of all ȷEEvᵃ-s concerned with the act. The stock of memory traces (sᵃmskaarᵃ-s) is referred to as accumulated kᵃrmᵃ (sᵃmchEtᵃ kᵃrmᵃ). It is the sum total of the ȷEEvᵃ's kᵃrmᵃ across lifetimes beginning with early evolution and includes: historical kᵃrmᵃ, geographical kᵃrmᵃ, religious kᵃrmᵃ, ethnic kᵃrmᵃ, and genetic kᵃrmᵃ. These are added on to individual kᵃrmᵃ. When any of these kᵃrmᵃ-s reach maturity they can express themselves. This may happen whenever the ȷEEvᵃ is ready: immediately, later in the current life, or in a subsequent life. Any delay in karmic consequences is due to the need for the maturation or ripening of kᵃrmᵃ.

That part of accumulated (sᵃmchEtᵃ) kᵃrmᵃ whose maturation originates the current birth and that comes to fruition in it is called praarᵃbdhᵃ kᵃrmᵃ (completely begun kᵃrmᵃ). Some of the praarᵃbdhᵃ kᵃrmᵃ selects those parents who can provide the appropriate genetic material and initial experiences that the ȷEEvᵃ has earned. Once commenced, praarᵃbdhᵃ kᵃrmᵃ continues until fully exhausted, just like an arrow that has been released from a bow.

The law of kᵃrmᵃ provides an explanation for the implementation of moral justice in the universe. Current suffering is due to past misdeeds, either in this life or a previous one; similarly, current well-being is due to past good deeds. Every opportunity for choice has a karmic consequence. The law of kᵃrmᵃ is the means by which the universe holds each being responsible for the gift of free will. Rebirth is an essential component for cosmic justice. Some kᵃrmᵃ-s must be worked through in nonhuman form. Therefore, no one has any guarantee that the next birth will be in human form.

Memory traces (sᵃmskaarᵃ-s) remain in the subtle field. They may be expressed in dreams or worked through mentally using the InnerTuning system.

THE PATH OF EGO REFINEMENT

The process of ego refinement takes many lifetimes as the jᴇᴇvᵃ proceeds to the Self (Aatmaa). Each lifetime provides an opportunity for the jᴇᴇvᵃ to make some movement along the path that is provided by the seven chᵃkrᵃ-s. The degree of movement in a lifetime is limited by our kᵃrmᵃ and our sense of dhᵃrmᵃ. Interspersed with progression there are inevitable periods of regression as blocks assert their power. There are also periods of consolidation in which no discernible progress occurs. These too are an important part of the process. Travel along the path must be at our own pace and in our own manner.

An individual who attempts to move along the path with conviction and determination is called a spiritual aspirant (saadhᵃkᵃ). The methods used are called spiritual practices (saadhᵃnaa). Traditionally, a guru (spiritual teacher) aids the spiritual aspirant—often imparting subtle knowledge that is otherwise unavailable.

An ego has no identity of its own. Ego energy acquires identity by means of attachment to a variety of beliefs, feelings, thoughts, behaviors, objects, and people. In order to bring the ego in tune with the flow of retᵃ, many of these attachments must be modified or eliminated. This process is known as "refinement of the ego." When all seven egos have been sufficiently refined, the remaining purified ego energy can transcend all three fields and function beyond them in perfect harmony with retᵃ. Finally, it may merge into the Self. This is liberation (mokshᵃ) and is a very rare event in the age in which we live, the Kᵃlᴇ yugᵃ.

A human birth is a precious gift. It should be understood as an opportunity to evolve spiritually or devolve spiritually. If we live in a dharmic manner we will evolve and our desires will become more refined; if we live in an adharmic manner we will devolve and our desires will become more gross and brutal. Bold determination is required for spiritual growth.

If it is assumed that the human population of the planet is approximately six billion then, even with the bull of dhᵃrmᵃ standing on one leg, there are approximately 1.5 billion people who have the potential to raise their awareness and attain significant ego refinement. The number of qualified gurus falls far short of that required. The emerging science of subtle energies may be what our age demands to help with this problem.

The Subtle Energies of Breath and Sound

Among the practices of InnerTuning that serve to refine ego are work with subtle breath and subtle sound. The former is known as svᵃrᵃ yogᵃ and the latter as naadᵃ yogᵃ. Historically, these two approaches to subtle energy have developed independently. They are combined in the teachings of Microchakra Psychology.

Through observing the breath, svᵃrᵃ yogᵃ eventually leads you to an ability to identify the different elements and guɴᵃ-s within it. This facilitates control of the chᵃkrᵃ minds.

Working with subtle sounds helps to purify and enhance connections among the microchakras. Eventually these practices lead to hearing specific sounds which reverberate in the universe (see Table 10.2) and ultimately to hearing your own fundamental note.

3

The Subtle Field

THE SUBTLE NERVOUS SYSTEM

The Tantric literature describes a network of subtle nerves (naaDEE-s) within the subtle field.[1] They are analogous to nerves in the physical body. However, they are nonmaterial channels of vibration. (The word naaDEE is derived from a Sᵃmskretᵃ word meaning "motion.") The subtle nerves provide pathways through which the life currents of praaNᵃ may move. There are various estimates of the number of subtle nerves; the most commonly cited is 72,000. All subtle nerves originate in a root plexus (khᵃndᵃ) in the first chᵃkrᵃ. It is generally agreed that the three subtle nerves that are of paramount importance are the left breathing channel (Edaa), right breathing channel (pEngᵃlᵃ), and a channel running through the center of the spine (sushumnaa), which itself consists of three channels that conduct *fire* and solar and lunar energies (see plate 4).

The subtle nerves vibrate at a much higher frequency than objects in the physical field. Known verbal or geometrical descriptions of them are probably only approximations. S. S. Goswami has reviewed many of the classical descriptions of the subtle nerves and noted their similarities and differences.[2] A comparison of modern authors on this subject will also show similarities and differences. As individual sensitivity and intuition are the primary tools for exploring and reporting on the world beyond the material, the lack of perfect interobserver agreement is to be expected.

The Central Channel (Sushumnaa)

Sushumnaa is located in the center of the network of subtle nerves. It commences in the root plexus (khᵃndᵃ), which is shown in plate 4 as a downward-pointing triangle within the first chᵃkrᵃ. Sushumnaa rises through the center of the triangle and continues its upward path through the centers of the six major chᵃkrᵃ-s (also depicted in plate 4) until it reaches a hollow space within the seventh chᵃkrᵃ (Brᵃhmᵃrᵃndhrᵃ).

The Tantric literature has described the diameter of sushumnaa as a tiny fraction of the thickness of a hair. A segment from the vertical plane of sushumnaa is shown in plate 5.

The left and right channels of sushumnaa form a figure eight pattern. Solar energy in the region of the left hemisphere of the brain crosses at the sixth chᵃkrᵃ level to the right channel (vᵃjrENEE) and flows down the right side of the body to the root plexus (khᵃndᵃ). From there it rises up the lunar left channel (chEtrENEE) to again reach the sixth chᵃkrᵃ region and complete the lower loop of the figure eight. The flow now crosses over to the area of the right hemisphere and finally returns to the region of the left hemisphere, thus completing the top loop of the figure eight. As they form the figure eight, both the left and right channels intersect with each chᵃkrᵃ.

The Left and Right Breathing Channels (Edaa and PEngᵃlᵃ)

The left breathing channel (Edaa) commences on the left side of the root plexus (khᵃndᵃ) and terminates in the left nostril. Along the way, it crisscrosses among each of the first five chᵃkrᵃ-s and bifurcates in the middle of the sixth chᵃkrᵃ. This channel carries lunar energy that feeds the lunar microchakras. Reverberations from praaNᵃ within this breathing channel energize the right cerebral hemisphere while cooling the left hemisphere.

The right breathing channel (pEngᵃlᵃ) begins on the right side of the root plexus (khᵃndᵃ) and ends in the right nostril. It also crisscrosses among each of the first five chᵃkrᵃ-s and bifurcates in the middle of the sixth. The right breathing channel carries solar energy and feeds the solar microchakras. Reverberations from praaNᵃ within this breathing channel energize the left cerebral hemisphere while cooling the right hemisphere.

All energy in the system of subtle nerves (naaDEE-s) emanates from sushumnaa. The left channel (chEtrENEE) supplies lunar energy to the left breathing channel (Edaa) and the right channel (vᵃjrENEE) supplies solar energy to the right breathing channel (pEngᵃlᵃ).

PRAAnᴬ-S

The Tantric and Vedic traditions identify five major praaNᵃ-s as part of the subtle field. Knowledge of the praaNᵃ-s, like the guNᵃ-s and the elements, aids in understanding the interrelationship of the physical and subtle fields. Each praaNᵃ is a type of vital energy.

PraaN^a aiding the functioning of each cell of the body is called vyaan^a.

PraaN^a operating in the throat and neck is called udaan^a. It assists in the formation of speech and thoughts. Ultimately, it helps in the process of dying.

PraaN^a energizing the fourth ch^akr^a in the region of the heart and lungs is simply called praaN^a.

PraaN^a in the area of the third ch^akr^a allows the secretion of digestive fluids to occur. Its name is s^amaan^a.

PraaN^a operating below the navel is called apaan^a. It assists all motions of expulsion associated with rectal and urogenital functions. These include defecation, urination, orgasm, and birthing.

In addition to the five major praaN^a-s, there are five minor praaN^a-s that control a) coughing, belching, and hiccups (naag^a); b) movement of eyelids (koorm^a); c) hunger, thirst, and sneezing (krek^al^a); d) yawning and sleep (d_{AV}^ad^att^a); and e) swelling (dh^an^anj^ay^a).

The Problematic Role of Apaan^a

Microchakra Psychology has a unique understanding of the role of apaan^a in many physical and emotional problems. It has been the clinical observation of the senior author that normal wear and tear coupled with lingering inner conflicts are the reason that apaan^a praaN^a (from here on referred to simply as apaan^a) frequently generates toxic fumes that invade the integrity of the higher ch^akr^a-s—causing a host of problems. These range in severity from sluggishness to psychotic episode. Bodily toxicity, constipation, unhealthy lifestyle, negative thinking, and emotional shock aggravate apaan^a problems. The unconscious desire to say "no" to life, to want to return to the womb, and to avoid responsibilities reverses the normal downward flow of energy in the right channel. Instead of descending, an upward trend occurs that puts the whole subtle energy system out of balance.

Normally, apaan^a dwells in the first ch^akr^a. If it invades the second ch^akr^a, one becomes preoccupied with sex and other exchange relationships. When apaan^a affects the third ch^akr^a, there are digestive disorders or expressions of rage that may be directed either inward toward oneself or outward toward others. There may be an excessive pursuit of worldly success and power. When apaan^a affects the fourth ch^akr^a, there can be unexplained pressures on the heart, arrhythmia, shortness of breath, and depression. When the fifth ch^akr^a is affected, one may hear voices giving advice that sometimes is misinterpreted as spiritual. One may at times speak out loud to oneself and not be aware of it. In addition, if the pods of apaan^a are large, one may even feel that one is a great leader of humankind. When apaan^a affects the sixth chᵃkrᵃ, schizophrenia or manic-depression may result. In the seventh chᵃkrᵃ, apaanᵃ may produce catatonia.

Problems that are sometimes believed to be associated with the rise of KuNDᵃlEnEE, a powerful subtle energy dormant in the first chᵃkrᵃ, may often be due instead to the influence of apaanᵃ on the higher chᵃkrᵃ-s. The senior author has had the opportunity to work with numerous people, many referred by the psychological community, whose apaanᵃ was responsible for creating havoc in their lives. They were all benefited by purifications and InnerTuning sounds, which gradually lessen the emotions of insecurity and fear. Practitioners of InnerTuning participate in a five-day purification twice a year (Spring and Fall). The varied benefits include the purification of apaanᵃ.

Apaanᵃ and the Cycle of Chᵃkrᵃ Activity

In human beings, energy cycles twice through all seven chᵃkrᵃ-s during each twenty-four hour period, with each chᵃkrᵃ successively becoming the most active. (A detailed discussion and chart of these energy cycles is given in chapter 10.) Energy drops from the seventh to the first chᵃkrᵃ in both the morning and evening. In the Tantric and Vedic traditions, this period is called Brahmᵃmuhoortᵃ, because, as noted below, it is the time of Brᵃhmaa, who resides in the first chᵃkrᵃ. Daily defecation, ideally before dawn and dusk, when energy is centered in the first chᵃkrᵃ, is one simple way to keep the apaanᵃ grounded.

The Breath of Life

Breath is the carrier of praaNᵃ, the force of vitality in the universe. It is the link between the three bodies and the key to psychospiritual development. Each inhalation draws praaNᵃ from the causal field to nourish the feeling body with the elements and the physical body with oxygen and other gases.

The five elements alternate their appearance in the breath. The Latin *spiritus* means "breath"; to be spiritual is to be aware of all elements in the breath. The following cycle will occur naturally during the course of an hour:

> *Aakaashᵃ*—4 minutes
> *Air*—8 minutes
> *Fire*—12 minutes
> *Water*—16 minutes
> *Earth*—20 minutes

Our reactions to external events are influenced by the element we are breathing. With some practice we can modify this cycle and summon whatever element we desire.

Forms of KuNDᵃlᴇNEE

The whole manifest universe is generated by Cosmic Potentiality (MᵃhaakuNDᵃlᴇNᴇᴇ) as it assumes the successive forms of KuNDᵃlᴇNᴇᴇ (Potentiality), Great Vibrancy (Mᵃhaashᵃktᴇ), and Vibrancy (Shᵃktᴇ). Vibrancy (Shᵃktᴇ) is the immediate creator of the universe; she produces numerous male and female deities to assist her. As mentioned earlier, these deities are both principles and beings. They serve as archetypes for the manifest world.

Every form is created by the universal KuNDᵃlᴇNᴇᴇ. After a form is completed, a dormant potential for future lives is stored at its base. In the case of human beings, the dormant KuNDᵃlᴇNᴇᴇ is located in the first chᵃkrᵃ. The word KuNDᵃlᴇNᴇᴇ is derived from the word for "curl" (kuNDᵃlᵃ). KuNDᵃlᴇNᴇᴇ is spoken of as curled or coiled like a serpent at rest.

Movement of KuNDᵃlᴇNᴇᴇ

For most people, KuNDᵃlᴇNᴇᴇ remains dormant in the first chᵃkrᵃ throughout their lifetimes—with one important exception. Every night, when the ego rests in sleep, KuNDᵃlᴇNᴇᴇ awakens and rushes upward through the central channel (Shᴇvᵃ naaDᴇᴇ) to be in the embrace of the beloved Shᴇvᵃ in the seventh (crown) chᵃkrᵃ. At the time of awakening she returns, unnoticed, to her abode in the first chᵃkrᵃ. During her ascent and descent (possibly several times per night), KuNDᵃlᴇNᴇᴇ notes the concerns of each chᵃkrᵃ mind and induces a dream to aid in overcoming them. Some dreams deliver a message and others are simply wish fulfilling.

Some sensitive spiritual aspirants (saadhᵃkᵃ-s) practice a sleep fast under expert guidance during the nights of the new and full moon. At these times, in deep meditation, they may observe the ascent of KuNDᵃlᴇNᴇᴇ.

Through persistent spiritual discipline KuNDᵃlᴇNᴇᴇ may move from the first chᵃkrᵃ to higher abodes. If complete contentment of the first lᴇngᵃ desires is attained, she will ascend to the second lᴇngᵃ. At this point, KuNDᵃlᴇNᴇᴇ may awaken and rise in the central channel (Shᴇvᵃ naaDᴇᴇ) to a second abode in the fourth chᵃkrᵃ. The serpentine form that manifested in the first lᴇngᵃ is transformed into a radiant benevolent goddess in the second lᴇngᵃ.

When the third lᴇngᵃ is activated and internalization of the senses increases, KuNDᵃlᴇNᴇᴇ may make her abode in the sixth (aagyaa) chᵃkrᵃ where she manifests as a deity that is half male and half female. This androgynous archetype (Ardhᵃnaarᴇᴇshvᵃrᵃ) symbolizes the unification of solar and lunar energy within.

The fourth abode of KuNDᵃlᴇNᴇᴇ will be in the somᵃ chᵃkrᵃ (see page 86) where she manifests as both the lord of desire and the goddess of desire (KaamAshvªrª-KaamAshvªrEE). While in embrace, instead of gazing at each other, these deities gaze upward toward the seventh chªkrª (sªhªsraarª) in anticipation of the final return to Stasis (Pªrªmª ShEvª).

As an aspirant makes genuine efforts to refine and integrate the three bodies, KuNdªlEnEE may at times naturally and gently arise to a higher abode. If this does not happen, it is simply that the time has not come. The genuine activation of KuNdªlEnEE is extremely rare. Some problems that have been associated with the rise of KuNdªlEnEE may be due to the activation of sister powers of the KuNdªlEnEE, which cause unusual experiences. Tªntrª does contain authentic methods for stimulating the rise of KuNdªlEnEE, but InnerTuning does not recommend their use. Instead of arising in the central channel, the awakened energy may rise in the left or right channel—with disastrous results. In a famous example, Gopi Krishna has described such a disaster.[3]

The Doorkeepers

Three doorkeepers (dvaarªpaalª-s) are found at the doors where the three channels meet in the first chªkrª: at the right-channel door the doorkeeper is Brªhmªdvaarª; at the left-channel door it is VEShNudvaarª; at the central-channel door it is ShEvªdvaarª.

The doorkeeper in the right channel prevents the rise of the toxic fumes of apaanª. This purpose is also served by other right-channel doors: between the first and second motivational principles (lEngª-s) and between the second and third motivational principles. If the doorkeepers should fail, apaanª might invade the integrity of the higher chªkrª-s. This could release stored negative memories, which have the power to activate the sister powers of the KuNdªlEnEE. Such premature awakening has the potential to cause a host of mental problems—some very severe.

Three similarly located doors in the left (lunar) channel serve to aid the rise of praaNª. The left-channel doors are strengthened through devotion (bhªktE) and unconditional love. Awareness of the left-channel door between the fifth and sixth chªkrª-s is of great value to the advanced aspirant. Establishing the first-chªkrª-hour toilet rhythm opens the right-channel door. Thereby, the flow of apaanª is directed downward. After defecation and cleansing in the first-chªkrª hour, when we sit for meditation, satvic praaNª with golden (sooryª) *aakaashª* is absorbed. This eventually opens the left channel door. When this door is fully open, the upward flow of lunar energy is maximized and the left-channel openings are fully empowered.

Advanced breath awareness, such as detecting the elements in the breath, opens the door of the central channel. This is also aided by the invocation of golden (soory^a) *aakaash^a* through the vocalizing of central-channel m^antr^a-s. This opening is a necessary prerequisite for the rise of the dormant KuNd^alEnEE. However, there is considerable risk associated with any attempt to deliberately open this door. Sister powers of the KuNd^alEnEE may be awakened prematurely and severely disrupt the nervous system. Hence deliberate efforts to open the central channel door (ShEv^advaar^a) are not recommended unless one is very spiritually advanced and has the guidance of a genuine guru.

The Last Breath
According to the K^aTH^a Up^anESH^ad (6.16):

> *There are a hundred and one channels of the heart.*
> *One of these passes up to the crown of the head.*
> *Going up by it, one goes to immortality.*
> *The others are for departing in various directions.*[4]

At the time of death, KuNd^alEnEE has to rise in the central channel; as she does she draws all impressions of the current life into her. She then departs from the body through one of ten gates: 1) anus, 2) urethra, 3) mouth, 4) right nostril, 5) left nostril, 6) right eye, 7) left eye, 8) right ear, 9) left ear, 10) bregmatic fontanel, in the region of the seventh ch^akr^a.

The gate through which KuNd^alEnEE departs is determined by the level of spiritual development the person has attained and the quality of awareness when the last breath comes. In those who lead adharmic lives, KuNd^alEnEE usually leaves through the anus or urethra. This may occur while literally defecating or urinating. The exit of KuNd^alEnEE from the first three gates is accompanied by apaan^a.

In most deaths KuNd^alEnEE, accompanied by praaN^a, leaves from the fourth gate and above. Udaan^a is the carrier of KuNd^alEnEE and is summoned by her at the time of departure. Those who have worked intensively with the left hemisphere (such as intellectuals, scientists, and scholars) leave through the right nostril. Fine artists and those who have done some selfless service leave from the left nostril. This includes those who have put their life on the line such as firemen, policemen, and soldiers. People who have done some deliberate (conscious) spiritual work go out of the right eye or the left eye. Very advanced saints go out of the right or left ear.

The tenth gate is only for those who have reached 7:7 (the seventh ch^akr^a's seventh microchakra) and lived with awareness of ret^a. Those who are able to leave from the tenth gate attain liberation (moksh^a) from the cycle of birth, death, and rebirth (s^amsaar^a).

Examination of a corpse may sometimes reveal the gate through which Kuɴdˡlɛɴɛɛ departed. Departure through one of the first two gates may be accompanied by signs of defecation or urination. When Kuɴdˡlɛɴɛɛ leaves from the third gate, the mouth is usually open (others ordinarily close it). When departure is from the nostrils, the face is pale with a pink area on the side of the nostril used. Departure from the eyes is indicated by a beam of light in either the right or left eye. When the ears provide the gate, there is a patch of pink on the ear lobe of the gate used. Departure from the tenth gate is accompanied by an opening the size of a pinprick or a tiny bulge in the area of the bregmatic fontanel.

CHᴬKRᴬ-S

Harish Johari explained the meaning of the term chᵃkrᵃ as follows:

> *Chakras* are psychic centers that cannot be described fully from a materialistic or physiological standpoint. Just as a painting cannot be described from the standpoint of lines and curves or varying shades of paints—even though these can be said to form the basic structure of a painting—similarly, *chakras* can not be described in terms of psychology, physiology, or any other physical science. Chakras are centers of activity of subtle, vital force . . .[5]

Chᵃkrᵃ-s are vortices of psychospiritual energy that radiate outward from the central channel (Shɛvᵃ naaɴɛɛ) of sushumnaa. One of the literal meanings of the word chᵃkrᵃ is "wheel." Tradition recognizes seven major chᵃkrᵃ-s distributed along sushumnaa. These are illustrated in plate 4. They, together with two minor lunar chᵃkrᵃ-s, form the starting point for Microchakra Psychology.

The chᵃkrᵃ-s are known by means of advanced practices for directing the senses inward and developing intuition. However, there are many differences in the reports about them. For purposes of developing a psychospiritual science, Microchakra Psychology regards both chᵃkrᵃ-s and microchakras as hypothetical constructs, just as the atom was a hypothetical construct for centuries before it was first seen in the twentieth century (years after the first atomic explosion). As psychospiritual science advances, our understanding and experiences of both chᵃkrᵃ-s and microchakras will expand.

Chᵃkrᵃ-s are traditionally visualized as luminous lotus flowers in the core of which a seed sound (bɛɛjᵃ mᵃntrᵃ) resounds. Pratyāgātmānanda observed that "Harmony or *chandas* is of the essence of the Divine and all its emanations and manifestations.

And quite fittingly, the lotus represents this."⁶ The lotus grows in the mud of lakes and ponds but cannot be stained by the mud, which just rolls off it. Similarly, the chᵃkrᵃ-s cannot be blocked by the dross and toxins found in the empirical world. Their flow of energy is frictionless.

The petals of the lotus symbolize subtle nerves (naaDEE-s), each of which resonates to a specific sound and can briefly retain varying amounts of sonic energy. If the hue of the petal is dull or muddy, the sensitivity to sound is decreased. Conversely, purity of the sounds can produce golden (sooryᵃ) *aakaashᵃ*. If abundant golden *aakaashᵃ* is produced during spiritual practice (saadhᵃnaa), the petals are energized and point upward. This increases the smoothness with which the chᵃkrᵃ rotates.

When the petals are full, the rhythm is perfect. At this point the seventh microchakra may open and release its lunar energy (the energy of contentment) into the central channel and quench the corresponding *fire* of desire. Contentment of all seven chᵃkrᵃ-s is a preparation for the upward movement of KuNdᵃlEnEE. It rises without any effort when we are unattached to any of the objects that appeal to the seven chᵃkrᵃ minds.

Chᵃkrᵃ Characteristics

The remainder of this chapter describes the seven major chᵃkrᵃ-s. The distinguishing characteristics of the seven major chᵃkrᵃ-s are as follows:

- ✦ Rotation: Each chᵃkrᵃ has its own specific plane and direction of rotation. The rotation of the chᵃkrᵃ-s and microchakras is nurtured by the purity of the sound that energizes the petals. The first and third chᵃkrᵃ-s rotate clockwise; all other chᵃkrᵃ-s rotate counterclockwise. Optimum rotation occurs when solar nourishment through the right channel is abundant and the petals are fresh. In the process, the right-channel petals—receptacles of nourishment—expand more and more and become increasingly vibrant. This, in turn, offers renewed impetus to the rotation and the field of radiance of the chᵃkrᵃ expands. At a certain level of radiance, the left-channel sounds enrich the petals. Consistency of the freshness of the petals on both sides determines the proper rotation of the chᵃkrᵃ. While the chᵃkrᵃ-s and microchakras are always rotating, the petals are always fixed.
- ✦ Element: The first five chᵃkrᵃ-s are related to a specific element. At some stage of spiritual practice (saadhᵃnaa) the shape (yᵃntrᵃ) and color of an element are internally recognized.

◆ Therapeutic Color: A particular color has a therapeutic effect on each chᵃkrᵃ.

◆ Sense Organ: Each chᵃkrᵃ has a connection with a sense organ.

◆ Organ of Action: Each chᵃkrᵃ energizes a specific organ in the body.

◆ Storehouse: Specific parts of the body serve as storehouses for energy associated with each chᵃkrᵃ.

◆ Sleep Habits: Sleep posture and duration of sleep are determined by the chᵃkrᵃ mind that is dominant in a person most of the time.

◆ Endocrine Gland: Each of the chᵃkrᵃ-s activates a particular endocrine gland.

◆ Symbolic Animal: The Tantric tradition designates a symbolic animal for each of the five elements and thus for the related chᵃkrᵃ as well.

◆ Developmental Period: As development proceeds from childhood to maturity, the person is challenged to fulfill the desires and potentials of each chᵃkrᵃ. The opportunity to do this unfolds, chᵃkrᵃ by chᵃkrᵃ, in six-year cycles for females and seven-year cycles for males. These cycles form sensitive developmental periods for establishing communication between the subtle and the physical fields. For instance, a boy in the second-chᵃkrᵃ age (between seven and fourteen) would find it easier to make openings in the left-channel microchakras of the second chᵃkrᵃ than he would when he is in another chᵃkrᵃ age.

◆ Celestial Connection: Each chᵃkrᵃ receives supplemental energy from a different heavenly body.

◆ Musical Sensitivity: Each chᵃkrᵃ reacts naturally to a specific type of musical instrument. However, all musical instruments are capable of influencing all chᵃkrᵃ-s when played skillfully.

◆ Petal Sounds: Each chᵃkrᵃ has a specific number of petals, each with its specific sound. As mentioned earlier, the petal sounds are the basis of the Sᵃmskretᵃ alphabet. In the lists of petal sounds for each chᵃkrᵃ given below, the first half of each list contains the sounds for the right channel in descending order and the second half of each list contains the sounds for the left channel in ascending order. Adding the suffix "m" to each petal sound vibrates the specific petal in both the right and left channels.

◆ BEEjᵃ mᵃntrᵃ: Each chᵃkrᵃ has a seed (bEEjᵃ) mantra that influences the central channel (ShEvᵃ naaDEE). These are taught only by certified InnerTuning teachers to qualified aspirants.

◆ Intoxicant: Intoxicants may temporarily break powerful conditioned reactions of long standing. They thereby permit expression of feelings otherwise suppressed. Consciously or unconsciously, some seek these intoxicants as a means to escape from the suffering caused by blocked feelings and emotions. Unfortunately, the tendency to addiction usually outweighs any possible benefits.

✦ Archetypes: Microchakra Psychology regards the gods and goddesses of the Tantric tradition as archetypal patterns of energy. These patterns are available to all people regardless of their cultural background. They represent ways of utilizing the specific energy available in a chᵃkrᵃ. Invocation of a celestial being by means of a mᵃntrᵃ (sound associated with the god or goddess) or yᵃntrᵃ (geometrical figure associated with the god or goddess) increases the availability of this subtle archetypal energy.

Kuɴdᵃlɛɴɛɛ is represented in each chᵃkrᵃ in the form of male and female archetypes. Among these are six female archetypes found in the first six chᵃkrᵃ-s; they are "sister powers" of Kuɴdᵃlɛɴɛɛ. All reside in the left channel except the sister power of the third chᵃkrᵃ, which resides in the right channel for as long as the first lɛɴgᵃ is dominant and the *fiery* triangle of the third chᵃkrᵃ is pointed downward. The sister powers, from the first to sixth chᵃkrᵃ-s respectively, are: Daakɛɴɛɛ, Rakɛɴɛɛ, Lakɛɴɛɛ, Kakɛɴɛɛ, Saakɛɴɛɛ, and Haakɛɴɛɛ.

When an archetype awakens due to proper spiritual practices (saadhᵃnaa), the aspirant (saadhᵃkᵃ) may be graced with a variety of abilities ranging from overcoming fear of death to knowing past and future. The sister powers have a ferocious as well as a benevolent aspect. Premature spiritual practices and the negative effect of apaanᵃ in the right channel may awaken the ferocious aspect, with results that are destructive of self or others. For this reason InnerTuning gives high priority to the *purification of the three bodies,* which stabilizes apaanᵃ.

As each chᵃkrᵃ is discussed below, its corresponding sister power is described. Just as there are varied descriptions of the chᵃkrᵃ-s in the literature, so also do the descriptions of the sister powers vary.[7] The descriptions given in this book draw from various classical sources as well as the understanding of Microchakra Psychology. They are intended only as a stimulus to reflection about the manner in which a chᵃkrᵃ functions. Unlike some Tantric approaches, *InnerTuning does not recommend that the sister powers be used as a basis for worship.* Any benefits provided by them will only deepen your entanglement in the first lɛɴgᵃ.

Stillness (Shɛvᵃ) also has a representative in each chᵃkrᵃ. These are listed in Table 3.1. In addition to the representatives of Stillness (Shɛvᵃ) and Vibrancy (Shᵃktɛ), various other deities may be associated with a given chᵃkrᵃ.

TABLE 3.1. THE REPRESENTATIVES OF STILLNESS (SHᴇvᴬ) IN NINE CHᴬKRᴬ-S

Seventh Chᵃkrᵃ	SHᴇvᵃ-Shᵃktᴇ united
Somᵃ Chᵃkrᵃ	Kaamᴀshvᵃrᴇᴇ-Kaamᴀshvᵃrᵃ
Sixth Chᵃkrᵃ	Ardhᵃnaarᴇᴇshvᵃrᵃ
Fifth Chᵃkrᵃ	Pᵃnchᵃvaktrᵃ
Hretᵃ Pᵃdmᵃ	Saakshᴇᴇ
Fourth Chᵃkrᵃ	ᴇᴇshaanᵃ SHᴇvᵃ (ᴇᴇshᵃ)
Third Chᵃkrᵃ	Rudrᵃ SHᴇvᵃ
Second Chᵃkrᵃ	Hᵃnumaanᵃ mᵃntrᵃ*
First Chᵃkrᵃ	Gᵃɴᴀshᵃ

*The Hᵃnumaanᵃ mᵃntrᵃ is used by those maintaining celibacy. The deity Hᵃnumaanᵃ is not associated with any particular chᵃkrᵃ; however, it restores the integrity of all second microchakras.

THE FIRST CHᴬKRᴬ
Root Support (Moolaadhaarᵃ)

Introduction

The element of the first chᵃkrᵃ is *earth*. As this chᵃkrᵃ rotates, it establishes sympathetic resonance with the earth and grounds the individual to the body of the planet.

Golden solar energy flowing down the right channel (vᵃjrᴇɴᴇᴇ naaᴅᴇᴇ), finds its root support in the first chᵃkrᵃ. There, the cooling earth absorbs solar heat and transforms it into the lunar upward flow of the left channel (chᴇtrᴇɴᴇᴇ naaᴅᴇᴇ).

The subtle body can be seen as a sphere with two poles: the seventh chᵃkrᵃ (sᵃhᵃsraarᵃ), the domain of Shᴇvᵃ, forms the upper pole and the first chᵃkrᵃ (moo-laadhaarᵃ), the domain of Shᵃktᴇ, forms the lower pole. The seventh chᵃkrᵃ represents the transcendent principle (beyond the tᵃtvᵃ-s and guɴᵃ-s). The first chᵃkrᵃ, in contrast, represents the foundation of physical manifestation.

The fetus in the womb is frequently positioned in the yoga posture of the "head-stand" so that most energy is available for the formation of the brain. As the time of birth approaches, the mother's contractions begin to massage the area of the baby's seventh chᵃkrᵃ. This stimulates the energy to begin its descent into the right channel (vᵃjrᴇɴᴇᴇ naaᴅᴇᴇ).

The natural birth of a welcome baby is the best assurance that an abundant amount of energy will flow down the right channel. If the first years of life offer supportive circumstances, then most of the seven rays of solar energy will descend to the first chᵃkrᵃ. This results in a healthy identification with the physical body in which the child feels grounded and centered. The breath can flow confidently and deeply, allowing the eyes to shine and preparing all senses for an abundance of exploration and expression.

The first chᵃkrᵃ provides instinctual energy necessary for meeting the basic survival needs of security, food, and shelter. Adults with a healthy first chᵃkrᵃ will completely embrace the *earth* element and have a clear sense of "me." There is also a sensitivity to others and a desire for knowledge. Energy will easily rise up the left channel and permit them to be in touch with their feelings. Evolution toward the second ʟᴇngᵃ may occur with ease.

If, on the other hand, the first experiences of life have produced emotions of insecurity and threats to survival then significant blockages will appear in the right channel. To overcome them, and to develop the will to do so, may require deep psychological work and meditation in adulthood.

Any difficulties that occur in utero, at the time of birth, or in the first three to three and a half years of life tend to create a network of blockages. As a result, insufficient energy descends in the right channel (vᵃjrᴇɴᴇᴇ naaᴅᴇᴇ). The practical consequence is that the person functions mostly from the right channel and the left hemisphere of the brain dominates life. There is little communication with feelings and, inadvertently, fantasy becomes a major part of life. This fantasy may cause unnecessary pressures to gain more and more money, sex, and power—in a futile attempt to compensate for the failure of all the solar rays to descend.

When energy is blocked in the first chᵃkrᵃ, a sense of physical identity is lacking, stimulating fears of abandonment, annihilation, or even the demands of meeting daily needs. Basic intuition is confused and ignorance prevails. Such a person's outlook is selfish, resulting in behavior that is cowardly, apathetic, or malicious.

Rotation

The first chᵃkrᵃ is parallel to the ground and rotates clockwise.

Element

The dominant element of the first chᵃkrᵃ is *earth*. Its color is yellow and its shape (yantrᵃ) is a square. Contact with the earth can give a feeling of security. Walking barefoot or sitting on the earth energizes the first chᵃkrᵃ and may create feelings of well-being.

Therapeutic Color

The therapeutic color for the first chᵃkrᵃ is red. This is the color of Vibrancy (ShᵃktE). In the physical field the color red is associated with praaN in the blood; without praaN blood is blue. When the first chᵃkrᵃ mind lacks stability and grounding, the frequencies of the color red have therapeutic value. Red facilitates the descent of solar energy in the right channel. It helps to build confidence and a sense of power, thereby counteracting feelings of insecurity.

Sense Organ

The nose is the sense organ of the first chᵃkrᵃ. The sense of smell is connected to the early brain. People who are well grounded tend to have a strong control over the sense of smell.

Organ of Action

The anus is the main organ of action for the first chᵃkrᵃ. Pressure to the heel may be used to facilitate the process of elimination. Squatting is a natural first chᵃkrᵃ posture.

Storehouse

The thighs are the storehouse of first-chᵃkrᵃ energy.

Sleep Habits

When awareness is preoccupied with the first-chᵃkrᵃ mind, the person is inclined to lie on the stomach for deep sleep. Insecurity and feelings of abandonment make the body want to cling to the earth. This clinging response is basic for young primates. Duration of sleep is twelve hours or more, as is common in children during the first six to seven years, the first-chᵃkrᵃ age.

Endocrine Gland

The medulla of the adrenal gland is connected to the first chᵃkrᵃ.

Symbolic Animal

The element of the first chᵃkrᵃ is represented by the elephant with its powerful body and enormous weight—when the elephant walks, the earth moves. The elephant has exceptional memory. It symbolizes bodily confidence as well as being grounded and centered.

The elephant described in the tradition is a mythical one with seven trunks representing the colors of the rainbow. When all seven rays, beginning as white light in the seventh chᵃkrᵃ, descend in the right channel to the first chᵃkrᵃ, the person is naturally energized by the complete spectrum of light.

Developmental Period

In the first chᵃkrᵃ, the developmental period for girls is from birth to age six; for boys, to age seven. With relatively good parenting, the child will be able to resolve the psychological complexes of the first chᵃkrᵃ (such as: fear of abandonment, insecurity, lack of basic identity) during this period. Young children are naturally right-hemisphere dominant. It is essential that this tendency be nurtured during the first-chᵃkrᵃ age. The right hemisphere is feeling, devotional, poetical, and intuitive. Premature emphasis on left-hemisphere activity will make it very difficult for the person to experience contentment from feelings later in life.

Celestial Connection

The first chᵃkrᵃ receives energy from the planet Mars.

Musical Sensitivity

Simple rhythms of pulsation are pleasing to the first-chᵃkrᵃ mind. The drum is often used to appeal to the first chᵃkrᵃ. A simple 1-2 rhythm is associated with the early brain and is used to train circus animals. It has strong attraction for children up to about three years of age. Afterward, a four-beat cycle (matching the number of petals in the first chᵃkrᵃ) is most representative of the first chᵃkrᵃ. Dancing to a four-beat rhythm helps to develop the first chᵃkrᵃ. Ideally, the four-beat cycle is appreciated by the sixth year. This gives a solid foundation for further development of body coordination and helps in space orientation and the reduction of insecurity.

The drum is associated with the first chᵃkrᵃ because its sound can assist energy to come down the right channel and produce a grounding effect. The hand motion used with many types of drums has a downward accent.

The quality of drumming determines which of the first microchakras in the higher chᵃkrᵃ-s will be affected. The beat cycle is the most important strategy that the drummer controls. Each chᵃkrᵃ is affected by a different beat cycle that corresponds to the number of lotus petals of the chᵃkrᵃ. The names of the cycles are in parentheses below:

> The 8-beat cycle (kahrvaa) pleases the first chᵃkrᵃ in adults (while children respond to a 4-beat cycle) and first microchakras. It is a combination of two 4-beat cycles.
>
> The 6-beat cycle (daadraa) pleases the second chᵃkrᵃ and second microchakras.
>
> The 10-beat cycle (jhᵃptaalᵃ) pleases the third chᵃkrᵃ and third microchakras.
>
> The 12-beat cycle (Aktaalᵃ) pleases the fourth chᵃkrᵃ and fourth microchakras.
>
> The 16-beat cycle, (teentaalᵃ), pleases the fifth chᵃkrᵃ and fifth microchakras.
>
> The 7-, 9-, 13-, and 17-beat cycles as well as more complicated cycles please the sixth chᵃkrᵃ and sixth microchakras.
>
> The hollow sound of a royal ancient Indian drum (the pᵃkhaavᵃjᵃ) activates the fifth chᵃkrᵃ. This drum is played sideways and the hand motion is accented upward—thus assisting the upward flow of energy in the left channel.

Petal Sounds

The four blood-red petals of the first chᵃkrᵃ respond to the following sounds:

Right channel:	vᵃ	व	Labial
	shᵃ	श	Palatal
Left channel:	SHᵃ	ष	Cerebral
	sᵃ	स	Dental

Intoxicant

Opium is the primary intoxicant of the first chᵃkrᵃ. It influences all solids of the body including bones and nerves.

Archetypes

Brᵃhmaa. Brᵃhmaa as the creative principle is the ruling deity of the first chᵃkrᵃ. It is important to give due consideration to Brᵃhmaa by keeping this chᵃkrᵃ pure and thereby reducing obstruction of the energy flow in the subtle channels.

Brᵃhmaa's four heads offer the ability to see in four directions simultaneously and to be in touch with the energies of the four directions. Energy from the east is associated with physical health. Energy from the south overcomes the fear of death. Energy from the west provides material wealth and popularity. Energy from the north gives the inspiration for spiritual evolution. Alternatively, each head symbolizes one of the four Vadᵃ-s, the ancient books of wisdom.

Brᵃhmaa's four arms each offer a benediction: the upper right hand shows the gesture for removing fear (abhayᵃ mudraa). The lower right hand carries a sacred water vessel, symbol of the cleanliness of the body. The lower left hand holds a scriptural scroll depicting Divine wisdom. The upper left hand offers a lotus that opens to the sun symbolizing the purity of the Brᵃhmᵃ muhoortᵃ—the first-chᵃkrᵃ hour in which Brᵃhmaa is easily invoked.

Brᵃhmaa creates the universe as an adult. Then he places himself in the first chᵃkrᵃ as a child—the child Brᵃhmaa (Baalᵃ Brᵃhmaa). He understands that the way to convert the ferocious DaakЕnЕЕ (see below) into her benevolent aspect is by attracting her to his innocence as a child. As DaakЕnЕЕ looks at the glowing face of the child Brᵃhmaa, her motherly instinct is aroused.

DaakЕnЕЕ. KuNdᵃlЕnЕЕ is represented by DaakЕnЕЕ in the first chᵃkrᵃ. Since the first chᵃkrᵃ is completely "me" oriented, DaakЕnЕЕ is shown with only one head. In her benevolent aspect, accompanying Brᵃhmaa, DaakЕnЕЕ wears a peach-colored dress, her eyes have genuine warmth, and she uses her weapons to overcome obstacles to spiritual growth such as attachment and greed. She holds the following weapons:

- ✦ Upper right hand: shield—to protect from physical and psychic attack
- ✦ Lower right hand: sword—for removal of obstacles
- ✦ Upper left hand: skull—conquest of the fear of death
- ✦ Lower left hand: trident—a symbol of creation, preservation, and transformation

In her destructive aspect, DaakЕnЕЕ has red skin and is dressed in the hide of a black antelope. She has fierce red eyes and fang-like teeth. She uses her weapons for a greedy pursuit of wealth, sexual conquest, and fame. The meaning of each weapon changes:

- ✦ Upper right hand: shield—saboteurs (see chapter 4) protecting themselves
- ✦ Lower right hand: sword—potential to kill others
- ✦ Upper left hand: skull—annihilation of nature's plan for a species to reproduce
- ✦ Lower left hand: trident—vengeance, jealousy, and competitiveness leading to
  total destruction of the planet Earth that is supporting all life

DaakɛnEE changes from her destructive to her benevolent aspect as the spiritual aspirant (saadhᵃkᵃ) evolves in the pursuit of liberation. The aspirant may facilitate this transformation by invoking the child Brᵃhmaa (Baalᵃ Brᵃhmaa) and maintaining the purity of innocent truth. Then, everything is called as it is seen; there is no room for any diplomatic evasion.

GᵃNAshᵃ. GᵃNAshᵃ is a godhead in the first chᵃkrᵃ who symbolizes grounding and centering as well as gregariousness and the joy of life. He is invoked as the remover of obstacles. At the command of ShEvᵃ, he is called upon at all ceremonies before any other deity.

GᵃNAshᵃ's upper right hand holds a hatchet with which to cut obstacles. His lower right hand offers the gesture of "fear-not" (abhayᵃ mudraa). When GᵃNAshᵃ awakens within us we handle obstacles with confidence and ease because there is direction through the grace of GᵃNAshᵃ.

His upper left hand holds a lotus that symbolizes the purity of the first chᵃkrᵃ period (Brᵃhmᵃ muhoortᵃ) that, at the equator, occurs two hours before sunrise. The further north or south of the equator one travels, the later is the first chᵃkrᵃ period (see page 267).

GᵃNAshᵃ's lower left hand offers a bowl of sweets with which he feeds a little mouse at his feet. The mouse represents the first chᵃkrᵃ "mouse mind" that is destructive and constantly nibbles at everything edible and inedible. In people, the constant desire to chew is an indication of the mouse mind out of control. The insecure first-chᵃkrᵃ mind also generates internal chatter without end. Feeding sweets to the mouse keeps the mouse mind in check. The "sweets" symbolize glucose or any other source of energy, both physical and psychological, which serve to control eating habits, anger, greed, and backbiting.

GᵃNAshᵃ's elephant head represents excellent memory. The large ears connote the importance of attentive listening. The trunk is an instrument of precision; it knows how to pick up a needle as well as a tree. Precise intuition regarding bodily needs is available from the sixth microchakra in the first chᵃkrᵃ. The pot belly of GᵃNAshᵃ symbolizes the contentment derived from healthy nourishment of the first chᵃkrᵃ.

The Elephant with a Rainbow of Trunks. A traditional representation of the descending spectrum of light is an elephant with seven trunks, one for each color of the rainbow. If any of the hues are weak or muddy, it means that a specific chᵃkrᵃ has a proportional number of microchakras blocked in the right channel. Negative emotions related to the affected color may drive the elephant wild and lead to unbelievable crimes and atrocities. The presence of GᵃNAshᵃ can control this elephant.

The First lɛngᵃ (Svᵃyambhoo)

The first chᵃkrᵃ is also the dwelling of the dormant Kᴜɴdᵃlɛɴee. In the center of the root plexus (khᵃndᵃ), represented by a downward-pointing triangle, is a Sʜɛvᵃ lɛngᵃ. This sign of Sʜɛvᵃ is shaped like an egg or leaf bud. A serpent, representing Kᴜɴdᵃlɛɴee, is coiled around it 3½ times, with its mouth closing the door to the central channel (Sʜɛvᵃdvaarᵃ), awaiting a time of awakening.

The name of the Sʜɛvᵃ lɛngᵃ in the first chᵃkrᵃ means "self-born" (Svᵃyambhoo)—one of the thousand names of Sʜɛvᵃ. The connotation is that the desires of the first lɛngᵃ come naturally to us all, they are self-born (that is, innate). This is very different from the desires of the second and third lɛngᵃ-s that need much spiritual practice (saadhᵃnaa) to emerge.

THE SECOND CHᴬKRᴬ

Support in Itself (Svᵃdhɛsʜᴛʜaanᵃ)

Introduction

The element of the second chᵃkrᵃ is *water*. As this chᵃkrᵃ rotates, it impels us into relationships with others. The "me" of the first chᵃkrᵃ is expanded to "me and you" and the ego becomes more refined through its relations.

Water is a potent purifier. Flowing water carries negative ions, and aspirants throughout the ages have sought rivers, waterfalls, and oceans as ideal places for spiritual practice (saadhᵃnaa). The positive aspects of *water* also have their polar opposites, primarily those associated with the emotion of fear. Fear is the major complex of the second chᵃkrᵃ.

Water has a tendency to mix with just about anything. Sharing and exchange come naturally. In the first-chᵃkrᵃ age, parents have to teach their children to share their toys with others. Later, in the second-chᵃkrᵃ age, it is natural for healthy children to give and take.

When energy flows freely in the second chᵃkrᵃ there is enjoyment of pleasure and acceptance of pain. Sensuality, sexuality, and conditional love are readily integrated into life. Exchange is honest. Gender identity is well established.

When second-chᵃkrᵃ energy is stagnant, feelings of separation and isolation tend to prevail. As an adult, emotions may be colored by fear, thus inhibiting sexuality or causing overindulgence. Fear of pain is very common. Sensuality may be rejected due to guilt associated with sex. There is frequent escape into fantasy. Exchange is often unfair and dishonest. Hesitancy (or outright rejection) regarding gender identity is often a problem. During the second-chᵃkrᵃ age, fantasy may be used to diminish fear. Artistic endeavors help to transcend sexual preoccupation. Some adults take to a religious life because they lack the courage to express their sexuality. Truly religious people know how to transform their sexual energy to the heart chᵃkrᵃ by selfless service and worship.

A fundamental desire of the second chᵃkrᵃ mind is the survival of the species. This is associated with an unconscious fear that the species might not survive. In this way, sexuality is linked to fear; as the threat to a species materializes, its rate of reproduction increases. This relation between fear of extinction and reproductive activity may be mediated by the morphogenetic field as it is described by Rupert Sheldrake in his *A New Science of Life: The Hypothesis of Formative Causation*.[8]

Rotation

The second chᵃkrᵃ is perpendicular to the ground and spins counterclockwise. However, the clockwise spin of the first and third chᵃkrᵃ-s tends to pull the second-chᵃkrᵃ energy downward. It requires assistance from the upward spin of the chᵃkrᵃ-s in the second and third lᴇngᵃ-s to maintain the upward spin of the second chᵃkrᵃ.

Element

The element of the second chᵃkrᵃ is *water* and the associated affects are fear and eros. The color of *water* is clear or pale blue and its shape (yantrᵃ) is a circle, similar to the appearance of a water drop. The secretion of both urine and sexual fluids are derived from the activity of the second chᵃkrᵃ.

Water can be an expression of feeling. In his book *The Hidden Messages in Water* Dr. Masaru Emoto reported on his experiments that demonstrated the differing effects of positive and negative thoughts on water. Water that had been exposed to kindness and care showed an amazingly beautiful crystal when frozen. It had six aesthetic protrusions similar to the six petals of the *water* yᵃntrᵃ of the second chᵃkrᵃ. The same water, when exposed to harshness, showed crystals that were uneven, incomplete, and distorted.[9]

If negative emotions can distort a molecule of water, imagine what they can do to the *water* mind! Adults are more than 70 percent water. If you harbor negative thoughts about yourself and you contain 100 pounds of water, this can weigh heavily on your psyche.

Therapeutic Color

The therapeutic color of the second chᵃkrᵃ is pink for females and orange for males. Pink can be called a lunar shade of the red frequency and orange a solar shade of the same. These shades give comfort and courage when in fear.

Sense Organ

The tongue is the sense organ of the second chᵃkrᵃ. It contains the receptors that discriminate the basic tastes. Ayurveda (ancient Indian medicine) recognizes six different tastes: sweet (*earth + water*), sour (*earth + fire*), salt (*water + fire*), bitter (*air + water*), pungent (*air + fire*), and astringent (*air + earth*).

Organ of Action

The genitourinary organs are the organs of action for the second chᵃkrᵃ.

Storehouse

The balls of the feet are the storehouse of second-chᵃkrᵃ energy. This storehouse is energetically linked with pressure points in the lower lip and tongue.

Sleep Habits

In the second-chᵃkrᵃ age, when fear dominates, deep sleep occurs in the fetal position. Fear directs the body to curl up in sleep, more or less like a circle (the yantrᵃ of a water drop). Fear can bring forth an unconscious desire to be back in the womb, to be safe and automatically taken care of—away from the challenges regarding "me-others" that arise in the second-chᵃkrᵃ age. Duration of sleep is ten to eleven hours.

In a healthy state, when fear is not dominant, the preference is to start out sleep on the back and later in the night to turn to the left side.

Endocrine Gland

The gonads are the endocrine glands of the second chᵃkrᵃ.

Symbolic Animal

The energy of the second chᵃkrᵃ is represented by the crocodile. In many ancient cultures, the crocodile was associated with sexuality; its oil and other parts of its body were used as aphrodisiacs. It is said that the crocodile calls for its mate during second-chᵃkrᵃ hours.

The crocodile is agile in water as well as on land. This agility is reflected in the mind of the second chᵃkrᵃ. The second chᵃkrᵃ mind tends to be easily influenced and molded by its environment. It is facile in adapting to others in a social situation. This is particularly helpful in circumstances requiring diplomacy. However, there is an accompanying tendency to insincerity and the shedding of "crocodile tears." Some businessmen may devour like crocodiles and charge mercilessly if they are trapped in the fearful second chᵃkrᵃ mind. This trait is alleviated only when energy rises to the fourth chᵃkrᵃ where conscience resides.

Developmental Period

The developmental period for females is from six to twelve; for males, seven to fourteen.

Celestial Connection

The second chᵃkrᵃ is enhanced by energy from the planet Mercury.

Musical Sensitivity

The rhythm of this chᵃkrᵃ is the flowing rhythm of the waltz: one-two-three. Tight-stringed musical instruments that are picked or plucked, such as the guitar, banjo, and harp, appeal to the second chᵃkrᵃ. These instruments produce few sustained tones.

Petal Sounds

The six orange-red petals of the second chᵃkrᵃ respond to the following sounds:

Right channel:	bᵃ	ब	Labial
	bhᵃ	भ	Labial
	mᵃ	म	Labial
Left channel:	yᵃ	य	Palatal
	rᵃ	र	Cerebral
	lᵃ	ळ	Dental

Intoxicant

Alcohol is the primary intoxicant of the second chᵃkrᵃ. It removes inhibitions and gives a false sense of courage and laughter. After a while these reactions turn into depression.

Archetypes

Veshnu. As the preserver, Veshnu tames the second chᵃkrᵃ wild crocodile that can devour overly sexual people. He permits dhᵃrmᵃ and good will to enrich relationships. Veshnu is the embodiment of the sᵃtvᵃ of the second chᵃkrᵃ and its upward directed flow of energy. As long as sexual desire is present, Veshnu is portrayed with a blue skin of great beauty. He sanctifies each dharmic act of sexuality. When all sexual desire is transcended his skin is said to be of a glorious transparent white. His four arms carry the following implements:

- ✦ The lower right hand holds a metallic club, which represents the earthly power that is needed to acquire material means to meet second chᵃkrᵃ goals. According to Microchakra Psychology, this power draws upon the energy flowing in the first microchakra of the left channel in the second chᵃkrᵃ (L2:1) (see chapter 5).
- ✦ The lower left hand offers a lotus, symbol of purity in relationships.
- ✦ The upper left hand holds a conch, a fifth chᵃkrᵃ instrument that comes from the ocean—the home of Veshnu. The sound of the conch creates an upward spiraling *aakaashᵃ*. It is a reminder that second chᵃkrᵃ attachments can be dissolved in fifth chᵃkrᵃ *aakaashᵃ*.
- ✦ The pointing finger of the upper right hand has a disc of light that continuously whirls around it. This is the dhᵃrmᵃ chᵃkrᵃ (wheel of dhᵃrmᵃ). Veshnu represents the continuity of life and the dhᵃrmᵃ chᵃkrᵃ symbolizes this. On occasion, the whirling disc must be used as a weapon to slay enemies of life's continuity. Some people are called to a dhᵃrmᵃ that serves this purpose.

Incarnations of Veshnu

The principle of preservation manifests in each yugᵃ according to the needs of evolution of the jeevᵃ. The classical ten incarnations of Veshnu reflect these needs.

1. Fish (Mᵃtsyᵃh)—Sᵃtyᵃ yugᵃ
   The cycle commences with Sᵃtyᵃ yugᵃ and fish populate the sea.
2. Tortoise (Kurmᵃh)—Sᵃtyᵃ yugᵃ
   Earth emerges out of the water. Fish evolve into amphibians and reptiles.
3. Boar (Vᵃraah)—Sᵃtyᵃ yugᵃ
   Boar represents mammals that can survive in marshy land.
4. Half-man/Half-lion (Nᵃrᵃsimᵃh)—Sᵃtyᵃ yugᵃ

Symbol of human evolving from animal.

5. Dwarf (Vaamᵃnᵃ)—Tʀᴀtaa yugᵃ

  Appearance of human in evolutionary process.

6. Rama with the axe (Pᵃrᵃsuraamᵃ)—Tʀᴀtaa yugᵃ

  Human as hunter.

7. Rama (Raamᵃchᵃndrᵃ)—Tʀᴀtaa yugᵃ

  Appearance of moral man. Rama was an exemplar of integrity.

8. All Attractive One (Kʀᴇshnᵃ)—Dvaaprᵃ yugᵃ

  Perfect artist. Expert in sixteen arts.

9. Enlightened One (Buddhaa)—Kᵃlᴇ yugᵃ

  Transcendence of suffering.

10. Destroyer of Unrighteousness (KaalkEE)—Kᵃlᴇ yugᵃ

  To appear in the distant future.

At the end of each yugᵃ the Earth is submerged in water. After a pause it reemerges from the water and evolution commences the next cycle.

Hᵃnumaanᵃ. Hᵃnumaanᵃ is an archetype of a man with simian features and a tail. He has extraordinary strength, a great capacity for loyalty, and the ability to assume any size. These and other attributes are described in the epic *Ramayana*. Hᵃnumaanᵃ is an archetype of celibacy and was created in the Tʀᴀtaa yugᵃ to help civilize the early brain by preventing an excess of sexuality. Today, his mᵃntrᵃ may be particularly useful during the second-chᵃkrᵃ age (which ends with puberty), for periods of celibacy, and for those who desire celibacy throughout life. The senior author's research suggests that the Hᵃnumaanᵃ mᵃntrᵃ helps to overcome fears of various types when chanted on specific tones designed on an individual basis.

RaakᴇnEE. Kᴜɴᵈᵃlᴇɴᴇᴇ appears as RaakᴇnEE in the second chᵃkrᵃ. She has two heads: "me" and "you." These represent two separate conflicts: the first conflict is between asexuality and sexuality; the second conflict is between sexuality and transcendence.

Asexuality reigns during the first-chᵃkrᵃ age. In contrast to the teaching of Freud and others, Microchakra Psychology holds the view that children do not have sexual feelings during the first six or seven years of life unless they receive unusual and inappropriate stimulation—in the form of touch or food. The latter includes red meat in any form that stimulates the sexual nerve endings and may lead to premature sexual stimulation and masturbation. During the right-channel age children should receive easily digestible proteins such as mother's milk and that from one-stomach animals such as sheep and goats. Other sources of easily assimilable protein include fermented soy, avocado, whole grain cereals, and limited amounts of seeds and nuts as paste. Organic forms of these products are to be preferred.

When girls and boys play together during the first-chᵃkrᵃ age, they simply assert their bodily identity. Children develop a feeling of gender identity in the second-chᵃkrᵃ age. When the conflict between gender neutrality and positive gender identity is greatest, RaakEnEE's two heads look in opposite directions. As the conflict is resolved and a positive gender identity is accepted, her two heads turn toward each other.

In many societies women are treated as second-class citizens. This begins in the second-chᵃkrᵃ age. During the first-chᵃkrᵃ age, boys and girls are treated more or less equally. However, in the second-chᵃkrᵃ age, girls receive spoken or unspoken messages that they are less important than the boys. The unfair treatment given to girls distorts the smooth flow of energy from the lotus of six petals of the *water* mind of the second chᵃkrᵃ. The distorting effect upon their self-image may last a lifetime, particularly if it is accompanied by a belief that sex is dirty or sinful.

The second conflict is shown when RaakEnEE's two heads look away from each other in a playful manner. On the one hand, a female accepts her gender identity and seeks a male friend to play with; on the other hand, she aspires to rise to the higher chᵃkrᵃ-s to find her social identity. RaakEnEE also symbolizes a similar conflict for the males. To the degree that these conflicts are resolved, the two heads of RaakEnEE turn to face one another. Resolution is strongly dependent upon support from the culture for healthy gender identity.

RaakEnEE in her benevolent form has skin of a luminous pink hue. She is covered by flowing silks of sunset red, adorned with a transparent shawl reminiscent of the new moon. She is a great inspiration for those who honor the upward flow in the second chᵃkrᵃ. Her weapons are:

- ✦ Upper right hand: axe—warns against overindulgence, detrimental to spiritual growth.
- ✦ Lower right hand: drum—following the lunar nature of sexual rhythm leads to perfection of various types of intimate relations. During the second-chᵃkrᵃ age, mastery of the 6-beat cycle in dancing enhances masculinity in boys and femininity in girls.
- ✦ Upper left hand: arrow—intuition about mate (L2:6).
- ✦ Lower left hand: skull—unconscious fear of extinction of the human race.

A prematurely awakened RaakEnEE, nourished by right-channel saboteurs, represents the second-chᵃkrᵃ mind out of control. Her appearance becomes fierce: her eyes are blood red and frightening canine teeth protrude from the mouths of both heads—expressing insatiable desires. Blood flows from her nostrils. The meaning of the weapons changes:

- Upper right hand: axe—impulse to kill, either physically, through slow rejection or hired assassin.
- Lower right hand: spear—replaces drum, aggressive expression of sexual impulses including aggressive masturbation. Suppression of sexual instinct and body development. May utilize shame or masochism.
- Upper left hand: arrow—separation from feelings due to guilt and/or intellectualization.
- Lower left hand: skull—excess of sexuality leading to weakness and death. Alternatively, it may lead to a denial of sexual feelings and gender rejection.

THE THIRD CHᴬKRᴬ
Palace of the Jewel (MaɴEpurᵃ)

Introduction

The element of the third chᵃkrᵃ is *fire*. In the physical body, it nourishes the process of digestion and maintains homeostasis. In psychological activity, it is the element that fuels the ego in all chᵃkrᵃ-s; the third chᵃkrᵃ ego (3:3) is the *fire* of the *fire*. It is concerned with assertiveness and personal power. The "me and you" of the second chᵃkrᵃ is now expanded to "me, you, and others" as power reaches beyond intimate relationships to status in a group or community.

When the third chᵃkrᵃ ego functions in a healthy manner, reason and emotion are balanced, we are content with our accomplishments, and personal power can be used to help others. The third chᵃkrᵃ egotistical desire for immortality has significantly diminished.

When energy flow within the third chᵃkrᵃ is restricted, we are burdened with an excessively rational view of life and preoccupation with the intellect. This is accompanied by intense striving for recognition and fame. There will be great pride in our own accomplishment. Motivation for personal power and domination of others is very strong. The ever-present fear of death is reflected in an insatiable desire for longevity and the immortality of our name.

An underdeveloped ego produces a follower mentality and right-brain orientation. However, this form of right-brain orientation does not have the benefit of being in touch with deeper feelings.

The third chᵃkrᵃ influences the area of the solar plexus. By sitting quietly at sunrise, it is sometimes possible to experience solar activity going on in the solar plexus. Tᵃntrᵃ illustrates the *fire* of the third chᵃkrᵃ by means of a downward-pointing triangle. The third chᵃkrᵃ tends to use its power for the protection of the second chᵃkrᵃ (family and friends) and the first chᵃkrᵃ (survival and property). One of the objectives of spiritual practice is to enable the downward-pointing triangle to reverse and point upward. This indicates that the selfish energy of the first lᴇngᵃ is now flowing upward to the fourth chᵃkrᵃ and a more loving attitude toward life in general is becoming established.

Rotation
The third chᵃkrᵃ is perpendicular to the ground and spins clockwise.

Element
The element of the third chᵃkrᵃ is *fire*. The color of *fire* is red and its shape is a triangle.

Therapeutic Color
The therapeutic color of the third chᵃkrᵃ is green.

Sense Organ
The eyes are the sense organ of the third chᵃkrᵃ. Light is an aspect of the *fire* element for which the eyes are receptors. When the *fiery* triangle of the third chᵃkrᵃ reverses and points upward, warmth, love, and enthusiasm may be expressed with extra *fire* in the eyes.

Organ of Action

The organs of action for the third chᵃkrᵃ are the digestive system and the legs from the knees to the feet. The digestive system is primarily related to the physical field. *Fire* feeds the liver, kidneys, pancreas, spleen, and other organs in the radius of the solar chᵃkrᵃ and maintains the body's homeostasis.

Storehouse

The trapezius area around the neck and shoulders is the storehouse of third-chᵃkrᵃ energy. The energetic link is to the eyes, pancreas, and knees.

Sleep Habits

When the third chᵃkrᵃ is dominant, deep sleep occurs lying on the back for eight to nine hours.

Endocrine Gland

The cortex of the adrenal is the endocrine gland of the third chᵃkrᵃ.

Symbolic Animal

The energy of the third chᵃkrᵃ is symbolized by the ram. Rams fight with their heads. When the third chᵃkrᵃ is dominant, people are very competitive and interested in conquering others. They place far more emphasis on results than on the process of attaining them.

Developmental Period

The developmental period for females is from twelve to eighteen; for males, it is fourteen to twenty-one.

Celestial Connection

The third chᵃkrᵃ is enhanced with energy from the Sun.

Musical Sensitivity

Bowed instruments such as the violin, cello, and sarangi are considered third chᵃkrᵃ instruments. As these instruments are played, they typically make use of the third chᵃkrᵃ storehouse of energy in the muscle between the neck and shoulders.

All melodies are created with seven notes. The ocean of seven notes is deep. The greater the musician, the more they realize the depth—which makes them humble.

Petal Sounds

The ten flame-blue petals of the third chᵃkrᵃ respond to the following sounds:

Right channel:	Dᵃ	ड	Cerebral
	DHᵃ	ढ	Cerebral
	Nᵃ	ण	Cerebral
	tᵃ	त	Dental
	thᵃ	थ	Dental
Left channel:	dᵃ	द	Dental
	dhᵃ	ध	Dental
	nᵃ	न	Dental
	pᵃ	प	Labial
	phᵃ	फ	Labial

Intoxicant

Cocaine and caffeine are third-chᵃkrᵃ intoxicants.

Archetypes

Rudrᵃ. Shᴇᴠᵃ's representative in the third chᵃkrᵃ is Rudrᵃ, who is portrayed as a white old man sitting on a bull and protecting dhᵃrmᵃ (through blocking destructive tendencies).

In his right hand Rudrᵃ carries a trident, the symbol of all three channels and their connection to the tripartite brain. The shaft is the strongest and represents the central channel and its connection to the early brain. It functions automatically through the principle of retᵃ. The prongs represent the left and right channels and their connections to the cerebral hemispheres. Evolution has created a mutually beneficial relationship between the shaft and the prongs. The prongs help to civilize the shaft through their power of reason and feeling. In turn, the shaft guides them to retᵃ and the eventual end of birth, death, and rebirth (sᵃmsaarᵃ).

In his left hand Rudrᵃ holds a drum. The rhythm of the solar chᵃkrᵃ (at both dawn and dusk) is extremely important. The drum is a reminder of this.

During the right-channel age, Rudrᵃ is naturally in meditation (that is, his destructive potential does not manifest) and he dwells in the left channel with the other male deities.

Unfortunately, beginning in the left-channel age, various practices that can spoil a child (described in later chapters) commence or intensify. These cause Rudrᵃ to awaken and manifest such destructive aspects as dominance, selfishness, jealousy, anger, competitiveness, intolerance, and vengeance. The awakened Rudrᵃ is portrayed as red and wearing a tiger skin. He shifts places with LakᴇɴᴇE (see below) and moves into the right channel where he contributes to blockages.

The awakening of Rudrᵃ keeps the third-chᵃkrᵃ triangle of *fire* burning downward and motivation locked into the first lᴇɴgᵃ.

LakᴇɴᴇE. The sister of KuɴdᵃlᴇɴᴇE in the third chᵃkrᵃ appears as the archetype LakᴇɴᴇE. She has three heads representing "me," "you," and "others." She is dark in color and garbed in yellow. Her face is as beautiful as the moon and her eyes shine brightly. Showing qualities of leadership, she holds the following weapons:

- Upper right hand: thunderbolt—mighty power of decision making
- Lower right hand: gesture of fearlessness—imparts courage
- Upper left hand: fire of purification—reminder to reverse the downward-pointing triangle of the third chᵃkrᵃ
- Lower left hand: arrow—upward flow of energy in left channel

When the destructive LakᴇɴᴇE is awakened by right-channel blocks driven by apaanᵃ-fueled saboteurs (see chapter 4), her beautiful countenance changes to that of a power-hungry hellcat with protruding fangs. The meaning of the weapons now becomes:

- Upper right hand: thunderbolt—royal symbol of vain power
- Lower right hand: gesture of ruthless power—projects brutality
- Upper left hand: fire—destructive fire projected on the world
- Lower left hand: arrow—pinpoint accuracy in targeting victims

This power-hungry LakᴇɴᴇE dwells in the left channel and supports the awakening of Rudrᵃ. The minds of the first lᴇɴgᵃ are encouraged to believe that they can do anything for their pleasure without any consideration for others, and that it is acceptable to destroy the Earth for their momentary pleasure.

At some point, LakᴇɴᴇE might shift her perspective and surrender to the wise old Rudrᵃ. Then they exchange places—LakᴇɴᴇE joins the female deities in the right channel and Rudrᵃ joins the other male deities in the left channel. The triangle of the third chᵃkrᵃ reverses to an upward direction and energy can proceed to the second lᴇɴgᵃ.

THE FOURTH CHᵃKRᴬ
Unstruck Sound (Anaahᵃtᵃ)

Introduction

The element of the fourth chᵃkrᵃ is *air* and the associated feelings are unconditional love and compassion. The ego in the fourth chᵃkrᵃ (4:3) surrenders the self-centered motivation of the first lɛngᵃ and becomes established in the other-centered perspective of the second lɛngᵃ (Baaɴᵃ lɛngᵃ). Then it is natural to dedicate yourself to a deity, a cause, a healing profession, or simply your family, particularly children and elderly parents or grandparents. Healing energy may flood the hands, which become extraordinarily sensitive to touch. Worship (upaasᵃnaa) is intense.

The sense of personal possession decreases; it is understood at a deep level that all belongs to the Divine. The motivation of a person with ample fourth-chᵃkrᵃ energy may not be understood by those still trapped in the first lɛngᵃ. However, in times of need, their capacity for nurturance will be appreciated.

In fourth chᵃkrᵃ awareness, there is no fear of dying and it is nearly impossible to kill another for any reason. Sometimes, however, fourth chᵃkrᵃ awareness is corrupted by religious or other fanatics who turn followers into executioners.

The fourth chᵃkrᵃ is the plane of balance, with three chᵃkrᵃ-s below and three above. It is a gateway to the Great Plane (mᵃhaa lokᵃ)—one of the planes of existence (lokᵃ-s) that are beyond spacetime. The fourth chᵃkrᵃ covers a greater area of the body than that of any other chᵃkrᵃ.

The fourth chᵃkrᵃ is called anaahᵃtᵃ because it is here that unstruck sound can first be heard. According to Microchakra Psychology, this occurs in the fifth microchakra of the fourth chᵃkrᵃ (L4:5).

Rotation

The fourth chᵃkrᵃ is perpendicular to the ground and spins counterclockwise.

Element

The element of the fourth ch^akr^a is *air*. The color of *air* is green. The shape is a hexagram.

Therapeutic Color

The therapeutic color of the fourth ch^akr^a is beige, brown, or gold.

Sense Organ

The fingertips are the sense organ of the fourth ch^akr^a.

Organ of Action

The skin is the organ of action for the fourth ch^akr^a.

Storehouse

The storehouse of fourth-ch^akr^a energy is the diaphragm. The energetic link is to the fingertips and breath. Healing energy may be directed to flow from the fingertips through proper control of the diaphragm.

Sleep Habits

When the fourth ch^akr^a mind is dominant, deep sleep occurs while lying on the left side with legs slightly bent. Duration is six to seven hours.

Endocrine Gland

The thymus is the endocrine gland associated with the fourth ch^akr^a.

Symbolic Animal

The energy of the fourth ch^akr^a is represented by the deer. The gentleness of deer eyes reflect a basic love energy. The leaping of the deer symbolizes the heart when it leaps in joy.

Developmental Period

The developmental period for females is from eighteen to twenty-four; for males, twenty-one to twenty-eight.

Celestial Connection

The fourth ch^akr^a is enhanced by energy from the planet Venus.

Musical Sensitivity

The energy of the fourth ch^akr^a may be best expressed through wind instruments such as the flute and oboe; these instruments tap naturally into the storehouse of energy in the diaphragm.

Petal Sounds

The twelve rusty-red petals of the fourth chᵃkrᵃ respond to the following sounds:

Right channel:	kᵃ	क	Guttural
	khᵃ	ख	Guttural
	gᵃ	ग	Guttural
	ghᵃ	घ	Guttural
	ngᵃ	ड़	Guttural
	chᵃ	च	Palatal
Left channel:	chhᵃ	छ	Palatal
	jᵃ	ज	Palatal
	jhᵃ	झ	Palatal
	njᵃ	ञ	Palatal
	Tᵃ	ट	Cerebral
	THᵃ	ठ	Cerebral

Intoxicant

Peyote, sacred mushrooms, and soma (juice of a plant used in ancient Vedic ritual) are intoxicants of the fourth chᵃkrᵃ.

Archetypes

EEshaanᵃ ShEvᵃ (EEshᵃ). ShEvᵃ appears in the fourth chᵃkrᵃ as EEshaanᵃ ShEvᵃ, (EEshᵃ means "Master"), embodiment of perfect balance of the energy of creation, preservation, and transformation—symbolized by the trident in his right hand. The drum in his left hand represents the twelve-beat cycle of the heart chᵃkrᵃ. This rhythm assists in freeing the aspirant of worldly attachments and kindling love for the inner sound (naadᵃ).

EEshᵃ, free of first lɛngᵃ attachments, is ever youthful, generous, and evocative of peace. He has three eyes and the holy waters of the Ganges (Gᵃngaa) river flow from his matted hair, symbolizing purity of the left channel.

EEshᵃ wears seven snakes as ornaments. These indicate transcendence of the emotions—the basis of attachment in all seven chᵃkrᵃ-s. EEshᵃ, with three eyes, personifies the harmonious coexistence of the internal reality with the external world.

KakENEE. The representative of KuNdᵃlENEE in the fourth chᵃkrᵃ is KakENEE. In her benevolent form, KakENEE embodies the swift *air* element with her ever-watchful upward impetus and devotional qualities. Invocation of KakENEE assures that the third chᵃkrᵃ triangle stays pointed upward and that KuNdᵃlENEE can take her abode in the fourth chᵃkrᵃ.

KakENEE is said to be of moon-like beauty with the gentlest of eyes that emit a mysterious green glow. She is draped in soft white silk and graces the aspirant with healing and peace of mind. She is the goddess of refined devotional arts and healing. KakENEE has four heads and four arms. Her heads symbolize:

+ First head: rapture of unconditional devotion
+ Second head: love of healing and visionary art
+ Third head: service through the phenomenon of nondoership
+ Fourth head: bliss (aanandᵃ) of complete faith in the deity

The symbols held by her four arms are:

+ Upper right hand: spear—pierces the illusory desires that prevent energy from rising
+ Lower right hand: skull—conveys freedom from the false identification with the body
+ Upper left hand: shield—protects from both physical and psychic influences
+ Lower left hand: sword—cuts away obstacles to spiritual growth

The destructive form of KakENEE emerges when the right-channel blockages and apaanic pods are activated through the rise of apaanᵃ to the heart chᵃkrᵃ. The four heads then represent:

+ First head: unrealistic expectations such as: "I am the next Savior"
+ Second head: trapped in frustration
+ Third head: victim of doership
+ Fourth head: suffering because of separation from Divine

The meaning of the symbols in the hands changes:

+ Upper right hand: spear—narrows the opening of the delicate passageway to the fifth chᵃkrᵃ
+ Lower right hand: skull—isolation and feeling unloved with a strong hatred toward the body to the point of suicide

♦ Upper left hand: shield—the defensive shield is weak and negative energy from others easily penetrates

♦ Lower left hand: sword—may use the sword to commit suicide

THE HRETᵃ CHᴬKRᴬ

Within the fourth chᵃkrᵃ (between the fifth and seventh microchakras) there is a mysterious small lunar chᵃkrᵃ called the Hretᵃ chᵃkrᵃ or Hretᵃ pᵃdmᵃ (lotus of the heart). It contains an inner sanctuary where the Divine Self dwells in profound silence within each of us. Complete devotion to an external deity will open the heart chᵃkrᵃ, as has been demonstrated by many saints in many traditions. Far fewer, however, have gone on to enter Hretᵃ pᵃdmᵃ. Their very devotion to the external Divine helps to prevent their discovery of the internal abode of Divinity. But this is only one obstacle. Ideally, entry to Hretᵃ pᵃdmᵃ is from the central channel and, in order to enter, all fifth microchakras of the fourth chᵃkrᵃ (R4:5, L4:5, and C4:5.) must be open. With deeper conviction and some struggle one can enter in this sanctuary if R4:5 is not open.

The effective use of sustained tone will serve to let energy flow into L4:7 and beyond to Hretᵃ pᵃdmᵃ. There, in that place which is quiet and full of love, you hear the inner sound (naadᵃ) of your Self. Further working with your breath, you will be guided onward to the fifth chᵃkrᵃ.

Discovery of Hretᵃ pᵃdmᵃ usually requires the personal guidance of a guru (see plate 6).

THE FIFTH CHᴬKRᴬ
Ultra Pure (VEshuddhᵃ)

Introduction

The openings in the fifth chᵃkrᵃ may be enhanced by energy flowing upward from the fourth chᵃkrᵃ. This upward flow may be due to an abundance of love for a deity or a cause. It may also be due to openings in 4:5 and 4:6 caused by listening to or producing sustained-tone music.

When 5:6 is ready to open, the aspirant searches for an external guru who will model a lifestyle to help in this task. When 5:6 is sufficiently open, an inner guru awakens to take over from the outer guru in leading the aspirant's energy to even higher levels of refinement.

The element of the fifth chᵃkrᵃ is *aakaashᵃ*. It is the purest of the elements—from which the others emerge and into which they ultimately dissolve. *Aakaashᵃ* provides the fifth chᵃkrᵃ awareness that the universe consists of varying sound frequencies against a background of profound silence. As a result of a spiritual lifestyle, the ten inner cosmic sounds known as naadᵃ (see Table 10.2) may be heard. After the final sound one is in ecstasy. Periodically, it is also possible to hear frequencies in the subtle and causal fields. The frequencies are called shrutE-s. They may combine to form words of wisdom or dictums known as rechaa-s. The ancient sages who heard them were the reSHE-s and the VAdᵃ-s (foundational teachings of the Vedic tradition) were their discovery.

Aakaashᵃ is also the basis for the fifth chᵃkrᵃ qualities of creativity, fluent communication, and nonattachment. Those in this awareness prefer long periods of silence (mownᵃ), which help in the internalization of all senses. The empirical world is seen as only a play (lEElaa) of the five senses when they are directed outward. It is described as "for the five" (prᵃpᵃnchᵃ).

In fifth chᵃkrᵃ awareness, social kᵃrmᵃ-s are few; the prime motivation is spiritual practice (saadhᵃnaa) and giving guidance to some students. With fourth chᵃkrᵃ desires transcended, devotion is more toward the sound of a mᵃntrᵃ than to the external form of the deity associated with it.

A person who has fifth chᵃkrᵃ awareness is a natural healer through voice (L5:4): by reciting a mᵃntrᵃ internally he or she can direct its vibrations anywhere. A fifth chᵃkrᵃ voice creates quality *aakaashᵃ* rather than expressing love (the domain of a fourth chᵃkrᵃ voice, L4:5).

In a mature fifth chᵃkrᵃ the central channel in the lower four chᵃkrᵃ-s is relatively free of the *fire* of desire. Suffering does not linger; it is transcended.

Rotation

The fifth chᵃkrᵃ is perpendicular to the ground and spins counterclockwise.

Element

The element of the fifth chᵃkrᵃ is *aakaashᵃ*. The color of this element ranges from all possible shades of blue to ultraviolet. The shape is that of the crescent moon.

Therapeutic Color

The therapeutic color of the fifth chᵃkrᵃ is ash gray.

Sense Organ

The ears are the sense organs of the fifth chᵃkrᵃ.

Organ of Action

The vocal cords are the organ of action for the fifth chᵃkrᵃ.

Storehouse

The storehouse of *aakaashᵃ* is in the head where this element has different qualities and hues.

Sleep Habits

When energy is concentrated in the fifth chᵃkrᵃ, sleep occurs while lying on the left side with legs outstretched. Duration is five to six hours.

Endocrine Gland

The thyroid is the endocrine gland associated with the fifth chᵃkrᵃ.

Symbolic Animal

The fifth chᵃkrᵃ is represented by a gray elephant with a single trunk. The inner guru rides on the elephant; that is, his advice is as solid as an elephant.

Developmental Period

The developmental period for females is from twenty-four to thirty; for males, twenty-eight to thirty-five.

Celestial Connection

The fifth chᵃkrᵃ is enhanced by energy from the planet Jupiter.

Musical Sensitivity

The instrument for the fifth chᵃkrᵃ is the human voice, especially when the *earth, water, fire,* and *air* elements are controlled. Other instruments that may be used to express the fifth chᵃkrᵃ are the conch and tambura (played solo).

Petal Sounds

The sixteen purple petals of the fifth chᵃkrᵃ respond to the following vowel sounds:

Right channel:	a	अ
	aa	आ
	E	इ
	EE	ई
	u	उ
	oo	ऊ
	ri	ऋ
	rrEE	ॠ
Left channel:	lri	ऌ
	lrEE	ॡ
	A	ए
	I	रो
	o	ओ
	ow	औ
	ung	अं
	ah	अः

Intoxicant

An intoxicant of the fifth chᵃkrᵃ is cannabis.

Archetypes

Pᵃnchᵃvaktrᵃ, the five-headed god, is the representative of Shᴇvᵃ in the fifth chᵃkrᵃ. He appears as the inner guru within L5:6, C5:6, and R5:6. His skin resembles pure crystal (a reference to the ultra purity of the fifth chᵃkrᵃ) and each head contains three brilliant eyes. Five pairs of large but delicate ears shine like crystal jewels. They symbolize nonverbal communication as well as attunement to inner sound (naadᵃ, shrutᴇ), inner wisdom (rechaa), and the finest single frequency that can be vocalized (prᵃNᵃvᵃ).

The five heads stand for the five minds based on each of the elements. They first must be balanced and then eventually dissolved into golden (sooryᵃ) *aakaashᵃ*, which breaks attachments to the world of objects.

SaakᴇNᴇᴇ. The representative of KuNdᵃlᴇNᴇᴇ in the fifth chᵃkrᵃ is SaakᴇNᴇᴇ.

Like Pᵃnchᵃvaktrᵃ, SaakᴇɴEE has five heads of exquisite beauty, each containing three eyes. She is light itself. In her four elegant arms she holds:

+ Upper right hand: scriptural scroll with a rosary (maalaa) around it. The scroll has instructions for vocalizing; the rosary aids repetition. The scroll also indicates inner wisdom and the role of mᵃntrᵃ as revealer of wisdom. The thumb and pointing finger of this hand are joined in a gesture of meditation (gyaanᵃ mudraa).
+ Lower right hand: gesture (mudraa) of granting boons—SaakᴇɴEE is the bestower of parapsychological potentials in the field of sound (naadᵃ) and communication. The elements of all chᵃkrᵃ minds are placed under the aspirant's control. Intuition for creative purposes also results from SaakᴇɴEE's grace.
+ Upper left hand: a white lotus—symbolizes the delicate voice fit for golden (sooryᵃ) *aakaashᵃ*.
+ Lower left hand: skull—signifies remaining unattached to the empirical world.

In her destructive aspect, when joined with other fifth microchakra blocks in the right channel, SaakᴇɴEE can create deep-rooted psychological problems, especially when apaanᵃ is high. These include hearing voices that control the person's actions and cause the suspension of reason.

THE SIXTH CHᴬKRᴬ

Commander (Aagyaa)

Introduction

The lotus of the sixth chᵃkrᵃ is pure white with two shiny white petals. The minds based on the five elements (tᵃtvᵃ-s) have now been transcended and the refined ego is beyond their pull (tᵃtvaatᴇᴇtᵃ). The sixth chᵃkrᵃ is located in the sushumnaa near the midpoint of the two eyebrows. It is sometimes called the "third eye" and is the seat of intuition. Among its endless possibilities, this intuition may be used to help balance the three guɴᵃ-s.

The availability of the Witness (saakshEE) is at its zenith, making it possible to observe the play of the senses (prapancha) without judgment. The polarity between solar and lunar currents is resolved into unity. There is a continuous conversion of energy from the second chakra to the sixth. As the veil of duality thins and awareness moves beyond the prism (C6:3), an aspirant of this magnitude has experiences beyond spacetime. The multicolored world of names and forms belonging to the five lower minds is replaced by a formless state of homogeneous white light.

Few karmic debts are left; such a person only has to teach a few disciples, often simply by being, and honor the truth that manifests within all. Everything is truly seen as an aspect of underlying Consciousness. The person in sixth chakra awareness is endlessly grounded, centered, and creative. The sixth chakra mind usually abstains from performing any of the central channel powers of which it may be capable. Sixth chakra relationships focus on the breath: tuning into each other's breath and harmonizing with it. Whatever relationships come are received with gratitude. Able to tune into cosmic humor, such a person may laugh a great deal.

In sixth chakra awareness, the mind easily becomes immersed in praNava, the fundamental unit from which all sound and speech come forth. PraNava literally means "ever fresh though ancient." PraNava—which manifests on the subtlest internal level—is sensed more as intuition than audition. In the company of such a person others may begin to hear their own inner sound (naada).

A person in sixth chakra awareness is directed by the inner guru to live the specific way of life that will support the natural attainment of the balance of the three guNa-s. People who have become dependent and who do not accept this responsibility continue to imitate their external guru. They may have difficulty parting and suffer unnecessarily. Wise gurus order such disciples to leave after training is completed. At this stage, total trust has to develop for the inner guru.

There is no self-consciousness about the body, and the usual preferences are to eat little and drink a lot of water, and to wear the color of the day (see chapter 10 for a discussion of the Tantric color of the day) or simply ochre or white.

Until the guNa-s are balanced there can be no significant period of meditation. In the struggle to balance the three guNa-s, dark spots can appear in the psyche. Tamas guNa and dark *aakaasha* dull the mind. Focused raja-s energy must be applied in order to overcome such obstacles. This requires careful observation, thought, and courage. Afterward, satva may be activated through concentration on a mantra and by producing soorya *aakaasha*, which is the ideal source of contentment for all the chakra minds. Focusing can then proceed to a higher level of refinement and ultimately lead to praNava. This may be followed by samaadhE.

Rotation

The sixth chᵃkrᵃ is perpendicular to the ground and spins counterclockwise.

Guɴᵃ-s (Beyond the Elements)

The sixth chᵃkrᵃ operates with the three guɴᵃ-s: tᵃmᵃs, rᵃjᵃs, and satvᵃ. Satvᵃ is white, rᵃjᵃs is red, and tᵃmᵃs is blue. The yantrᵃ of the sixth chᵃkrᵃ consists of two petals.

Therapeutic Color

The therapeutic color of the sixth chᵃkrᵃ is clear white.

Sense Organ

The sense organ of the sixth chᵃkrᵃ is the pineal gland and the sense is intuition.

Organ of Action

The organ of action of the sixth chᵃkrᵃ is the pituitary gland.

Sleep Habits

When the inner guru begins to awaken, it prompts the person to search for a guru outside to continue the spiritual work from past lives. These fortunate people have accumulated enough spiritual praarᵃbdhᵃ to proceed in the direction of liberation. When they meet a teacher, they face the challenge of opening the sixth chᵃkrᵃ. During this period, their sleep habits are very important. The guru may advise them to sleep for four hours on the left side or in a special yoga posture. If they are under forty years of age and in good health, they may be advised to do sleep fasts on the new and full moon.

Developmental Period

The usual developmental period for females is from thirty to thirty-six; for males, thirty-five to forty-two. The ability to meditate can be fully accomplished during this period as can subtle discrimination in daily behavior patterns. Intuition may also come to full blossom.

Celestial Connection

The sixth chᵃkrᵃ is enhanced by energy from the planet Saturn.

Musical Sensitivity

The sixth chᵃkrᵃ is most sensitive to the human voice.

Petal Sounds

The two luminescent-white petals of the sixth chᵃkrᵃ respond to the following sounds:

Right channel:	ha	ह	guttural/aspirated
Left channel:	ksha	क्ष	compound

Intoxicant

The intoxicant of the sixth chᵃkrᵃ is deep meditation and ability to merge with Divinity by capturing the nectar of the moon (amretᵃ) during a full moon.

Archetypes

Ardhᵃnaarᴇᴇshvᵃrᵃ is the representative of Shᴇvᵃ-Shᵃktᴇ in the sixth chᵃkrᵃ. The left side of this deity is portrayed as female and the right side as male. This androgynous figure signifies the unity of Shᴇvᵃ and Shᵃktᴇ. In the first and second lᴇngᵃ-s the male deities were usually representatives of Shᴇvᵃ. Now in the third lᴇngᵃ, there is no purely male deity. Polarity has been transcended by the singularity of Shᴇvᵃ-Shᵃktᴇ. They are as inseparable as moon and moonbeam.[10]

Ardhᵃnaarᴇᴇshvᵃrᵃ has three eyes; the left and right eyes represent the moon and sun respectively while the third eye indicates *fire*. When the third eye is activated, total one-pointedness occurs and awareness rises beyond the prism (C6:3). The third eye also symbolizes the abode of goddess Kuɴdᵃlᴇnᴇᴇ in the sixth chᵃkrᵃ. It is her illuminating presence that opens the door to nonduality. A yogi feels the unity of male and female within the physical body.

Ardhᵃnaarᴇᴇshvᵃrᵃ has two arms. The right hand carries the trident signifying the balance of the three guɴᵃ-s. The left hand holds a drum (dᵃmᵃroo), which makes a two-beat rhythm. It attracts sound energy from the two petals of the sixth chᵃkrᵃ. The drum is also a reminder of the crucial role of prᵃɴᵃvᵃ in the sixth chᵃkrᵃ where awareness merges into Consciousness and the drop becomes the ocean (adhyaatmᵃ yogᵃ).

Haakᴇnᴇᴇ. In the sixth chᵃkrᵃ, Kuɴdᵃlᴇnᴇᴇ is represented by Haakᴇnᴇᴇ. As the embodiment of sᵃtvᵃ, Haakᴇnᴇᴇ is a vibrant white color. Her six heads indicate the dissolution of the five elements into the Supreme Intelligence (Mᵃhᵃt), fueled by golden (sooryᵃ) *aakaashᵃ*. Haakᴇnᴇᴇ has six arms. The three right hands each form a gesture (mudraa):

- Upper right hand: gesture of fearlessness (abhayᵃ mudraa)
- Middle right hand: gesture of granting boons (vᵃrᵃ mudraa)
- Lower right hand: holds a book—symbolizing the bestowal of knowledge (vᴇdyaa mudraa)

The three left hands each hold a symbolic object:

- Upper left hand: drum (dᵃmᵃroo)—the hollow rhythmic sound of the drum is the call to go beyond gender duality and beyond the prism (C6:3).
- Middle left hand: beads (rudraakshᵃ maalaa)—rosary that symbolizes the eyes of Rudrᵃ Shᴇvᵃ. To look with Shᴇvᵃ's eyes of total nonattachment is a prerequisite for perfect balance. Then sushumnaa breath can happen at will and you can enter meditation. Breath itself becomes the mᵃntrᵃ. You simply listen to the sound of the inhalation—SO—and exhalation—HUM. In contrast with the usual repetition (jᵃpᵃ) of mᵃntrᵃ, this is called "no repetition of repetition" (ᵃjᵃpᵃ jᵃpᵃ).
- Lower left hand: skull (kᵃpaalᵃ)—reminder of our true nature (svᵃbhavᵃ) as That (Tᵃt).

In her destructive form Haakᴇnᴇᴇ represents a pattern of sixth microchakras in the right channel, which can lead to multiple personalities.

THE SOMᴬ CHᴬKRᴬ

Somᵃ means "nectar" (amretᵃ) or "moon." The somᵃ chᵃkrᵃ is located in the pericarp of the seventh chᵃkrᵃ. Even though regarded as a minor chᵃkrᵃ, its influence on the psyche of advanced spiritual practitioners may be far reaching.

The nectar flowing into the somᵃ chᵃkrᵃ originates in a smaller chᵃkrᵃ, the Kaamᴀshvᵃrᴇᴇ chᵃkrᵃ. After passing from this chᵃkrᵃ, the nectar is refined by a symbolic cow (Kaamᵃdhᴀnu). It then flows into the somᵃ chᵃkrᵃ, where it may be used by those whose egos are sufficiently refined.

Kaamᴀshvᵃrᴇᴇ chᵃkrᵃ. The Kaamᴀshvᵃrᴇᴇ (Goddess of Desire) chᵃkrᵃ is a small eight-petaled lotus; within its heart is a full moon seated in the crescent of the new moon. Inside the circle of the full moon is a downward-pointing triangle, the a-kᵃ-thᵃ triangle. Within the a-kᵃ-thᵃ triangle, Kaamᴀshvᵃrᵃ and Kaamᴀshvᵃrᴇᴇ are seated. Kaamᵃ means "desire" and ᴇᴇshvarᵃ means "lord." Kaamᴀshvᵃrᵃ is Shᴇvᵃ (Stillness) while Kaamᴀshvᵃrᴇᴇ is Shᵃktᴇ (Vibrancy).

The a-k^a-th^a triangle is called the womb or matrix of the universe (j^ag^adyonEE). The base of the triangle represents desire (EChhaa); the right side of the triangle stands for knowledge (gyaan^a); the left side of the triangle represents action (kreyaa). These are eternal potentials of Sh^aktE, which she uses to create the manifest universe. They provide the essence of the nectar to the symbolic cow (Kaam^adhAnu).

Seated above the a-k^a-th^a triangle, in the physical body, is a hollow space between the two cerebral hemispheres. It is a projection of Br^ahm^ar^andhr^a (also known as the "cave of Br^ahmaa"). Br^ahm^ar^andhr^a has three distinct parts. The lowest third is called the "cave of the bumblebee" (Bhr^amr^a guhaa). When an aspirant (saadh^ak^a) tunes into this cave, the intoxicating drone of the bumblebee is heard from all directions, including from within.

The middle third of the Br^ahm^ar^andhr^a is the "calm cave" (nErjh^ar^a guhaa; literally, cave without ripples). Here there is no sound as such but the *aakaash^a* of the drone brings the aspirant even deeper within.

The top third of the Br^ahm^ar^andhr^a is called the "blind cave" (andh^akoop^a). Here no sound or *aakaash^a* can appear. It is said that when awareness is in the blind cave, no one can help us. There we are on our own between the memories we brought with us (s^amskaar^a-s) and the spiritual practices (saadh^anaa) we have done in this life.

At the top of the blind cave is the tenth gate. It corresponds to the bregmatic fontanel. To leave the body through this gate at the time of death is the greatest desire of those who have been dwelling in third lEng^a awareness.

Before Kund^alEnEE can pass through the tenth gate, it must first mix with subtle (sookshm^a) praaN^a in the Br^ahm^ar^andhr^a. This subtle praaN^a is produced from praaN^a by accumulated golden (soory^a) *aakaash^a* and by the absorption in pr^aN^av^a over many lifetimes.

Kaam^adhAnu. Between the KaamAshv^arEE ch^akr^a and the som^a ch^akr^a, Tantric tradition places a mystical cow called Kaam^adhAnu. Harish Johari explained the symbolism of Kaam^adhAnu:

The color of Kamadhenu is white. She has the face of a crow [one of the most intelligent of birds], which stands for alertness; the horns of a cow, which symbolize nourishment; the neck of a horse, which symbolizes strength; the tail of a peacock, which is associated with fantasies and dreams; and the wings of a white swan (*hamsa*), which stand for the quality of discrimination. Her forehead is *ahamkara* (the ego) and her eyes are human, of pure nature.[11]

Kaam^adh_Anu receives the three streams of nectar produced by the Kaam_Ashv^ar_{EE} ch^akr^a and transforms them into streams of enhanced nectar, which she passes to the som^a ch^akr^a through her four udders. Kaam^adh_Anu symbolizes the power of the aspirant (saadh^ak^a) to receive nectar and to enhance it for use by the som^a ch^akr^a.

Som^a ch^akr^a. The som^a ch^akr^a is represented by a lotus of twelve petals that surrounds a crescent moon, the dispenser of nectar. The crescent moon is silver color and the lotus petals are a milky white.

On a full moon night, the flow of nectar is activated in the blind cave of Kaam_Ashv^ar_{EE} ch^akr^a. An aspirant (saadh^ak^a) with a pure and healthy body is able to capture the nectar by focusing on the som^a ch^akr^a and invoking Kaam^adh_Anu.

The higher dimension that is made available through this nectar (amret^a) shakes the reality of the ordinary waking state: opposites may merge and transcendent experiences occur with ease. The som^a ch^akr^a offers a prelude to contentment. When, through systematic spiritual practice, we allow ourselves a "taste" of the amret^a, our worldly attachments begin to weaken.

Som^a ch^akr^a experiences can be very intoxicating, especially when the availability of the nectar coincides with hearing of the inner sound (naad^a). The ego has been refined to the point where, in meditation, the breath is almost absent. Technically, this means that the praa_N^a from the left and right breathing channels (_Edaa and p_Eng^al^a) becomes available to sushumnaa to begin the awakening of Ku_Nd^al_En_{EE} or to lead Ku_Nd^al_En_{EE} higher up from the fourth ch^akr^a.

At this point m^antr^a is only by means of association, which has been built up through lifetimes of practice. The tone of one's breath becomes completely in tune with the cosmic tone. This is reflected in the gentle sweet sound of the breath when the rate of breathing in meditation is two breaths per minute. The sound of the inhaled breath resonates as SO and the exhaled breath as HUM. Hence SOHUM (That is me), wherein That is external.

In the depth of meditation and complete stillness of the mind—when the breath is one per minute—attention may be directed to the som^a ch^akr^a. Then the sound of the breath changes to HUMSA (I am That), wherein That is internal.

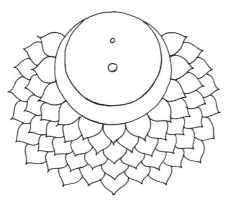

THE SEVENTH CHᴬKRᴬ
Thousand Petal Lotus (Sᵃhᵃsraarᵃ)

Introduction

The seventh chᵃkrᵃ is the storehouse of *aakaashᵃ*, the finest of the elements within eightfold nature and the space in which manifestation occurs. It is caused by static sound as described in the Lᴇᴇlaa model.

Dark blue or black *aakaashᵃ* becomes more refined as its color changes to gray, red, purple, violet, and finally gold. This is accomplished by a voice that has mᵃntrᵃ sᴇddhᴇ and chants with pure praaɴᵃ (that which is inhaled through the nose). When a mᵃntrᵃ is chanted in this manner, the golden (sooryᵃ) *aakaashᵃ* energizes the petals of this majestic chᵃkrᵃ—a prerequisite for naadᵃ sᵃmaadhᴇ.

Table 3.2 provides a detailed description of *aakaashᵃ*.

TABLE 3.2. TYPES OF *AAKAASHᴬ* AND REPRESENTATIVE CAUSES

Black aakaashᵃ	Explosion of bomb • Cannon • Gun fire • Severe thunder
Gray aakaashᵃ	Shouting • Screaming • Scratching chalk board
Maroon aakaashᵃ	Heavy Metal • Angry Rock
Red aakaashᵃ	Folk music • Jazz • Humor • Laughter • Stories • Soap Operas • Emotional situations
Blue aakaashᵃ	Classical music • Spiritual poetry • Epics • Philosophy
Violet aakaashᵃ	Dhrupᵃdᵃ • Kᴀraanaa (Forms of Indian classical music)
Ultraviolet aakaashᵃ	Sacred mᵃntrᵃ with devotion

With sufficient devotion as the ultraviolet *aakaash*ᵃ is increased, it divides into chᴇddaakaashᵃ and brᵃhmaakaashᵃ. The former accumulates in the right hemisphere as green *aakaash*ᵃ. The latter accumulates in the left hemisphere as yellow *aakaash*ᵃ. When these accumulations are great enough, the special mᵃntrᵃ prᵃɴᵃvᵃ is invoked. Prᵃɴᵃvᵃ is a super subtle way of chanting the mᵃntrᵃ AUM. Chanting the sound of "A" increases the yellow *aakaash*ᵃ in the left hemisphere. The sound of "U" increases the green *aakaash*ᵃ in the right hemisphere. The sound of "M" increases the sooryᵃ *aakaash*ᵃ in the early brain. As sooryᵃ *aakaash*ᵃ expands it gradually replaces both the yellow and the green *aakaash*ᵃ. When the whole seventh chᵃkrᵃ is filled with soorya *aakaash*ᵃ, the aspirant may intuit the original separation of Potentiality from Stasis. The sound of this separation is also called prᵃɴᵃvᵃ and is described in the Lᴇᴇlaa model presented in the previous chapter.

In this way, the practice of prᵃɴᵃvᵃ permits individual awareness to return to Consciousness. Needless to say, this practice will be effective only when undertaken by a very advanced aspirant who is capable of great depth of sentiment, purity of breath, and accuracy of pronunciation.

Rotation
The seventh chᵃkrᵃ is parallel to the ground and spins counterclockwise.

Element
The seventh chᵃkrᵃ operates beyond the elements and guɴᵃ-s, yet it is the storehouse of a variety of types of *aakaash*ᵃ from black *aakaash*ᵃ to golden (sooryᵃ) *aakaash*ᵃ. It is also the storehouse of the seeds of the guɴᵃ-s.

Sense Organ
The sense organ of the seventh chᵃkrᵃ is the pituitary gland.

Organ of Action
The organ of action of the seventh chᵃkrᵃ is the pineal gland.

Sleep Habits
Such a person is beyond habits of sleep and sleeps any amount or not at all.

Symbolic Animal
There is no symbolic animal for the seventh chᵃkrᵃ. The inner guru has shifted from the fifth to the seventh chᵃkrᵃ.

Developmental Period

The developmental period for females is from thirty-six to forty-two; for males, forty-two to forty-nine. This is the period in life in which one can experience more complete contentment. From there onward, it would be natural to gradually dedicate more and more time to the internalization of the senses and still be living a normal life as a kᵃrmᵃ yogi.

Celestial Connection

The seventh chᵃkrᵃ is influenced by the Moon except during sᵃmaadhE.

Musical Sensitivity

When the seventh chᵃkrᵃ is active, one tunes into the silent reverberation (anaahᵃtᵃ) of prᵃNᵃvᵃ, the smallest fraction of a sound frequency.

Sounds

The internal sound associated with the seventh chᵃkrᵃ is prᵃNᵃvᵃ.

Archetypes

The deity of the seventh chᵃkrᵃ is ShEvᵃ-ShᵃktE without distinction.

SᵃmaadhE-s

Even in meditation (with less than four breaths per minute) and in stillness, the elements are still active and produce experiences of varied colors in the seventh chᵃkrᵃ. However, when the guNᵃ-s are completely balanced and breathing ceases completely, a sᵃmaadhE experience occurs. The varied colors then merge into white light.

SᵃmaadhE is a state where the ego is totally submerged in the Self for a period of time, as it is in deep sleep. However, in sᵃmaadhE the person is sitting and the spine is perpendicular to the earth; whereas in sleep the person reclines with the spine parallel to the earth. An accumulation of sᵃmaadhE experiences may result in the egoless personality of a saint who is cognizant of the Divine presence in all forms of life.

Different people find different methods of experiencing sᵃmaadhE. As the senior author is cognizant of the tradition of naadᵃ yogᵃ, he can provide more detail about those methods. Various classes of temporary mergings with Consciousness (sᵃmaadhE-s) may be identified:

+ Root (jᵃDᵃ) sᵃmaadhE (7:1)—occurs while sitting buried underground. Alternatively, herbs and other plants are used to prepare chemically induced sᵃmaadhE.

✦ Water (jᵃlᵃ) sᵃmaadhᴇ (7:2)—occurs while seated underwater.

Both jᵃᴅᵃ sᵃmaadhᴇ and jᵃlᵃ sᵃmaadhᴇ demonstrate the parapsychological ability to live without prᵃnᵃ for extended periods of time. These demonstrations are intended to help people understand the vast potential within the human and to transcend the limits of reason.

✦ Fire (agnᴇ) sᵃmaadhᴇ (7:3)—leaving this body while executing one's duty creates merit for the next birth. Microchakra Psychology hypothesizes that C6:3 will be open in the next life for these heroes, hence making it easier for them to pursue their Divinity.

✦ Air (vaayu) sᵃmaadhᴇ (7:4)—is based on complete devotion (bhᵃktᴇ) to Divinity and absorption in service and unconditional love for the universe. This devotion produces chᴇddaakaashᵃ, a special *aakaashᵃ* that fills the mind with devotion to the Divine.

✦ Aakaasha sᵃmaadhᴇ (7:5)—occurs when attention is directed toward inner sounds (naadᵃ). The practitioner of naadᵃ yogᵃ pursues, in a gradual manner, finer and finer levels of sound. Eventually (perhaps after several decades) the ability to produce pristine golden (sooryᵃ) *aakaashᵃ* emerges. Absorption of this *aakaashᵃ* helps reduce the rate of breathing.

✦ Sᵃguɴᵃ sᵃmaadhᴇ (7:6)—happens when both nostrils are evenly open and the three guɴᵃ-s are balanced, leading to the experience of the individual Divinity uniting with Consciousness.

✦ Nᴇrguɴᵃ sᵃmaadhᴇ (7:7)—is a state in which the enlightened saint is pure Consciousness, one without a second. Necessary remaining actions due to praarᵃbdhᵃ are undertaken with neither desire nor attachment (nɪshkᵃrmyᵃ sᴇddhᴇ). They are completely governed by retᵃ. Unlike the other six sᵃmaadhᴇ-s, which are temporary states, nᴇrguɴᵃ sᵃmaadhᴇ results in a permanent state of liberation (mokshᵃ). In the state of nᴇrguɴᵃ sᵃmaadhᴇ, external breathing gradually comes to a standstill and the brain lives off stored praaɴᵃ. This stimulates each neuron and its related structures to maximal activity and consequent conversion into light—aptly called enlightenment.

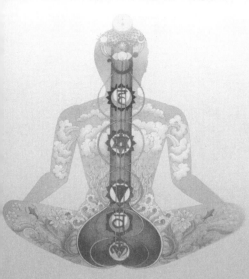

4
Basic Microchakra Dynamics

EIGHTFOLD NATURE AND THE PLAYS OF LIFE

As discussed in chapter 2, the Tantric and Vedic traditions teach that all manifestation is based on eightfold nature. Microchakra Psychology is built on this insight. Vibrancy (ShᵃktE) is the all-encompassing energy of the universe, which may be perceived from different points of view. Modern physical science has identified four basic types of energy that underlie all phenomena of the material world. These are the gravitational, electromagnetic, strong nuclear, and weak nuclear energies. This understanding is primarily derived from a quantitative analysis of energy. Einstein's famous equation, $E = mc^2$, represents a triumph of this approach.

In contrast to the physical sciences, psychology requires a view of energy that is primarily qualitative and that enables a systematic understanding of human experiencing. The concept of eightfold nature does much to meet this need. This suggestion may be clarified through use of the theoretical idea of "traits."

Traits

A trait is a shorthand description of a human quality. Examples are: industrious, sociable, gullible, mean, careful, earthy, fiery. Such descriptors provide an approximate understanding of the way in which a person thinks or behaves. For accurate understanding, the trait name must be supplemented with additional information. The last two examples—earthy and fiery—show that some components of eightfold nature are already reflected in common language. This indicates that a modicum of awareness of the role of eightfold nature in our lives already exists. Microchakra Psychology greatly expands this awareness. Table 4.1 below gives the dominant trait associated with each chᵃkrᵃ.

TABLE 4.1. DOMINANT TRAIT OF EACH CHᴬKRᴬ

Seventh Chᵃkrᵃ (beyond guN ᵃ-s)	Contentment
Sixth Chᵃkrᵃ (guN ᵃ-s)	Intuition
Fifth Chᵃkrᵃ (*aakaash ᵃ*)	Creativity
Fourth Chᵃkrᵃ (*air*)	Feeling
Third Chᵃkrᵃ (*fire*)	Assertiveness
Second Chᵃkrᵃ (*water*)	Fluidity
First Chᵃkrᵃ (*earth*)	Stability

The way in which each trait functions by means of its related chᵃkrᵃ is elaborated in the following descriptions of the play of nature at each stage of life.

Developmental Ages

As we have seen, the first five chᵃkrᵃ-s are each dominated by one element that determines the basic goals of that chᵃkrᵃ. The sixth chᵃkrᵃ is beyond the five elements and is dominated by the guN ᵃ-s. The seventh chᵃkrᵃ transcends eightfold nature and all its plays. It connects with contentment leading to Stillness. In the first six chᵃkrᵃ-s, play is associated with the thoughts, feelings, and sensations necessary to meet the goals of the chᵃkrᵃ. Play also includes the obstacles that arise in the attempt to meet these goals.

Each chᵃkrᵃ and its related play is dominant during a different stage of life. Each stage presents certain challenges—which are met with varying degrees of success. Today, in the Kᵃlᴇ yugᵃ, most people do not move beyond the challenges of third- or fourth-chᵃkrᵃ play. A few occasionally meet a challenge belonging to a more advanced stage. The following paragraphs describe the activities associated with each chᵃkrᵃ and outline the major tasks associated with the period of its development. The outline given is for an idealized time and culture that can support its members as they strive to meet these challenges.

First-chᵃkrᵃ play is represented by the archetype DaakᴇnᴇE. Her single head signifies a one-dimensional view of the world where awareness is focused on "me" and first chᵃkrᵃ goals—the basic needs of survival. The element *earth* is the primary fuel of the first chᵃkrᵃ and enables these needs to be met. The most important of these needs is for nourishing food and a sense of being at home in our body. When *earth* is ample it contributes a sense of *stability* to the personality. We may be said to feel grounded. The quality of *stability* leads to related traits of confidence and curiosity. Freedom to explore the environment is a natural outcome of feeling secure and well-grounded.

The first-chᵃkrᵃ age (females: 0–6 and males: 0–7) includes the following developmental tasks:

- ✦ Overcome first-chᵃkrᵃ age insecurities
    - ▪ Fear of abandonment
    - ▪ Fear of being small and dependent
    - ▪ Fear of lacking knowledge
- ✦ Establish strong sense of physical identity
- ✦ Establish desire to survive and flourish
- ✦ Establish trust with parents and others

Second-chᵃkrᵃ play is represented by the archetype RakᴇɴEE. Her two heads signify a two-dimensional view of the world where awareness is focused on "me and you." The element of *water* is the primary fuel of the second chᵃkrᵃ. *Water* mixes easily with *earth*. This enables one to meet the need for exchanges with other people. These exchanges include those based on family, friendship, sexuality, and business. The trait of *fluidity* indicates that the *water* element empowers honest and straightforward interpersonal relations. *Water* permits some degree of mixing with another.

The second-chᵃkrᵃ age (females: 6–12 and males: 7–14) includes the following developmental tasks:

- ✦ Overcome second-chᵃkrᵃ age fears
    - ▪ Fear of pain
    - ▪ Fear of sexuality
    - ▪ Fear of isolation from peers
- ✦ Establish gender identity
- ✦ Establish enjoyment of pleasure
- ✦ Establish honest relationships with others

Third-chᵃkrᵃ play is represented by the archetype LakᴇɴEE. Her three heads stand for a three-dimensional view of the world where awareness now encompasses "me, you, and others." This is the basis for developing a social identity and a sense of membership in a community.

The *assertiveness* or power that comes with a highly competent third chᵃkrᵃ is also accompanied by the danger that this power may corrupt. It is one thing to be acknowledged by your mate in second-chakra play; it is quite another to be acknowledged by many people in third-chᵃkrᵃ play. Considerable energy from the fourth chᵃkrᵃ must be available to prevent third chᵃkrᵃ power from being abused.

In modern society, third chᵃkrᵃ power is often accompanied by an excessive sense of competitiveness and a desire to be "number one." Among the results may be zealotry and "type A" behavior. However, if you possess true leadership qualities, you will be a kind "king" or "queen;" that is, you will not be dictatorial.

The third-chᵃkrᵃ age (females: 12–18 and males: 14–21) includes the following developmental tasks:

- ✦ Overcome third-chᵃkrᵃ age fears
  - ▪ Fear of mortality
  - ▪ Fear of failure
  - ▪ Fear of rejection
  - ▪ Fear of responsibility
  - ▪ Fear of losing beauty
  - ▪ Fear of losing power
- ✦ Establish balance of rational and emotional
- ✦ Establish oneself as an independent thinker
- ✦ Establish control over urges for personal power
- ✦ Establish a meaningful social identity
- ✦ Establish contentment with one's accomplishments
- ✦ Establish moral courage to become a martyr

Fourth-chᵃkrᵃ play is represented by the archetype KakᴇnᴇE. Her four heads symbolize *earth, water,* and *fire* as well as *air*—the primary element of the fourth chᵃkrᵃ. The *air* element enables the human capacity for *feeling* in all its forms, which reaches its height in devoted love. KakᴇnᴇE's four heads also indicate that there are now four psychological dimensions associated with awareness at this level. In addition to awareness of "me," awareness of "you," and awareness of "others," there is also an awareness of Divinity—a Cosmic Intelligence that pervades all and governs all.

You can enter this fourth dimension only through the surrender of first lᴇngᵃ ego and a heightened development of *feeling*. Reason, which has great value in meeting the goals of the first three plays, has little value in the play of the heart. Devotional poets may now be far better guides than those whose reasoning is based solely on sensory experience and knowledge.

In the Bhᵃgvat GEEtaa, Sri Krishna (as an incarnation of the Supreme) informs Arjuna (representative of the best in the human spirit):

From him who is pure, restrained, self-subdued
And intimately offers with devotion
A leaf, flower, fruit, or water,
I accept.[1]

With mind immersed in Me, devoted to Me;
Sacrificing to Me,
Surrendering yourself to Me as Supreme;
Thus having yoked to Me,
You will reach Me alone.[2]

Elsewhere, the Supreme teaches that it is not form but sincerity that opens the door to the fourth dimension.

Whoever desires to worship with faith
Whatever form
I grant him that same faith to be unflinching.
Endowed with that faith,
He engages himself in the worship of that form
From which he procures his desires
Verily, which are prescribed by Me.[3]

Many other spiritual teachings have emphasized the importance of the connection between love, worship and Divinity. In the *Old Testament* for example, there are numerous stories of devotion to the Lord. The book of Deuteronomy stresses the importance of this devotion:

And you shall love the Lord your God with all your heart, and with all your soul, and with all your might.[4]

The *New Testament* teaches:

Above all, clothe yourselves with love, which binds everything together in perfect harmony. And let the peace of Christ rule in your hearts, to which indeed you were called in the one body. And be thankful. Let the word of Christ dwell in you richly; teach and admonish one another in all wisdom; and with gratitude in your hearts sing psalms, hymns and spiritual songs to God.[5]

Fourth-chᵃkrᵃ play has several particularly significant features. The fourth chᵃkrᵃ itself is a point of balance, since three chᵃkrᵃ-s lie above it and three below. It radiates into a larger area (roughly that of the heart and lungs) than does any other chᵃkrᵃ.

The fourth chᵃkrᵃ marks the first opportunity to rise above the "iron chains" of the first lɛngᵃ. To do so requires faith and passionate commitment to the world beyond the senses, either in the form of a deity or a cause. If it is a cause then the faith and the hope are that one day the desired results shall be manifest.

A direct connection between the fourth chᵃkrᵃ and the seventh chᵃkrᵃ is possible. The pure and intense devotion of a saintly being can set up sympathetic resonance in the seventh chᵃkrᵃ and movement toward liberation—without energy having to pass through the fifth and sixth chᵃkrᵃ-s. Those less than saintly, however, may fall in love with the experience of loving the Divine. Then they remain caught in the "silver chains" of the second lɛngᵃ. In this state, they may temporarily merge with the deity.

The fourth-chᵃkrᵃ age (females: 18–24 and males: 21–28) includes the following developmental tasks:

- ✦ Establish voluntary surrender of ego
  - ▪ Commitment to a deity or
  - ▪ Commitment to a cause
- ✦ Establish sense of compassion
- ✦ Establish sense of nonkilling
- ✦ Establish sense of unconditional love

Fifth-chᵃkrᵃ play is represented by the five-headed archetype, SaakɛnEE. The fifth head represents the element *aakaashᵃ* and the fifth psychological dimension: an awareness that sound underlies all creation. In order for the fifth chᵃkrᵃ to be active, some of the attention of the senses, particularly sound, must be shifted inward. This enhances sound sensitivity and *creativity*. The other elements dissolve in *aakaashᵃ*, permitting new connections to be created in all three bodies. It is hypothesized that in the physical body, this involves changes in neurochemical pathways.

The inner guru dwells in the sixth microchakra of the fifth chᵃkrᵃ. When awakened, it leads to further refinement of ego and engagement with the third lɛngᵃ.

The fifth-chᵃkrᵃ age (females: 24–30 and males: 28–35) includes the following developmental tasks:

- ✦ Establish free movement of energy and spontaneity

- Eliminate all rigidities that prevent energy moving with the speed and abundance necessary to activate the third lɛngᵃ
  - ✦ Establish excellent communication and teaching skills to pay back karmic debts
  - ✦ Establish highly aware use of sound and speech
  - ✦ Establish profound sound sensitivity throughout the body
  - ✦ Establish chantings and meditations filled with sooryᵃ *aakaashᵃ*
  - ✦ Establish contentment of desires from the first five chᵃkrᵃ-s and thereby discover the art of internalization of the senses

Sixth-chᵃkrᵃ play is represented by HaakɛNEE, an archetype with six heads. The sixth head represents the guN ᵃ-s: tᵃmᵃs, rᵃjᵃs and sᵃtvᵃ. When these three guN ᵃ-s are in balance, awareness may transcend the world of the five elements and, via *intuition,* enter the sixth dimension, which is the plane of knowledge. This is the locus of Cosmic Intelligence (Mᵃhᵃt). The human mind is permitted to apprehend parts of it through *intuition* alone—never by reasoning or feeling. It is toward this realm and beyond that the inner guru points. *Intuition* teaches the further refinement of intuition until, ultimately, the jɛɛvᵃ can surrender completely to retᵃ. The utilization and refinement of intuition in the sixth chᵃkrᵃ is the sixth-chᵃkrᵃ play. It is close to inner Divinity and refined energy from the sixth chᵃkrᵃ can be brought down to all the sixth microchakras in the lower chᵃkrᵃ-s to divinize their play.

The sixth-chᵃkrᵃ age (females: 30–36 and males: 35–42) includes the following developmental tasks:

  - ✦ Establish ability to practice advanced meditation
  - ✦ Establish androgynous nature
  - ✦ Establish ability to retain sooryᵃ *aakaashᵃ* and release inferior *aakaashᵃ*
  - ✦ Establish self-control and transcendence of the senses
  - ✦ Establish sense of non-doership
    - Study Vᴀdaantᵃ
  - ✦ Establish highly intuitive mind guided by retᵃ
  - ✦ Establish single focus on liberation

Seventh-chᵃkrᵃ play. The seventh chᵃkrᵃ is beyond eightfold nature; hence there is no play associated with it—at least in the usual sense involving subject and object. Instead, there are only various types of sᵃmaadhɛ (temporary merging in the Self). The waking state life is full of *contentment,* in which the person is unattached and has an intuition of Reality.

The seventh-chªkrª age (females: 36–42 and males: 42–49) includes the following developmental tasks:

◆ Discriminate between Self and not-Self (vEchaarª)
◆ Establish the awareness that pleasure and pain are the same
◆ Establish the ability to see lEElaa (cosmic play) in all situations
◆ Establish the awareness that one's death is a transformation into the causal field
◆ Establish complete contentment—no regrets
◆ Liberation from all attachments

If all challenges, with the exception of liberation, have been met at the end of the seventh-chªkrª age, then the cycle of seven stages repeats in the causal field. There the concern is more with abstract thought and obedience to retª in all planes of existence (lokª-s).

MICROCHAKRA FUNDAMENTALS

The microchakras are formed by the intersection of each chªkrª with the three channels: the intersection with the right channel (vajrEnE) segments it into seven microchakras; in a similar way, segmentation of a chªkrª into seven microchakras occurs in the left channel (chEtrnEE) and in the central channel (ShEvª naaDEE). This division of each chªkrª into twenty-one microchakras is shown in the depiction of the first chªkrª (see plate 7).*

The seven major chªkrª-s together contain 147 microchakras—49 microchakras in each channel. The fundamentals of Microchakra Psychology described in this book are primarily built upon the microchakras of the right and left channels with some reference to those in the central channel. The microchakras of the central channel are related to parapsychological abilities (sEddhE-s). The Tantric tradition relates that these abilities will come automatically to those of advanced spiritual development. They warn that, even then, they are to be avoided as distractions that enhance egotism and hinder further spiritual advancement.

---

*It should be noted that each microchakra contains seven microchakras, each of these contains seven microchakras, and so forth in a vast progression of refinement until all differentiated energy returns to white light. However, there is no practical way to work directly with microchakras below the initial level of twenty-one; nor does there seem to be any need to do so. Therefore, they do not enter into the formulation of Microchakra Psychology.

Microchakra Openings and Blocks

Ch^akr^a-s and microchakras are located in the feeling body and are functioning perfectly at all times. However, the access to the microchakra in the physical body can become blocked. Calling a microchakra "blocked" is only a manner of speaking, like saying, "The sun is rising." It would be more accurate, albeit cumbersome, to say that the physical pathway to the microchakra is blocked. Blockage may commence at any level—from organ to molecule. It proceeds to the quantum interface between the physical and subtle fields.

A microchakra is termed "open" when all seven rays of the solar spectrum pervade that microchakra, and it is designated as "blocked" when all seven rays are absent. This is true in all three channels. Microchakra Psychology represents degrees of opening on a seven-point scale ranging from 1 (blocked or minimal vibration) to 7 (completely open or maximum vibration).

Blocks are formed differently at different stages of early life, beginning with the child's prenatal experiences and during the birth experience itself.

Conception

At conception the right and left channels are completely blank—a "tabula rasa."

The Fetus

Some blocks may develop during the fetal stage if the mother experiences any of the following while carrying the child:

1. Various types of physical injury or infections
2. A poor diet
3. Use of certain drugs or inhalants
4. Sexual intercourse during the late stage of pregnancy

Birth

At birth, all of the microchakras are in a neutral state (neither opened nor blocked) with two exceptions:

1. The microchakras that have become blocked during pregnancy
2. In the fifth, sixth, and seventh ch^akr^a-s most microchakras in the left channel are open

These left-channel openings explain why some very young children show amazing intuition and openness to all life. These natural assets usually disappear by puberty, as most cultures do not provide an environment necessary to maintain the required openings.

The functioning of blocks and openings is different in the left and right channels.

The Right Channel

All fetuses have solar energy in the cerebral cortex. When the baby is ready to be born, the mother's contractions massage its head and the energy begins its gradual descent in the right channel from the top of the seventh chᵃkrᵃ to the bottom of the first chᵃkrᵃ. The amount of time required is equivalent to one-half of the first-chᵃkrᵃ age. In girls, this process requires three years; in boys it takes three and a half years. The downward descent of energy in the right channel is a perilous journey. During this time the human child is quite helpless. It is dependent upon the wisdom and love of the adults who are caring for it—usually the parents, particularly the mother. If the care is optimum, all microchakras in the right channel will be opened and the total spectrum of light in the first chᵃkrᵃ—represented by the elephant with a trunk of seven rainbow colors—will arrive.

Unfortunately, optimum care is the exception and not the rule. Many child-rearing practices are blemished, usually through ignorance of the subtle energies. The result is impaired flow of energy in various microchakras of the child. These blocked microchakras of the right channel form obstacles to ego refinement and are part of the karmic package with which the individual must cope.

Once a block is made in a right-channel microchakra there is no known way to remove it or open it to any degree. That is why the first three or three and a half years are a critical period that requires the utmost attention to the needs of the child.

The Left Channel

Beginning in the second half of the first-chᵃkrᵃ age, right-channel development is complete (all openings and blocks have been established). When the hot solar energy reaches the bottom of the right-channel, it is cooled by the *earth* in the first chᵃkrᵃ and converted to lunar energy. This lunar energy then ascends in the left channel toward the "third eye" and crosses over to its ultimate destination in the right hemisphere of the brain. The greater the degree of opening at the base of the right and left channels, the more copious will be the flow of energy up the left channel.

Though a *right*-channel block cannot be removed, the effect that it has can be greatly mitigated by using the mind and InnerTuning practices to open the corresponding microchakra in the *left* channel. Energy ascending in microchakras of the left channel will compensate significantly for the blocks of the right channel. Openings and blocks may form in the left channel at any time in life. Their formation is a consequence of life experiences and determined psychospiritual practices (saadhᵃnaa).

Champion and Saboteur Patterns

A single opening or block is usually not enough to have a major influence on the functioning of a chᵃkrᵃ. However, if three or more openings are vibrating in unison, their combined energy helps to move a chᵃkrᵃ in the direction of goal achievement. Such a pattern of openings is called a *champion pattern*. It champions the ego as it moves toward its goal. Similarly, three or more blocks vibrating together form a *saboteur pattern,* which inhibits attainment of the chᵃkrᵃ's goals. Identifying and overcoming saboteurs is a major task for those practicing InnerTuning.

Both champions and saboteurs form patterns of triangles, squares, pentagons, hexagons, or septagons, depending upon the number of microchakras participating. These patterns are also referred to as "diagrams." The microchakras need not be contiguous: for example, 1:2, 3:2, and 4:2 form a triangle of second microchakras; 2:5, 3:5, 4:5, and 6:5 form a square of fifth microchakras. The combinations encountered most frequently are triangles and squares; pentagons are more rare, while hexagons and septagons seldom occur.

Saboteur Activity

The power of a saboteur is strengthened when apaanᵃ is flowing upward in the right channel; it is weakened when the flow is downward. The Three-Body Purification designed by the senior author (described in chapter 10) help to weaken saboteurs and break the connections between their microchakras. For instance, after a purification, a saboteur square may be reduced to a triangle.

Even though no new blocks develop in the right channel after the right-channel age, the blocks already there can form saboteur patterns at any point in life. These patterns have both intelligence and force, which can generate intrapsychic struggle. For example, you may decide to work as a volunteer for a charitable cause. Suddenly and unexpectedly a number of other demands on your time make it very difficult to implement this decision. All spiritual progress occurs by overcoming obstacles. The saboteurs, in great variety, are there to provide these obstacles.

An adharmic (not following dhᵃrmᵃ) lifestyle provides plenty of apaanᵃ—the fuel of saboteurs. It may cause a downward-pointed saboteur triangle to turn upward. This triangular pattern then recruits more microchakras as it grows into a square, pentagon, or (in the worst cases) a hexagon or septagon. Intense effort is required to reverse such a development and systematically reduce the saboteur from septagon to hexagon to pentagon to square. The square must then be reduced to an upward pointed triangle, and then "flipped" into a downward direction. Finally, the pieces of the triangle must be separated. When their unity is broken, a single microchakra block has no power.

Living a dharmic lifestyle helps to keep the saboteurs in check. If we do not care for our body, and allow tᵃmᵃs and rᵃjᵃs to utterly suppress sᵃtvᵃ, then the saboteurs will flourish and completely control our life, as we slide along the path of psychospiritual devolution.

Champion Activity

In the left channel, the champion patterns are strengthened by the upward flow of lunar energy. A champion pattern may first consist of a downward directed triangle. At some point the triangle "flips" to an upward direction. Champions may also start as upward directed triangles.

The energies of the champions offset those of the saboteurs and move the chᵃkrᵃ toward its goals. If the energy flow of the champion is downward, it is helpful to first lɛngᵃ goals. The flow must be upward in order to support the goals of the second and third lɛngᵃ-s.

Special Microchakra Connections

Certain specific types of connections between microchakras play special roles in the dynamics of their interactions.

Complementary Connections

When the reversal of the major and minor terms describing one microchakra form the description of a second microchakra, the connection between the two microchakras is called a "complementary connection." For example, the connection between 3:6 and 6:3 is a complementary connection. Any influence on one microchakra has a sympathetic effect on its complement.

Solar and Lunar Connections

The first, third, and fifth chᵃkrᵃ-s are predominantly solar chᵃkrᵃ-s. Their representative microchakras are also solar. In the same way, the second, fourth, and sixth chᵃkrᵃ-s and microchakras are predominantly lunar. The importance of the distinction between solar and lunar connections arises in a variety of contexts, particularly in the properties and the use of corresponding musical notes and scales.

Hretᵃ-Chᵃkrᵃ–Seventh-Chᵃkrᵃ Connection

There is a potentially direct connection between Hretᵃ pᵃdmᵃ and L7:4. If a devotee is able to enter Hretᵃ pᵃdmᵃ and continues with extraordinarily intense devotion, then this connection may be actualized. The consequence is that the energy of the devotee will have risen to the seventh chᵃkrᵃ without having to pass through the fifth and sixth chᵃkrᵃ-s, as is usually the case.

Many saints from many traditions have enjoyed the bliss of the special *aakaashᵃ* (chᴇddaakaashᵃ), which is available in L7:4. It is the basis of devotional (bhᵃktᴇ) sᵃmaadhᴇ. There is, however, a problem with such an attainment. The individual is locked into L7:4 and cannot proceed higher. In order to attain liberation (mokshᵃ), one must pass beyond 7:7. These aspirants will be reborn as very high beings.

Blocks and Environmental Pollution

A polluted environment pollutes access to the chᵃkrᵃ-s. The impaired functioning that results creates attitudes and habits that lead to further pollution of the environment. It is imperative that aware human beings break this vicious cycle. In addition to pollution, the planet has been weakened as its oils, minerals, and metals have been drained from it.

The global condition of planet Earth is a reflection of the *earth* chᵃkrᵃ of all the earth's creatures. The earth breathes, pulsates, contracts, expands, dries, and moistens according to its dhᵃrmᵃ. Industrialized society has interfered with this process by burying toxic waste in the earth, polluting underground streams and using fertilizers that have harmful side effects. Accordingly, the first chᵃkrᵃ is polluted by food grown in this contaminated earth. In addition, our advanced technology has spawned fear on a vast scale. We have had two world wars and innumerable smaller ones. The fear of nuclear, chemical, and biological terrorism is part of life in the twenty-first century. Human fear is a pollutant of the earth and of the food that grows in it. Our polluted food weakens the functioning of the first chᵃkrᵃ and makes it difficult to obtain contentment from what we eat. This is one of the factors in the current epidemic of obesity.

In a similar manner, water contaminated by the by-products of industry pollutes the second chᵃkrᵃ. Exchange is the function of the second chᵃkrᵃ and pollution of this chᵃkrᵃ diminishes the quality of exchange. "What's in it for me?" becomes the sole criterion of exchange. Pride in ethical behavior slips as greed rises. Ethical behavior becomes defined as the ability to get away with it. Sexual activity is exploited by greed in innumerable ways. As the second chᵃkrᵃ becomes weaker, the amount of fear that is repressed increases and the desire to alleviate the fear through sexual activity increases. The contentment derived from such sex decreases. In addition, the overactive second chᵃkrᵃ mind is attracted to perversions.

The element of the third chᵃkrᵃ is *fire*. Modern society is organized around increasing "gross national product" and encouraging consumerism. This not only leads to a waste of the resources of the planet but also to inflated egos, as people measure themselves and others in terms of their capacity to consume and possess. In mindless service to consumerism, we burn the resources of the planet and damage its ionosphere, even though it is obvious that we are cutting the branch on which we are sitting.

The fourth chᵃkrᵃ provides love, devotion, worship, and the ability to see humanity as one family. Its fuel is the *air* of the air. We pollute this most important fuel by our dependence on burning hydrocarbons. We have reached the point where, on certain days, our air quality is described by some meteorologists as "unacceptable." The skin is the sense organ of the fourth chᵃkrᵃ. It is often covered with synthetic fabrics, which prevent air from reaching it. As a consequence, the pores of the skin cannot breathe and the skin's defenses become weak. When the skin of the hands is damaged by household chemicals, the sensitivity of touch is diminished. This is particularly noxious for babies and lovers.

The element of the fifth chᵃkrᵃ is *aakaashᵃ*. Different frequencies and timbres of sound create different kinds of *aakaashᵃ*. These range from those that are heavy, dense, and filled with tᵃmᵃs to those that are light, calming, and brimming with sᵃtvᵃ. The former keep us bound to the empirical world; the latter move us in the direction of transcendence. The more gross the individual psyche, the greater will be the attraction to tᵃmᵃs-dominated sound. Conversely, the more subtle the psyche, the greater the attraction to sound containing sᵃtvᵃ.

The present electronic age has reached a pinnacle in the use of loud and harsh sound as a means of entertainment. The effect of this bombardment on the nervous system leads to impairment of hearing—the most subtle of the five senses. With prolonged exposure to abusive sounds, characteristics of the fifth chᵃkrᵃ, communication, spontaneity, and creativity suffer severe and often lasting damage.

If the elements of the first five chᵃkrᵃ-s are polluted, they will impair the balancing of the guNᵃ-s in the sixth chᵃkrᵃ, and prevent true meditation.

A BRIEF SURVEY OF THE MICROCHAKRAS

The quiddity of each microchakra (*earth, water, fire, air, aakaashᵃ*, guNᵃ-s, or contentment) is always a representative of that chᵃkrᵃ where the quiddity is most completely expressed. For example, all *fire* microchakras (i.e., all third microchakras) may be regarded as representatives of the third chᵃkrᵃ, whose dominant element is *fire*. In this manner, the quiddity of each chᵃkrᵃ mind contributes to the functioning of all other chᵃkrᵃ minds (see plate 8).

The following paragraphs give some indication of how this process operates in the play of the chᵃkrᵃ-s. For purposes of simplification, any distinction based on the three channels is minimized. The descriptions below are based on the assumption that the microchakra is completely open and making its full contribution of energy. The significance of blocks is discussed elsewhere.

The Paradox of the Key Microchakras. The key microchakras are L1:1, L2:2, L3:3, L4:4, L5:5, L6:6, and L7:7. In order to maintain the play associated with a chᵃkrᵃ, nature (prᵃkretᴇ) conspires to keep these microchakras blocked. This forces the person to keep striving for the goals of the chᵃkrᵃ. When a key microchakra is finally opened through following dhᵃrmᵃ and spiritual practice (saadhᵃnaa), the energy that has been used to open it now aids in opening higher microchakras.

First-Chᵃkrᵃ Microchakras

1:1 Stability (*Earth*) within *Earth*
The flow of *earth* within *earth* is called the body of the *earth* (first) chᵃkrᵃ. It makes the greatest contribution to the overall stability of the first chᵃkrᵃ. The first chᵃkrᵃ is then grounded and in tune with bodily rhythm. There is a strong feeling of security—which helps us to be fun loving and gregarious.

1:2 Fluidity (*Water*) within *Earth*
The adult human body is approximately 70 percent water. This microchakra permits the flow associated with bodily water to be well integrated into the overall sense of the physical body. There is a healthy capacity for sexual exchange and a fundamental honesty in all interpersonal exchanges.

1:3 Assertiveness (*Fire*) within *Earth*
The *earth* element is enriched with assertive energy, which helps to attain the goals of the first chᵃkrᵃ: food, shelter, sense of physical power, and effectiveness. Since these goals can be attained with relative ease, there is a tendency to be cooperative with others and responsible in relationships.

1:4 Feeling (*Air*) within *Earth*
Earth-related activities are approached with feeling. One example is gardening. The *fire* element may enable one to enjoy this activity with competency; however, it is the *air* element that permits a feeling of deep connection with nature to accompany

it. There is a desire to touch the earth, to see things grow and to nurture all living things. If 4:1 is also open then feelings of gratitude toward the earth for supporting us all are likely to arise.

1:5 Creativity (*Aakaash^a*) within *Earth*

Self-expression reveals that we are at home on the planet Earth. Creativity is used to enjoy life. Eating habits are healthy and there is adequate chewing. There is a tendency to praise the earth in both speech and song, especially if 5:1 is also open.

1:6 Intuition within *Earth*

There is an intuitive awareness of how to work with the *earth* element to obtain the goals of the first ch^akr^a. Discernment in what food to eat and to grow is present. A capacity to nurture the planet Earth through a deep understanding and appreciation of it is part of the awareness of this microchakra. This capacity is enhanced if 6:1 is also open.

1:7 Contentment within *Earth*

The goals of the first ch^akr^a have been attained.

Second-Ch^akr^a Microchakras

2:1 Stability (*Earth*) within *Water*

The play of the second ch^akr^a involves interpersonal exchange. The primary element enabling this exchange is *water*. When *earth* within *water* is flowing, confidence for participation in this play is strengthened. Family and friends are particularly important.

Differences in bodily fluids (hormones, etc.) help to define gender and a strong *earth* contribution to *water* strengthens the body of the second ch^akr^a. In this way, it helps to make gender identification clear and unambiguous.

2:2 Fluidity (*Water*) within *Water*

This is a key (paradoxical) microchakra wherein blocked energy helps to meet the goals of this ch^akr^a. Nature (pr^akretɛ) wants us to maintain this block in order to preserve the species. Opening leads to transcendence of this goal and the upward flow of energy to the next ch^akr^a.

2:3 Assertiveness (*Fire*) within *Water*

Assertiveness within the context of gender occurs, for example, when a lover dresses in a manner designed to charm. In the business realm, dress may be selected to impress or intimidate. In a diplomatic situation, an attempt is often made to create the impression of genuine friendship.

2:4 Feeling (*Air*) within *Water*
Gentle touch, both physical and spiritual, is the chief contribution of the *air* element to play that is fueled by the primary element of *water*. Exchange of touch is most refined in a loving couple. There is a gratitude for being a partner in the process of creation.

2:5 Creativity (*Aakaash^a*) within *Water*
Exchange is facilitated by clear expression and keen listening and speaking to others. During intimate communication with a mate or friends, the expansion due to *aakaash^a* enhances feelings of closeness. There is an ability to express feelings in folk singing.

2:6 Intuition within *Water*
This opening taps into wisdom, which helps one to choose a good mate, friend, or business associate.

2:7 Contentment within *Water*
The major issues of the second-ch^akr^a play are resolved.

Third-Ch^akr^a Microchakras
3:1 Stability (*Earth*) within *Fire*
This microchakra provides a sense of stability to the assertiveness that accompanies the operation of the *fire* element. Hence the third-ch^akr^a play of establishing one's social identity—through work, family, and community—is given a solid base from which to operate.

3:2 Fluidity (*Water*) within *Fire*
Assertiveness is conducted in an honest and forthright manner. Sexuality is purely for physical pleasure of the ego. This opening may permit a person to be a good matchmaker—selecting a mate for a relative, friend, or other.

3:3 Assertiveness (*Fire*) within *Fire*
This is a key microchakra, which nature (pr^akretɛ) wishes to remain blocked so that we strive to meet the goals of the third ch^akr^a and develop a sense of autonomy in so doing. When open, it permits us to see ourselves and others with complete

objectivity. This then leads naturally to an opening in L3:7 and a desire to soften the ego and move on to the second lɛŋgᵃ.

3:4 Feeling (*Air*) within *Fire*

The feeling and caring for others that naturally accompanies the *air* element directs the assertiveness of *fire* in that direction. This helps to refine the ego and enables the truly confident expression that wins people's hearts. We accomplish the goals of the third chᵃkrᵃ by gaining acceptance in a community and identifying with its goals. This community may be a social group, a religion, or a nation. Identification may be so strong that we willingly give our life for the community.

3:5 Creativity (*Aakaashᵃ*) within *Fire*

The voice sensitivity that accompanies *aakaashᵃ* permits clear articulation of our views with confidence and precision. We are not subject to stage fright. This opening may be at the root of a convincing and hypnotic voice.

The creativity associated with *aakaashᵃ* may express itself in the visual arts—since the eye draws most of its energy from the *fire* element.

3:6 Intuition within *Fire*

Having an intimate relation with the same-sex parent results in considerable confidence in pursuing goals by rational means.

3:7 Contentment within Fire

The goals of the third chᵃkrᵃ have been met.

Fourth-Chᵃkrᵃ Microchakras

4:1 Stability (*Earth*) within *Air*

This microchakra is the body of feeling. It enables us to explore the depth of our feelings and facilitates entry into the fourth dimension of devotion and service—an aspect of life that is outside the experience of the first lɛŋgᵃ. The deeper we can feel life, the more natural devotion and service become. This capacity, and all other fourth chᵃkrᵃ capacities, is normally easier for females than for males—partly because the lunar right hemisphere is usually more active in females.

4:2 Fluidity (*Water*) within *Air*

There is no expectation of receiving anything in return for what is offered. The idea of exchange that accompanied fluidity in the lower chᵃkrᵃ-s is now rare. It is replaced by an unstoppable flow of love and caring. Energy from this microchakra can be used to purify the profit-oriented second ch^akr^a. The brother-sister bond helps to establish close relationships with the opposite gender.

4:3 Assertiveness (*Fire*) within *Air*

The opening of this microchakra is accompanied by a significant refinement of the ego. As the fire of unconditional giving flows, this refinement precludes any expectation of acknowledgment. The capacity for surrender to that which is higher and subtler increases. This is sometimes done through a "dance of ecstasy," which surrenders the ego to a deity. Similarly, the heart may dance and leap with joy when surrender to a cause seems to be effective.

4:4 Feeling (*Air*) within *Air*

This is a key microchakra. In order for it to open, four or five fourth microchakras need to be open. These openings permit an accumulation of sufficient devotional energy to open this microchakra. Then there may be total and unconditional giving. This is sometimes called religious ecstasy.

4:5 Creativity (*Aakaash^a*) within *Air*

The flow of *aakaash^a* within *air* permits the uninhibited expression of devotional feelings. Creative ways of showing love and surrender can be manifested, such as singing, particularly with a sustained tone.

4:6 Intuition within *Air*

The opening of 4:6 is dependent on the relation with the opposite-sex parent. In this microchakra intuition enters into the capacity for feeling. The probability that the deity or cause to which we surrender will be an aspect of the one Truth is greatly increased. In other words, we will think and behave according to dh^arm^a and draw ever closer to ret^a.

4:7 Contentment within *Air*

The minimal amount of time necessary is spent on first lɛng^a goals and the lifestyle is one devoted to the second lɛng^a.

Fifth-Ch^akr^a Microchakras

5:1 Stability (*Earth*) within *Aakaash^a*

This microchakra provides body to the voice. When it is open, the voice is full and resonant; creativity has a solid base from which to proceed.

5:2 Fluidity (*Water*) within *Aakaash*[a]

The voice will have a clear, flowing quality. Abstract values related to personal integrity, such as promises, will be pure and transparently honest. Creative expression will reflect fluidity.

5:3 Assertiveness (*Fire*) within *Aakaash*[a]

This microchakra provides the courage to allow the breathing rate to drop significantly and to enter altered states, fostering internalization of the senses (pr[a]tyaahaar[a]). Creative *fire* is kindled and expressed through arts of all kinds. The person may have the mind-set of an inventor.

5:4 Feeling (*Air*) within *Aakaash*[a]

This feeling for *aakaash*[a] permits a very skillful and loving approach to tonality. The voice is used to express love of sound and chanting expresses a full range of sentiment. The voice may be honey sweet and can be used to do healing. People with this opening tend to be carefree and have a cosmic sense of humor.

5:5 Creativity (*Aakaash*[a]) within *Aakaash*[a]

When this key microchakra is opened, the capacity to hear beyond the normal range emerges. You may hear one or more of the classical ten inner sounds (see Table 10.2) until finally you hear your own naad[a] (fundamental frequency) constantly. Interest in liberation intensifies. You have the flexibility to dwell in any place, no matter how noisy. However, your preference will be to live in a secluded place where silence reigns. The ability to hear all forty-nine tones in an octave emerges. If 4:5 is also open, you will be able to chant them.

Spiritual practice is focused upon connecting your own fundamental frequency with that of the universe, with the grace of the inner guru.

5:6 Intuition within *Aakaash*[a]

Intuitive awareness helps to establish control over the lower elements and attention is focused on discriminating among the gu$_N$[a]-s. The inner guru awakens when L5:6 and C5:6 are both open. R5:6 is blocked in most people. However, if it is open it will be easier to awaken the inner guru. The inner guru will advise you on how to divide your attention among the three fields and will help in moving energy further upward.

Most trained professional advisors have this microchakra slightly open.

5:7 Contentment within *Aakaash*[a]

All attachments to spacetime cease. In the Indian subcontinent, such a person may choose to live as a wanderer without a home (avᵃdhootᵃ), whose bed is the earth and roof is the sky.

Sixth-Chᵃkrᵃ Microchakras

In the sixth chᵃkrᵃ, the guɴᵃ-s are dominant. The elements have ceased to be active and remain only as abstractions that are available to intuition. People in sixth chᵃkrᵃ awareness can use these abstractions to master the activity of the elements in their own lower chᵃkrᵃ-s.

6:1 Stability (*Earth*) within Intuition

This opening permits you to perceive the earth as a living breathing being. The phrase "Mother Earth" comes alive. You feel that you are a citizen of the planet and that your body is a temple for which you are responsible. Fasting becomes easy.

6:2 Fluidity (*Water*) within Intuition

Those with this microchakra open can master the *water* element in themselves. They can turn thirst off at will; their fast can be liquid as well as solid. If 2:3 or 3:2 are also open, there is no karmic obligation to reproduce. They can very easily become celibates if they so choose.

6:3 Assertiveness (*Fire*) within Intuition

There is mastery of the *fire* element. The downward flow of solar energy and the upward flow of lunar energy is clearly seen in yourself and others. If C6:3 is also open you may see the auras of others. This opening is equivalent to surrendering the sixth chᵃkrᵃ ego. It permits entry to the feeling of the Cosmic Intelligence within— a necessary prerequisite for advanced meditation. An opening in 6:3 makes it natural to rise before sunrise for spiritual practices.

6:4 Feeling (*Air*) within Intuition

Compassion reaches its zenith. The pain of others is felt deeply and it is possible to take on the burden of the pain and negative karmᵃ of others. There is devotion toward the Divinity within oneself.

6:5 Expression (*Aakaashᵃ*) within Intuition

Paranormal abilities with respect to sound exceed their presence in 5:5. There is communication with your own inner deity by means of the inner guru (5:6–6:5 connection). The quality of sooryᵃ *aakaashᵃ* produced while chanting is so superb that stone walls and metal construction can absorb and retain it.

6:6 Intuition within Intuition

Profound knowledge of naad^a yog^a (yoga of sound) unfolds from within if 6:5 is also open. If 6:4 is also open, then knowledge of sv^{a}r^a yog^a (yoga of breath) will unfold. When the inner guru is awake and L6:6 and C6:6 are open, as you focus on your dh^{a}rm^a, an intuition of Reality may emerge.

6:7 Contentment within Intuition

You are almost free of the guN^a-s, though s^{a}tv^a still retains a slight influence. You are content with your knowledge of the universe and have no further desire to "know" anything from outside. "As it is here, so it is there" (Y^{a}thaa PEndA T^{a}thaa Br^{a}hmaandA) has been actualized.

Seventh-Ch^{a}kr^a Microchakras

The microchakras in the seventh ch^{a}kr^a are dedicated to various ways to merge with the ocean of Divinity.

PARENTING CONSIDERATIONS
AND THE RIGHT-CHANNEL AGE

As mentioned earlier, during the first half of the right-channel age (the first three years of a girl's life and the first three and a half years of a boy's life), the full spectrum of solar energy slowly descends down the right channel. If there is no interference with this flow, it will energize each microchakra in the channel and keep it open. This makes parenting practices during this time crucially important.

Conception

Parenting includes planning for conception under the best conditions possible. When parents view the time of conception as very special, it will be reflected in the newborn. Ideally, in preparation for conception, both parents will maintain a healthy diet, exercise daily, and use massage and breathing exercises for several months. They avoid drugs. Such discipline and meaningful sacrifice help to create optimal conditions for the conception of a child.

Pregnancy

During pregnancy, a healthy diet and appropriate exercise for the mother are crucial. Specific yoga postures used throughout pregnancy may make birthing a lot easier. Sexual intercourse after approximately the first twenty weeks of pregnancy is to be avoided. In the serene environment of the womb, the baby experiences penile thrusting as a violent intrusion, which it interprets as aggression. It engages in defensive reactions to protect itself and thereby creates blockages in the microchakras of its sixth and seventh chᵃkrᵃ-s. The effects of these aggression-caused blockages manifest deep within the developing brain and may predispose one to violence and militant behavior later in life. Inexplicable aches and pains (both physical and mental) later in life may also be due to these early blocks. Other forms of sexual intimacy, however, may relax the mother's body and prepare her for an easier childbirth.

Pregnancy is an especially important time for the father to serve as a buffer against outside influences that could potentially disturb the mother. Any stress experienced by her leaves an impression on both her and the unborn.

Observations of the normal conditions of a fetus reveal that most of the time the body rests in the womb with head downward, as if in the yoga posture of the headstand. Thus when the mother is sitting, standing, or walking, gravity assures a maximum supply of blood to the developing fetal brain.

David B. Chamberlain has reviewed the literature pertaining to the sensory and motor capacities of the fetus and provided a summary. The following paragraphs are primarily based on his findings.

Around three weeks gestational age, the first heartbeat appears. By the tenth week, the swallowing reflex begins and the mouth may be opening and closing. Rotation of the head and waving of the arms and legs occurs. Around twenty weeks, the fetus can suck on its toes, rub hands and feet together, and yawn.

Touch sensitivity appears as early as eight weeks. The stroke of a single hair elicits protective movements when the cheek is touched. Over the next few weeks, touch sensitivity appears sequentially in the genitals, palms, soles, and abdomen.

At fourteen weeks, the taste buds have developed. When sweet tastes are given, swallowing increases; if the taste is bitter, swallowing diminishes. The fetus is also capable of detecting odiferous compounds in the amniotic fluid.

Hearing involves the skin and bones as well as the ears. Researchers have demonstrated that the fetus reacts to sound at sixteen weeks, eight weeks before the ear is completely developed.[6]

Chamberlain noted:

These findings indicate the complexity of hearing, lending support to the idea that receptive hearing begins with the skin and skeletal framework, skin being a multireceptor organ integrating input from vibrations, thermo receptors, and pain receptors. The primal listening system is then amplified with vestibular and cochlear information as it becomes available.

Many studies now confirm that voices reach the womb. . . . Intonation patterns of pitch, stress, and rhythm, as well as music, reach the fetus without significant distortion. A mother's voice is particularly powerful because it is transmitted to the womb through her own body reaching the fetus in a stronger form than outside.[7]

Testing vision in utero is not feasible, but studies of premature infants show that focusing and tracking develop by thirty-four weeks.

Around sixteen weeks a fetus may either defend itself or withdraw from the needle during amniocentesis. It shows irregular heart rate and the breathing rate may not return to normal for several days. This demonstrates the sensitivity of the fetus to pain.

The above facts negate the view, held by science for many decades, that infants do not feel or react to pain and that crying in the neonate is simply to open the lungs rather than to express distress.

Birthing

When the time arrives for birthing, the mother goes through contractions that propel the child from the womb and through the birth canal. The energy that accumulates in the rapidly growing brain of the child plays a significant part in the birth process and may, in fact, initiate it. The child's head needs the contractions as a massage for regulating the flow of energy throughout its body.

It is therefore not the mother's body alone that determines the duration of the period of contractions. The needs of mother and child are intertwined. Their communication establishes the overall duration of the contractions.

Birthing actually starts to take place once the energy begins to move downward from the baby's head. The first cry of the newborn is only possible if enough energy has moved from the head to the neck and lung areas.

When a baby is born, and for a few months thereafter, awareness resides in the seventh chᵃkrᵃ much of the time. In the ancient Indian tradition, babies are referred to as a Divine Form (Brᵃhmaa roopᵃ). The purity of their innocence together with their often amazing intuitiveness led to this appellation.

In general, premature birth causes the rotation of the chᵃkrᵃ-s to speed up. This may contribute to a restless temperament. A late birth may slow the rotation of the chᵃkrᵃ-s, thereby requiring extra incentives to attain normal accomplishment.

Natural Birth and Obstetric Practice

In most societies throughout human history, childbirth has usually occurred in the privacy of the home. The mother was attended by other women experienced in birthing: family, friends, or midwives. At the time of birth, she would assume a posture that permitted gravity to assist the baby's entry into the world, such as kneeling, squatting, or standing with bent knees. The mother was engaged in a profound and sacred event wherein her feelings and intuition were given central importance.

In her book *Gentle Birth Choices,* Barbara Harper has traced the change in American birthing practices from the traditional focus on home and midwife to the current focus on hospital and obstetrician.[8] She notes that in 1900, 95 percent of American births took place at home. In the 1990s, 95 percent took place in a hospital. This trend began in the nineteenth century and was initiated by the high mortality rate that surrounded childbirth (sixty-five percent greater in 1900 than today). This mortality rate was often caused by poor nutrition and unsanitary conditions. Medicine offered a welcome solution.

> The rapid development of the field of obstetrics in the late 1800s and early 1900s, coupled with the growth of related medical technology and hospital procedures, began to make women feel inadequate about their ability to give birth. They no longer trusted their bodies, their instincts, or the wisdom of their grandmothers. Doctors increasingly discredited women birth attendants and eventually controlled the education and licensing of midwives.[9]

The transfer of authority to obstetricians meant that birth became a medical problem to be solved by the best technology possible. A pregnant woman was turned into a patient. The materialistic model of science governed the training of the obstetricians and came to dominate the woman's view of birth itself.

> This view of birth stripped women of the chance to experience the emotional and social aspects of childbirth. In other words, women became baby machines, treated like repositories of little uteruses that contained little fetuses, all of which were subject to the control of the physician. During the 1940s, 1950s, and 1960s, the birth process was turned into an assembly line managed by skilled technicians and machines. Time limits were established for the first and second stages of labor, with some hospitals actually instituting the policy that a woman could only be in the delivery room for a specific length of time. With the development of oxytocic drugs to induce or speed up labor, doctors could manage birth even more effectively. Drugs were given to slow a labor until the doctor or the delivery room was ready; then Pitocin could be used to get the labor going again. Cesarean sections replaced the use of high forceps, and fetal monitors helped detect fetal distress that resulted from the use of drugs and anesthesia. One intervention inevitably

led directly to the next, until every birth was a medically managed, staged, and produced event.[10]

This approach to birthing obviously demonstrates understanding of the physical field alone. It is as if one machine is replicating another machine.

In the 1970s, the French obstetrician Frédérick Leboyer challenged several of the assumptions underlying the mechanistic model of birth. In his book *Birth without Violence,* Leboyer gave a heart-rending account of what birth must be like from the perspective of the suffering infant subjected to standard obstetric practices:

When children come into the world, the first thing they do is cry.

And everyone rejoices.

"My baby's crying!" the mother exclaims happily, astonished that anything so small can make so much noise.

And how does everyone else react?

The reflexes are normal. The machine works.

But are we machines?

Aren't cries always an expression of pain?

Isn't it conceivable that the baby is in anguish?

What makes us assume that birth is less painful for the child than it is for the mother?

And if it is, does anyone care?

No one, I'm afraid, judging by how little attention we pay to a baby when it arrives.

What a tragedy that we're all so determined to believe that this "thing" can't hear, can't see, can't *feel* . . .

So how could "it" feel pain?

"It" cries, "it" howls. So?

In short, "it" is an object.

But what if "it" is already a *person?*[11]

In 1995, Chamberlain reported:

My own attention was drawn to birth trauma by clients remembering birth in hypnosis . . .

The great majority (but not all) were actively protesting inappropriate conditions or actions at the time of birth. With ringing clarity they identified what was wrong: the pressure of forceps on their heads, cold rooms, bright lights, needle injections, repeated heel jabs for blood, stinging or blurring eye medicine, being suspended by their feet, hasty cutting of the umbilical cord, separating them from their mother, and isolating them in nurseries. Their cries were cries of pain and protest.[12]

Since the 1970s, many people—both physicians and laity—have joined the struggle to provide a more humane and gentle approach to childbirth. The struggle continues to the present day. Accounts of it and alternative approaches to birth may be found in the writing of Susan L. Diamond[13] and Henci Goer,[14] among others.

The impact of birthing practices upon the microchakras of the right channel will be discussed in detail in the chapters on the three lɛngᵃ-s.

Bedtime

In industrialized societies most parents put their baby to sleep in a separate room. From the viewpoint of babies, it must be confusing that in the daytime they are cared for with sweet words, caring hands, and admiring exclamations, while at night, they are suddenly left alone in a dark room.

Jackson described the Spartan attitude behind this inconsistent treatment of the most helpless members of society:

> One mother told me how a friend of hers locked her two-year-old in her bedroom every night, ignoring her screams, which would go on for up to an hour. When the child did finally submit, exhausted, to sleep, her body would be pressed against the closed bedroom door on which she had been hammering. Her mother would then go and pick her up, and put her back into bed.
>
> 'I feel awful listening to it,' said the friend. 'The mother says, "Oh, she'll learn that I won't go up to her and it's useless making that noise." But it's been going on for weeks now, and it doesn't seem to be getting any better.'
>
> This is the kind of child abuse our society tolerates, because it is in the name of socially educating our children.[15]

Sleeping with one or both parents influences three crucial microchakras: R4:4 (heart of the heart), R4:7 (contentment of the heart) and R2:2 (the core of fear). The baby that has the good fortune to sleep with his or her parents will never wake up in a dark room alone—a parent is always within hand's reach. Intense experiences of fear and disorientation are bypassed. The intelligence of the skin—a measure of buoyancy of the immune system—is nurtured through caring touch and breastfeeding. The close proximity of parents at night allows the baby's skin to relax and be receptive. As a result, the breath deepens, thus slowing inhalation and exhalation. Contentment is experienced.

Proximity, and an occasional caress from the parent sleeping nearby, nurtures a baby's subtle body. Couples who have slept with a newborn never forget the precious moment when, early in the morning, one parent finds the baby gently tracing the facial features of the parent who is still asleep. It is an experience of paramount importance when baby sees and feels the unchanging facial expression of a parent. This provides a balance for the fact that in the daytime, the baby usually sees the parent with constantly changing facial expressions. Deep bonding and profound feelings of security occur at these moments. The depth of relaxation experienced in the skin contact is unique.

Some parents place their baby in a crib beside their bed. The mother first lies with the baby until she sleeps deeply, then places her into the crib. This is an excellent solution when either baby or parents are very sensitive to each other's movements during sleep. Any squirm or sound can still be clearly heard.

It is good, right from the beginning, to put the baby to sleep on her back with her head slightly raised. Sleeping on the stomach is unhealthy and restricts breathing; it is related to insecurity. A baby who sleeps with her parents usually adapts rather quickly to sleeping on her back. When the baby is fast asleep, she can be turned on her left side. Nonbreastfed babies and babies who sleep alone tend to become more jittery, possessive, aggressive, resentful, depressed, or colicky.

Breastfeeding

In recent decades, science has pointed to the importance of breastfeeding during the first forty weeks for optimal functioning of both the immune system and digestive tract of the baby. Breastfeeding must be done on demand. It generates beta endorphins in the brain that create heartfelt contentment—thus nurturing R4:7.

Breastfeeding is crucial to the opening of R4:5. Baby's suckling creates a warm red *aakaash*[a] that nourishes R4:5. When suckling mother's left breast, baby's left nostril will be open; during right breast suckling, the right nostril opens. The *aakaash*[a] created by the left nostril open versus the right is of a different hue. Both forms of *aakaash*[a] during suckling are needed to open R4:5. In hearing mother's heartbeat and feeling its pulsation, a natural synchronization happens that intensifies the experience of *aakaash*[a]. An echo of the *aakaash*[a] that opens R4:5 resounds in R3:5, R2:5, and R1:5.

Small pauses may occur during suckling that bring forth an even subtler *aakaash*[a]. Baby's breath actually may momentarily stop, leaving the baby surrounded by a luminous *aakaash^a* of "audible" stillness. This may add to the eventual sweetness of the baby's voice. Most babies laugh and giggle profusely during this period.

Breastfeeding nurtures R4:4 by way of its intimate skin contact in which individual boundaries dissolve. When mother allows one-pointed attention during breastfeeding, a unique silent communication vibrates R5:5 in the baby. Thereby a fertile soil is created for profound sound sensitivity later in life.

When the time for weaning arrives, baby lets the mother know unmistakably by biting or by avoiding the smell of the breast.

Importance of the Royal Treatment

Too much contrast between daytime and nighttime treatment creates conflicting feelings in infants. At night they feel unwanted, abandoned, and they cry and cry for the comfort of the parent. Often they go through a stupor before falling asleep. There is nothing to hold on to but a blanket or a teddy bear while they are trapped alone in a crib. Loneliness, abandonment, and inferiority register: "I am not good enough to have anything better." The ground for early fantasizing is laid. They struggle to get love and care when in need. This struggle may follow them throughout life since these early desperate impressions are buried very deep in their memory. Later in life they may become great achievers as *the world becomes the mother substitute.* In personal relationships, they often seek the unconditional loving mother they never had. This problem may be magnified if the other person needs the same unconditional love.

During the right-channel age, efforts to discipline the child should be minimal. Rather, they should be given unconditional love and treated like a little prince or princess. Toward the end of this period, the ego of the first ch^akr^a will have naturally strengthened. This strength will show in several ways: they will reject the bottle, begin to ask for their own room, spend more time by themselves, and be more sharing with other children.

SIGNS AND CAUSES OF OPENINGS AND BLOCKS

Based on the extensive observations of the senior author, Microchakra Psychology has identified detailed indicators of openings and blocks, as well as examples of actions that may open or block each microchakra. They offer invaluable guidance for parents, particularly of children in the right-channel age, but are also helpful throughout life, as they provide information that can guide the application of

InnerTuning techniques. They are given in the following three chapters, with a chapter devoted to each of the three lɛngᵃ-s. However, they should be used with the following warning in mind.

WARNING !

+ The material on openings and blocks provided in the following three chapters represents probabilities only—not certainties. Sometimes a champion pattern will negate the effect of what would otherwise be an experience that would produce a block. Similarly, saboteur patterns may prevent expected openings from happening.

+ Often several signs of a block or opening will be presented. Not all of these signs need be present in any given case. Some might be seen in one case and others in a different case.

+ The examples of openers and blockers used in this book are the senior author's personal observations in cultures where he has lived (India, America, and Europe). There may be other examples in these cultures or in other cultures of which he is not aware.

+ **DO NOT RUBRICIZE.** In his *Toward a Psychology of Being*, Abraham Maslow advised that we avoid attaching labels (rubrics) to people.[16] For example, if an individual is showing a number of symptoms of third-chᵃkrᵃ blockage, one should not call him or her a "third-chᵃkrᵃ person." All people have all seven chᵃkrᵃ minds and all are the Self, which is beyond them all.

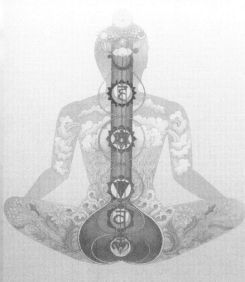

5
Openings and Blocks in the First Leng^a

The first lɛng^a is comprised of the first three ch^akr^a-s (see plate 9). In this chapter the specific signs and causes of openings and blocks of the microchakras of the right and left channels of each of these three ch^akr^a-s are presented in detail.

THE FIRST CH^AKR^A
R1:1 and L1:1

Right Channel 1:1

Signs of an opening. Children's eyes are clear and soft and radiate an earthly wisdom. They feel free to follow the impulse of curiosity and to explore the environment. Adjustment to the basic circadian rhythm of sleeping shortly after sunset and awakening shortly before sunrise happens naturally. Sleep is deep with moderate dreaming. The anal sphincter is relaxed. Bowel movements occur daily without any problem.

Children are energetic, calm, and self-accepting. They feel secure enough to leave the parents and play with other children. There is enjoyment of the moment.

Causes of an opening. Baby's space in the womb is secure with no threatening intrusions. After birth, as much contact as possible is maintained between the infant and the bosom of the mother. Toddlers benefit from much loving touch from parents and close relatives, particularly grandparents. Good nutrition is particularly important for this opening as well as other first microchakra openings.

Signs of a block. When this microchakra is blocked, the child has difficulty in sharing space with others. There is greater likelihood of colic and, later, chronic constipation or diarrhea. The child is locked into "me first" awareness and takes whatever she can regardless of the needs or wishes of others. The ability to sit or be still is almost absent.

Saboteurs love blockage in R1:1—it ensures their supply of apaan^a.

Causes of a block. These include: a) trauma during pregnancy, b) the shock of birth itself, c) any removal of the infant from the mother for long periods of time, d) no physical contact with the grandparents and other close relatives, e) not feeding the child when he cries for food, f) hitting the child for playing with her feces, and g) starvation or malnutrition during the first three years of life.

Foods that are processed, heavy, or fried add to the intensity of the block.

Left Channel 1:1

Signs of an opening. The *earth* of the *earth* in this microchakra contributes to the efficient flow of information through all cells of the body. The resulting cellular wisdom gives the body an awareness of its own identity as well as a general physical well-being and strength. Together, these provide a basic self-confidence. The corresponding feeling of self-acceptance precludes any form of masochism. Life is lived in a relaxed manner. Physical labor is engaged in with enthusiasm.

Of particular significance is the contribution of this energy to the flexibility of the spine—crucial to overall health. After puberty, spinal flexibility permits a motionless sitting posture that can be maintained for at least twenty minutes. The opening of L1:1 contributes to a clear flow of the cerebrospinal fluid.

The wisdom of the body fed by this opening promotes habits of moderation in both sleeping and eating and eliminates the desire to eat unhealthy foods. The sense of smell, the most basic of the senses, is very keen. Stools are moist, long, continuous, and float naturally, indicating good health (fiber makes stools float; undigested fat makes them sink).

Because the sense of survival is well established, a person with this opening will take no pleasure in killing other creatures and will do so only if life itself is threatened.

Generally, the whole character of the left channel changes when L1:1 is open. It is easier for champion patterns to form. When L1:1 is blocked, it is easier for saboteurs to form.

Signs of a block. L1:1 is a key microchakra and nature (pr^{a}kretɛ) uses a feeling of insecurity to keep it partially blocked. This insecurity is based on a powerful fear for survival that is encoded in the circuits of the early brain. Through this insecurity, contentment of the first ch^{a}kr^a mind is difficult to obtain, so the person is kept busy working toward first ch^{a}kr^a goals of wealth and personal power. Life seems a struggle. If, however, persistent engagement in spiritual practices repeatedly brings contentment, nature will eventually give way and permit this microchakra to fully open.

A block in L1:1 causes unconscious attempts to find the weak or missing *earth*. Stomping heavily, rather than walking normally with the heel first, may be a sign of this. The style of eating is also affected. Overeating or gorging occurs in an effort to secure a feeling of bodily identity. This is a way of allaying both ignorance about self-identity and the fear of dying—the fear that the survival goal of the first chᵃkrᵃ will not be met.

Eating habits often lack normal discrimination—such as eating foods that are too hot or too cold. Intoxicants may be used indiscriminately, particularly opiates, sedatives, raw alcohol, and tobacco.

Other physical symptoms, clearly visible when asleep, include a habitually angry face, stiff chin, and loud heavy breathing through the mouth. Smell, the sense of the first chᵃkrᵃ, may be weak.

Lack of self-confidence and distrust of others are basic characteristics of this block. There is often a refusal to explore new knowledge; instead, ignorance is embraced.

Negative energy from obstruction of this microchakra contributes to an unruly temper. Anger may be suppressed until there is a drastic and violent outburst. In some cases, hostility is directed to the survival of others. The unconscious attitude is, "I have been deprived so why shouldn't you?" The intensity of this hostility varies from spiteful acts to murder. Hunting animals or even killing other people is a source of pleasure. Abortion can be used as a form of birth control with no qualms.

The hostility toward life activates a perverted pleasure in witnessing suffering or bloodshed. It may also lead to various sexual perversions such as foot fetishes and chain fetishes. In some cases, the negative energy is directed toward the self and contributes toward various types of masochism. Habitually wearing black leather clothing is a possible indicator of this block.

There is propensity to constipation.

LI:I played a special role in human evolution. Before any cortex emerged, the animal was governed simply by the emotions and instincts of the early brain. Solar energy was brought down the right channel to RI:I with the aid of gravity. When it was converted to lunar energy by LI:I it arose in the left channel to stimulate cells that would experience feeling (as distinct from emotion) and lead to the emergence of the right hemisphere.

RI:2 and LI:2

Right Channel 1:2
Signs of an opening. When a child is deeply asleep and R1:2 is open, the child will squirm or cry before urination. A child may play without a parent being present

as this opening significantly reduces the fear of abandonment. Trust in parents increases and there is a closer feeling toward the grandparents.

After twenty weeks children are usually given solid foods (in mashed form) while they continue to nurse. A sign that R1:2 is open occurs if they no longer desire to nurse after forty weeks.

Causes of an opening. An opening in R1:2 is due to an intimate relation with the opposite sex parent.

Signs of a block. Blockage of this microchakra contributes to the search for oral gratification. The child may suck his thumb and, even after age three, may not easily give up the bottle. The underlying fear stems from a lack of solid grounding and physical identity. This may express itself as fear of the dark or bed-wetting. Any separation from the parents causes anxiety.

Feelings of insecurity may also give rise to an insatiable need for attention, even negative attention. Thus, the child's behavior may appear to consist predominantly of chronic naughtiness and occasional temper tantrums. Another form of negative behavior, closely related to bed-wetting, is either unconscious or deliberate failure to give notification before urinating.

If the child is punished for innocent exploration of its genitals, a fearful or negative attitude toward the genitals may develop—thus blocking this microchakra. Possible consequences, either precociously or later in life, are proneness to severe sexual guilt, environmental (not genetically caused) homosexuality, or sexual sadism.

If a little boy feels deeply rejected by his father he may reason as follows: "Daddy likes Mommy. If I were more like Mommy, Daddy would like me." He may then proceed to imitate his mother and suppress his masculine tendencies. A similar situation can arise between a little girl and her mother.

The degree to which any of these conditions may manifest in behavior depends on the presence of additional blockages in R2:2 and R2:3.

Causes of a block. Reasons for blockage in this microchakra include: a) general negativity of the mother toward the child, b) lack of contact with the opposite-gender parent or surrogate, c) punishment of the child for fondling genitals, especially if punishment comes from the mother, d) thumb-sucking and use of pacifiers.

Left Channel 1:2

Signs of an opening. Children who have the second microchakra within the first chᵃkrᵃ (L1:2) open by the end of the right-channel age (three for girls; three and a half for boys) want to have their own bed and no longer sleep with the parents.

The combination of *earth* with *water* in this microchakra contributes to a strong gender identity. Adults who have this microchakra open have a heterosexual temperament. Thoughts and feelings related to homosexuality do not arise. There is a soft and considerate attitude toward all members of the opposite sex regardless of physical attractiveness, age, or demeanor. This is particularly true if the sixth microchakra of the first chᵃkrᵃ (L1:6) is also open. This opening is associated with a low level of violence; play and gentleness in sexual exchange is the norm. Orgasms are full and vigorous as 2:7 opens during this time.

Some people with this opening may, during puberty and early teens, go through a period of homosexual fantasy or activity. This passes, and the power of the opening asserts itself.

Signs of a block. In the adult, the enduring consequences of blockage in this microchakra are closely linked to the overall state of affairs in the second chᵃkrᵃ itself. Blockage in this microchakra makes a person a homosexual. If the homosexual impulse is denied, impotence or frigidity may result. If there is enforced engagement in heterosexual sex, it is accompanied by gradual repulsion and subconscious feelings of guilt. Alternatively, there will be a focus on personal gratification, with little concern for the partner.

Fear or hatred of the opposite sex may arise. There is a tendency to express sexual energy by force, either in the form of rape, sadistic sexual brutality, or perversion. In some instances, sadism may be directed against the self and the person may derive sexual excitement from being tortured. A block of this microchakra could generate attraction to group sexuality for the mutual support that it provides.

Shyness and fear of the opposite sex may be present. This can develop into a chronic feeling of incompetence in exchanges with the opposite sex or an inability to relax in their presence.

The negative energy formed by the block contributes toward confusion regarding sexual identity. There may be a desire to dress like the opposite sex (transvestism, mostly found in males) and the hairstyle chosen may be similar to that of the opposite-sex parent that was in fashion during childhood. In more severe cases, a complete change of physical gender is sought (transsexualism). Confusion about sexual energy can even lead to sexual activity with animals (bestiality).

Aggressive behavior and philosophy are another possible consequence of this block; for example, "Do unto others before they do unto you." There is enjoyment of violent, aggressive stimulation. This includes watching videos that portray killings, beatings, or other forms of suffering inflicted upon people or animals. Cockfights, bullfights, and dogfights as well as boxing matches become attractive forms of entertainment.

The need for oral gratification is not outgrown but merely transformed by age. Adults seek to satisfy this need by compulsive sucking of ice cubes, chewing gum, or smoking a pipe, cigar, or cigarette. This occasionally manifests as a persistence of the infantile habit of thumb sucking into adulthood.

Failure of this microchakra to open causes some individuals to develop fears that they have been short-changed in comparison to others. This can then lead to jealousy over money, friends, fame, looks, talent, or anything else. It is difficult to deal with this jealousy or to conceal it. Various forms of stealing, including kleptomania, may be performed without guilt.

The fear of darkness often carries over into adult life. A feeling of unease in a darkened room and need for a night-light in order to sleep is typical. There may be frightening dreams and nightmares.

It is a common observation that a badly frightened animal or bird may suddenly urinate and/or defecate. A vestigial remnant of this reflex mechanism can afflict people with this block. They may suffer from chronic diarrhea.

If the sixth of the second is open but the second of the first is blocked, the person may marry yet still have homosexual relations.

If the third of the first is open (the ego in relation to physical identity) and the second of the first is blocked, the individual may camouflage homosexual tendencies so well that they are not recognized by others. The attraction to same-sex partners will be enhanced if the blockage was produced in connection with dislike or fear of the opposite sex.

RI:3 and LI:3

Right Channel 1:3

Signs of an opening. When this microchakra is open, children have a self-accepting and uncomplaining attitude. They are interested in playing with other children of the same age. There is usually no fear of strangers and personal relationships with adults other than the parents are easily established.

An opening in this microchakra leads to healthy pride in accomplishment. Children under two years of age may point triumphantly to the feces they have "made" (if they have the opportunity to view it). The child who has constructed something from building blocks will be insistent that adults come to look at it.

Causes of an opening. Energy flow in this microchakra is helped by careful nurturing and encouragement of the child's attempts at accomplishment. When very young children reach for an object that they should not touch, it helps to move the object rather than pull the child away from it. This is less of an assault on their effort. Of course, it is best to not have any such objects within the child's reach in the first place.

Use of crayons helps to open R1:3 and develop hand-eye coordination.

Signs of a block. When this microchakra is blocked, children tend to play alone without human presence. When they do play with other children, they will compete rather than cooperate. In some cases, they act as bullies.

Causes of a block. The most common causes of a block are either pressuring the child toward accomplishments or, alternatively, discouraging the child's efforts at achievement. Parents may also strengthen the block by the habit of prying the child's fingers apart to retrieve objects from them.

When a child repeatedly fails to achieve unrealistic goals set by the parents, he or she may dwell on feelings of failure. This is a situation that increases blockage in R1:3.

Left Channel 1:3

Signs of an opening. When the third microchakra in the first chᵃkrᵃ is open, there is a sense of being well grounded and an ease with one's physical identity. Healthy assertion comes naturally. The element of *fire* in the first chᵃkrᵃ flows freely throughout the body.

Children take joy in demonstrating a newly acquired skill such as swimming or bicycle riding. In adults, there is a wholesome pride in accomplishment. This is usually accompanied by a self-accepting, uncomplaining attitude. There is little need to prove physical strength or superiority. Feelings of competitiveness are minimal. Enjoyment of sports or games, even competitive ones, is not accompanied by a compulsion to win.

Signs of a block. When L1:3 is blocked, *fire* spreads out of control. This shows itself in a variety of aggressive expressions. For example, walking heavily, shaking hands roughly, slamming doors, shouldering other people aside in crowded elevators or subways, and driving in an encroaching manner. Great pains may be taken to develop musculature to an unusual degree and to be admired for it. This "show-off" mentality may extend to a desire to be watched while engaged in sexual activity. The identification with physical strength and power peaks with this block.

There is enjoyment of physical domination of others and participation in contact sports such as boxing or wrestling. The competitive attitude extends toward nature as well and pleasure is taken in rigorous physical activities under harsh conditions; for example, mountain climbing and white-water canoeing.

The insecurity to which this block contributes works against the attitudes of compassion and generosity and toward those of greed, possessiveness and miserliness—"I had to earn it, now you go earn it" is an attitude that fits this pattern.

The absorption in one's own *fire* obscures awareness of the solar energy of the dawn. It is very difficult to arise before the sun. Thus fear is not converted (see chapter 9) and the block is strengthened.

Though enjoyment is derived from the use of muscles, their overstressed use leads to the need for more sleep in order to recuperate.

Other possible symptoms of this blockage may be: a) harsh hunting eyes, b) masturbation to relieve aggressive energy, c) preference for bright warm colors, particularly red (the missing *fire* element) and d) use of mind-contracting drugs such as opiates and sedatives.

Psychosomatic problems in the area of elimination may be present. Unconscious attitudes may resemble the trait of "anal-retentiveness" as discussed by Freud. Some people may have a tight upper lip.

RI:4 and LI:4

Right Channel 1:4

Signs of an opening. When this microchakra is open a natural flow of give and take with others is part of the person's physical identity. This is the *air* of the *earth;* praaNᵃ flows freely. Children with this opening readily make friendships and maintain them. Sharing toys and other possessions comes easily. The existence of others is readily recognized. Actions are not taken without first considering the possible effect on others. There is play for the pure enjoyment of it.

Mothering propensities appear in both sexes. Children offer help to younger siblings voluntarily. They sympathize with and attempt to succor wounded animals. This helping propensity is seen in the child's effort to aid the parents with simple tasks. Some children offer spontaneous help to visitors or even strangers in the street.

Causes of an opening. Energy flow through this microchakra benefits from unconditional love, especially from the mother. Encouragement and constructive punishment from the parents helps to open R1:4.

Signs of a block. When this microchakra is obstructed the child is neither able to make friends nor to treat its playmates in a friendly manner. The capacity to share toys is lacking. The child feels unloved and so may experience resentment and anger. Stealing and other forms of dishonesty may occur. The child believes that his parents were unfair to him and therefore sees no reason to be fair to others. Objects may be handled in an unnecessarily rough manner.

The lack of compassion associated with this block may lead to sadistic pleasures such as disturbing ant hills, maiming spiders, kicking dogs, and tormenting zoo animals.

Causes of a block. Blockage in this microchakra is produced if the child feels unwanted and unloved by the mother, who usually is the primary source of unconditional love. These feelings will undoubtedly result if the mother's love becomes conditional and is withdrawn as a punishment.

Frequent physical punishment also contributes to blockage of this microchakra. There is a similar result if the parents treat the child as a possession rather than as a person.

Left Channel 1:4

Signs of an opening. A nurturing and mothering quality is present. There is an acceptance and compassion for physical suffering in self and others. Neighbors and others are related to with concern and interest. There is a natural desire to preserve and encourage all forms of life.

Signs of a block. Lack of compassion is characteristic of this block. The world is perceived as cruel and stealing can be justified without guilt. There may be sadistic pleasure in hurting others.

It is very difficult to share with others or to make friends. In the extreme, this leads to a reclusive lifestyle. A tendency toward depression results from a blocked 1:4. Self distrust and distrust of others enhances this problem. Relief may be sought through drugs or alcohol. Sometimes attempts are made to get the attention and sympathy that others get through normal friendship by developing hypochondriasis and complaining about ailments to anyone who will listen.

The belief system of those with this block is influenced by the lack of compassion and sharing. They tend to be rigid in outlook and advocate a system of strict punishments and rewards as the basis for social functioning.

R1:5 and L1:5

Right Channel 1:5

Signs of an opening. The element of *aakaash*ª is still pure and contributes to a child's honesty of expression. Children show considerable curiosity about the environment and relate to it from a creative level. This includes the manner of using toys and playing games or solving puzzles. There is a general free expression of well-being. Verbal skills are good and there is pleasure in communicating with others. Their bodies respond to music and they enjoy dance. All of these benefits add to their enthusiasm for living. There is no need for a pacifier. In times of danger, they are not shy in letting their voices be heard and recognized by the parents.

Causes of an opening. Children who teethe on toys made of natural substances (like beeswax) are able to open this microchakra more easily. This opening is also formed by means of fruits and vegetables that provide oral satisfaction, such as small whole apples and pears or the thick end of a carrot; these cannot be swallowed yet satisfy the itch of teething gums.

A colorful variety of foods in an aesthetic setting is helpful, as is encouraging a child to try different foods from different cultures. Encouraging vocal expression is an important opener of R1:5.

Signs of a block. In children, indications of a block of this microchakra are facial expressions of crying, especially when asleep, and lack of vocal confidence. There may be an obsessive use of sound with loud vocal expressions. The voice may be deep and guttural or piercing and high pitched. It may have a narrow range, as insecurity prevents use of the full range.

If the child's environment is too authoritative, stuttering may be the result. The child feels perplexed by the anger and misunderstanding he generates in impatient and authoritative adults. After the third-chªkrª age, such children may have an uneven opening of the mouth when speaking.

Causes of a block. Causes of blockage in this microchakra include: a) letting the child cry itself into a stupor before falling asleep, b) permitting the child to cry alone for long periods of time, c) giving drugs to induce sleep, d) using a pacifier, e) frequent use of foul language by parents, f) forcing or permitting the child to overeat, and g) preventing free vocal expression.

The possibility that R1:5 will become blocked is increased if R6:1 is blocked due to undernourishment while in the womb. R6:1 has registered the scarcity of nutrition at the level of the guNª-s and inhibits R1:5, which influences the chewing of food.

Left Channel 1:5

Signs of an opening. People with this opening can hear themselves when they speak and are sensitive to the effect of their speech on others. They are usually good communicators. Their temperament is creative, gregarious, and fun loving. Life is filled with merriment, dancing, and a general joy of living.

Skill in verbal communication does not necessarily correlate with the ability to sing or chant, even though both may use the same basic energy. As evidence, we may note that some famous singers had stuttering problems that disappeared whenever they engaged in singing rather than speaking. The senior author has worked with people with severe stuttering problems who can chant with ease. This lack of correlation is simply one instance of the general fact that expression of the basic energy available to a microchakra may take different directions.

If this microchakra opens in the first half of the first-chᵃkrᵃ age the person may be overly frank and loud later on in life (especially if the sixth microchakra of the first chᵃkrᵃ is blocked).

Signs of a block. Blockage is expressed by extremes in vocalization (either too much or too little). There may be fear of self-expression or, on the other hand, compulsive talking and monopolization of the conversation as a "protective" shield. When addressing a single person, the speech volume may be geared to addressing a large crowd. Especially in the case of males, obscenities rather than appropriate adjectives may be used and remarks clouded with profanity and scatological references.

The effect of this block on humor, enjoyment of jokes, satire, caricature, and so on, is an emphasis on crudeness, coarseness, and vulgarity. Slapstick and violent humor are particularly relished; conversely, there is little sensitivity to subtler humor and sophisticated wit.

Tight string and percussion instruments that produce a thrill and a feeling of movement in the body are preferred. Loud, earth-shaking music, played at full volume, is enjoyed, as it numbs this block.

The person has a lack of awareness of the sound of the breath, which may be loud, snorting, or gasping. Sounds of coughing and nose blowing that feel normal to the person who has this block are perceived by others as uncommonly or even offensively loud. Subtleties of tone and emotion are not registered. Lack of sensitivity to sound contributes to a whining or nagging voice. Severe blockage can produce stuttering.

When partially blocked, there may be difficulty in pronouncing the petal sounds of the first chᵃkrᵃ that require clear distinction among "sᵃ", "shᵃ" and "ꜱʜᵃ." Proper distinction between the sounds "vᵃ" and "bᵃ" may also be absent. More energy than is normal may be expended in pronouncing these sounds.

When asleep, the face may appear to be crying, reflecting a feeling of fundamental deprivation. This block can lead to a dislike of one's own *aakaashᵃ* and thus dislike of many features including facial appearance.

The persistent desire for oral gratification leads to habitual pipe and cigar smoking. There may be frequent ingestion of tobacco, an anodyne that masks emotional pain. Compulsive chewing may occur independently of the ingestion of food.

RI:6 and LI:6

Right Channel 1:6

Signs of an opening. Children with the sixth microchakra of the first chᵃkrᵃ open have balanced control over the first-chᵃkrᵃ functions of sleeping, eating, urination, and defecation. This is accompanied by an intuitive sense of security and a capacity to play independently of the parents without fear of abandonment. Relationships with other adults are relatively free and independent. In the first half of the first-chᵃkrᵃ age children with this opening sometimes test their parents or teachers by doing something that they know is naughty. For example, they may put some forbidden object in the mouth and sheepishly look at the parents to see how they react.

Causes of an opening. This opening is likely to be greater in children raised in the countryside where there is greater proximity to the earth. Challenges to the survival instinct also strengthen it. Parents may occasionally present food to the child without any choice.

Signs of a block. When this microchakra is blocked there is little or no sense of physical security and children easily feel abandoned. They may be very dependent upon their parents and not function well outside their orbit. Even though such children can be early accomplishers, they feel weak inside and lack self-confidence. It is common for them to fear strangers.

Causes of a block. Fathers, often the main authority figure, contribute to blockage of this microchakra if they are weak in character, make the child feel unwanted, have little contact with the child, or are overly strict.

Forcing the child to play alone too much too soon will produce a feeling of abandonment that enhances the block. Allowing the child regularly to watch television for many hours per day has a particularly negative effect. The passivity promoted by this medium inhibits the development of the intuitive and discerning capacities of the sixth microchakras that require engagement with the real world. The probability of an inner world excessively tied to fantasy is increased.

Left Channel 1:6

Signs of an opening. The sixth of the first is the guide of the first chᵃkrᵃ. When it is open there is confidence regarding bodily identity and survival.

The distinction between foods that are beneficial to health and those that are not is intuitively known, and there is a natural attraction to wholesome foods. The energy of this microchakra supports sitting at ease with a relaxed body and relaxed first chᵃkrᵃ mind. This relaxation may be done at will. The needs of the body are met with relative detachment.

If help for survival is needed (as when lost in a forest), intuition acts like an inner navigator and provides a sense of the geographical direction in which to search for help.

Satisfaction is obtained from directly working with the physical manifestation of the *earth* element in such forms as soil, clay, or wood.

Signs of a block. People who have the sixth microchakra of the first chᵃkrᵃ blocked may have poor eating habits and a lethargic body and mind. Defecation is possible only after eating. Physical movements are often clumsy. They may be subject to intense mood swings—and even manic-depressive symptoms, such as an explosive temper on the full moon followed by depression on the new moon (or vice versa).

The lack of a sense of basic identity contributes to general mental confusion and the feeling that life has no purpose. The mental confusion leads to such symptoms as a) a greatly diminished capacity for decision making and a preference to take orders, b) lack of understanding of others (it is difficult to understand others if you don't understand yourself), c) poor sense of economics, d) secret engagement in various perversions.

R1:7 and L1:7

Right Channel 1:7

Signs of an opening. Ideally this microchakra opens by the end of the right-channel age. Evidence of its opening includes an abundance of physical energy and a joy of life. To the degree that this microchakra is blocked, development of the second chᵃkrᵃ will be inhibited or delayed.

When the seventh of the first is open, most of the other microchakras of the first chᵃkrᵃ are also likely to be open. Energy flowing in this microchakra gives the individual a sense of physical well-being and comfort with no tendency toward restlessness or hyperactivity. There is a capacity to sit quietly for extended periods without discomfort; thus the later struggle to sit quietly for meditation is minimized. Bodily movements have greater than average flexibility.

Causes of an opening. Energy flows in the seventh microchakra of the first chᵃkrᵃ when contentment of the physical body is experienced. This is helped when parents allow toddlers to touch and enjoy food in their own imaginative ways—even though a considerable mess may result. A prepared parent places an old sheet under the child's chair and allows play to continue until contentment is reached.

In general, playing with the earth helps this microchakra to open. This includes sitting on the grass with coccyx touching the earth or sand. This helps the whole spine to become like an antenna.

Signs of a block. A child with R1:7 blocked may frequently show general restlessness and such other symptoms as crankiness, anger, possessiveness, and biting.

Causes of a block. Children need to play in the mud and have the earth as part of their life. Parents who do not permit this because of their fastidiousness or fear of germs contribute to a block of R1:7.

Sometimes a parent is discontent with his or her own body and frequently expresses this feeling in the presence of the child. The child may then imitate this feeling. Even if the child's body is perfect, the discontent will register in R1:7.

Left Channel 1:7

Signs of an opening. There is a sense of physical comfort and well-being in one's body. The body itself is loose and supple and able to sit comfortably for long periods, a prerequisite for meditation later in life.

No sense of security is found in the accumulation of wealth or land alone. There is an avoidance of overeating, overfatigue, and excessive concern with earthly matters.

Temporary satisfaction may be produced by a good meal. The requirements for a satisfying meal are excellent food combinations and delicious taste. The deepest contentment from food is achieved through cooking for oneself. In addition to a good meal, a good bowel movement and a good workout contribute to the temporary opening of R1:7. Ideally, these experiences would occur on a daily basis and cumulatively contribute to a full opening.

Signs of a block. Blockage in the seventh microchakra of the first ch^akr^a may produce a variety of physical symptoms: a) overeating, b) undereating, c) oversleeping, d) undersleeping, e) restlessness (demonstrated by such behavior as shuffling feet, drumming fingertips, and frequent change of posture), f) overexertion, g) underexertion, h) poor circulation in legs, swollen ankles, weak ankles/arches, cold feet, leg cramps, i) migraine headaches (if first ch^akr^a tensions push apaan^a up the right channel toward the head).

The psychological symptoms associated with this blockage may include: a) inability to accept one's body, b) inability to relax and feel content at the level of the physical field, c) tendency to delay release of feces, d) feelings of inferiority because of being unable to take care of one's own survival, e) insatiable appetite for wealth, f) feelings of emptiness and general lack of purpose—attraction toward nihilistic philosophies.

THE SECOND CH^AKR^A
R2:1 and L2:1

Right Channel 2:1

Signs of an opening. R2:1 is the source of gender identity based on solar energy. Children with this microchakra open have admiration and affection for both parents. They usually do not resist discipline provided that the parents are consistent with their affection. Toward the end of the first-ch^akr^a age they understand fear of the dark and find ways to deal with it.

Causes of an opening. Within the central channel and the circuits of the early brain lies the instinct to imitate. By imitating their mothers and identifying with them, little girls develop their femininity. In a similar manner, little boys imitate their fathers and develop their identification with masculinity.

Signs of a block. Children with this microchakra blocked may continually test their acceptance by pinching, biting, pushing, or fighting. Behaving like the opposite-gender parent may occur as a means of attracting attention. If the child experiences repeated states of fear, the sense of touch will not develop normally and the fingers may become stiff. There may be premature genital exploration during the right-channel age.

Causes of a block. Blockage of R2:1 may be caused by the following: a) a lack of identification of the child with the same-gender parent, b) a lack of contact with the opposite-gender parent, c) use of a pacifier, d) trauma in weaning, e) eating fried fatty meat.

Left Channel 2:1

Signs of an opening. Whereas R2:1 is the source of gender identity based on solar energy, L2:1 is the source of gender identity based on lunar energy. This follows from the fact that it is the left channel that carries lunar energy to the right hemisphere of the brain.

Adults are capable of feeling and enjoying a sense of polar difference when with someone of the opposite sex. Once having selected a partner, they do not easily become bored in the relationship (provided L2:3, is also open). They will accept the role of spouse joyfully.

The first of the second, like the first of the first, promotes a desire to refrain from killing unless absolutely necessary. This opening offers a good foundation for the health of the body provided plenty of good water is consumed frequently.

Signs of a block. Blockage of the first microchakra in the left channel of the second chᵃkrᵃ (L2:1) causes unstable gender identity. This may result in repression of sexual desires in order to escape the issue. Alternatively, obsession with sexual thoughts may arise in an attempt to discover a sexual identity. Later in life, other symptoms of this weak identity may include: a) frigidity, b) impotence, c) exhibitionism, and d) perversions. If L2:1 does not open by the age of 12 in girls and 14 in boys, the temperament will be bisexual.

Fantasizing in the second-chᵃkrᵃ age is a natural phenomenon as the child encounters fears and discovers a sexual identity. In adulthood, habitual fantasizing may reinforce second chᵃkrᵃ and second microchakra blocks.

In males, fantasy may interfere with sexual activity and lead to premature ejaculation. In the masochistic male, it may result in late ejaculation.

Doubts about gender may lead to discomfort with both sexes, particularly the opposite sex. There may be experimentation with homosexuality or bisexuality. This results more from fear of the opposite sex than from feelings of repulsion (as is the case if the second microchakra in the left channel of the first chᵃkrᵃ is blocked). If the person marries, there may be homosexual relations outside the marriage. Sadistic or masochistic tendencies may appear in the marriage relationship as an expression of the struggle with bisexuality.

Either of the extremes of sexual exhibitionism or asexuality may be associated with this block. The latter may be reflected in premature renunciation of sexuality for ostensibly spiritual purposes.

The difficulty in forthright exchange caused by this blockage may produce various forms of dishonesty including lying, cheating, and stealing. This behavior may be compulsive, as in kleptomania. Or it may result in living on a dishonest source of income even if outwardly it appears legitimate. Habit may make the person believe in his or her own lies.

A person with this block may feel at war with mother, father, and society, and break laws in order to "get even." Sometimes such a person feels guilty and seeks to be caught in order to be punished. If aggression is sufficiently strong, another person may be attacked when not on guard—denying them a fair chance to defend themselves.

Lack of *earth* within *water* tends to make the overall character weak; it is often difficult for people with this deficiency to take a stand. They may see this lack as a virtue and pride themselves on their agnosticism. Magic, witchcraft, and hypnosis are possible sources of entertainment and vicarious power.

Insensitivity related to sexual exchange increases with age and ever more perverted relationships are often sought in desperate attempts to open the block. Graceful aging is also inhibited by this block. The harder and less pretty the face becomes with age, the more makeup is used. Self-dislike tends to increase and thoughts of suicide may accompany depression.

There is a propensity to abuse alcohol, the intoxicant of the second chᵃkrᵃ.

R2:2 and L2:2

Right Channel 2:2
Signs of an opening. This microchakra is the *water* of the *water* and is the core of fear. Children with this microchakra open readily obey the opposite-gender parent particularly if that parent is acknowledged as an authority in the family by his or her spouse.

Causes of an opening. The opening of this microchakra is facilitated when there is a healthy upbringing by the entire family: parents, grandparents, and siblings. This contributes to a deep sense of belonging, which lessens fear. Among other benefits, this permits openness to the opposite sex.

Signs of a block. Children with this microchakra blocked may show withdrawn behavior alternating with aggression.

Causes of a block. Obstruction results if the child does not sleep with the mother during the first three years of life. If there are nightmares concerning abandonment, they will add more layers of fear to R2:2.

Obstruction is also caused by premature stimulation and fondling of the genitals for sexual pleasure. This is more likely to occur in cases of extreme emotional deprivation and fear. It can also occur if the child has been fed tamsic foods (such as meat paste or fried foods) that irritate the sensitive nerve endings of the genitals. Circumcision in boys and girls during the first year also deepens fear and blocks this microchakra.

Left Channel 2:2

Signs of an opening. L2:2 is a key microchakra. As long as it is not completely open, contentment of the second ch^{a}kr^a mind cannot be attained. Deep in the central channel and partaking of the fear circuits of the brain is a fear of extinction of the race. This fear demands reproductive activity. Therefore, at the unconscious level, it works to maintain a block in L2:2 and prevent contentment of the sexual drive. This block is not present in those living in third-lɛng^a awareness or who have opened L6:2. They are moving beyond the pull of eightfold nature and do not fear for the race as they proceed toward the eternal Self. They have no karmic obligation to reproduce in this life as they have fulfilled this obligation in past lives.

Whereas nature works to prevent full opening of L2:2, it does not prevent partial opening. This partial opening contributes to a healthy pride in one's sexuality and an open attitude toward sexual activity. There is healthy passion, healthy orgasm, and little difficulty in maintaining fidelity. The preference for fidelity will be increased even further if the second microchakra in the third ch^{a}kr^a (L3:2) is also open. A heightened sense of union and bliss will occur with orgasm, which will be achieved easily—without pain, fear, or melodrama. A buoyant sense of well-being and physical energy occurs after sexual activity if 2:1, 1:6, and 1:7 are also open.

Orgasmic experience is so satisfying that the need for intercourse is less frequent than would otherwise be the case. Husband and wife can sleep together for months without having intercourse. They are so close emotionally and in such a strong marital union that sex isn't necessary to confirm their love for each other.

The flow of energy in this microchakra causes a person to be honest and straightforward in business and other aspects of life. It adds to creativity and to the heightening of sensual awareness, especially taste sensitivity. It also increases tolerance for pain.

Signs of a block. Sexual feelings are severely impacted by insufficient opening in this microchakra. Sexual appetite may be insatiable or, alternatively, fear of sexuality may be constant. These general tendencies are accompanied by a variety of specific sexual symptoms: a) inability to experience orgasm, b) painful intercourse, sometimes causing the person to feign climax, c) hysterical behavior during intercourse as energy spurts forth in violent erratic jerks with dramatic sounds being made, d) premature climax, e) intensification of sexual fantasy, f) menstrual problems, g) frequent urinary infections, h) prostate difficulties.

When L2:3 is also blocked, the following symptoms may occur: i) dishonesty in business and other aspects of life, j) low tolerance for pain, k) propensity for alcoholism, l) difficulty in expressing creativity, m) hypochondria, n) alternation of repressed and withdrawn behavior with aggressive behavior.

R2:3 and L2:3

Right Channel 2:3

Signs of an opening. When the third microchakra within the second chᵃkrᵃ is open, exchange is asserted in an honest and direct way. Children are able to take pride in their accomplishments and function within the normal rules of discipline whether in the playground, the classroom, or the home.

Causes of an opening. Parents demonstrate forthright exchange between themselves and with others. The child absorbs the sense of surrender to each other that they see in the parents.

Signs of a block. When R2:3 is blocked the child lacks assertiveness in exchange relations. An introverted child may internalize aggression and deny herself the joy of being with others. In following rules and discipline the child is timid because of fear of rejection. She attempts to please as compensation for her lack of ability to engage in forthright exchange. As an adult, there will be difficulty in finding the love of a mate.

Extroverted children will direct aggression outward and may bully other children. They dislike obeying rules or submitting to discipline and may cheat if the opportunity arises. They generally are rebellious and difficult to manage.

Causes of a block. The major cause of blockage in the third microchakra of the second chᵃkrᵃ (R2:3) is poor quality of exchange between the parents, with little love or affection and the dominance of one over the other. Divorce or separation before children pass the second-chᵃkrᵃ age (and can understand) may also deprive them of any model for healthy exchange between parents.

Any aggression toward the child, such as beating, causes the child to hurt others; if the child is withdrawn, this aggression turns inward and the child may hurt itself or become depressed.

Left Channel 2:3

Signs of an opening. Adults with this microchakra open relate to sexuality with naturalness and ease. They approach their sexual abilities with confidence. Their sexual desires are neither ignored nor suppressed. Instead, they are satisfied with a minimum of melodrama. Sexual fluids flow easily and generously. After making love, they feel satisfaction and are no longer compelled to think about it.

People with *fire* flowing within *water* have a mature and poised attitude toward sexuality. They have no need to play dominance games with their partner, nor do they feel the need to have many children to prove their virility and sexuality. They can be emotionally close and are able to sustain a meaningful long-term relationship.

The energy of this microchakra expresses itself both as sexual exchange and as business exchange. When sexual satisfaction is present, there tends also to be financial contentment; that is, whatever is earned is felt to be sufficient for the family's needs.

Signs of a block. Adults with this blockage believe that the satisfaction of their exchange goals requires the conquest of an opponent. They also assume that others see the world in the same way. However, their sexual conquests do not bring them any real satisfaction so they are driven to seek a variety of sexual partners—who often have the same block. They desire to be seen with a sexually attractive partner as a trophy to validate their prowess.

Such a person usually does not find a satisfactory relationship because of the inability to surrender the sexual ego to anyone. While with one partner, there may be fantasizing about someone else. An exception to this unhappy situation may occur if the person connects with someone who has this microchakra (L2:3) open. Such a mate might be of help in overcoming the block, provided that they are deeply loved by the partner with it.

This block may affect sexual and family relationships in many other ways. For example: a) the sight of an attractive person of the opposite sex may cause either nervousness or flirting; b) a great deal of energy is wasted in sexual fantasizing; c) sex may be used to manipulate and dominate another; d) when a relationship fails, there is a tendency to blame either the supposed inadequacies of the partner or the marriage of one's own parents; e) some people may engage in sexual bragging or exhibitionism, including the use of provocative outfits; f) men may fantasize about a harem; g) compulsive buying is sometimes used as a substitute for sexual satisfaction.

Additional symptoms of this block include: h) a search for sensual pleasure from various foods, which may lead to excessive consumption of meat and proteins that stimulate increased sexual desire; i) holding on to photos and other mementos of past relationships and constantly looking toward the past or future—since the present can never be sufficiently satisfying; j) women may brag about being a mother or having many children as a way of reassuring themselves about their femininity; k) women may hold on to their children longer than is healthy; l) excessive efforts may be expended to make the home beautiful, as it becomes an unconscious symbol of personal sexuality; m) frequent eye blinking while communicating.

Money is seen as the universal comforter when the third of the second is blocked. Vigilance is maintained to assure that full value in all transactions is achieved, since there is a strong fear of being cheated. There is great pride in the roles of moneymaker and entrepreneur—tasks at which considerable competency is often acquired.

Adults with both R2:3 and L2:3 blocked have a compulsive need for a variety of sexual partners. They look at the opposite gender in terms of conquest and victimization. Their egos experience gender identity as an independent identity that tends to override all other identities.

R2:4 and L2:4

Right Channel 2:4

Signs of an opening. When the fourth microchakra within the second chᵃkrᵃ is open children are compassionate and gentle. They are able to express physical tenderness and older children will gladly help younger ones. Even in very young children, a natural mothering quality can be apparent.

Causes of an opening. Empathic and loving qualities in children arise as a result of an abundance of physical affection and touch from parents. In some cultures, children as young as six may carry littler ones (in right-channel age) on their hip. Being carried in this way and grasping the front of the one carrying helps to open R2:4.

Signs of a block. The blocked energy of this microchakra may be shown in a variety of ways:

1. Some children may become overly dependent upon the mother. If the child is more aggressive, it may express affection toward the mother by excessive touching or clinging. On the other hand, if the child is more passive in nature, there can be a pronounced avoidance of touching. Touching is not a neutral activity but carries either a strong positive or a strong negative significance for the child with this particular blockage.

2. In relation to other children, touching may be employed as a socially acceptable means of expressing aggression, as in the case of excessive tickling or other petty forms of physical contact.

3. Another characteristic of a child with this blockage is a tendency to suppress awareness of bodily needs or to postpone attending to bodily functions such as urinating—until they have to go in a hurry. This situation is different from a child simply not wanting to interrupt its play.

Causes of a block. Energy does not flow through this microchakra unless the touch of the parents actively expresses considerable tenderness and affection. The touch of the mother is particularly important. Blockage will be produced if she is uncomfortable in holding the child or her touch is erratic and conditional.

Left Channel 2:4

Signs of an opening. Those with this opening are compassionate and gentle. There is no embarrassment associated with sexual feelings and exchange. Others can be touched emotionally without a dependence upon physical touch, though physical touch can also be used most supportively. It is not difficult to make friends on a nonsexual basis or to discriminate between a friend and a lover. There is no need to cling to another for emotional support, so friendships are easily made.

Energy flowing through the fourth of the second promotes a healthy brother-sister relationship; it also enhances the endurance of pain. Not much time is spent preoccupied with pain. Women are very willing to endure the pain of natural childbirth.

No display of embarrassment takes place in dealing with bodily needs and functions—of one's self or children.

Signs of a block. The skin is the organ of action of the fourth ch^{a}kr^a and the fingertips are the sense organ. Hence use of the hands for giving and receiving touch is an important expression of the state of the fourth ch^{a}kr^a and its representative fourth microchakras.

Blockage in this microchakra may manifest through the fear of touch. Since the block was originally caused by either inadequate love or even conditional love, great uncertainty surrounds the act of expressing love. A fear that the other may respond with rejection or hostility inhibits the positive use of touch. Thus a dislike to touch or be touched may develop.

The fear of touch may even extend to touching or massaging oneself.

Rather than arousing fear, touch may be compulsive with an excessive need to touch and/or be touched. Examples of this are: a) relating to children only through tickling them—sometimes to the point of sadism, b) needing the sexual partner to provide the parental touching that was never received, and c) constantly touching others to demonstrate affection.

Because of the centrality of touch in forming a person's attitude toward the body, a block in this microchakra may generalize to a discomfort with the whole body. That can lead to embarasssment about a variety of bodily functions including sneezes, burps, flatulence, and urination.

Touching others can be a form of giving. The impaired capacity for touching that has just been described is, at a deeper level, a diminished capacity for giving. There is difficulty in feeling good about giving even though there is a desire to do so. Fear of losing something acts as a saboteur. Accordingly, giving is only done with the expectation of receiving something in return, usually something better; that is, more profitable. Fear of being hurt prevents surrender to a partner.

R2:5 and L2:5

Right Channel 2:5

Signs of an opening. An opening in R2:5 allows the child to articulate emotions and feelings without inhibition. It provides a good range to the voice for expressing emotions.

Causes of an opening. The parents' example of clear and uninhibited vocal expression as well as singing and playing music contributes to this opening. The use of nursery rhymes helps in this endeavor.

Signs of a block. The child may have a fearful, constricted, or whining voice. Self-consciousness, shyness, or fear of expressing feelings may appear. The fear of expression of feelings and emotions most often leads to suppression. Thus a great obstacle to the understanding of feelings and emotions in adult life is born. Inadvertently, confusion and chaos become a part of relationships.

Causes of a block. If the parents have neglected the sonic aspect of the child's development or have been unresponsive to its vocal expression then blockage of this microchakra results. If children are screamed at and frightened it may even result in stuttering, especially if they are beaten frequently as well.

Left Channel 2:5

Signs of an opening. An opening in the fifth microchakra of the second chᵃkrᵃ (L2:5) contributes to the overall effectiveness of the voice in communication. More specifically, it enables articulation of feelings and emotions without inhibition. The body of the voice has full range. The flow of *aakaash^a* within *water* helps the tongue in its dual functions of tasting and articulating.

Adults are able to express emotions and feelings, including sexual feelings, easily. They are good talkers whom others enjoy hearing, rather than compulsive talkers whom many would like to silence. They are also good listeners who encourage others to express themselves freely, thereby making communication more meaningful.

This microchakra allows communication to be honest and open. Consequently, others will know precisely where they stand. Vocal expression is given in the service of honest exchange of energy.

There is a preference for flowing emotional music and enjoyment of making music oneself, especially with fretted stringed instruments. If both R2:5 and C2:5 are also open then folk or love songs can be sung most beautifully.

This microchakra also permits creative energy to be easily channeled into arts and crafts. It permits people to laugh openly.

During meditation, the deep-pitched sounds of water flowing may be heard as if at a great distance.

Signs of a block. When obstruction occurs in the fifth microchakra of the second chᵃkrᵃ (L2:5), the use of the voice for direct honest communication is impaired. Thus, there is difficulty in using the voice to express personal feelings, emotions, needs, or opinions.

Adults, as well as children, may speak with a whining, nagging, complaining quality. If the fourth microchakra of the second chᵃkrᵃ (L2:4) is open, they may be able to make their voices sound seductive. In some cases, silence is used to trigger nurturing feelings in others, particularly members of the opposite sex. Alternatively, in attempts to elicit motherly or fatherly feelings in others, they may appear needful, dainty, or pitiful. If assertiveness is sufficiently high, an effort may be made to overcome the block by compulsive talking.

Since direct expression is absent, this block frequently leads to engagement in ambiguous verbalizing, making it difficult for others to know where they stand. This may be helpful in some business or diplomatic situations, but in most relationships it tends to create problems.

In addition to impairing speaking, this blocked energy also weakens listening and musical ability. It produces inattentive listeners who may easily engage in frequent interruption of others. The ability to carry a tune is absent; this is often related to the incapacity to listen to music with genuine enjoyment. Consequently, playing music or singing does not offer an emotional outlet.

Attention is captured, however, by communications of a sexual nature. A fondness may be shown for sexual humor especially indirect sexual jokes involving double entendre.

R2:6 and L2:6

Right Channel 2:6

Signs of an opening. A child with this opening is bright eyed and fearless. She trusts her parents and feels free to ask them anything. She will also claim her parent's lap at will. In exchange situations there are no inhibitions due to fear or insecurity.

Causes of an opening. Stories about those who have faced difficulties and overcome them help to awaken the intuition of R2:6. The child may be taught that painful events sometimes come as a friend in disguise and that it is unwise to just seek what is pleasurable while avoiding the painful. The young child should not be subjected to scary stories that induce real fear.

Signs of a block. When R2:6 is blocked, a child fears abandonment by his parents. There is timidity and hesitancy in interpersonal relations. These children tend to attract bullies.

Causes of a block. Trust between parent and child may be compromised in a variety of ways:

1. The parent may be too strict a disciplinarian. Too many "no's" and the child learns evasion rather than trust.
2. The parent may be lax as a disciplinarian. Rather than learning trust, the child learns to stretch the limits.
3. The parent may make the child feel guilty when he does something wrong. Guilt is not a basis for trust.

Left Channel 2:6

Signs of an opening. Adults with the sixth microchakra of the second ch^{a}kr^a (L2:6) open have considerable control over their second ch^{a}kr^a feelings and desires. Even if some of the lower microchakras in the second ch^{a}kr^a are blocked, they can momentarily behave as if the blocks are not bothersome.

When C2:6 is also open a keen sense of discernment develops with respect to the selection of a mate and to sexual expression. Available sexual energy can be manipulated to the best advantage of both partners. If desired, this energy may be channeled for nonsexual uses, such as art or spiritual pursuits. It is not dissipated in fantasy.

Furthermore, an opening here allows excellent communication with your mate. If this microchakra forms a square of openings with L6:2, L5:6, and L6:5, then intuitive communication with your mate will be of a rare quality.

People with this opening have no fear of rejection and abandonment and feel perfectly comfortable when by themselves. Hence they are able to spend considerable periods of time alone without any feelings of loneliness.

Sensitivity to *water* enhances discrimination among types of food and refines eating habits.

Signs of a block. A block in the sixth chᵃkrᵃ and its representative microchakras results in poor discernment and difficulty in decision making. In L2:6 this manifests as lack of control of the lower stages of the second chᵃkrᵃ.

It will be recalled that the basic requirement for the development of intuition is trust. Children with the sixth microchakra of the second chᵃkrᵃ (L2:6) blocked distrust their parents and emotional closeness cannot develop. They may engage in masturbation while in the early second-chᵃkrᵃ age, that is, age six to eight for girls and seven to nine for boys.

Fear can paralyze emotion during sexual activity. Even if the relationship with a loved one is secure, fear of rejection may be haunting.

This block makes it stressful to sustain a period of celibacy (such as after the first twenty weeks of pregnancy). Lack of discernment pertaining to exchange often causes poor choices in sexual and business partners. Sometimes, however, the person is attracted to those who have this microchakra open—an opportunity to alleviate the block.

If a block here in the left channel is accompanied by a similar barrier in the right channel, the lack of discernment may lead to becoming a prostitute or gigolo.

As with the sixth of the first, the blockage of the sixth of the second contributes to a follower mentality. The person may go along with the decisions of others simply because of the fear of rejection. The need to please others becomes particularly hard to overcome if the sixth of the third is also blocked. There is usually an attraction to jobs that require a minimum of personal decision making.

It is difficult to find self-expression through arts and crafts since the mind is so filled with fear. Nevertheless these activities, as well as sports, should be encouraged.

R2:7 and L2:7

Right Channel 2:7
Signs of an opening. A few of the children who are born with the first lᴇɴɢᵃ active may open this microchakra. For those children with the second or third lᴇɴɢᵃ active

it is more likely to open. If it does, they could be celibate throughout life provided L2:2, L2:3, L6:2, and L3:2 are also open.

Causes of an opening. The child is allowed to play nude and prevented from experiencing any fear, especially at night. This is best accomplished by sleeping with the parents or next to them.

Signs of a block. There is discontent in the relationships with family, friends, or business partners.

Causes of a block. R2:7 will be blocked if the child is forced to wear pants all the time and not allowed to play nude at least several hours per day.

Left Channel 2:7

Signs of an opening. Healthy sexual activity facilitates the opening of this micro-chakra. If this happens, the contentment experienced after orgasm has lasting effects. When this microchakra is permanently open, orgasm is of very high quality. Couples who both have this opening may have transcendent experiences. The memories of such states of awareness are so powerful, and the experiences of satisfaction so enduring, that desire for sexual activity greatly reduces. A sense of detachment develops toward sex.

People with this opening develop an acute understanding of their biological needs and the needs of their partners. The body's sexual needs are surprisingly few. Sexual activity may be compared with eating. The body requires a basic minimum of food for survival and health and everything beyond that is sheer indulgence. Similarly, much sexual activity is psychological or emotional indulgence rather than simply responding to our own needs or the needs of our partner.

A woman with this microchakra open develops a sensitivity to her natural monthly cycle and finds union most gratifying during ovulation. Her contentment is such that sexual desires are unlikely to arise during the remainder of the month.

There is no impulse to be conspicuous in order to attract the opposite sex. Instead, the tendency is to dress in a nonprovocative way and to abstain from challenging behavior, gestures, postures, or language.

Signs of a block. In many cultures, the seventh of the second is usually blocked in children. When it is blocked in an adult, such a person will always be concerned about the body and sexuality at some level. A block here also contributes to difficulty in accepting the supernatural since an experience that goes beyond physical sensation cannot even be imagined. Without genuine sexual contentment it is difficult to teach proper sexual functioning to children. Blockage in the key microchakra L2:2 will make it very difficult to open L2:7 for an extended period of time. Usually, contentment will last only while engaged in sex and shortly thereafter.

Sublimation of Sexual Energy

It is the dhᵃrmᵃ of the second chᵃkrᵃ to help produce sexual energy and the natural desire to express it—in both genders, from puberty onward. This energy may be converted to fourth-chᵃkrᵃ energy through physical activity, arts and crafts, worship, devotion, and selfless service. It may be further converted to sixth-chᵃkrᵃ energy by someone who has developed sufficient sound sensitivity to work with an accomplished teacher of mᵃntrᵃ. Then advanced practices, such as working with bᴇᴇjᵃ mᵃntrᵃ-s and with prᵃɴᵃvᵃ (a specialized way of chanting the mᵃntrᵃ AUM) may be employed. The accumulated sooryᵃ *aakaash* produced by these practices deepens the meditative state.

THE THIRD CHᴬKRᴬ

It is
It is my power
It is my will
It is my time
I am the greatest
Alas but not forever
Not even ever
It is because
It just is

S. Bhatnagar

R3:1 and L3:1

Right Channel 3:1

Signs of an opening. The child relates easily to others and shows confidence in social situations. There is much giggling, laughter, and sharing.

Causes of an opening. Imagination is enlisted in the development of this microchakra. Various roles are played such as mommy, daddy, doctor, nurse, and astronaut.

Signs of a block. When R3:1 is blocked, social interaction is marked by feelings of insecurity, fear of failure, and even fear of success. Children are withdrawn and may run into another room to avoid a guest.

Causes of a block. This microchakra is blocked when parents condition their love upon the child's accomplishment: showing love when the child succeeds in a task and withdrawing it when the child fails. Criteria for success are perceived as being in the hands of authority figures and as an adult one experiences major obstacles to the opening of L3:1—one's social identity. If L3:6 has not been opened by that time, the situation can become critical and may lead to contemplation of suicide.

Left Channel 3:1

Signs of an opening. When the first microchakra within the third chᵃkrᵃ (L3:1) is unobstructed we can successfully make a place for ourself in society. We will have a healthy self reliance and ability to assert our independence through work. We feel that we are useful and contributing members of society whose services are valued. This acceptance strengthens our self-image as competent and achieving. Regardless of whether or not society's criteria of "success" are met, a positive ego identification is manifested. Suicide is never contemplated unless this microchakra in the right channel is blocked and combines with other right-channel blocks to cause severe emotional difficulties.

Signs of a block. Children with the first microchakra of the third chᵃkrᵃ (L3:1) closed often exhibit a compulsion to achieve and to be "special" in order to win parental approval and love. In other words, these children, haunted and driven by feelings of insecurity, make extraordinary efforts in an attempt to obtain personal validation and recognition from the important adults in their lives. They are victims of conditional love.

Adults with this block experience a similar insecurity in relation to employers and the society at large. The first fruit of this insecurity is indecision regarding occupation and social role. Alternatively, the decision may be impulsive and based on a perceived opportunity rather than love of the work. Once employed, feelings of insecurity and inferiority breed a lack of confidence in the ability to perform satisfactorily. The possibility of future accomplishments is similarly constrained. Even when the person feels capable of handling a prospective challenge there is a reluctance to try because of fear of failure.

Lack of confidence about job performance may lead to anxiety, stresss, and depression. Feelings of inferiority regarding accomplishments frequently produce withdrawal and self-blame. The slightest failure strengthens this negative self-image and inhibits further attempts at assertiveness. If aggressive, blame may be directed toward society rather than self; the mate may be attacked. When severe depression occurs, so may contemplation of suicide—especially if 3:6, 4:4, and 4:6 are also blocked in the left channel.

R3:2 and L3:2

Right Channel 3:2

Signs of an opening. In this microchakra the *fire* of the third chᵃkrᵃ is reduced by the effect of *water*. The ego becomes less aggressive and more capable of social interaction. Boys are willing to play with girls and vice versa. Children are able to form healthy relations with others. Sharing comes naturally.

Causes of an opening. Encouraging a child to play with other children helps to open this microchakra. An older sibling may have an advantage if a younger one is looking up with admiration. The opening is also facilitated by parents who model healthy social exchange and enjoy the company of friends.

Signs of a block. When this microchakra is blocked a child may be withdrawn due to lack of social skills. This lack may be aggravated for an only child.

Causes of a block. If children are repeatedly left wet and unclean, the second microchakra of the third chᵃkrᵃ (R3:2) becomes blocked. Circumcision also blocks this microchakra. The failure of parents to admire their children for who they truly are contributes to this block.

If a child habitually hides in the shadow of an older sibling, he or she may feel protected and not develop this microchakra.

Left Channel 3:2

Signs of an opening. In L3:2 sexual identity is strengthened by establishing a wholesome sexual relationship. When this microchakra is open, relations with the opposite sex are simple and warm with no need for domination of the partner.

This opening contributes to a healthy marriage in several ways: a) it provides a wise combination of reason and emotion for the selection of a partner, b) there is contentment with a monogamous marriage, c) exchange with the mate is done on the basis of equality, d) there is no difficulty in surrendering the sexual ego to the mate (if L2:1 and L2:3 are also open), e) communication between partners is noncompetitive.

Signs of a block. A block of L3:2 often expresses itself as a complex of sexual inferiority. This may be shown in various forms of promiscuity. The need for a variety of partners leads to temporary sexual arrangements suitable to both partners. If this variety cannot be obtained, considerable time and energy is spent thinking about it, wishing for it, and fantasizing it.

Individuals with this obstruction have a need to feel sexually powerful. They are sexually and physically aggressive and manipulative. A constant search for a better aphrodisiac, a new position or technique, another source of sexual energy, and a chronic need to prove virility are parts of the pattern. Wanting and needing to have the love of the whole world leads to frantic maneuvers such as making oneself as indispensable to as many people as possible. This is usually at the expense of one's mate, with whom there is no genuine relationship.

People with this block may speak or act so as to embarrass the opposite sex and make them uncomfortable in social situations. If severely blocked (the first and seventh microchakras of the second chᵃkrᵃ are also blocked in the right channel), they may engage in vicarious promiscuity by becoming a procurer. Those who are introverted may engage in excessive masturbation.

Another indication of this negative energy is a relationship with the opposite sex characterized by moodiness, melodrama, and a temperamental attitude.

On the physical side, weakness caused by excessive use of sexual energy can result in vaginal difficulties, prostate trouble, or low energy level. A strong attraction to caffeine or cocaine may lead to an addiction to these substances.

R3:3 and L3:3

Right Channel 3:3

Signs of an opening. The third microchakra of the third chᵃkrᵃ (R3:3) is the seat of the ego. It is the *fire* within the *fire* chᵃkrᵃ. When it is open, a child attracts immediate attention because of the special shine in the eyes. Confidence and healthy self-assertion are the result and lay the ground for refinement of ego later in life. A child with R3:3 open has the good fortune that Rudrᵃ is in meditation (meaning that various destructive potentials do not manifest). Such a child has even and centered eyes and a large peripheral vision.

Causes of an opening. Parents can assist the opening of R3:3 by encouraging a child in its various endeavors and praising even the smallest of accomplishments. This microchakra is opened by the child's positive sense of accomplishment: "Look what I did!"

Signs of a block. When the third of the third is closed, egotistical and stubborn qualities flourish that may lead to cruelty in adult life for those who are extroverted. On the other hand, introverts with this block will be attracted to a codependent relationship.

Causes of a block. The common practice of cutting the umbilical cord before it stops pulsating is traumatic for the infant and blocks R3:3. Close observation shows that, after delivery, the umbilical cord pulsates with diminishing intensity. A little patience permits severance as soon as pulsation ceases and thereby avoids trauma. The baby will accelerate the cessation if it is allowed to suckle the mother's breast while still attached to the umbilical cord. Suckling causes release of a pituitary hormone (oxytocin), which helps the mother to expel the placenta and gradually reduce the pulsation in the umbilical cord. By this time, the infant begins to adjust to its new environment and the cord may be safely cut.

Premature cutting of the umbilical cord has far-reaching consequences; once R3:3 is blocked it takes a lot of systematic effort later in life to open L3:3.

Too much pressure on a child for accomplishment also blocks this microchakra. Blockage also develops when the child does not receive genuine admiration from people other than its parents.

Left Channel 3:3

Signs of an opening. When *fire* within *fire* (L3:3) is open, self-assertion flows easily. Self-examination is objective and both talents and shortcomings are accepted with equanimity. Realistic goals are set and likely to be attained.

Because self-assertion is easy, it is also easy to surrender the ego. Some with the third microchakra of the third chᵃkrᵃ open surrender the ego in service to an institution such as a church or charitable foundation.

Objective perception of self and others foster the capacity to be a good diagnostician, therapist, or teacher of either secular or spiritual matters.

Desires are focused on completing the accomplishments related to the first lᴇɴɢᵃ and being free to move on.

Visual ecstasy may occur in meditation; the eyes appear as tunnels through which all the universe passes. The meditator merges with the vision.

Signs of a block. When adolescents have the third microchakra in the third chᵃkrᵃ (L3:3) blocked, they feel that they need to prove their power and strength to the world. They possess a very competitive attitude in games, sports, and almost all areas of life.

Great pride in worldly accomplishments is characteristic of this block. It is manifested through a craving for power and authority and a desire to be regarded as important by others. The more difficult something is to achieve, the more intense is the struggle to obtain it. Activities are undertaken for self-aggrandizement rather than for the purpose of serving others. The sense of self-worth is usually perceived solely in terms of personal accomplishments and the accumulation of personal power in the physical field.

Great value is placed on "rugged individualism"—the individual alone is seen as being personally responsible for any "success" or "failure" in life. This attitude has been parodied in the story of the wealthy man who bragged that he was born in a log cabin—which he built himself.

People with this microchakra blocked believe that they own their energy and that they can do with it whatever they wish. They cannot entertain the idea that energy is not a personal possession, but rather a universal gift that flows through them for their responsible use. Instead, the energy is often used in pursuit of some form of immortality in the hope that society will remember them after they are gone. Since any insight into the true source of power is lacking, it may easily be misused. Those with this block are likely to rebel in some manner against any social institution that requires them to surrender some of their power, at least until they themselves occupy the position of power.

Hemispheric functioning is unbalanced. The left hemisphere is overactive, leading to excessive rationality. Emotional and intuitive capacities are weak or crippled. The sense organs of the third chᵃkrᵃ are the eyes and they may display considerable restlessness as the overactive left hemisphere continuously scans the external world.

The competitive attitude that is characteristic of this block is often associated with either an inferiority complex or a superiority complex: "I will show them that I am not inferior" or "I will show them how superior I really am."

Too much egotistical responsibility is often assumed—resulting in anxiety or stress. Stimulants such as coffee, tea, amphetamines, and cocaine are used in the effort to accomplish more.

There is a tendency to sleep on the right side at night; hence activating the right hemisphere. During the day, the system attempts to balance itself by keeping the right nostril open. This keeps the left hemisphere active and produces a more solar, rational, and aggressive chemistry. Consequences of this activity may include anxiety and distrust of others, as well as the habit of looking others in the eyes in order to check them out. A general state of restlessness and inability to sit still usually accompanies this block.

The blockage of *fire* within *fire* may cause stress-related illnesses and a propensity for eye trouble due to inefficient and excessive use of these sense organs.

In those adults who are generally passive, this block causes a weak sense of purpose.

R3:4 and L3:4

Right Channel 3:4
Signs of an opening. When R3:4 is open, the child will seek opportunities to be helpful to others. He or she will be friendly to strangers and will like to make others laugh.

Causes of an opening. Plenty of opportunity to spend time with other children supports the opening of R3:4. Interactions strengthen self-confidence and teach the child empathy. Energy flow in this microchakra is enhanced when the child is encouraged to help his or her parents in minor tasks around the house or to help younger children.

Signs of a block. With R3:4 blocked, a child is reluctant to help others. He or she feels alone and can see no reason to associate with other children. When forced to, such children can respond only with aggression.

Causes of a block. The primary cause of this block is lack of parental love or any other supportive and caring environment. Criticism or embarrassment blocks this microchakra.

Left Channel 3:4

Signs of an opening. When the fourth microchakra of the third chᵃkrᵃ (L3:4) is open, assertiveness is directed toward helping others. This opening makes a person a good neighbor, friend, and citizen who wants to see others happy and wishes the world to be a better place. There is genuine concern for those who need help—including complete strangers. A clear ethical and moral sense prevails, accompanied by a natural tendency to give to charitable or philanthropic organizations.

The flow of *air* within *fire* permits excellence in careers involving public service or the healing professions. There is generally good eye-hand coordination and skilled manual dexterity. If the fifth microchakra of the third chᵃkrᵃ (L3:5) is also open, artistic talent may be present. Concentration on work for long periods of time is done with ease.

When negative emotions arise, they are usually managed creatively. They may be transformed through work or sublimated through service to others. Aggression is usually directed inward. To most of the world there is an appearance of being light-hearted and helpful.

Signs of a block. Blockage in the fourth microchakra of the third chᵃkrᵃ (L3:4) is a major obstacle to spiritual evolution. Egocentricity and lack of compassion reign. It is not possible to entertain the idea of giving without receiving something in return. The lifestyle is usually focused on maintaining an image of personal power and a willingness to do almost anything in its pursuit. This includes lying, stealing, and various types of betrayal including treason; even murder is not excluded. The temptation of these adharmic acts is increased with increased social position. "Power corrupts and absolute power corrupts absolutely."[1]

No capacity exists for solid, sincere relationships with others. Friendships are likely to be superficial. A person with this block cannot be trusted or depended upon, and has no problem knifing someone else in the back. Phony images may be displayed, as well as a false reputation as a do-gooder.

Because of feelings of isolation and separateness from other people, this block creates moodiness, melancholy, and introverted loners. In social situations, such a person is hypercritical of others and competitive with a domestic partner; in a work situation, there is no ability to cooperate or function well with fellow workers, even though considerable skill and idealism may be exhibited in planning.

R3:5 and L3:5

Right Channel

Signs of an opening. A child with the fifth microchakra of the third chᵃkrᵃ (R3:5) open is able to communicate with confidence.

Causes of an opening. The role of the parents is to encourage the child to vocalize, both in speaking and singing. When children initiate conversation with adults it is wise not to treat them as intruders but to teach them to take turns in conversation.

Signs of a block. If R3:5 is blocked, a child will be shy in speaking before others. He or she will be afraid to argue and cannot use singing as a means of expression, even when feeling good.

Causes of a block. Discouraging a child's vocal expression or instilling the feeling that it is intruding when it speaks leads to a block. The old saying that "Children should be seen and not heard" is advice that will create a block in R3:5.

Parents who are dishonest with their children block the flow of energy in this microchakra. Children sense dishonesty and it adversely affects their own self-expression.

Left Channel 3:5

Signs of an opening. When the fifth microchakra of the third chᵃkrᵃ (L3:5) is open, rationality can be expressed with great clarity. Speech is logical, careful, and clear. You are aware of the impact of your words. You can use the power of speech to have significant influence over others. There is a natural ability to listen carefully. This opening makes excellent actors, as well as lecturers and public speakers, who are particularly effective when speaking about their own occupation or profession.

The expressive power available may be directed toward music and the person may be a good singer if the fifth of the third is also open in the right channel and in the central channel. There is generally an above average appreciation and preference for music with some degree of sophistication, that is, music with more harmony than rhythm, such as classical and symphonic music. Loud, noisy music is usually avoided. Sustained-tone music is not likely to be appreciated unless the fifth micro-chakra of the fourth chᵃkrᵃ (L4:5) is also open.

Often creative and artistic abilities are displayed, as well as the ablity to be a good teacher of the fine arts, including painting, drawing, and sculpting.

Signs of a block. Blockage of the fifth microchakra in the third chᵃkrᵃ (L3:5) ordinarily manifests as difficulty in expressing ideas logically and rationally. Verbalization is poor and there is an inability to relate openly and naturally in social situations. Speaking to others, especially in front of groups or when meeting strangers, causes self-consciousness.

Instead of being free, verbal expressions and emotions are censored. Spontaneity is threatening because of a need to feel in control at all times.

Other characteristics of this block are a coarse, aggressive voice or a hesitant whining one. Lack of the ability to sing well or carry a tune is common, stemming from a deafness to tone.

There is a tendency to be argumentative. Only in the heat of an argument can the inhibitions of verbal expression be overridden.

R3:6 and L3:6

Right Channel 3:6

Signs of an opening. If a child looks toward the same-sex parent as a role model, that is a sign that R3:6 is open. This is particularly important for the third chᵃkrᵃ since it provides the motivation for the child's social identity.

Causes of an opening. The relationship with the same-sex parent is the foremost influence on the flow of energy within the sixth microchakra of the third chᵃkrᵃ (R3:6). A good relationship enhances the energy flow; conversely, a poor relation-ship inhibits it. Hence this microchakra has a profound effect upon the self-image of the child as a social being through its positive or negative identification with the same-gender parent.

Parents who encourage the child's curiosity and exploration of the environment nurture R3:6. Encouragement includes providing games and toys that enable the child to feel and express a sense of accomplishment.

Signs of a block. Poor relations with the same-sex parent indicates a block in R3:6. This block also causes lack of discrimination in social situations.

Causes of a block. Lack of encouragement in exploration is detrimental to the flow in this microchakra.

If the child is prematurely forced into abstract and intellectual activities this microchakra is impaired. Young children are naturally right-brain dominant and should be allowed to remain so until they are ready to start school around age six—then they may be truly ready to stimulate the left hemisphere with mathematics and other forms of logical thinking.

Left Channel 3:6

Signs of an opening. The sixth microchakra contains the guiding energy of the third chᵃkrᵃ. This microchakra is infused with the sixth chᵃkrᵃ abilities of self-governance, intuition, and discernment. Thus, understanding of the lower microchakras in the third chᵃkrᵃ occurs and this leads to the ability to steer the desires of these microchakras. This capacity is strengthened if the seventh of the third or the third of the sixth is also open.

A heightened visual perception results from this opening. Creative thinking is enjoyed and there is an attraction to the exploration of new subjects. Pondering the "imponderable" gives inspiration.

This opening is particularly helpful for deeper psychological insights. It confers the ability to see with objectivity the ego's patterns of behavior. We encounter here for the first time a certain degree of objectivity about ourselves—the foundation for objectivity regarding others. It is natural for those with this energy flowing to comprehend people's psyches accurately by interacting and observing. Most psychological theories are based on perceptions of human behavior seen from this level of awareness.

The dawn of understanding that the rational self alone fails to offer a deep insight into life commences here. The transition to the feeling and intuitive selves can now commence. Energy is ready to move from the first lᴇngᵃ to the second.

A fairly confident outlook on life is typical. It is easy to focus intentionally on the positive aspects of a situation and deliberately refrain from investing energy in disagreeable aspects. Humility and modesty tend to increase.

The capacity for self-criticism is based on openings in 3:6 and 6:3. It is healthiest when there is a triangle of thirds and a square of sixths.

Signs of a block. Usually a block in L3:6 is based on a block in R3:6 as a result of a poor relationship with the same-gender parent in the early years of life. If this negative identification with the same-gender parent continues, the block in L3:6 causes a lack of control over the flow of energy in the lower microchakras of the third chᵃkrᵃ. The person is basically a follower needing someone else to lead since the ego lacks confidence. Consequently, there is a preference to follow instructions from a "superior." A person with this microchakra blocked tends toward passivity and is right-brain oriented. A few may be aggressive and, with considerable struggle, rise to positions of leadership.

The temperament tends to be masochistic and it may be hard to give up attachment to suffering. This is directly related to the very common feeling of "not being good enough," and carrying the perceived criticism of the same-gender parent from childhood.

A person with this block is usually oblivious to subtler energies and realms. There is a tendency to believe that spiritual sciences have been developed as psychological "crutches" for others who are weaker. On the other hand, a religion maybe joined out of fear of the unknown.

Psychedelic drugs have a strong effect on this microchakra (among others), opening it widely momentarily, which can be the beginning of a genuine belief in a higher power. Even so, regular use of such drugs, while possibly opening small doors, closes larger ones.

R3:7 and L3:7

Right Channel 3:7

Signs of an opening. When R3:7 is open, a child feels content with his accomplishments, which he repeatedly calls to the attention of the parents.

Causes of an opening. The third chᵃkrᵃ provides the motivation for social identity. Parents who are content with their own accomplishments and directly or indirectly communicate this feeling to the child inspire her seventh microchakra in the third chᵃkrᵃ (R3:7) to open.

Signs of a block. When this microchakra is blocked, the child cannot be happy while sitting still. There is discontent with accomplishments.

Causes of a block. Parents who are discontent with their accomplishments convey a subtle vibrational message to the child that blocks this microchakra. In the ideal case, children would not hear any remarks of discontent or dissatisfaction regarding their parents' accomplishments during the first-chᵃkrᵃ age.

Left Channel 3:7

Signs of an opening. There is an increase in the ability to refrain from action and simply observe. The experience is that of being a vessel through which energy is passing. The view of the objective world undergoes a marked change. Some basic truths of the Tantric and Vedic traditions are no longer simply understood intellectually but are validated experientially. These include the insight that the ego has no independent existence apart from Consciousness, and that all seemingly individual actions are simply components of LEElaa—the Divine play.

The sense of personal suffering ceases to exist. Eagerness now arises to raise the energies beyond the first lɛngª, the abode of egotism, and to begin the search for the higher Self.

Contentment is derived from the smallest accomplishments; little is desired from the world. Instead the person desires to understand how it all began and how to return to the Source. Spiritual practices, including sitting and meditation, come naturally. States of looking through *air* to *aakaash*ª may be experienced.

There is a preference not to look into people's eyes. Instead, the focus is on the aura that surrounds them and expresses the whole being. Those with this opening are ideal students for a true spiritual teacher since they have given up attachments to worldly accomplishments.

There is no desire for immortality and an appreciation that all is an expression of the one Consciousness is readily attained.

Signs of a block. When the seventh of the third is blocked, the individual remains caught in "doership" and no contentment comes from achievement. The person is questing and thirsty—never satisfied. There is no capacity to surrender worldly attachments and experience that which is beyond the tangible. Neither is there a capacity to surrender life if duty should require it.

After retirement, feelings of worthlessness may lead to depression.

6
Openings and Blocks in the Second Lᴇɴɢᵃ

The second lᴇɴɢᵃ is comprised of the fourth and fifth chᵃkrᵃ-s (see plate 10). In this chapter the specific signs and causes of openings and blocks of the microchakras of the right and left channels of each of these chᵃkrᵃ-s are presented in detail.

THE FOURTH CHᴬKRᴬ

It is love that I have
I have love beyond limits
I merge in service
In love I worship
In worship I feel loved
Goodness is in me
I am in goodness
It is because
It just is

S. Bʜᴀᴛɴᴀɢᴀʀ

R4:I and L4:I

Right Channel 4:1

Signs of an opening. The skin is the work organ of the fourth chᵃkrᵃ and maintaining it in a wholesome state helps to keep R4:1 open. There is an important complementary connection between R1:4 and R4:1. Timely cleansing and changing of diapers keeps the baby's body satvic; the skin is vibrant and is filled with healthy sensations. These, in turn, allow for the development of positive feelings. A child who is in contact with these feelings reflects that the foundational microchakra for feeling (R4:1) is open. Whether or not this is the case requires attentive observation of the child, usually by the parents.

Causes of an opening. Hearing and reading stories of great lovers of the Divine, religious heroes, and others who have great compassion help to open R4:1. In addition, healthy physical sensation in the skin aided by regular massage with seasonal oils helps to open this microchakra (for example, coconut oil in the summer and almond oil or mustard oil in the winter).

Signs of a block. The child with R4:1 blocked is not in touch with the depth of sensations of the body. Impatient and socially withdrawn behavior may be present. Lack of understanding of satvic energy is the major cause of heart chᵃkrᵃ blockages.

Causes of a block. If the child is fed nonvegetarian foods, such as red meat pastes, during the first year of life the *earth* of the *air* will be weakened. Fried foods given during this period will also block R4:1. Both red meat pastes and fried foods are difficult for the liver to tolerate. These foods add to tᵃmᵃs. They cause irritation to the nerve endings and anger.

Left Channel 4:1

Signs of an opening. The opening of L4:1 initiates a major shift in self image as the second lᴇɴgᵃ starts to become active. An external deity (often derived from a religion) assumes a central role in life. You perceive yourself not only as a physical being but also as a religious being (this perception will be stronger if the third of the fourth is also open). Life becomes more of a flow and less of a struggle to meet needs, both real and imagined. There may be a feeling of being born again as the refinement of ego energy takes a major step forward. This is often accompanied by a desire to focus on the here and now and spend less time with the old habits of thinking about the past and the future.

This opening inspires new behaviors, such as the consecration of food before eating.

If both L4:1 and R4:1 are open then the *earth* of the *air* flows strongly and the body becomes more flexible. A natural upright sitting posture can be held without discomfort for as long as two hours. There is the ability to rise with ease in any direction from this posture (in the first half of life). This flexibility and agility permits a state in which the body is completely forgotten and the person is lost in the stillness of turning inward.

Signs of a block. Blockage in the first microchakra of the fourth chᵃkrᵃ (L4:1) makes it difficult to move beyond the first lᴇɴgᵃ. Individuals may go through life completely ruled by the desires of the first three chᵃkrᵃ-s. They usually contend that there is no meaningful component to life that is not based in the physical world.

The subtle and causal fields remain inaccessible as experience of satvic energy does not enter their lives.

Tension in the legs and shoulders is common. Consequently, the ability to sit for an extended period of meditation is lacking. Feelings are weak due to lack of *earth* in the *air*.

R4:2 and L4:2

Right Channel 4:2

Signs of an opening. When *water* of the *air* is flowing easily, there is an ability to play equally well with both boys and girls. Feelings may linger; for example, children may talk about how much they enjoyed being with friends and express a desire to see them again.

Causes of an opening. The second microchakra of the fourth chᵃkrᵃ (R4:2) is opened through nonsexual relations with members of the opposite sex. The brother-sister relationship is extremely important in opening R4:2. In cases where there is no sibling of the opposite sex, neighborhood children who are almost as close as brothers or sisters are of great help. The brother-sister relationship is satvic.

During the first-chᵃkrᵃ age (six or seven years), it is psychologically healthy for children to see each other nude; the same is true for adult family members in such natural situations as showering.

Signs of a block. A condescending attitude toward children of the opposite gender indicates that R4:2 is blocked.

Causes of a block. The lack of a brother, a sister, or playmates of the opposite gender blocks this microchakra as does lack of contact between mother-son and father-daughter.

Left Channel 4:2

Signs of an opening. A good brother-sister relationship indicates that L4:2 is open (the closer this relationship, the wider will be the opening). Whether this relationship involves one's genetic brother or sister, or a relative or friend who is like a brother or sister, this bond provides the first opportunity to relate to a member of the opposite gender without the pulls of male-female polarity. In India, a brother-sister day is celebrated twice a year to honor the sanctity of this relationship. Nonsexual loving feelings open this microchakra. Adults who have L4:2 open are much more likely to have friends of the opposite sex.

Pure *water* flowing through the second microchakra of the fourth sensitizes the hands. Bodywork professionals who incorporate therapeutic touch in their practice are much more effective when this microchakra is open.

Signs of a block. When the second of the fourth (L4:2) is blocked, it is not possible to relate to the opposite gender in a pure (satvic) fourth chᵃkrᵃ manner; thoughts of sensuality and sexuality tend to intrude. A wholesome brother-sister relationship is absent. It is difficult to distinguish between a sexual and a nonsexual touch. Giving unconditional love is not possible, nor is real friendship with someone of the opposite sex.

People with this block are unable to distance themselves from their body, to which they cling as the sole source of both pleasure and pain. Their awareness seldom encompasses more than the physical field and they are immersed in a continuous search for sensual gratification.

R4:3 and L4:3

Right Channel 4:3

Signs of an opening. Good interaction with other children is a sign that R4:3 is open.

Causes of an opening. The child opens the third microchakra of the fourth chᵃkrᵃ (R4:3) by playing and sharing with other children. Hence children learn to meet the desires of someone else.

Parents of an only child have an extra responsibility to ensure that their child has plenty of opportunity to play with other children. Within a single-child family context, the child is primarily receiving and has relatively little opportunity to give. In families with two or more children, birth order influences the opportunity for giving and caring versus receiving. The eldest child has more frequent opportunities for giving.

The opening of this microchakra is inspired by telling the child stories of selfless service. Stories of saints from all religions may provide models of second lᴇɴɢᵃ philosophy and behavior.

In some cultures and religions, bowing is a common practice. This helps to open 4:3. Bowing takes place to a deity, grandparents, parents, teachers, or elders. The act of bowing causes the adult ego to learn to surrender and thereby increase its refinement.

Sometimes a private temple or a small sanctuary is constructed in the home. A baby statue of the Divine can play an inspiring role—the child sees how parents wash and dress the baby deity and put it to sleep by drawing curtains over the door of the sanctuary. Any model of selfless service can help open R4:3, such as watching parents do volunteer work.

Signs of a block. When R4:3 is blocked there is no faith in deities or any other higher powers. There is an inability to surrender the ego either in prayer or to a cause that helps the planet.

Causes of a block. This microchakra is likely to be blocked when: parents do not model prayer or surrender of the ego, do not display commitment to a higher cause, or do not celebrate festivals meaningfully.

Left Channel 4:3

Signs of an opening. As we have observed earlier, the second lƐngᵃ commences at the fourth chᵃkrᵃ. Whereas the *fire* of assertiveness burned in the service of "me" in the first lƐngᵃ, in the second it becomes more refined in order to meet the wishes of the "other," particularly a cause or a deity. Tuning into *fire* within *air* inspires love for the form of the deity. People with this opening will not feel self-conscious about offering praise or thanksgiving to an invisible force in the universe. They recognize that there are powers in the universe that may be called upon in time of need and that can aid in spiritual evolution.

As the ego refines, there is recognition that individual energy is the universal Vibrancy passing through the three fields. The person realizes that he or she is not the possessor of the Vibrancy nor the "doer." "Not my will but Thy will" is the attitude when nondoership has dawned.

With this more realistic attitude of nondoership, the person often becomes devoted to serving a social or religious institution that is engaged in bettering the human condition and bringing cosmic ideals into manifestation. Such individuals act in harmony with the karmic laws of the universe. Focus is on the dharmic action and not on the result. The Bhᵃgvat Gᴇᴇtaa explains:

> *That karma that is performed as daily obligatory duty*
> *Devoid of attachment*
> *Free from desire or hatred*
> *Without any desire for result*
> *Is declared to be satvic.*
>
> *On the contrary, that karma that is performed*
> *With desire to obtain some result*
> *With ego or again exerting much*
> *Is declared to be rajsic.*[1]

Those with this microchakra open may prepare themselves to function with a pure (satvic) energy. When 4:4 is also open, they are present-oriented and thereby create fewer repercussions. Satisfaction comes from simply knowing that they are living in a dharmic manner. They are able to see value in all life; they endeavor to do no harm.

The sense of personal possession weakens since it is understood that the things of this world are necessarily transitory and will have to be left behind when death arrives. It makes more sense to regard all possessions as belonging to eightfold nature.

Giving takes place without expecting anything in return. It is unconditional. People with this energy available will readily satisfy the sexual desires of their mates.

Their joy is devotion and service to the deity. They have great compassion for those who suffer. The flow of *fire* within *air* makes them eager to share the bounty of love produced by their heart chᵃkrᵃ-s.

Such people experience a true inner freedom that permits tremendous enjoyment of life. On the other hand, when they do experience personal suffering, they can relinquish awareness of their body and become detached from it.

Signs of a block. Adults with this microchakra blocked have difficulty in accepting the possibility of moral forces in the universe generally and in their own lives in particular. Their lack of a basic capacity to surrender the ego to a higher force locks them into the first lᴇɴɢᵃ. They are unable to worship or give thanks to a higher power with any sincerity. They may deny the possibility of higher states of awareness altogether. Doubts and resistance make it very difficult for them to learn from a spiritual teacher or anyone else with knowledge of the subtler realms.

This block also affects their attitude toward social institutions that might offer them an opportunity to surrender their ego in service. They may be antagonistic toward such institutions and be unwilling to aid them, except financially in return for public recognition of their generosity.

This block often contributes to feelings of loneliness and depression—one consequence of being trapped in the first lᴇɴɢᵃ. Attempts may be made to mask these feelings through intense bouts of sports, television viewing, shopping, drinking, partying, and even reading or talking.

R4:4 and L4:4

Right Channel 4:4

Signs of an opening. Gentleness in behavior and eyes full of love and surrender indicate that R4:4 is open. This microchakra is the center of the heart chᵃkrᵃ. It is the fountain of unconditional love.

Causes of an opening. Unconditional love on the part of the parents helps to produce a child who, later in life, will be able to give unconditional love. In addition, the flow of *air* within *air* is stimulated by the touch of the infant's skin against the mother's bosom. During the right-channel age, this flow is activated by frequent skin contact with the bosom during nursing and when sleeping at hand's reach during the night.

Massaging the baby with seasonal oil before bathing helps with this opening.

A minimum of forty weeks of breastfeeding is very important. If the baby bites the nipple repeatedly after forty weeks, weaning can begin. Otherwise, breastfeeding may continue if necessary until the age of three.

Signs of a block. When R4:4 is blocked, one can neither give unconditional love nor recognize it when expressed by others. The possibilities of love do not extend beyond the conditional.

Causes of a block. The main cause of blockage in R4:4 is the failure to have received unconditional love. Lack of breastfeeding and skin contact with the mother are major contributors. All baby mammals need frequent touch.

Left Channel 4:4

Signs of an opening. Those with this opening are in touch with satvic energy and sense the subtle field. They feel full to overflowing with love toward a deity, moral cause, or humanity in general. They have complete faith in their belief system, whatever it is. Attaching little importance to their own accomplishments, they act instead for the benefit of others.

Devotees (bhᵃktᵃ-s) may experience such spiritual intoxication that they may literally dance with joy. (Every professional classical dancer wishes to achieve this feeling.) It is *air* within *air* that enables such ecstatic movements.

For a woman, an opening in L4:4 awakens nurturing qualities. On the cosmic scale, she may identify with the archetypal mother of the universe. On the family scale, she embraces motherhood, physically, psychologically, and spiritually. Her breast milk flows freely.

People with this opening usually have a deerlike softness in their eyes. An unusual light shines in their skin. Devotees may develop a very mellow expression on the face.

Pleasant aromas may be perceived as the fourth chᵃkrᵃ attracts the awareness of the inner sense of smell. Healing vibrations may flow in the hands.

During meditation, the rate of breathing may drop significantly. Spontaneous gestures (mudraa-s) may occur in response to the subtle energies flowing within. The body becomes the perfect seat, enabling experiences of serenity and equilibrium.

Causes of an opening. The fourth microchakra of the fourth chᵃkrᵃ (L4:4) is a point of balance. It is in the center of the fourth chᵃkrᵃ, with three chᵃkrᵃ-s below and three chᵃkrᵃ-s above. It is also the 'heart of the heart,' with three microchakras above and below it. L4:4 is one of the key microchakras and is extremely difficult to open. In women, the discomfort and pain of natural childbirth, as well as the self-sacrifice required to raise a child, can help to open it. Men and childless women, who have not yet paid back the child-rearing debt in their evolution, will require effort to open it. To do so requires almost a constant outpouring of love and devotion. This may be done through worship of a deity or loving dedication to a cause for the betterment of the planet or its inhabitants.

A Devotee of Sʜᴇvᵃ who served at the cave of Vashishta Temple above Rishikesh in the Himalayas (circa 1971)

Signs of a block. When the fourth of the fourth (L4:4) is blocked there is little access to unconditional love. Consequently, parenting is bound to bring a lot of hardships. A woman does not obtain optimal enjoyment from motherhood, nor does a man obtain deep satisfaction from fatherhood.

Sometimes the man may harbor feelings of jealousy over the woman's ability to create new life and over the attention that the child receives. The mother may be shy and hesitant in expressing motherly feelings—even to the point of suppressing them altogether due to social pressures. Blockage of L4:4 may inhibit the capacity of the breasts to produce milk. It may also influence the mother's attitude toward them. She may be so attached to the pre-partum shape of her breasts that she is reluctant to nurse.

Another manifestation of this block is lack of faith in any aspect of Divinity. Even if at moments one does believe, there is no ability to sustain faith. Furthermore, the idea of a personal deity or deep commitment to a worthy cause may not be acceptable.

R4:5 and L4:5

Right Channel 4:5

Signs of an opening. A pleasing voice accompanies an opening in R4:5. The ability to enjoy music comes naturally. There may also be a love and appreciation for sustained-tone music, particularly if 3:5 is also open.

Causes of an opening. Breastfeeding on demand is the primary cause of this opening. All fifth microchakras are nurtured by sound of good quality. To open the fifth microchakra of the fourth chᵃkrᵃ (R4:5) these sounds need to occur within the context of love. If mother sings to the infant during breastfeeding, its lips and whole body absorb the vibrations. Lullabies, soft music, and happy stories (particularly before bedtime) inspire the opening of this microchakra. Hearing expressions of intimacy and affection between the parents or watching them participate in worship or chanting also contributes to this opening.

Exposure to foreign languages enriches nuances in the child's sound sensitivity and assists in opening R4:5.

Signs of a block. R4:5 blocked may lead to tone deafness. The severity of tone deafness depends on additional blocks in 5:1, 5:4, 5:5, 5:7, and 6:5.

Causes of a block. If the umbilical cord becomes wrapped too tightly around baby's neck, R4:5 may become blocked along with other fifth chᵃkrᵃ blockages.

Failure to provide the experiences necessary for this opening, such as breastfeeding, allows blockage to develop in R4:5. Fear of *aakaashᵃ* strengthens this blockage in the right-channel age.

Left Channel 4:5

Signs of an opening. Adults who have this opening may enjoy listening to sustained-tone music. When either speaking or singing, they have a soothing, soft and mellow quality of voice. Even when angry, their voices do not become discordant. They usually will not lie for personal advantage, especially when 5:2 is also open.

When energy flows through the fifth of the fourth, many creative ideas may be produced. (If the recipient is overly feeling-oriented the ideas may not be realized.) The energy of this microchakra allows for spontaneity and uninhibited expression of devotional feelings.

If the fifth microchakra of the fourth chᵃkrᵃ (L4:5) has not opened in childhood, work with appropriate sounds may open it during the adult years. This includes listening to bells, gongs, conches, chants, and sustained-tone music such as that produced by the tambura. Singing and producing sustained tones is also helpful.

Signs of a block. People who have the fifth microchakra of the fourth chᵃkrᵃ (L4:5) blocked are unable to sing well. There may be tone deafness if L5:1, L5:2, and L5:4, among others, are also blocked. Chanting may seem like an impossible dream or an absurdity. They have difficulty listening to sustained-tone music. When doing so, they may feel dizziness, shortness of breath, boredom, or simply annoyance. Sometimes they may fall asleep or feel as if the earth is moving, or have no reaction.

R4:6 and L4:6

Right Channel 4:6

Signs of an opening. The flow of energy in this microchakra is influenced by the relation with the opposite-sex parent and plays a major role in normal ego development. A positive loving relationship between father and daughter or mother and son is a sign that this microchakra is open. Parent substitutes (such as grandparents) may also contribute to this opening.

Causes of an opening. To be effective in this role the opposite-gender parent, or parent substitute, must remain unconditionally loving during the first-chᵃkrᵃ age.

Signs of a block. If a child is unable to turn to the opposite-sex parent for unconditional love, then R4:6 will be blocked.

Causes of a block. Blocks arise when a) unconditional love cannot be provided to an opposite-gender child due to such obstacles as the parent's lack of sufficient authority within the family unit, b) excessive leniency or strictness in disciplining the child, c) emotional or physical distance from the child, or actual hatred of the child.

If a parent did not receive unconditional love in his or her own childhood, then he or she may unconsciously feel jealous of or even undermine the child who is loved by the opposite-gender parent.

Left Channel 4:6

Signs of an opening. People with this opening tend to be compassionate and loving. They have a devotional temperament. However, they also exhibit considerable objectivity. There is not just faith, but an experiential feeling and understanding of Divinity, particularly if L6:4 is also open.

Such people are intuitive about the thoughts and feelings of family and close friends. Intuition may be supplemented by psychic abilities, such as healing touch and clairvoyance. Discrimination is used in directing love and healing energy, especially if other sixth microchakras are joined in a champion pattern.

During worship, there may be subtle body experiences. These may include seeing the subtle body of another, hearing the fundamental note of another or picking up their odor. These parapsychological abilities may be present when the breath is in one element but not another.

An opening in L4:6 also increases the probability that other microchakras beneath it in the fourth chᵃkrᵃ will be open and helps to guide feelings associated with them.

If openings in L4:6 and L2:6 are joined, the person will be able to choose a loving mate.

Causes of an opening. Openings of the sixth microchakra in the fourth chᵃkrᵃ (L4:6) may be brought about by going on pilgrimages to holy sites, performing sincere worship, chanting, and doing daily spiritual practices. Openings may also be developed by expressing true love and gratitude for the opposite-gender parent.

Signs of a block. Control over fourth chᵃkrᵃ feelings is usually lacking with L4:6 blocked. Those with this block may suffer intense emotional pain when they absorb the pain of others and are unable to release it. This happens when some microchakras in the fourth chᵃkrᵃ are open but the sixth microchakra is blocked.

In a family, one person's resentment against their own mate may develop to such an extent that they may consciously or unconsciously turn the affections of a son or daughter against the other parent.

The sense of touch is not fully developed. Adults are not able to express "fatherly" or "motherly" love to the opposite gender. There is a lack of both feeling and understanding of higher laws and higher chᵃkrᵃ-s.

R4:7 and L4:7

Right Channel 4:7

Signs of an opening. When R4:7 is open, the child is perfectly content. The face, chin, and forehead are without tension. The skin glows and the eyes are shining and soft. The child has a well-composed smiling face because it has received an abundance of touch, love, and security, and has shared laughter together with the family.

Causes of an opening. In order for the seventh microchakra of the fourth chᵃkrᵃ (R4:7) to open, a baby has to revel in a profusion of unconditional love. The mother plays in delight with the baby and they smile and laugh together. The mother breastfeeds the baby. Throughout the day, caring touch is available when the baby needs it.

The importance of loving touch for R4:7 to open cannot be emphasized enough. It determines the quality of sensitivity and the texture of baby's skin and the functioning of the heart chᵃkrᵃ in general.

Imagine being the baby receiving this loving touch, moving from one lap to another: from parent to grandmother, grandfather, sister, brother, aunt, uncle, neighbor, close friend, and back again.

Massage from both parents stimulates the breathing channels of both the lunar and solar hemispheres, enhances vibrancy of the skin and creates fourth chᵃkrᵃ contentment. One of the best ways to prevent feelings of "I am not good enough and worthy to be loved" is to help R4:7 to fully open.

At night the baby experiences contentment by sharing the same bed with both parents or at least with one parent within arm's reach. When all microchakras in the heart chᵃkrᵃ are open, contentment registers in 4:7.

Signs of a block. The failure to experience deep contentment indicates that this microchakra is blocked. This block may be the seed of a touch-hungry personality and be accompanied by a sad look and a raised chin during sleep (an expression of deprivation).

Causes of a block. A block is caused by repeated experiences of disappointment due to blockages in the lower microchakras. For example, this block can occur in children who have been the center of attention during the day but are isolated in a separate room at night. The severity of this block may be increased if a sibling detracts from the attention that the child normally receives.

Left Channel 4:7

Signs of an opening. Spiritual practice (saadhᵃnaa) is a joy and there is contentment with spiritual attainments. A gentle embrace gives the feeling of being loved. Compassion flows easily toward all.

This microchakra brings forth natural healers whose touch and even mere presence has a healing quality. They feel all energy to be Divine energy.

When the seventh microchakra of the fourth chᵃkrᵃ (L4:7) is open, along with most of the other microchakras of the fourth chᵃkrᵃ, the dormant KuNDᵃlᴇnᴇᴇ moves her abode from the first to the fourth chᵃkrᵃ. The second lᴇngᵃ now replaces the first lᴇngᵃ as the dominant source of motivation.

The thymus gland becomes strong and the body's capacity to heal itself increases.

Signs of a block. A longing to receive love from the deity is an indicator that L4:7

is not open. Because this spiritual yearning is unsatisfied, more and more intense fourth chᵃkrᵃ feeling is desired as compensation. Unless the seventh microchakra of some other chᵃkrᵃ is open contentment is not seen as an attainable goal in life.

THE FIFTH CHᴬKRᴬ

Sound is in aakaashᵃ
Aakaashᵃ is in sound
Silence is in aakaashᵃ
Aakaashᵃ is in silence
In sound I am Divine
Divine is sound in me
We are one-song
Uni-verse that is
It is because
It just is

S. BHATNAGAR

R5:1 and L5:1

Right Channel 5:1

Signs of an opening. When the *earth* of *aakaashᵃ* is solid, the voice is strong. There is a capacity to easily imitate the voice of others as well as the voices of animals and birds.

Causes of an opening. While breastfeeding, R5:1 in the baby opens if a) mother's diet is organically nutritious, b) she eats appetizing and unprocessed foods, c) she eats in a pleasant environment and uplifted state of mind.

The opening of R5:1 is aided by hearing a variety of sounds from a loving mother. Family members who have strong and authoritative voices enhance the opening. It is also facilitated by listening to different languages, by singing, and by hearing the rhythms of drums, cymbals and bells.

Signs of a block. A weak voice—whiny or cracking and lacking in solidity—indicates that R5:1 is blocked.

Causes of a block. A block may be caused by the absence of sufficient releasers for R5:1. It may also be caused by a) repeatedly hearing loud noises, shouting, or screaming, b) crying before sleep (long crying dries the throat, which contributes to this block), c) having the mouth covered by an adult's hand in a desperate attempt to force crying to stop.

Left Channel 5:1

Signs of an opening. When the first microchakra of the fifth chᵃkrᵃ (L5:1) is open, one aspires to cosmic identity. This is in contrast to the fourth chᵃkrᵃ aspiration to worship an outwardly projected deity. The paramount desire of people with an opening in L5:1 is to move to a higher state of awareness, that is, to sense the omnipresence of the deity. Hence they prefer to remain in *aakaashᵃ* and merge into silence.

The cells of the body may resonate with the planet in what can be called planetary identification. There is no doubt in sensing Divinity everywhere, even in a stone.

This opening is a requirement for a spiritual teacher to efficiently teach stillness of being. Such a teacher can stabilize *aakaashᵃ* within and serve as a mirror for others. Students who sit quietly with such a teacher also begin to recognize *aakaashᵃ* within. This helps them to shed disguises and false self-images. Attention is drawn more and more to the space between words and the space between thoughts.

Attunement to *aakaashᵃ* also lessens self-criticism and self-blame. Instead, objectivity about the self increases and the seed of nonattachment is sown.

People with this microchakra open tend to either dress in white or to wear the Tantric color of the day (see chapter 10). If they belong to a religious group, they will wear the color of their tradition.

Signs of a block. When the first of the fifth (L5:1) is blocked there is no identification with either the planet or the cosmos. The voice lacks the ability to sustain a tone and speaking is usually in a monotone. The voice may be low-toned, guttural, and throaty or high-pitched and annoying. Restlessness prevents sitting in a stable posture for meditation, a problem aggravated by impurities in the *aakaashᵃ*. There may be a fear of *aakaashᵃ* because prolonged silence sounds deafening. Those with this blockage may be compulsive talkers in an unconscious hope that the block will be removed.

If you have this obstruction you lack a universal perspective on life and have no sense of the Divine. The capacity to mirror yourself and see yourself as others do is absent. In other words, you are not able to view yourself with objectivity and detachment. Life seems puzzling and chaotic. It is difficult to move beyond the first lƐngᵃ. You may be self-critical even to the point of doubting your sanity. When unwell or depressed, solace is sought in seclusion rather than through the company of others because you find it very difficult to give voice to your feelings.

You are able to do spiritual practices based on devotion and the *air* of the fourth chᵃkrᵃ but not those based on sound and the *aakaashᵃ* of the fifth chᵃkrᵃ—unless there is an opening elsewhere in the fifth chᵃkrᵃ.

Plate I. The human body and the three fields that pervade it: Purple represents the causal field that is created by luminous sound and accessed through the overtones of the sounds of the chᵃkrᵃ-s. Gold represents the subtle field that is created by illuminated sound and accessed directly by the sounds of the chᵃkrᵃ-s. The physical field is created by audible sound and affected by both the tones and overtones of the chᵃkrᵃ-s.

Plate 2. The temple of eightfold nature links Earth to the highest reaches of the cosmos. The three rectangles at the base of the figure are steps leading to the temple. The main body of the temple is formed by an earth-colored (yellowish) square that symbolizes the element of the first chᵃkrᵃ (*earth*). Within the temple sits a lɛngᵃ (egg-shaped icon). For ages it has been used by aspirants as a means to adore the Divine.

The lɛngᵃ rests on a base representing the womb of the universe (jᵃgᵃdyonɛɛ). The total symbolism suggests the universe as the source of the manifest world represented by the egg. This egg is the source of all desire.

The blue water and base of the cone stand for the element of the second chᵃkrᵃ (*water*). The top of the cone forms a red triangle symbolizing the third chᵃkrᵃ. In the background is the sunlight that is the main source of third chᵃkrᵃ energy (*fire*). Normally, in the darkness of the Kᵃlɛ yugᵃ, *fire* burns downward and fuels our basic desires. In the sanctified atmosphere of the temple, however, the *fire* points upward toward the higher chᵃkrᵃ-s. This upward striving is also represented in that part of the six-pointed star that points up. The downward pointing portion represents the higher energies that are reaching below to help lift the aspirant. The six-pointed star is green, the color of *air* that resides in the fourth chᵃkrᵃ. In the center of the star is a second lɛngᵃ, representing more refined desires. Above the star is a gray crescent moon—symbol of the fifth chᵃkrᵃ and its element *aakaashᵃ*. The crescent moon supports a third lɛngᵃ, which contains the colors blue, red, and white. These represent tᵃmᵃs, rᵃjᵃs, and sᵃtvᵃ respectively. At the top of the third lɛngᵃ is the Sᵃmskretᵃ symbol for AUM, the primal sound of creation from which all elements and guɴᵃ-s have issued.

Plate 3. The tripartite brain: The blue-haired male face represents the solar energy of the left hemisphere. The brown-haired female face represents the lunar energy of the right hemisphere. Both gaze at the early brain from which they have evolved and which they are helping to refine. The early brain is represented by a hooded cobra in the area of the sixth chᵃkrᵃ. The pathway directly above it is the route by which advanced yogis may leave their bodies. It is discussed at greater length in chapter 2 where the somᵃ chᵃkrᵃ is described.

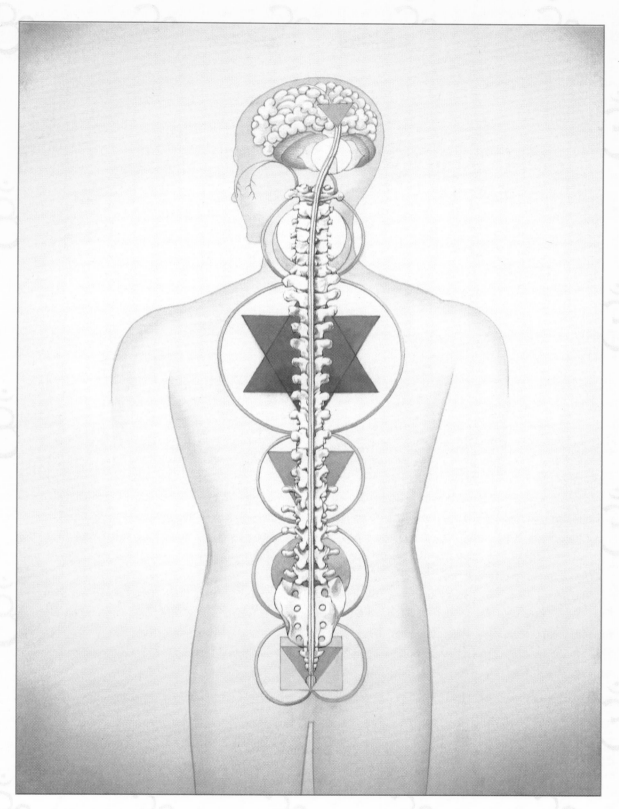

Plate 4. The three primary naaDEE-s—Edaa (left breathing channel), pEngᵃlᵃ (right breathing channel), and sushumnaa (carrier of *fire* and solar and lunar energies)—are the three subtle nerves of paramount importance. Note that the painting illustrates the fact that chᵃkrᵃ energy influences the body from the back.

Plate 5. Sushumnaa surrounded by ᴇdaa and ᴘᴇɴɢᵃlᵃ: Right-channel solar energy (vᵃjrᴇɴᴇᴇ) spirals down from the seventh chᵃkrᵃ to the first in a clockwise motion. This is depicted by orange-gold circles (sun) with an attached triangle showing the downward spiral. When this male solar energy reaches the first chᵃkrᵃ, it is absorbed by the cooling *earth* element, which converts it to a female lunar energy. This lunar energy then rises in the left channel (cʜᴇtrᴇɴᴇᴇ) with a counterclockwise motion. It is represented by a silver crescent (moon) and attached tear showing upward spiral of energy toward the seventh chᵃkrᵃ.

In the center is the central channel (Sʜᴇvᵃ naaᴅᴇᴇ). It is shown as fiery orange-red flames penetrating both vᵃjrᴇɴᴇᴇ and cʜᴇtrᴇɴᴇᴇ. It carries information from all lives of the jᴇᴇvᵃ—from existence as an amoeba to the present life. All filled and unfulfilled desires are recorded here.

Intensity of desire manifests as intensity of *fire* in the central channel. As long as there are unfulfilled wishes, there is the *fire* of desire. When a desire has been fulfilled, no *fire* is present; this is symbolized by ashes. Unfulfilled desires of the central channel impel us in the current life. Liberation may be symbolized as all *fire* converted to ashes.

The painting depicts the solar heat of ᴘᴇɴɢᵃlᵃ (right breathing channel) in flame-shaped magenta. The cooling energy of ᴇdaa (left breathing channel) is depicted with blue waves of water.

Plate 6. Inner sanctuary of Hretᵃ pᵃdmᵃ: With the grace of the guru, this inner sanctuary of the Divine Self is accessed. We are then able to love unconditionally and to feel the world to be our child.

Plate 7. Artistic portrayal of 21 microchakras within the first chᵃkrᵃ: Each major chᵃkrᵃ is reflected as a microchakra. For artistic purposes, the appropriate color of each chᵃkrᵃ has been replaced by the color of the channel in which it is located. The seven microchakras of the right solar channel are portrayed in gold. The seven microchakras of the left lunar channel are portrayed in silver. Those of the central channel are portrayed in red.

Plate 8. Artistic portrayal of the 147 microchakras in their respective channels with their elements showing faintly in the background.

Plate 9. The iron chain of the first lɛŋgᵃ: The first three chᵃkrᵃ-s are portrayed with their appropriate symbols and elemental colors. Within each chᵃkrᵃ are the twenty-one microchakras in the color of their channel. These three chᵃkrᵃ-s are bound by the iron chain of the first lɛŋgᵃ. *(continued)*

(Plate 9 continued) Outside the iron chain the artist has depicted each chᵃkrᵃ element with a corresponding animal that is attracted to it (sometimes fatally) through the sense related to that element: bee for smell (*earth* of first chᵃkrᵃ), fish for taste (*water* of second chᵃkrᵃ), moth for sight (*fire* of third chᵃkrᵃ). Each chᵃkrᵃ element also contains within it a second animal signifying a dominant characteristic of that chᵃkrᵃ mind: hoarding like ants, flitting like butterflies, striking out like cobras.

In the background are the therapeutic colors. Red for the first chᵃkrᵃ, pink and orange for the second chᵃkrᵃ, and green for the fourth chᵃkrᵃ.

Plate 10. The silver chain of the second lɛngᵃ: The fourth and fifth chᵃkrᵃ-s are portrayed with their appropriate symbols and elemental colors. Within each chᵃkrᵃ are the twenty-one microchakras in the color of their channel. These two chᵃkrᵃ-s are bound by the silver chain of the second lɛngᵃ.

Outside the silver chain the artist has depicted each element with a corresponding animal that is fatally attracted to it through the sense related to that element: elephant for touch (*air* of fourth chᵃkrᵃ) and spotted deer for sound (*aakaashᵃ* of fifth chᵃkrᵃ). Each chᵃkrᵃ element also contains within it a second animal signifying a dominant characteristic of that chᵃkrᵃ mind: chasing mirages (represented by the gray deer of the fourth chᵃkrᵃ) and grandeur of being represented by the peacock of the fifth chᵃkrᵃ.

In the background are the therapeutic colors, gold for the fourth chᵃkrᵃ and gray for the fifth chᵃkrᵃ.

Plate II. The golden chain of the third lɛngᵃ: The sixth and seventh chᵃkrᵃ-s are portrayed, bound by the golden chain of the third lɛngᵃ. Within each chᵃkrᵃ are the twenty-one microchakras in the color of their channel.

    The two swans signify the dominant characteristic of the sixth chᵃkrᵃ mind—transcendence. The multicolored light represents the illumination resulting from union with the Self above the seventh chᵃkrᵃ.

Plate 12. Representation of pranic and apaanic memory pods: Shown here are the fourth microchakras of the third chᵃkrᵃ for both the right and left channels (symbolized by the gold hexagon). The ten blue petals emerge from the red fire of the third chᵃkrᵃ. They are alternately divided into five that symbolize the apaanic pods (thorny holly leaf) and five that symbolize the pranic pods (graceful pattern). Note that received and emitted light is vibrant from the pranic patterns and dull in relation to the apaanic patterns.

Plate 13. A sage sits in meditation at the Vashishta Temple above Rishikesh, India. This is a legendary cave where Lord Rama's guru, Sage Vashishta, did his saadhᵃnaa.

R5:2 and L5:2

Right Channel 5:2

Signs of an opening. A pleasant melodious voice is a sign that R5:2 is open, as is the aspiration to higher values.

Causes of an opening. Sweet gentle talk to the baby helps to open this microchakra. Gentle sustained-tone string music is also a releaser of this energy.

Signs of a block. Blockage in R5:2 is reflected in the lack of fluidity in the voice. It may also be scratchy and generally unpleasant.

Causes of a block. Any obstruction to the flow of energy to the head while in the womb may cause a block. This can happen, for example, if the umbilical cord becomes coiled around the neck of the fetus.

Left Channel 5:2

Signs of an opening. The voice has a flowing quality. The body is very light and feels as if it consists mostly of space. If C5:2 is also open, there is an awareness of living in a timeless space beyond duality. Reflective of this weightless flow, one walks as if floating. This opening leads to a relatively fearless life without needing weapons for defense. This opening may make out-of-body awareness possible.

Living up to higher values brings enjoyment. Rich and exotic foods, or even foods in great variety, are not appealing. Preference is for a simple diet of fruit, vegetables, pulses, herbs, grains, and a few seeds or nuts.

If the second of the fifth in the central channel is also open, the highs in the voice are quite clear and melodic.

Practicing nudity in seclusion helps to open this microchakra in the central channel and reduce identification with the body. Adherents of the Naga (nude ones) sect in India are noted for their devotion to the practice of nudity. They live in the mountains away from society.

Signs of a block. When the second microchakra in the fifth chᵃkrᵃ (L5:2) is blocked, it can lead to a fear of speaking the truth. Fears of seclusion, punishment, or embarrassment may arise as obstacles. There may be a strong attraction to someone of the opposite sex who has a soothing voice.

Some people create melodies in an attempt to open this microchakra.

R5:3 and L5:3

Right Channel 5:3

Signs of an opening. When R5:3 is open, the *fire* in the child's voice has a good range, awareness of color is strong, and play is creative.

Causes of an opening. Exposure to refined, sustained-tone music and voice helps to open R5:3 as does the sight of yᵃntrᵃ-s with beautiful colors—drawn for various auspicious ceremonies. Watching mobiles adds to this opening.

Signs of a block. When R5:3 is blocked, the range of the voice is limited and may crack at high pitches. The color sense may be weak and play lacks creativity.

Causes of a block. Disturbing, unpleasant, or frightening visual scenes (whether actual or from media) during the first forty weeks after birth obstruct the flow in R5:3.

Left Channel 5:3

Signs of an opening. When L5:3 is open, both sight and hearing become internally oriented. Any time the eyes are closed, there is the possibility of hearing the inner sound (naadᵃ). This use of the "inner ear" permits reception of a variety of naadᵃ-s.

When the third of the fifth is open, the approach to life is steady. Gentleness, modesty, courage, forgiveness, and self-control are prominent qualities. Greed, malice, and vanity are absent. A capacity to relieve demoralization or cowardliness in others, and to awaken in them silence and detachment from feelings, is also accessible.

When L5:3 surrenders its ego, a host of possibilities for parapsychological abilities opens up. For example, if this microchakra joins in a triangle with L4:3 and L6:3, there will be no difficulty in perceiving the subtle energy flow in other people.

If an opening in C5:3 accompanies an opening in L5:3, there may be an ability to visualize internally; that is, people with this opening may be able to see their own internal organs or even the internal organs of others.

If one has an extrovert personality, one may develop a powerful and resonant voice that conveys a convincing message. The truth of the message, of course, will depend on the degree of openness in the fourth and sixth chᵃkrᵃ-s.

Signs of a block. When speaking loudly, the voice tends to be unpleasant. At higher pitches, it is cracking and disagreeable. For these reasons, a counterfeit voice may be adopted—one that is believed to sound better than the natural voice.

Those with this block tend to take a long time before they speak and they edit out what they feel they should not say. Thus, in conversing with others, they lack sincerity and spontaneity. If assertiveness is high, they may speak rationally for hours in an attempt to open this microchakra.

Some with L5:3 blocked train their voice theatrically in an attempt to overcome the block. The result may be a voice that is artificial and pretentious. Large numbers of people may believe them but those who are very close to them will not believe.

R5:4 and L5:4

Right Channel 5:4

Signs of an opening. When R5:4 is open, the voice is extraordinarily sweet, tender, and full of love. In the second-ch^akr^a age, these children are drawn to singing.

Causes of an opening. Hearing soft vocal expressions of unconditional love and tenderness serve to open fourth microchakras in general and R5:4 in particular. For example, children might be told "I love your fingers," "I love your eyes," "I love your toes."

Listening to sustained-tone music contributes to this opening.

Signs of a block. Blockage may cause an inability to speak in a tender and loving manner. At times, the voice may be high toned and scratchy or low toned and rough.

Causes of a block. Loud sounds heard during pregnancy will cause blockage in R5:4. Later, the absence of a melodious speaking voice in surrounding adults—especially the mother—tends to block this microchakra.

Loud arguments and fighting between the parents serve as blockers—as does any expression of violence or hatred. The sound of aggressive videogames and TV programs also harms this microchakra.

Left Channel 5:4

Signs of an opening. A person born with this microchakra open has an extraordinarily sweet and melodious voice, a "saintly" voice full of orange/red *aakaash^a*. If the microchakra is opened later in life, the person may become a healer utilizing both sound and touch. All who possess this opening have great compassion; they can readily feel the pain of others even at a distance. They are very forgiving and tend to be full of laughter and merriment. When they walk, it may appear as if they are moving on air.

Their mastery of *aakaash^a* is such that a special space surrounds them to which others are attracted. This applies even to children who are normally afraid of *aakaash^a* since it makes them feel spacey.

To help others reduce or forget their psychological pain, these wonderful beings may sing or chant. Some popular singers also have this microchakra open and their sweet voices and songs have relieved the pain of millions of hearts.

Signs of a block. When the fourth microchakra of the fifth ch^akr^a (L5:4) is blocked, there may be an ability to sing but the voice will lack sweetness. It is very difficult to chant and produce soory^a *aakaash^a*.

Some popular singers with this block express a common frustration that both they and their audience are experiencing. They show this by screaming as much as singing. They may attract a large audience who also feel like screaming. This audience provides the singer with attention, popularity, and money. The ego of the singer is frequently not mature enough to handle this adulation and seeks escape in mind-contracting drugs.

Others with this block may be attracted to singing classical sustained tones in an attempt to open it.

R5:5 and L5:5

Right Channel 5:5

Signs of an opening. Babies are awake much more than average. After eighty weeks, they refuse to sleep during the day. Children relish silence and *aakaash*ᵃ. They are keen listeners who hear in a very special way.

Causes of an opening. The fifth microchakras in the fifth chᵃkrᵃ contain the essence of *aakaash*ᵃ. This element requires silence for its absorption. Regular experiences of singing with intermittent silence, when the baby's body is relaxed and most receptive, aids the opening of R5:5.

Families who have learned to share moments of silence together strengthen this microchakra.

Signs of a block. The lack of sensitivity to sound and its effect in everyday life is an indicator that R5:5 is blocked.

Causes of a block. Radio, TV, and other appliances that detract from silence in any way are the natural enemies of this microchakra. This is particularly true in the right-channel age. The burden of continuous talk numbs this microchakra. Loud music with deep sounds of drumming will ensure this block.

Left Channel 5:5

Signs of an opening. The fifth microchakra of the fifth chᵃkrᵃ (L5:5) is one of the key microchakras and hence very difficult to fully open. When it does fully open, there is a desire for prolonged silence and to live alone so that energy can be directed inward and deeper.

Those with L5:5 open prefer silent communication by means of gesture or writing. When they do speak it is with reverence. The voice has a crystal-clear quality that can calm and relax others. Chanting is very ethereal and elevating. Laughter is frequent with an open sound full of *aakaash*ᵃ. Healing can occur purely through the use of sound.

Foreign languages are learned with such clarity that pronunciation is indistinguishable from that of native speakers.

This opening may bring forth genuine interest in liberation. Spiritual practice (saadhᵃnaa) is focused on connecting the person's own fundamental pitch (naadᵃ) with the pitch of the universe.

When the sense of hearing is internalized, the fundamental sound of the universe (naadᵃ) becomes clearly audible. This sound puts the aspirant in a blissful state. If internalization does not develop, clairaudience (sensing distant external sounds) might make its appearance. Attachment to this power may hinder spiritual growth unless pursuit of internalization is continued with the guidance of a teacher.

Aspirants (saadhu-s) with this opening can provide others with mᵃntrᵃ-s that can have an immediate and powerful effect, provided that they are pronounced accurately and intoned with devotion. Knowledge is shared only with those who are true seekers.

Individuals with the fifth of the fifth open can hear the blissful intonation in the teacher's voice, both in chanting and in speaking. They may even hear two or three voices when a naadᵃ yogi chants special mᵃntrᵃ-s. Constant practice leads them to appreciate the harmonic relation with cosmic sound. Then, one day they get very close to naadᵃ sᵃmaadhᴇ (see following discussion of seventh chᵃkrᵃ). In this final unitive awareness, breath at times is gradually suspended. No eating is needed at this time. Illumination takes place for as long as this state lasts or can be made to last.

At dawn, the open nostril vibrates at C natural; the recessive nostril is somewhat higher. At dusk, the open nostril is almost C sharp as the body wants to gradually recline.

Signs of a block. There is a lack of any of the varied abilities that are available when this microchakra is open. One may practice long speech fasts in an attempt to open this microchakra.

R5:6 and L5:6

Right Channel 5:6

Signs of an opening. The child speaks clearly and has a good memory for words. There is an ability to instantly mimic someone else's voice. This mimicry may reflect an opening or be an attempt to achieve one. Speech is well pronounced. Very special centered deep eyes show wisdom from past lives. There is an extraordinary ability to survive in life-threatening situations. This opening facilitates the awakening of the inner guru later in life.

Causes of an opening. Parents who use special prayers or mᵃntrᵃ-s before eating, putting children to sleep, or during bathing help them to open R5:6. It is important to expose children to silence and *aakaashᵃ* at these times through quietude before and after the sounds. As children absorbs *aakaash^a*, they learn that sound and silence may be used to sense the unseen.

Signs of a block. Clarity of speech comes slowly.

Causes of a block. It is blocked by the absence of family who can provide the necessary stimulation of sound and silence.

Left Channel 5:6

Signs of an opening. As this microchakra begins to open, the person is guided to a teacher and there is an intense desire to be with the teacher as long and as often as possible.

After 5:6 has opened and the inner guru has awakened, there is control over the lower microchakras in the fifth ch^akr^a. Duality based on the elements is nearly eliminated. Consequently, experiences of dissolution commence on this level. Fear of *aakaash^a* has long disappeared and, in its place, love of *aakaash^a* reigns.

The distinction between the elements and the gu n^a-s is fully felt and now the focus is on balancing the gu n^a-s. The contrast between the s^atv^a of the early morning hours and the t^am^as of the night is clearly experienced.

Everything is now seen as vibration rather than form. Living and dying are perceived as very similar to waking and sleeping. There is a deep appreciation of the cosmic humor of existence and the person may laugh frequently, aloud or silently. The cosmic wisdom (rechaa) present everywhere in the universe can be interpreted.

The transition of awareness from the second l ng^a to the third l ng^a commences. It may manifest itself in many different ways; for example, action may occur in a spontaneous manner synchronized with intuition, or creativity may flow abundantly. Alternatively, the world may be renounced and the rest of one's life devoted to the search for personal liberation. This is most likely if 6:1, 6:4, and 6:6 are also open.

Having this microchakra somewhat open makes the person an excellent therapist or fine teacher.

Because of the great sensitivity to sound that stems from this opening, naad^a s^amaadh is possible—especially in the early morning hours.

Since the faculty of hearing is now under voluntary control, the amount of attention given to a sound is a matter of deliberate decision. Neither the highest or lowest pitches nor the loudest or softest sounds can cause disturbances. The manner in which a person's own sound affects others is fully understood and used accordingly.

Because of this opening, m^antr^a-s are heard from within and contemplation turns into meditation.

L5:6 combined with R5:6 determines the regard we have for the inner guru as well as the quality of the intuition that guides us to a human spiritual teacher.

The sense of dhᵃrmᵃ resides in this microchakra. If the sixth microchakras in the right channel and the central channel are also open, the inner guru is fully awake.

When C5:6 is also open, it is possible to "tune in" to exactly how other people are feeling and where their awareness happens to be at the moment. Such a person is a natural teacher who works with a restricted number of students or disciples.

Signs of a block. The sixth microchakra in the fifth chᵃkrᵃ (L5:6) is the command center for sound sensitivity and creativity. If this microchakra is blocked there is no ability to guide the flow of information within the first five microchakras of the fifth chᵃkrᵃ. Sooryᵃ *aakaashᵃ* is not well absorbed. Those with this blockage are unable to direct or control their creativity. In fact, they have little quality creativity and their lives are characterized by rigidity and lack of spontaneity. They may frequently interpret spontaneity in others as "irresponsible behavior." *Aakaashᵃ* does not flow smoothly in the body and voice.

The concept of guᴺᵃ-s is not clearly understood. There is little capacity to make proper use of *aakaashᵃ* produced from quietude or from the recitation of mᵃntrᵃ-s. It is difficult to sit quietly for meditation. Intuitive appreciation of dhᵃrmᵃ is unavailable and the inner guru remains asleep. One may be attracted to serve a guru in an attempt to open this microchakra. However, true gurus only allow a spiritually qualified person to serve them.

R5:7 and L5:7

Right Channel 5:7

Signs of an opening. Those children with R5:7 open are afraid of loud sounds. However, they themselves can make sounds in the third and fourth octaves or even the fifth octave.

Causes of an opening. Religious communities all over the world have used sound during rituals. Prayers, songs, chants, bells, conches, cymbals, and so on are universal tools used to tune members to the vibrations of the community. R5:7 responds with an opening if special ceremonies are performed for the infant; when, for example, the baby is given a name, takes the first solid food or comes of age within his or her spiritual community. If the ceremony takes place in the spirit of the second lᴇɴgᵃ, the adults naturally radiate the link between special sounds and spiritual contentment—and the infant absorbs the same vibrational connection.

Hearing gentle lullabies chanted in sustained tones before sleep also inspires the opening of R5:7. When children regularly hum happily to themselves, R5:7 is nurtured.

The opening of R5:7 is fostered by deep communication between mother and infant. Periods of deep silence may occur when they simply gaze into each other's eyes. The sounds of suckling during breast feeding produce that type of delicate *aakaash*ᵃ that may occasionally dissolve the minds of the lower four chᵃkrᵃ-s and thereby open R5:7.

Mother and baby may together "unite" in the *aakaash*ᵃ produced by their intimate meetings. At these times, large amounts of endorphins are produced in the brains of both mother and baby and they become one. That oneness creates dissolution of the lower minds and the opening of R5:7. Properly understood, breastfeeding is a sacred act. At a minimum it is a normal act, yet many "modern" societies prohibit its practice in public places, thereby contributing to the blockage of microchakras within its new citizens.

Signs of a block. When R5:7 is blocked, there is little sensitivity to sound and little inclination to direct attention inward. Even rare musicians who hear notes very clearly and have a perfect pitch may not be sensitive to sound. At times, when deeply absorbed by their playing, their hearing may internalize. They still need to break their habitual reaction to the notes in order to hear the pure sound.

Causes of a block. Loud noises block R5:7. Examples are screams, loud arguments, the sound of heavy machinery, natural disasters, and armed conflicts.

Left Channel 5:7

Signs of an opening. When the seventh microchakra of the fifth chᵃkrᵃ (L5:7) is open complete contentment is experienced in silence and stillness (naadᵃ sᵃmaadhᴇ). Any attachments to the empirical world cease. In India holy men with this opening often live without a home. Wherever they wander, they are always at home—for they know that their only true home is the universe. Their eyes may be flooded with a crystal light and their bodies smell pleasant. Their awareness reaches beyond the play of the elements. Their only aspiration is to live in the sixth chᵃkrᵃ and experience the compassionate viewing of the play of the elements in others, while mastering the guɴᵃ-s in themselves.

These people may choose not to do much in the world that utilizes the energy of the first five chᵃkrᵃ-s. Instead, they may prefer to live in silence and not initiate vocal activity except that which vibrates their own systems or answers direct questions. Miracles may be performed through them without their knowledge; others may make them aware of it as in the following well-known story.

THE LEPER AND THE HOLY MAN

There was a famous holy man who avoided touching people. He was very involved in balancing his own guɴᵃ-s. One day a leper heard him chant and give a talk in a local temple. It occurred to the leper that if he could somehow get a touch from this holy man his leprosy would be removed. Since he knew the path that the holy man followed when he went to bathe in the river, the leper went there and sat on the steps leading down to the river. He sat there for many years.

One dark winter day, as the holy man was walking down the steps, he tripped. Reaching to balance himself, he placed his right hand upon the head of the leper who was seated silently near his feet. The leper knew that it was the holy man who had touched him and instantly yelled out, "Thank you! Thank you! Thank you!" Witnesses to the happening reported that the leprosy almost instantly dissipated.

We can believe that the curing of the leprosy was due to the faith of the leper or to the healing energy that flowed in the holy man's hands or to a combination of the two. The principle of synchronicity should also be remembered as well as the teaching of the Bhᵃgvat Gᴇᴇtaa that no one is the "doer" other than eightfold nature.

The voices of holy men may sound completely hollow and without personal emotions. They possess a precise and subtle vocal ability with which to soften the tenth gate by means of an extremely delicate vocal vibration called prᵃɴᵃvᵃ.

The advantage of an open L5:7 is that *aakaashᵃ* is absorbed most readily since it is the element of the fifth chᵃkrᵃ. With this opening *earth, water, fire,* and *air* can be dissolved in the voice and mᵃntrᵃ-s can be chanted to produce sooryᵃ *aakaashᵃ*.

The universe is experienced as nonlocal (as explained in chapter 1). Time can bend or even stop. Information does not travel—it is there synchronistically. There is no difficulty in accepting that nature is playing a game of hide-and-seek. The attachment with the elements is minimal and there is a desire to transcend eightfold nature.

Signs of a block. When the seventh of the fifth is blocked, people are caught in polarities. They believe that sound can only be produced by striking two objects together. They are unable to accept the possibility of silent sound or to appreciate the vibration that underlies the physical world. No contentment is found in the *aakaashᵃ* produced by mᵃntrᵃ-s.

If this microchakra begins to open, sitting on the guru's seat (aasanᵃ) helps to further open this microchakra.

7

Openings and Blocks in the Third Lᴇɴɢᵃ

The third lᴇɴɢᵃ is comprised of the sixth and seventh chᵃkrᵃ-s (see plate 11). In this chapter the specific signs and causes of openings and blocks of the microchakras of the right and left channels of each of these chᵃkrᵃ-s are presented in detail.

THE SIXTH CHᴬKRᴬ

It is
It is in me
You are in me
All is in me
The good and the bad
The right and the wrong
It is all in me
I am the whole
and all is in me
It is because
It just is

S. Bʜᴀᴛɴᴀɢᴀʀ

R6:1 and L6:1

Right Channel 6:1

Causes of an opening. Proper nutrition for both mother and baby will help to open R6:1.

Causes of a block. During pregnancy mother and baby are bound together in all three fields, yet even after the umbilical cord is cut the bond continues in the subtle and causal fields. R6:1 is vitally important to the strength of this bond because it sits at the nexus of the two higher fields.

During the last twenty weeks of pregnancy, R6:1 becomes blocked if the mother a) has an inadequate diet, b) eats in a depressed state of mind or in an unpleasant environment, c) has any addictions that affect the baby and interfere with baby's intuitive nature, d) feels insecure in her role as mother.

During the course of life, if apaanᵃ stations repeatedly in R6:1, pods of apaanᵃ will form causing either anorexia, obesity, or other disorders. These conditions are difficult to overcome. However, spiritual work aimed at opening L6:1 may provide the means.

Left Channel 6:1

Signs of an opening. The activity of the elements that dominate the first five chᵃkrᵃ-s firmly ties awareness to the empirical world. In the sixth chᵃkrᵃ, the more abstract guNᵃ-s replace the elements as the regnant energy. It is mastery of the guNᵃ-s that permits final transcendence of the world of experience. This process commences in the first microchakra of the sixth chᵃkrᵃ (L6:1).

When this microchakra is open, identification with the desires and thoughts of the lower five chᵃkrᵃ-s are easily witnessed. No longer at the mercy of the rational solar pulls of the left hemisphere or the emotional lunar pulls of the right hemisphere, functioning is based directly upon original intuition associated with the early brain. The body is experienced as a possession and a temple.

When C6:1 is also open, awareness of *earth* in the breath of others comes naturally. Sitting quietly (darshᵃnᵃ) with a teacher in whom this microchakra is open creates a feeling of weightlessness for the students. For the duration of the sitting, they feel extremely secure and comforted.

As is the case when the first microchakra in the fifth chᵃkrᵃ is open, those whose first of the sixth is open have a mirrorlike quality. They may take on any identity or role at will. This freedom from ordinary restrictions may make them seem to be lacking in principle (just the opposite is true). In the presence of such advanced saints, others feel exalted and undisturbed by spiritual obstructions.

The positive energy of this microchakra induces great sensitivity to the qualities of the guNᵃ-s. Any imbalance in tᵃmᵃs, rᵃjᵃs, or sᵃtvᵃ is readily detected.

When sitting up on a full-moon-night fast with those who have this opening, one will easily stay awake. Their energy counteracts the tᵃmᵃs that produces sleep.

Food sensitivity is also increased and those with this opening prefer to eat grains, pulses, and a few vegetables simply cooked.

Signs of a block. When no energy is flowing through the first of the sixth the capacities just described will be absent. Until the age of puberty, all microchakras in the sixth chᵃkrᵃ in the left channel are somewhat open.

R6:2 and L6:2

Right Channel 6:2

Causes of an opening. Massaging the baby with appropriate oils will facilitate the opening of R6:2.

Causes of a block. Vigorous intercourse after the first twenty weeks will cause R6:2 to become blocked.

Left Channel 6:2

Signs of an opening. When the second microchakra within the sixth chᵃkrᵃ (L6:2) is open, an urge to perform spiritual practice (saadhᵃnaa) arises spontaneously. The majority of those with this opening remain householders while some take to the path of renunciation. They have no karmic obligation to reproduce and may choose to be celibate. If they marry, they can engage in sexual activity to respond to the desire of their spouse. Gravity does not pull their sexual energy down so they do not experience compulsive sexual drive.

All sexual energy is converted from bᴇndu (a normal form of life force) to ojᵃs (life force of a higher vibration), giving the skin a radiance. No energy in any form is wasted; all of it is conserved inside and used with care. One relates equally well to any person of either sex.

Those with energy flowing in this microchakra have mastery over *water* in themselves. They can turn off thirst at will. Thus, when they fast, they can abstain from liquids as well as solid foods. They are also able to detect *water* in the breath of others.

Sensitivity to the guɴᵃ-s signifies that this microchakra is open. The nature and vibrations of food may be detected with ease. Enormous creative ability is available, including the spontaneous capacity to produce cosmically oriented art and poetry.

Those renunciates who have L6:2 open feel no need to work in exchange for the things they need. It is taken for granted that those things will come to them—and that is generally what happens. Devotees bring offerings in return for darshᵃnᵃ (sitting quietly and absorbing the teacher's energy).

When this microchakra is open, there may be an awareness of previous incarnations of self or others. Predictions of the future may also occur.

Signs of a block. When the second microchakra of the sixth chᵃkrᵃ (L6:2) is blocked, desire for attention from the opposite sex lingers on. Regulating sexual urges and transforming energy for creative purposes is difficult but possible. Control of breath or other practices geared toward spiritual development is unintelligible to those whose second of the sixth is blocked.

R6:3 and L6:3

Right Channel 6:3

Causes of an opening. Dim light is nurturing to R6:3. Normal indoor daylight and dim light at night teach the baby the difference between day and night. These precautions protect the light sensitive pineal gland, the sense organ of the sixth chᵃkrᵃ.

The complementary connection to R6:3 is R3:6—the relation with the same-sex parent. It is a lot easier to open R3:6 if R6:3 is already open.

Causes of a block. If the light in the delivery room is harsh or dazzling, R6:3 will be blocked. It is common sense that after nine months in the darkness of the womb, the baby needs gradual and gentle exposure to light. During the first forty days, the baby should not be left in the bright sunlight without shade.

Left Channel 6:3

Signs of an opening. An open L6:3 allows recognition of *fire* in the breath of others. The duration of *fire* in the breath can also be lengthened, shortened, or sustained, or the dominance can be switched to another element.

The ability to meditate begins to blossom with the flow through L6:3. This opening is nurtured by being awake in the first-chᵃkrᵃ hour (Brᵃhmᵃ muhoortᵃ). The causal body becomes radiant in the *fire* transmitted through the opening in the third of the sixth.

If the first and second microchakras of the sixth chᵃkrᵃ are also open, one is freed from the dominance of tᵃmᵃs guNᵃ. Those with these openings are then only influenced by the rᵃjᵃs and sᵃtvᵃ guNᵃ-s. They have a great deal of intensity about them for they always want to convert any tᵃmᵃs that is around into sᵃtvᵃ. They do so very rapidly by means of high energy rᵃjᵃs. When the sixth chᵃkrᵃ becomes fully open even this activity is no longer necessary because then the guNᵃ-s no longer hold sway.

People with this opening have the potential to see clearly the downward flow of the solar energy and the upward flow of the lunar energy, both in themselves and others.

The third microchakra of the sixth chᵃkrᵃ (L6:3) is very difficult to open. However, when it is open, it contributes to the strength of the causal ego and plays a very important part in spiritual development. If the inner guru (L5:6, C5:6, and R5:6) is fully open, it will guide the aspirant toward an opening of this microchakra. On the other hand, if the inner guru is only partially open, it may guide the aspirant to an external guru, whose word is taken as truth and to whom the benefit of any doubt is given. This will all be in an effort to open L6:3.

When L6:3 is open it functions as a prism (though much less intense than C6:3). When inner vision is directed upward through this prism, we are beyond spacetime and the experience is of white light. When vision is directed downward through the prism, we are within spacetime and the experience is of multicolor light and the world of names and forms. The strength of this prism is increased significantly if C6:3 is also open.

When the prism has been established, the darkness of the planet Saturn (which shadows the light) is gradually removed from the sixth chᵃkrᵃ.

Signs of a block. If you have the third microchakra of the sixth chᵃkrᵃ (L6:3) closed, it is not possible to liberate yourself from the domination of *fire*. You will remain caught in the rᵃjᵃs and tᵃmᵃs guɴᵃ-s and will not be able to feel completely free from the solar and lunar pulls on the left and right hemispheres of the brain.

The desire to impress others lingers. It may manifest in decorating yourself in front of a mirror and being concerned with an impressive appearance. A preoccupation with fame persists. Even spiritual leaders and aspirants can be affected. Real refinement of ego remains difficult.

Psychologically, you may experience unease and restlessness and indulge in futile pursuits to satisfy seemingly unquenchable desires.

Historically there have been incidents of disciples with this block betraying their gurus by stealing their knowledge or followers or both. This situation is worsened by blockage in R4:6 and R6:4. It is easy for such people to lie to themselves and others.

R6:4 and L6:4

Right Channel 6:4

Causes of an opening. The practice of placing a newborn infant upon the bosom of the mother facilitates the opening of R6:4. Every cell responds to the mother's loving touch. The texture and shine of baby's skin becomes more radiant and the foundation for security and calm is established. The bond between mother and infant is strengthened in all three fields.

Causes of a block. If the fetus experiences aggression while in the womb R6:4 will be blocked. Rough handling after birth, including the placing of the baby on a cold weighing scale, blocks this microchakra. If the baby is held upside down and slapped, blockage is certain.

Left Channel 6:4

Signs of an opening. When L6:4 is open, identification with feelings has lessened considerably. When the fourth of the sixth forms a pattern with the fourth microchakras in the chᵃkrᵃ-s below it, most identifications with feelings may be transcended. If a square of sixth microchakras is formed (see chapter 4), intuition becomes the dominant form of mentation.

People who open this microchakra are gifted with mastery over *air*; they can guide this element at will and detect it in others. They can undertake the most extreme austerities, and therefore take the most arduous vows. (Should these vows be broken, difficulties will result later in life or in subsequent lives.)

If the first, second, and third microchakras in the sixth chᵃkrᵃ are also open, then control of the tᵃmᵃs guNᵃ may be achieved. Individuals may now concentrate their efforts on freeing themselves from the pull of the rᵃjᵃs guNᵃ. At this point, with some help from central channel openings, the KuNDᵃlᴇɴᴇᴇ will automatically start to rise toward the third lᴇɴgᵃ from her second base in the fourth chᵃkrᵃ.

Compassion reaches its zenith when the fourth of the sixth is open. Sensitivity is so great that the pain of others will be felt, whether that of a human, animal, or plant. An ability develops to take on the burden of the kᵃrmᵃ-s and pain of others when additional fourth microchakras are joined with it in a hexagram.

If those with this opening also have an opening in C6:4 they can sense whether a microchakra is open by holding their breath. They are able to hear the sound of a block, as if it were coming through a hollow tunnel.

If there is an accompanying opening in L6:7 then the *fire* in C5:6 can be extinguished and the inner guru will stay awake for further guidance. The gratitude to the outer guru remains everlasting.

Signs of a block. If L6:4 is completely blocked it is difficult to experience yourself as a spiritual being. As breath slows down in meditation, fear may arise and L6:4 may become restricted. However, if L6:4's complementary microchakra L4:6 is open, then thoughts of the opposite-gender parent may come to allay the fear. Alternatively, you may cling to a deity.

R6:5 and L6:5

Right Channel 6:5

Causes of an opening. Because in the womb all sounds are filtered through the mother's body, the newborn baby's first exposure to outside sounds marks a transformational point.

For the first time, the baby is able to directly apprehend the element of *aakaashᵃ*. The quality of that *aakaashᵃ* sets the tone for baby's subsequent relationship to this element. For this reason a major Indian tradition holds that the Gayatri mᵃntrᵃ—whispered into baby's left ear immediately after birth—will maintain the baby's inherently divine nature. The Gayatri mᵃntrᵃ has the capacity to keep the three lɛngᵃ-s connected so they feel like one. As the mᵃntrᵃ is whispered, a small metal rod (steel, silver, or gold) the size of a thick toothpick is coated with a dab of honey and placed between baby's lips. The first taste represents the nectar from the somᵃ chᵃkrᵃ.

The sacred hollow sound of a conch in the distance—just as baby's ears are about to appear—would also offer a magnificent welcome to the newborn. The sound of conch is one of the ten inner sounds (naadᵃ) that are naturally available to all babies in the womb. Therefore, the baby would feel at home with that sound and the special *aakaashᵃ* it creates, while it can inspire and energize a powerful pushing action in the mother. In ancient India there used to be a custom that, outside of the delivery room, drums were played and bells were rung. Drums and bells also belong to the inner sounds (naadᵃ-s).

In general, an open R6:5 fertilizes the ground so that later in life the person will be able to use sound and silence for spiritual development.

Causes of a block. Loud sounds while the baby is still in the womb can cause a block of R6:5. They may also cause blockage during delivery. Mother's screams of pain can be a contributory factor. The intensity of the pain can be diminished by appropriate coaching during pregnancy and birthing. Mother can be taught to use her breath in such a way as to minimize the pain with long sounds of both "Aaa" and "Eee." Universally, baby's first sound is "Aaa!" It is the sound of arrival. When mother responds to baby in this manner, she can express the joy of its arrival and help herself to work with the pain.

Left Channel 6:5

Signs of an opening. In order for advanced meditation to take place, it is very important that L6:5 be open. It provides a starting point that allows the breath to sustain a rate of four breaths per minute or less.

The flow of energy within this microchakra enables the detection and mastery of *aakaashᵃ* in both self and others. A temporary merging with the Self while hearing internal sounds (naadᵃ sᵃmaadhɛ) frequently occurs in deep meditation. This requires that the fifth microchakras of the lower five chᵃkrᵃ-s join with the fifth microchakra of the sixth chᵃkrᵃ.

Since L6:5 also controls the middle ear, it is important in the maintenance of physical balance against the pull of gravity.

The fifth microchakra in the sixth chᵃkrᵃ is the first location where the subtle symphony of the universe becomes audible. Those with this microchakra open have complete understanding and mastery of the esoteric as well as the exoteric uses of sound, including the ability to hear and respond to eternally reverberating wisdom (rechaa-s), which they find exhilarating. On the other hand, they also appreciate silence and nonverbal communication and they understand the value of speech fasting. For decoding the deeper meanings of the rechaa-s the sixth of the sixth must also be open in both the left and central channels. They love soory^a *aakaash^a* as it helps them to connect with C6:5.

Signs of a block. When the fifth microchakra of the sixth ch^{a}kr^a (L6:5) is blocked, complete mastery over all the five elements cannot be achieved. Consequently, full control of the thoughts and desires of the lower five minds is lacking.

R6:6 and L6:6

Right Channel 6:6

Causes of an opening. The pineal gland, sense organ of the sixth ch^{a}kr^a, is extremely light sensitive. Delivery in a dimly lit room minimizes the shock to the pineal gland and to the eyes. During the first forty days after birth, use of a small night-light will stimulate the pineal function and help R6:6 to open. During this tender period, it is also best to keep the baby indoors during the daylight hours. Thus, the baby is not directly exposed to the rays of the sun, which could disrupt the functioning of the light sensitive sixth ch^{a}kr^a.

Causes of a block. Any manipulation of the right or left side of the head during delivery, such as the use of forceps or any other form of forced pulling, causes R6:6 to be blocked.

Left Channel 6:6

Signs of an opening. All men and women have both male and female hormones. When 6:6 is open, a man can perceive and accept female qualities in himself and other men. The reverse is true for women.

When L6:6 is open, the guN^a-s may be balanced and control of the thoughts and desires of the lower five minds is possible. Intuition of Reality can be available.

If people with this opening also have the sixth of the sixth in the central channel (C6:6) open, all three lEng^a-s will operate in harmony. Accordingly, these people will be very centered in their spiritual identity. They will also have the ability to detect the elements in the breath of others. Their more refined energy can influence the grosser energy of others, thus helping them to advance spiritually. That is why people make difficult pilgrimages to visit saints.

The lifestyle of those with the sixth of the sixth open is distinctive. They employ only a limited repertoire of consciously selected gestures, postures, and movements.

That is, they have certain ways of sitting, certain hand gestures, certain movements, which are their "signatures." They are never seen in odd, haphazard positions. Both their fasts and diets are very regular and very pure. In fact, their whole existence seems to flow in a simple, pure, and tranquil way. They are true spiritual masters and are revered by both aspirants and nonaspirants.

Individuals with this opening have a great capacity for discernment. They understand how energy manifests and returns to its source. Their knowledge of the yoga of breath (svᵃrᵃ yogᵃ) may be profound. It unfolds from within rather than being obtained from external teachings.

Because of their insight, and the example they set by their way of living, these people make the very best teachers for sincere students. Having achieved a perfect balance of masculine and feminine energies, they dedicate their lives to entering a state of union with the inner Divinity. They rise above religions, refusing any hierarchical position.

Signs of a block. People with this block are unable to achieve mastery over all of the five elements and are also unable to experience contentment of the lower five chᵃkrᵃ minds. They cannot transcend religious beliefs.

R6:7 and L6:7

Right Channel 6:7
Causes of an opening. Immediately following birth, after the mouth and nose are cleansed, the infant is placed on the mother's abdomen and allowed to nurse. This assures that the baby's first experience is one of contentment. It also reinforces the natural skills of clinging and nursing.

In an ideal delivery, gravity is used to assist the mother; she semi-squats, assisted by midwives who hold her by the armpits. The baby is welcomed as a Divine gift. The neck and base of skull are received with a soft warm cotton blanket. After the birth, joyful chants are repeated. Tuneful tones and overtones are comforting to the baby.

Causes of a block. Any amount of pressure or hard touch on top of the sixth chᵃkrᵃ region of the head, during delivery, blocks R6:7. Examples of blockers are forceps, vacuum extraction, and drugs given for delivery.

Left Channel 6:7
Signs of an opening. When the seventh microchakra of the sixth chᵃkrᵃ (L6:7) is open, an extraordinarily high quality of contentment prevails. The person is almost free of the guɴᵃ-s, though sᵃtvᵃ still retains a slight influence. The intuition of Reality brings total contentment.

Signs of a block. When the seventh microchakra of the sixth chᵃkrᵃ (L6:7) is blocked, none of the capacities described above are available.

THE SEVENTH CHᵃKRᴬ

It is
It is only appearance
It is neither me nor you
nor is it in the whole
Illusion is in me
Illusion is the whole
It is beyond all illusions
All illusions are beyond it
It is because
It just is

S. BHATNAGAR

R7:1 and L7:1

Right Channel 7:1

Causes of an opening. Proper nutrition during the first twenty weeks of life contributes to the opening of R7:1.

Causes of a block. Lack of adequate and organically nutritious food for the well-being of mother and child, during the first twenty weeks of life, causes R7:1 to become blocked. If the mother's diet is healthy, but she eats in an unpleasant environment or in a depressed state of mind, this microchakra will close.

Obesity in children and adults usually finds its origin in this microchakra, especially if the complementary R1:7 is also blocked. Obesity in many cases is an expression of discontent in relation to food, which stirs issues of insecurity. To mask insecurity and boredom, people eat indiscriminately.

Left Channel 7:1

Signs of an opening. When the first microchakra of the seventh chᵃkrᵃ is open (L7:1) the sense of smell is completely internalized. Hence all experiences of smell are from the subtle plane. Externally produced smells are not noticed. Fine aromas do not please nor do unpleasant aromas disturb.

When the breath stops and the ego merges into the Self—as a wave settles into the sea from which it emerged—sᵃmaadhᴇ is said to occur. During sᵃmaadhᴇ the brain lives off praaɴᵃ stored through long years of advanced spiritual effort, especially the performance of certain respiratory disciplines. If L7:1 is open, an *earth* sᵃmaadhᴇ (jᵃdᵃ sᵃmaadhᴇ) may be attained through spiritual exercises aided by roots, plants, and extracts that have psychedelic properties.

R7:2 and L7:2

Right Channel 7:2

Causes of a block. After approximately the first twenty weeks, the fetus is sufficiently formed to respond to the experiences of the mother. Normal sexual intercourse then creates stress for the fetus that registers in the second microchakra of the seventh chᵃkrᵃ. Abstinence from intercourse during this period is required if the parents wish to maintain an opening in this microchakra of their child. They can find other types of sexual activity to express their love.

Left Channel 7:2

Signs of an opening. When the second microchakra of the seventh chᵃkrᵃ (L7:2) is open, the sense of taste is completely internalized. Hence all experiences of taste are from the subtle plane. Externally produced tastes are not noticed. Fine tastes do not please nor do disgusting tastes disturb. Sᵃmaadhᴇ may be attained while breathing the *water* element (jᵃlᵃ sᵃmaadhᴇ) and may be maintained while sitting underwater for an extended period of time. Enough praaɴᵃ is stored in the brain that no damage will occur.

R7:3 and L7:3

Right Channel 7:3

Causes of a block. This microchakra represents the ego in the context of the seventh chᵃkrᵃ, the chᵃkrᵃ for contentment. If the mother has ambivalent feelings concerning her pregnancy or is resentful of it, this microchakra responds by blocking the natural flow of energy and warmth to the baby. It also shuts down if the mother does not receive support and cheerfulness from significant others, particularly her husband.

A domineering and angry attitude of either mother or father, or repeated fights between them, has a negative effect upon R7:3. The tender ego of the baby translates the negative vibrations from the parents as impediments to its natural state of blissful contentment.

One consequence of this block is that the important connection between the third chᵃkrᵃ and the seventh chᵃkrᵃ is weakened.

Left Channel 7:3

Signs of an opening. When the third microchakra of the seventh chᵃkrᵃ (L7:3) is open, the sense of sight is completely internalized during meditation. Hence all experiences of sight are from the subtle plane. Externally produced sights are not noticed. Fine sights do not please nor do foul sights disturb.

The *fire* (agnᴇ) element is stored to sustain a sᵃmaadhᴇ that an advanced yogi can enter at will. Such yogis are usually in a state of surrender to the Divine wherein actions are taken without desire. In other words, these yogis are intuitively tuned to retᵃ (natural law) and live in the present moment. They act as the autonomic nervous system of humanity.

R7:4 and L7:4

Right Channel 7:4

Causes of a block. It is important to avoid creating any pressure on the fetus during the last two trimesters of pregnancy. Overly strenuous exercise—particularly if it leads to overbending or twisting of the spine—may block the fourth microchakra of the seventh chᵃkrᵃ (R7:4). Accidental falls can have the same effect. The receptors for touch in the skin respond to such pressures.

When the baby's movement is restricted, the skin registers negative memories. No amount of touch will compensate. Feelings of being unloved will prevail unless they are overcome by psychospiritual practice.

Left Channel 7:4

Signs of an opening. When the fourth microchakra of the seventh chᵃkrᵃ (L7:4) is open, the sense of touch is completely internalized. Hence all experiences of touch are from the subtle field. Externally produced touch is not noticed. Gentle touches do not please nor do rough touches disturb. Feelings, positive or negative, also generate no reaction. Unconditional love for the Divine prevails.

Love for one's own Divinity (bhᵃktᴇ sᵃmaadhᴇ) is achievable, and—through praaɴᵃ stored in the brain—sustainable.

R7:5 and L7:5

Right Channel 7:5

Causes of a block. Harsh or frightening sounds during the last two trimesters of pregnancy block this microchakra. Doctrinaire child-rearing practices, such as adhering to a strict feeding schedule or letting an infant cry, do the same.

Left Channel 7:5

Signs of an opening. When the fifth microchakra of the seventh chᵃkrᵃ (L7:5) is open, the sense of sound is completely internalized. Hence all experiences of sound are from the subtle field. Externally produced sound is not noticed. Harmonious sounds do not please nor do discordant sounds disturb. Sᵃmaadhᴇ may be attained while absorbing *aakaashᵃ*. It is derived from internally produced sound (naadᵃ sᵃmaadhᴇ). A noisy environment cannot disturb this sᵃmaadhᴇ.

R7:6 and L7:6

Right Channel 7:6

Causes of a block. During delivery, if the sides of the head are manipulated by hands, forceps, or vacuum extraction, an imbalance is created in the functioning of this microchakra. This affects all of the microchakras in the region of the head where balanced energy is essential for the growth of discernment.

Left Channel 7:6

Signs of an opening. When the sixth microchakra of the seventh chᵃkrᵃ (L7:6) is open, the realization dawns of the vast spiritual power that is now available and of the need to decide how to use it. Some choose to proceed to open the seventh of the seventh and then leave the body. Others choose to come down to the fifth of the seventh and live as wandering saints.

Whether or not to accept followers is another decision that must be made. There are those who decide to live alone, or with only one disciple. The disciple sees to the holy one's needs—which are few—even to the point of helping to dispose of the saint's body after death.

With this microchakra open, saguɴᵃ (with guɴᵃ-s) sᵃmaadhᴇ may be experienced at will. This is the penultimate state of sᵃmaadhᴇ where the only focus is on the tenth gate (see chapter 3).

R7:7 and L7:7

Right Channel 7:7

Causes of an opening. During natural childbirth, intrauterine contractions initiate the downward flow of energy in the right channel. The contractions provide a massage for the fetus's head and facilitate the opening of the seventh microchakra of the seventh chᵃkrᵃ—critical to feelings of contentment.

The importance of the natural head massage due to contractions cannot be emphasized enough. We have seen in chapter 4 that an intuitive communication between mother and child determines the duration of the contractions. For some children, the massage needs to be long and intense in order to allow energy to begin its descent into the right channel. A longer or shorter experience of struggle in the birth canal may have significance beyond our understanding. An unnecessary interference with this struggle will not only inhibit the descent of the seven rays of light in the right channel, but also disrupt the infant's very first experience of "me" and "other," with lasting effect.

Causes of a block. In cesarean birth, the infant not only lacks the stimulus of the contractions, it also does not undergo the struggle and, thereby, does not develop the intelligence of the skin as much. Besides blocking the seventh microchakra of the seventh chᵃkrᵃ, there are other consequences of this experiential deprivation. Because of the lack of having to struggle, cesarean children tend to be more self-centered and may be subject to a prolonged prince or princess complex. They may feel that they deserve things without effort. When they are exasperated, they may experience unpleasant sensations in their skin. They often have difficulty with physical activity; for example, it takes a lot of extra motivation to get the body to exercise. Similar symptoms may occur in cross-breech babies and others whose head does not appear first.

Blockage can also be produced by pressure to the central part of the head before, during, or just after delivery, through physical or vacuum extraction. The soft fontanels are particularly vulnerable to this pressure.

Left Channel 7:7

Signs of an opening. When L7:7 is open, all the guNᵃ-s have been transcended and the person may experience sᵃmaadhE beyond the guNᵃ-s (nErguNᵃ sᵃmaadhE). There is a readiness to leave the body at any time (but there is no preoccupation with death). No attachment to any sensation, feeling, or thought remains. Preparing for the release of the final breath, the person merges with the Witness (saakshEE) and tranquilly observes the detachment from the three bodies, to which one has been chained since last conception.

The lifestyle of those whose seventh microchakra of the seventh chᵃkrᵃ is open is worthy of great respect. They have no likes or dislikes, no preferences, plans, goals, or complaints. They are beyond the polar opposites.

One such saint—Ram Tirth, a mathematician turned swami—expressed such a state of being in this way:

Pleasure or Pain
Loss or Gain
Fame or Shame
Are All the Same.

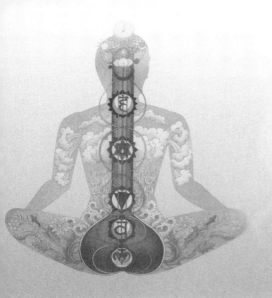

8
Advanced Microchakra Dynamics

MEMORY

Memory and the Channels

Microchakra Psychology suggests that all memory is stored in the three channels. The right channel contains those memories that have been constructed during the right-channel age. After this time, all memories of the current life are stored in the left channel. The central channel contains the sum total of accumulated wisdom and memories from all past lives. These are rarely accessed consciously.

Also stored in the central channel are the instinctive patterns acquired in the long evolutionary climb. Some of these are discussed in chapter 9. The "collective unconscious" postulated by Carl Jung[1] and the "morphogenetic field" postulated by Rupert Sheldrake[2] may also be accessed by means of the central channel.

At the time of death all information in the left channel regarding fulfilled and unfulfilled desires, memories, and accumulated wisdom from the present birth is passed to the central channel. This is done by means of the seventh microchakras of each chᵃkrᵃ. Kundᵃlᴇnᴇᴇ then rises and takes with it all the contents out of the central channel as it leaves the body. These contents become part of the accumulated (sᵃmchᴇtᵃ) kᵃrmᵃ in preparation for the next birth. Hence memory is the basis for the cycle of birth, death, and rebirth.

> *Krishna speaks:*
> *Many of My births have passed away, Arjuna.*
> *I am cognizant of all of them.*
> *You, super aspirant, know none.*
> BHᵎGVAT GEETAA IV.5
> (BHATNAGAR TRANS.)

Habit

In any psychology, particularly one that espouses personal growth, the power of habit must be given appropriate consideration. A classic statement of this power was provided by William James:

> Habit is thus the enormous fly-wheel of society, its most precious conservative agent. It alone is what keeps us all within the bounds of ordinance, and saves the children of fortune from the envious uprisings of the poor. It alone prevents the hardest and most repulsive walks of life from being deserted by those brought up to tread therein. It keeps the fisherman and the deck-hand at sea through the winter . . . It dooms us all to fight out the battle of life upon the lines of our nurture or our early choice, and to make the best of a pursuit that disagrees, because there is no other for which we are fitted, and it is too late to begin again. It keeps different social strata from mixing. Already at the age of twenty-five you see the professional mannerism settling down on the young commercial traveler, on the young doctor, on the young minister, on the young counselor-at-law. You see the little lines of cleavage running through the character, the tricks of thought, the prejudices, the ways of the "shop," in a word, from which the man can by-and-by no more escape than his coat-sleeve can suddenly fall into a new set of folds. On the whole, it is best he should not escape. It is well for the world that in most of us, by the age of thirty, the character has set like plaster, and will never soften again.[3]

James' observation, made in the nineteenth century, is still very applicable today. From his era until the rise of cognitive science in the 1960s, the concept of habit held a central place in psychology. It was buttressed by two methods for strengthening or weakening habits: classical (Pavlovian) conditioning and instrumental (Skinnerian) conditioning. Though it recognizes that the power of habit is important, neither the concept nor the procedures of conditioning are given emphasis in Microchakra Psychology. The subtleties of ch^{a}kr^a mentation require a different approach.

Memory and the Microchakras

In the subtle field, memory is stored in *pods* that are directly connected to the microchakras. Each pod may receive information from its microchakra or send information to it.

A microchakra with its pods functions as a unit that contributes to current information processing and experience. This unit may be described as a unit of energy/information wherein the energy is the quiddities of eightfold nature (supplied primarily by the microchakra) and the information is supplied primarily by the pods. There are two types of pods: *praanic pods* and *apaanic pods* (see plate 12).

Praanic pods contribute to the opening of a microchakra. They contain memories of events wherein praaɴᵃ (the vital life force) was flowing freely. Pleasant and joyful experiences register in the praanic pods.

Apaanic pods contribute to the blockage of a microchakra. They contain memories of toxic events and traumas filled with apaanᵃ.

Pods are intrinsically related to the quiddities and enhance or hinder their purity. A given pod contains many different memories. These are discussed using the theoretical concept of "schema."

Schemas

In almost any psychology it is necessary to have some method for theorizing about the contents of memory. Contemporary cognitive science often uses the concept of "schema" to represent the hypothesized structure of a memory. There is significant variation in the manner in which this concept has been used in cognitive science. Microchakra Psychology adapts the concept to the larger theoretical framework that it teaches, extending its theoretical properties into the nonmaterial fields.

Schemas often represent a combination of thought, feeling, and action—either above or below the threshold of awareness. This combination may include verbal and nonverbal material. In a schema representing a close relative, such as an aunt, there may be numerous subschemas. These represent the many memorable times you have spent with her and of dialogues that you have had. If these times have helped to open up L1:3 and L3:3, for example, their respective praanic pods will contain the relevant portions of that "aunt" schema.

A confident speaker would have a triangle of fifth microchakras (L1:5, L2:5, L3:5) open along with their associated praanic pods. These pods contain schemas of past successfully delivered speeches. The energy/information from this combination of microchakras and pods will give further clarity and life to the current speech.

A collection of schemas forms a schematic network. The adult schematic network contains a vast amount of information about the external world together with personal experiences and opinions that range from wise to unwise. Some of these opinions are simply echoes of the views of others, some are based on careful investigation and reasoning, and some have come from repeated difficult experiences. They all serve to either help or hinder psychospiritual growth.

Two simultaneous processes can bring about changes in a schema: a) *assimilation,* the addition of new information to the schema, and b) *accommodation,* the adjustment of the schema to the implications of the new information. These definitions are based on the work of the Swiss psychologist Jean Piaget, who introduced them in the 1920s. He thereby anticipated the rise of cognitive science by some forty years. Microchakra Psychology hypothesizes that assimilation and accommodation are continuously occurring as information arrives. Major efforts at personality change place significant demands on these processes.

Scripts

A script is a sequence of thoughts or actions. Scripts, like schemas, are thought forms that originate in the causal field. They specify the progression that an ego should follow in order to attain a specific goal of its chᵃkrᵃ. Hence there are first chᵃkrᵃ scripts through seventh chᵃkrᵃ scripts. For example, a first-chᵃkrᵃ cooking script specifies the items to be assembled for a recipe and the order and manner of combining the ingredients.

Individuals have many scripts for expressing their values and their affects. These scripts help them to do such things as make ethical decisions, participate in social organizations, communicate their viewpoints, and show their feelings.

Children, from their earliest years, are taught scripts by their parents and other adults: how to prepare for bed, how to greet the neighbors, what to do on the way to school, etc. Teenage rebellion is partly the desire to cast off scripts written by others and to commence to write one's own first-lEngᵃ scripts.

If an individual is eventually attracted to the path of ego refinement, old scripts will have to be dropped or revised. When energy rises to the higher lEngᵃ-s, the possibility of new scripts that utilize these energies emerges. Some of the practices of InnerTuning involve examining and rewriting one's scripts.

For an extensive discussion of the topic of scripts see Tomkins (1987).

INFORMATION PROCESSING
AND THE SEVEN CHᴬKRᴬ MINDS

When we experience ignorance or uncertainty about a topic our thinking about it may be momentarily halted, confused, or numbed; there is no clear path forward. Information is a reduction in that uncertainty. This reduction may take place through observation, reasoning, feeling, or intuition. By means of its microchakras, each chᵃkrᵃ has access to all these methods of processing information. Information always commences in the thought body, then flows to the feeling body, and finally enters the physical body. The continuous engagement of a chᵃkrᵃ in the processing of information from all three bodies makes a chᵃkrᵃ a "mind." Each chᵃkrᵃ mind can operate independently or in conjunction with one or more other chᵃkrᵃ minds.

Each mind attempts to reach the goals of its play, as described earlier, and achieve contentment.

Awareness

Awareness is frequently compared to a screen upon which images appear. This analogy is useful as a first approximation. However, a screen usually consists of a homogeneous substance such as a movie screen or blank wall. The screen of awareness is not homogeneous but varies with circumstances. It is permeable and easily modified by a variety of factors including intoxicants and the guᴺa-s. The effect of lethargy (tᵃmᵃs) is obvious, as drowsiness alters our awareness. The increasing effect of purity (sᵃtvᵃ) on awareness is an important consequence of continued spiritual practice. As we ascend the path of ego refinement, the accompanying field of awareness also becomes more refined. Awareness reaches its ultimate state of refinement when it is able to merge with Consciousness.

The analogy of awareness as a screen may also be inhibiting to those whose awareness is felt to be vibrating all around them. They may, instead, feel the world happening as a Divine play of life (ʟᴇᴇlaa), which exists on the authority of Consciousness.

The Threshold of Awareness. Information processing in the chᵃkrᵃ-s and microchakras is constantly happening whether we are aware of it or not. In the former case, it is said to occur above the threshold of awareness; in the latter case, below the threshold. This distinction may be particularly helpful when we need to seek the source of some of our thoughts and feelings.

Types of Mentation

Microchakra Psychology refers to the varied information processing activities of a chᵃkrᵃ mind as "mentation." There are four primary types of mentation: observing, intuiting, feeling, and reasoning. Microchakra Psychology asserts that psychospiritual growth requires improvement in all aspects of our information processing: observing, reasoning, feeling, and intuiting. Many of the methods of InnerTuning are designed to help bring about this improvement. It is by means of mentation and behavior that schemas in the left channel are modified. Some modifications move one toward the repayment of karmic debt; others create more debt. For example, building the skills of a nurse aids one in repaying those debts involving service to others. Building the skills of a robber moves one in the opposite direction.

Each individual has a unique path back to the Self. The manner in which we employ the gift of mind determines this path. Sri Ātmanandendra advises us to be grateful for the human birth we have at hand. There is no guarantee that the next birth will provide an equal opportunity to advance our spiritual awareness.

Observing

Observing is a function of the third chªkrª and third microchakras. It is dependent upon the element of *fire* as sight and the sense organ of the eyes. When the eyes are directed outward we can observe the flow of information in the external environment. This observation has many types of sophistication associated with it, which range from the innocence of a baby to that of a trained observer such as a detective or microbiologist.

Observation may also be directed inward toward the other three functions: we can observe ourselves intuiting, feeling, or reasoning. Whether the term "observation" is referring to external observation or internal observation can usually be determined from the context of its use. In the context of psychospiritual growth, it usually refers to internal observation and, as such, is of unique importance. Through observation a chªkrª mind learns about its own processes and how to improve them or transcend them and pass its energy to the next higher chªkrª.

Observation involves creating a distance between the object or process observed and the ego that does the observing. In some cases the ego is so attached to the object or bound up in the mental process that it is difficult or impossible to take sufficient distance to observe.

The ability to observe is derived from that aspect of Consciousness known as the Witness (saakshEE). To directly avail oneself of the Witness, the third-chªkrª downward-pointing *fire* triangle must reverse. A second opportunity arises after the inner guru awakens and one is beyond the elements.

Intuiting

Intuiting requires direct resonance in harmony with the causal field in order to receive information from it. Acquisition of information in this way requires neither feeling nor reason, though they may sometimes play supportive roles. The sixth chªkrª and the sixth microchakras are the source of this ability.

First-lEngª intuitions are concerned with the everyday world. For example, in the first chªkrª, L1:6 may provide direction to a person who has been wandering in the woods and suddenly realizes "I am lost." In the second chªkrª, a vibrant L2:6 may leave no doubt that a certain person should be your mate for life. Third chªkrª decisions regarding career choice are made with great confidence if L3:6 is open.

Second-lEngª intuitions relate to progress beyond an ordinary view of life. In the fourth chªkrª, the principle goal is to surrender ego to a Divine form or cause. An opening in L4:6 makes this surrender occur with certainty. Similar certainty regarding the instant irrevocable recognition of your guru is attained if L5:6 is open in conjunction with openings in L1:6 and L4:6.

Third-lɛngᵃ intuitions pertain to transcendence of the elemental world. When L6:6 is open, intuition is focused on liberation. Sri Swami Satchidānandendra discusses this in his book *Intuition of Reality*.[4] Reason and feeling are gradually transcended in approaching the ultimate Reality.

In all lɛngᵃ-s, intuition may receive wisdom that is connected to the individual's past lives or to the past lives of the whole human species.

Feeling

Feeling is produced in the subtle body by the movement of the elements. By means of the fourth microchakra in each chᵃkrᵃ the ego is able to detect this movement/feeling in all microchakras where it is occurring. For example, activity of the *earth* element may be reflected in such descriptive terms as solid, firm, rooted, or unshakable. Often the elements are blended together and the resultant feeling is complex. Sometimes it is also just floating below the threshold of awareness. The popular technique of "focusing," initially described by E. T. Gendlin,[5] can be helpful in making optimum use of complex feelings that fluctuate around the threshold of awareness.

Reasoning

Reasoning is the preferred method of mentation for many people operating in the first lɛngᵃ. This is reinforced by a cultural bias in favor of reason and against feeling and intuition. Like the other forms of mentation, reason is a skill that can be improved with instruction and practice.

In each chᵃkrᵃ mind, reasoning is a task performed by the ego. There are two types of reasoning: deductive and inductive. In deductive reasoning, if the premises are true, the deduction necessarily follows from them. It is an explication of the truth latent in them. In inductive reasoning, even if the observations are true, they are only a sample of all possible observations and therefore the induction is a probability—not a certainty. Here are two examples:

1. Mommy gets angry when my toys are in a mess. (Premise)
2. My toys are in a mess. (Premise)
3. Mommy will get angry. (Deduction)

1. Jane made a nasty face at me. (Observation 1)
2. Billy said I was stupid. (Observation 2)
3. Roger squirted water at me. (Observation 3)
4. My classmates don't like me. (Induction)

Like the other forms of mentation, the fundamental purpose of reason is to pursue truth and ultimately to contribute to a chᵃkrᵃ mind that vibrates with truth. However, reason is very susceptible to untruth. This is partly due to the fact that the first lɛngᵃ is the home of powerful emotions that may distort reason and establish false premises as part of an ego's belief system.

THREE FUNCTIONS OF THE EGO

In all cases actions are performed by the
guNᵃ-s created by nature.
Underdeveloped ego thinks "I am the doer."

BHᵃGVAT GEEtaa 3:27
(BHATNAGAR TRANS.)

The above passage from the Bhᵃgvat GEEtaa asserts the power of eightfold nature in comparison with the relatively frail and easily misled ego. It is particularly true for the egos of the first lɛngᵃ. In the second lɛngᵃ, the egos have become more refined and are less likely to become confused. In the third lɛngᵃ, eightfold nature itself is transcended and loses its power over the ultrarefined amount of remaining ego—which values no goal other than liberation from all seven chᵃkrᵃ minds.

A jɛɛvᵃ works out the praarᵃbdhᵃ kᵃrmᵃ of its present birth through the egos, so an increased understanding of how they work will help us to make best use of praarᵃbdhᵃ karmᵃ. Each ego can function in three different ways: Player, Observer, or Me-maker. Any of these functions may call upon the ego's powers of mentation. These functions may take place both above and below the threshold of awareness.

Player. When functioning as a player, an ego uses its current structure (ego-schema) to interact with an environment and pursue its goals. The environment is represented in awareness and may be the external physical environment or the internal environment of thoughts, feelings, and intuitions.

In the first lɛngᵃ, an ego may play such roles as son, husband, father, mechanic, coach, and citizen. In the second lɛngᵃ, roles may include worshipper, priestess, social worker, nurse, and chanter. In the third lɛngᵃ, only one role is possible: aspirant for liberation from all seven chᵃkrᵃ minds.

Observer. An ego functions as observer when its activity is limited to that component of mentation called observing, described above.

Me-maker. When an ego uses the processes of assimilation and accommodation to change its own schema (ego-schema) it is functioning as Me-maker.

Egos and the Microchakras

The third microchakra contains the *fire* energy in the chᵃkrᵃ and so functions as the assertive leader or ego of the chᵃkrᵃ mind. In attempting to reach the goals that life has assigned to its chᵃkrᵃ, the ego must create itself by asking questions and making decisions—hence it is also called the Me-maker. The Me-maker may draw upon the resources of the other microchakras as it performs its tasks. For stability, it utilizes the openings of the first microchakra. The energy available in the second microchakra helps it in interaction with others. From the fourth microchakra, it is able to receive a capacity to feel and empathize. This serves as a balance to its own natural power of reasoning. The fifth microchakra helps the Me-maker to express itself and to generate creative approaches to its goals. Potentially offering the most help is the sixth microchakra. It is the intuitive capacity of the chᵃkrᵃ mind and the source of its greatest wisdom. Decisions based on clear intuition surpass those based on reason. If the Me-maker is mature enough, it will be able to surrender to the decisions of the sixth microchakra. The seventh microchakra will register contentment only when the goals of the chᵃkrᵃ mind have been met.

EGOS AS DOERS

Both as player and as Me-maker, an ego engages in a variety of relationships with the objects surrounding it, which are listed in Table 8.1. In the terminology of Franz Brentano, a nineteenth-century psychologist, these may be regarded as "mental acts." Microchakra Psychology sees them as commencing in the thought body.

TABLE 8.I. SOME BASIC ACTS OF AN EGO

Binding
Imitating
Choosing
Identifying
Disidentifying
Willing
Imagining
Denying
Surrendering
Listening
Aligning

An ego implements these activities by drawing upon its powers of mentation and its access to other microchakras—within its own chᵃkrᵃ and through sympathetic resonance with other chᵃkrᵃ-s.

Binding

Binding refers to a theoretical step in schema formation. It occurs when the Me-maker establishes an affective relationship with an object. The affect becomes part of the schema and may be thought of as being like a glue that holds the object within the rest of the ego-schema. Hence an ego may relate to various objects through such ties as love, gratitude, and disgust. Sometimes the binding is complex, such as when the ego loves, fears, and is distressed by the same object. When bindings contribute to blocks, effort must be directed at weakening or severing them.

Through the concept of binding, Microchakra Psychology introduces the subtle feeling field as an integral part of a schema and gives it causal significance. The assimilation and accommodation of a schema is causally influenced by the affective states that are part of it. For example, if fear has been stored in a schema, it influences the reception of any new information that the schema attempts to assimilate.

Attachment. Whereas the term "binding" has been introduced to refer to a theoretical step in schema formation, the term "attachment" has been widely used by others to refer to a variety of relationships in the physical world. These relationships are the consequence of binding. As S. Goldberg has observed: "Attachment theory is no longer a single theory. There are as many versions of attachment theory as there are attachment researchers."[6] Several spiritual traditions speak of "unattachment" when stressing the power of spirit to overcome matter. Microchakra Psychology uses the term in a similar manner in some contexts.

Imitating

The task of building an ego-schema cannot be avoided. There are two general approaches to it: imitative and imaginative. Imitation is helpful when emphasizing our similarity to others; imagination is useful for discovering and emphasizing our distinctive qualities. Recent research has shown that simple forms of imitation are innate.[7] Infants as young as twelve days are able to reproduce a protruded tongue, a yawn, and a pout when they are modeled by an adult standing before them.

Imitation is a powerful means by which the Me-maker constructs its own ego-schema. There are many times, particularly in the first-chᵃkrᵃ age, when imitation is a useful and appropriate method for ego development. After the first-chᵃkrᵃ age, it remains a useful method for development of a variety of skills such as bicycling, swimming, typing, and chanting. However, after the first-chᵃkrᵃ age, its use in construction of the ego-schema should be highly selective. Inappropriate use will simply become a way of establishing saboteurs, such as imitating the bad habits of friends.

In the second-ch^{a}kr^a age the need to begin the process of self-actualization comes to the fore. It is a very difficult task and clever manipulators of children and young adults know how to work the situation to their advantage. Uniforms for various youth groups (religious, sports, military) are provided. The fragile ego is encouraged to believe that it has done its job by putting on the uniform and imitating the behavior of the other group members. The consumer society peddles an endless variety of objects, which parents must afford so that their offspring can imitate their friends. The parents themselves are subject to the same pressures. *Imitation can never open any seventh microchakra and provide contentment.*

Choosing

The need to choose between one or more objects or goals arises with varying frequency before the ego of each ch^{a}kr^a mind. The implications of the choice range from trivial to serious. In the second and third lɛng^a-s, choices tend to conform to dh^{a}rm^a. The possibility of failing to make a dharmic choice is greatest in the first lɛng^a. Saboteur patterns, including blind imitation, often make the adharmic (not dharmic) choice appear easier. The ego and its champion patterns must be strong enough to overcome the temptations of the easy choice. Whatever the decision, its consequences will appear on the karmic credit card.

Identifying

As the Me-maker attempts to construct a healthy ego-schema, it is aided by champion patterns of microchakras and inhibited by saboteur patterns. At any point in time, the ego-schema is the result of these positive and negative factors. If asked the question, "Who are you?" the ego will respond by describing the contents of its schema. It believes that it is what it has constructed.

An ego is engaged in identifying whenever it uses the pronoun "I:" "I am strong." "I am weak." "I own a house." "I am homeless." "I am rich." "I am poor." "I am healthy." "I am sick." Any of these statements may stand for the current situation as perceived by a first-lɛng^a ego that has identified with them. They all represent a temporary pattern of eightfold nature that praar^{a}bdh^a karm^a may change at any time.

Despite the danger of misusing the pronoun "I," work on ego-schemas must proceed. InnerTuning practitioners recognize this and, when it is a practical necessity to apply the pronoun "I," try to do so with an awareness that it is only a manner of speaking about a specific ch^{a}kr^a mind.

Disidentifying

The psychiatrist Roberto Assagioli has made the following statement:

We are dominated by everything with which our self becomes identified. We can dominate and control everything from which we dis-identify ourselves.

In this principle lies the secret of our enslavement or of our liberty. Every time we "identify" ourselves with a weakness, a fault, a fear, or any personal emotion or drive, we limit and paralyze ourselves. Every time we admit "I am discouraged" or "I am irritated," we become more and more dominated by depression or anger. We have accepted those limitations; we have ourselves put on our chains. If, instead, in the same situation we say, "A wave of discouragement is *trying* to submerge me" or "An impulse of anger is *attempting* to overpower me," the situation is very different.[8]

The first step in disidentifying with an object is for the ego to bring its power of observation fully upon it. When observation is directed inward at the ego's own schema, it creates a distance between the ego and that object within the ego-schema that has been selected for disidentification.

Suppose that I am angry with someone who has made a derogatory remark about me. Since this is an interpersonal relationship, it involves the ego of the second chᵃkrᵃ. To reduce identification with the anger, I might say, "My second chᵃkrᵃ ego is getting angry." I then quiet all speech, including subvocal speech, as much as possible. Sitting still, observation is directed inward toward the binding of anger that exists between the ego and that someone. As observation continues, distance between the observing ego and the anger increases. Saboteurs will arise in an attempt to reduce this distance and abort the process. Many of these will be thoughts about how justified I am to be angry. Even though I have a right to be angry, I do not want this anger in me. It generates apaanᵃ and chains me to the first lᴇngᵃ. I use my will (see below) to dismiss the saboteurs and keep my attention focused on observing the anger. As the anger becomes more distant, the ego may voluntarily summon the element of *aakaashᵃ* and direct it toward the anger. All other elements dissolve in *aakaashᵃ*, including the *fire* element that is at the root of anger. By repeating this process as often as necessary, the binding of anger between ego and the other may be weakened and miniaturized or even eliminated. In a similar way, bindings consisting of other negative affects may be weakened or removed by working directly on an ego-schema.

Willing

The term *willing* refers to the effort (*fire*) used by an ego to attain the goals of its chᵃkrᵃ mind and ultimately its contentment. At times, willing involves simple concentration and direction of the *fire* of the ego; at other times it requires skillful use of mentation. When willing is informed by the ego's sixth microchakra, it functions with wisdom. Without the effort of will no goal may be attained. The goal may be hoped for or its attainment imagined but only through willing can progress be made toward actual achievement. Willing is assisted by champion patterns and resisted by saboteur patterns.

Willfulness. Willing itself may be corrupted by saboteurs. The ego sets false goals that are unrealistic and pursues them with determination. This pursuit is not an example of willing but of willfulness. The sabotaged ego justifies its own acts of folly. This is exemplified when a first-ch^a^kr^a^ ego insists on eating large amounts of food or repeatedly ingesting a drug that it knows is harmful to the body. Sometimes the saboteurs are then able to magnify their influence further by turning willfulness into addiction.

Refinement of willing. As ego ascends the path of refinement, there is a corresponding refinement of willing. The errors of willfulness are usually limited to the first lɛng^a^. In the second lɛng^a^, the ego is attempting to serve other forces in the universe and adjusts its willing to do so ("Not my will, but Thy will"). By the time ego reaches the third lɛng^a^, willing has merged with ret^a^—it now has no goals apart from those of the Cosmic Intelligence (M^a^h^a^t).

Believing

Our beliefs form the foundation of our actions. They determine the nature of our relations with others, the effect on our karmic credit card and the manner in which each ch^a^kr^a^ mind functions. Owning the beliefs of others keeps one tied to the first lɛng^a^.

Intensity of belief. Beliefs vary in intensity from those that the ego holds lightly to those that are held with great passion. The latter may include those with which the ego has completely identified. It is nearly impossible to go beyond them.

Acquisition of belief. Beliefs are acquired through all four methods of mentation. The earliest beliefs are usually based on feeling. They may switch rapidly with changes in feeling, such as the change from "You don't love me!" when Mommy denies a request to "You love me" when an unanticipated gift appears. Later, the child acquires many beliefs through imitation of family members, peers, or television characters. It will also acquire beliefs through its independent exploration of the environment.

Truths and lies. The S^a^mskret^a^ phrase "s^a^t-chɛt-aanand^a^" is sometimes employed as an expanded reference to the indescribable T^a^t ("that which is"; i.e., Consciousness). The phrase may be translated as "Being-Consciousness-Bliss" or as "Truth-Consciousness-Bliss." S^a^t means either "being" or "truth." For Consciousness they are the same. This is the level of absolute purity. Truth is purity and light; it is s^{a}tv^a. Untruth is impurity and darkness; it is t^{a}m^{a}s. To be liberated is to discover absolute Truth, to become a gyaanEE (an actualized being who has transcended any distinction among knower, knowing, and knowledge). Until then, it is necessary to cope with various approximations to Truth.

One of the chief responsibilities of the spiritual aspirant is to seek the truth in each situation in which decisions must be made. This truth may be acquired by reason, feeling, or intuition. It must be recognized, however, that something that appears to be truthful is dependent upon the current schematic network of the seeker. An "objective fact" that may appear as true to one may appear as false to another. The situation that is created by war illustrates this. To one young person, it may appear as true that to express patriotism by joining the military is dharmic. To another, it may appear true that to be a conscientious objector is dharmic. Both must act according to their own perception of dh^{a}rm^a; otherwise they will be hypocrites tending toward devolution.

As the spiritual aspirant seeks the truth, it may be necessary to overcome saboteurs. One of their main tactics is to cause a lie to appear as a truth (or vice versa). In this way, the ego may be tricked into serving the goals of the saboteur.

As energy moves beyond the first lEng^a, it usually becomes easier to locate dh^{a}rm^a when a problematic situation arises, provided that we have the courage to deal with it.

Imagining

Normally our senses are engaged with the external environment and schemas derived from it. However, we may also imagine schemas different from the way things are in the immediate empirical world. These imaginings can serve a variety of purposes including a) entertainment—it may be fun to imagine going on a trip to a foreign country, b) skill development—by imagining ourselves to be better debaters, golfers, pianists, lovers, and so on we can refine the schemas associated with these activities and thereby improve them, c) invention—it is through reworking schemas in the mind that the proverbial "better mousetrap" may be discovered, d) anticipation—the ability to imagine what others might do often facilitates relations with them.

Imagination is fed by the *aakaash^a* of the fifth ch^{a}kr^a and the fifth microchakras. The *aakaash^a* loosens the bindings of schemas enough to permit them to enter into novel combinations with other schemas. Unfortunately, saboteurs as well as champions are able to avail themselves of imagination. In these cases, Microchakra Psychology refers to the activity as "fantasizing." Fantasies are often a clue as to which saboteur patterns are active.

Imagining can often be a very important act for the implementation of dhᵃrmᵃ. A person may have an intuition of the path ahead, but lack the details to proceed. Imagination may provide them. Maslow's term "self-actualizing creativity" may be interpreted as referring to such situations. Jung had a related concept of "individuation."

Microchakra Psychology teaches that once the second and third lᴇngᵃ-s have been activated, a portion of their energy should be directed downward to add to the refinement of the first lᴇngᵃ. This is referred to as "divinizing" the animal brain and thereby the body. It is simply the enhanced use of the energy of sᵃtvᵃ when engaged in the varied activities of the first lᴇngᵃ. Imagination can be of great assistance in doing this.

Denying

Each ego encounters various painful situations: "Daddy does not love me as much as my sister," "I felt so very foolish," "I can't believe my wife wants a divorce," "How could they fire an employee as loyal as me?" "Why is God doing this to me?"

A healthy ego with its supporting champion patterns can face the truth presented by any situation—no matter how painful. On the other hand, if the ego is immature or weakened by saboteurs, it may be unable to face the truth. It finds the pain overwhelming. In such a case, the ego may resort to denial. The truth of the matter is bent and twisted until a schema is formed that is more acceptable to the weak ego. This process of distortion usually occurs below the threshold of awareness. The ego is unaware that it is denying a truth. In psychoanalytic theory, denial is one of the ego defense mechanisms.

Those eager to move along the path of psychospiritual development may sometimes fall into denial. They wish their progress to be rapid and convince themselves that it is—by denying blockages within the first two lᴇngᵃ-s.

Surrendering

The surrender of ego takes many forms, each of which is important to psychospiritual development. The act of surrender is not formally recognized until the second-chᵃkrᵃ age when the possibility strongly emerges and Rakᴇnᴇᴇ appears with two heads. Yet, even in the first-chᵃkrᵃ age, children, particularly younger siblings, may learn to defer to the wishes of others. In some cultures, they are taught to bow with respect to their elders.

The egos of the first lᴇngᵃ are naturally aggressive in pursuit of their goals. Bowing is a gesture (mudraa) that can help to refine them. However, bowing must be accompanied by an appropriate sentiment or it is simply a cultural practice done from habit. The feeling may combine aspects of gratitude, reverence, devotion, love, and loyalty. These flow from fourth microchakras. In many modern societies, overt bowing is regarded as abnormal behavior or the sign of a sycophant. The internal bow is easily substituted. Simply permit the feelings that you wish to express to wash over the ego. You will know that you are bowing.

In India, one common gesture of bowing is to simply place both hands before the chest with palms together and fingers pointed upward. It may be accompanied by the mᵃntrᵃ namᵃstᴀ, which means "I bow to the Consciousness in you."

Listening

The primary method of refining the ego is through recognizing one's dhᵃrmᵃ and following it. For many this is not easy, but it is the essential first step in spiritual development. Yet dhᵃrmᵃ alone will not necessarily take you to the subtler levels of mind. The development of sound sensitivity, on the other hand, may be most useful in accomplishing this. The emergence of sensitivity to *aakaashᵃ,* sooryᵃ *aakaashᵃ,* and the relationship between voice tone and breath are signposts that you will meet along the way.

Aligning

Aligning, in the sense used here, refers to the alignment of the ego with retᵃ. This is possible only in the third lᴇngᵃ when very little ego remains (L6:3 and C6:3). Such an aspirant is beyond the minds and the need to use mentation, and is able to simply align with retᵃ in a manner similar to a migratory bird aligning with magnetic currents of the planet.

PRINCIPLES OF GROWTH AND CHANGE

The flow of information through the microchakras is the basis for a growing, changing, and complex individual. This flow is subject to at least six basic principles. Reflection on these principles from time to time may aid in appreciation of how all three bodies (physical, thought, and feeling) function as a single psycho-spiritual instrument.

The Principle of Releasing

Observers of animal behavior have noted that some stimuli may release specific innate patterns of behavior. They call these stimuli "releasers." An example is a red spot at the tip of a herring gull's beak. Upon seeing it, the baby gull will open its mouth to receive food.

In a similar (but more complex) manner, mᵃntrᵃ, yᵃntrᵃ, and mudraa release patterns of energy flow in the chᵃkrᵃ-s and microchakras. As a science of subtle energies advances, more will be learned about these innate relations.

The Principle of Adaptation

Adaptation refers to the changes in the threshold of awareness that occur due to changes in background stimulation. For example, if the noise of traffic outside your apartment is considerable, your threshold of awareness may automatically shift upward so that you are less often aware of the noise and disturbed by it. In this case, a higher threshold for detecting sound helps to block out unwanted external sounds.

When attention is directed inward, however, the goal is to lower the threshold of sound detection. This is not easy, as many powerful saboteurs work against such achievement. However, those who are successful find that their own thoughts and other sounds can reach awareness from surprisingly low levels of intensity. The practice of silence (mownᵃ) is an important aid in lowering the threshold. Eventually, when certain patterns of microchakras are open, one can hear the classical ten inner sounds (see Table 10.2).

The Principle of Readiness

In the early twentieth century, the psychologist E. L. Thorndike articulated a principle of readiness that stressed the importance of adequate preparation for learning. Such a principle is of paramount importance for those on the psychospiritual path. Premature effort only creates disappointment and strengthens saboteurs. By keeping the principle of readiness in mind, aspirants are able to set a realistic pace based on the current state of their own microchakras.

The Principle of Synchronicity

The principle of synchronicity refers to the simultaneous occurrence of two events with no physical connection. This principle is most understandable through a model of the universe as nonlocal, as is seen when a baby attended by a grandmother at home suddenly awakes and cries, and its mother, several miles away, starts to ooze milk.

The Principle of Emergence

The principle of emergence refers to those situations where two or more entities are combined to produce a third entity whose qualities are unpredictable from its constituents. An example is the combination of hydrogen and oxygen to produce water.

The psychospiritual path is filled with surprises as thoughts, feelings, intuitions, and synchronistic events emerge from seemingly nowhere. In this way, Cosmic Intelligence responds to the efforts of the aspirant.

The Principle of Transcendence

Transcendence takes place in each lɛngᵃ. First-lɛngᵃ transcendence is the surrender of the first three chᵃkrᵃ minds to the second lɛngᵃ. Second-lɛngᵃ transcendence is the surrender of the minds of the fourth and fifth chᵃkrᵃ-s to the third lɛngᵃ. Third-lɛngᵃ transcendence is the surrender of the minds of the sixth and seventh chᵃkrᵃ-s to the Consciousness that we all are.

AFFECTS

The term *affective state* refers to feelings and emotions. The term *affect* alone is used as a shorthand for "affective state." Each such state is characterized by distinctive activity in the thought body, patterns of elements and guɴᵃ-s in the feeling body, and neurochemical and organic activity in the physical body.

Positive and Negative Affects

The distinction between positive and negative affects is a common one—with some variation in the way it is made. In Microchakra Psychology, when an affective state accompanies progress to the goals of a chᵃkrᵃ mind, it is called a *positive affect*. A positive affect derives its energy from openings in the microchakras and associated praanic pods. Examples of positive affect are: joy, nurturance, pride, and love.

On the other hand, when an affective state accompanies a situation that thwarts progress of a chᵃkrᵃ mind, it is called a *negative affect*. These derive their energy from blocks and apaanic pods. Examples of negative affect are: fear, distress, guilt, and vanity.

It is important to note that these definitions are from the perspective of the ego of the chᵃkrᵃ that is seeking to attain its goal. From the perspective of kᵃrmᵃ, an evaluation as "positive" or "negative" may be different. For instance, an individual who has been fired from his job may experience the negative affect of distress. This is what his third chᵃkrᵃ ego is registering. This distress will impel him to look for another job and he may find one more in line with his spiritual path. In hindsight, the negative affect had a positive benefit. Life is filled with many such examples. It is also true that positive affect may produce a negative result from the perspective of kᵃrmᵃ. Too much time spent in joyous play may detract from effort toward spiritual growth.

Positive affects are usually accompanied by some form of pleasure and negative affects by some form of pain.

Early and Later Affects

Both the positive and negative affects are divided into those that occurred early in evolution and those that developed later. The early affects have their primary locus in the central channel and the early (subcortical) brain. Joy and fear are examples of early affects.

The later affects are derived from the early affects but obtained their distinctive qualities primarily through the lunar right hemisphere of the cortex with some assistance from the solar left hemisphere and processes of socialization. Examples of later affects are pride and guilt.

Affects and Spiritual Development

Table 8.2 lists some common affects that are of most interest to the task of spiritual development. These affects, and others, may blend with each other in innumerable combinations.

TABLE 8.2. SOME COMMON AFFECTIVE STATES

Early Positive Affects	Early Negative Affects
Ego Enhancing	Ego Contracting
Joy	Fear
Interest	Anger
Play	Distress
Nurturance	Disgust
Assertiveness	
Later Positive Affects	**Later Negative Affects**
Ego Enhancing	Ego Contracting
Eros	Shyness
Confidence	Shame
Pride	Guilt
Hope	Sadness
	Envy
	Hate

Later Positive Affects	Later Negative Affects
Ego Refining	**Ego Inflating**
Love	Possessiveness
Gratitude	Greed
Serenity	Vanity
Ego Transcending	
Contentment	
Bliss	

Life is a dance of the 147 microchakras, and much of this dance is based upon the affects. We can learn to refine them and use them for our spiritual advancement, we can permit society to control them—and thus control us, or we can allow some affects to run rampant and cause us to devolve. Our current affects are a measure of where we are on our evolutionary journey. Affect is a major means by which our kᵃrmᵃ speaks to us.

Sensations and Drives

The most powerful forms of eightfold nature are stored in the central channel and early brain in the form of drives: to breathe, to eat, to drink, to copulate, to avoid pain. These drives preserve the individual and the species. When necessary, they can easily overwhelm a comparatively weak ego and sweep it away as they proceed to their goals.

The evolutionary path that led to these drives first produced the capacity to experience sensations of pleasure and pain. The sensations and the drives form an ever-present background against which the affects conduct their dance.

Science and the Affects

Naturalistic Observation

An affective state cannot be fully understood without considering its relationship with all three bodies. Nevertheless, the difficult quest to understand affect has been advanced by some who have focused on its physical expression alone. In 1872, Charles Darwin published *The Expression of Emotion in Man and Animals,* which has remained a classic in the field. Examples of his astute observations are quoted in chapter 9. Despite the work of others who continued the tradition of Darwin, the study of affect was rejected by many in the scientific community for much of the twentieth century. These scientists regarded it as an "epiphenomenon," which might accompany behavior but had no causal significance. They were unaware of the feeling and thought bodies.

Another form of naturalistic observation of affect did continue throughout the twentieth century. It took place in the context of counseling and psychotherapy. A large literature emerged, from a variety of theoretical perspectives, describing case histories of those who struggled with severe negative affect.

Experimental Observation

Beginning in the 1960s, significant theoretical and experimental work concerning the affects started to emerge. Much of it focused on new ways to study the facial expression of different affects. The experimental study of affect is now continuing at an accelerating rate.

Of particular interest is recent research aimed at understanding how neural circuits and neurochemistry relate to the affects. Most of this research has been conducted from a strictly materialistic point of view. Nevertheless, a few researchers acknowledge that emotion may involve more than the purely physical. For instance, near the conclusion of his comprehensive *Affective Neuroscience,* J. Panksepp states:

> During the past few decades, three esteemed senior neuroscientists have forcefully disagreed with the traditional and radically monistic *identity* view of the brain-mind debate, siding instead with the perspective that mind is in some essential way separable from the material entities of the brain. First I will summarize the views of Wilder Penfield, a pioneering neurosurgeon who first demonstrated that localized stimulation of the temporal lobes could yield a remarkably faithful subjective reexperiencing of seemingly forgotten events. . . . Next, I will focus on the views of Roger Sperry, who won the Nobel Prize in 1981 for his work on the distinct and separate forms of awareness within each of the cerebral hemispheres. . . . Finally, I will summarize the more radical views of Sir John Eccles, a Nobel Laureate in 1963, who worked out the details of how neurons synaptically generate electrical signals of excitation and inhibition.
>
> After highly productive scientific careers, these scholars chose to dwell on the essential nature of the human spirit. Each found solace, understanding, and hope in the conviction that a distinction between mind and brain functions not only was real but also constituted a vital distinction for understanding the human brain and nature.[9]

Another neuroscientist who appreciates the inadequacies of materialism is Candace Pert. In her groundbreaking book, *The Molecules of Emotion,* she wrote:

If information exists outside of the confines of time and space, matter and energy, then it must belong to a very different realm from the concrete, tangible realm we think of as "reality." And since information in the form of the biochemicals of emotion is running every system of the body, then our emotions must also come from some realm beyond the physical. Information theory seems to be converging with Eastern philosophy to suggest that the mind, the consciousness, consisting of information, exists first, prior to the physical realm, which is secondary, merely an out-picturing of consciousness. Although this is about as radical as my scientist's mind will let me get, I'm beginning to understand how such a view could coexist comfortably with the kind of science I've been doing.[10]

The Stages of an Affect

Affects go through three main stages. The first stage is called *appraisal* and occurs in the causal field; the second stage is called *feeling* and occurs in the subtle field; the third stage is called *emotion* and occurs in the physical field.

Appraisal

The ego of each chᵃkrᵃ mind is continuously monitoring and appraising its environment for signs of change. This is in agreement with the position of R. Lazarus who described the physical organism alone:

> The *fundamental premise* is that in order to survive and flourish, animals (especially humans) are constructed biologically so that they are constantly engaged in evaluations (appraisals) of their changing relationships with the environment. Appraisals involve detection and evaluation of the relevant adaptational conditions of living that require action. These appraisals determine the emotional state, which involves efforts to respond adequately to the adaptational implications of what is happening.[11]

This monitoring may be above or below the threshold of awareness. When a sign of change is detected, appraisal of its meaning for the whole organism takes place in the thought body. Appropriate feelings are then generated in the feeling body through activation of the elements therein. If the intensity of feeling is sufficient, it will be followed by emotional expression in the physical body. For example, imagine the situation of a man who is quietly walking down a jungle trail, rounds a bend and comes face to face with a tiger. The instantaneous appraisal of danger is innate and forms part of the central channel: adult humans have learned to fear tigers through millennia of experience. The appraisal of threat occurs in the thought body and generates the feeling of fear or terror in the feeling body. This feeling explodes into emotional expression in the physical body, activating relevant brain circuits, biochemicals, and behavior, which produce such symptoms of fear as pounding heart, rapid breathing, and cold sweat.

Some appraisals are instantaneous and the next phases follow immediately. This is particularly the case for the early affects that have had innate triggers for millennia. Some appraisals take longer. Ambiguous situations are one example of this. Often we have heard someone say: "I didn't know whether to laugh or cry."

Feeling

Eons of evolution have formed an innate link between the activity of eightfold nature and the feelings that the ego experiences. A feeling is generated within a chᵃkrᵃ mind by the movement of the elements and the influence of the guN ᵃ-s. The ego of the chᵃkrᵃ temporarily attaches to the feeling and identifies with it.

Earth provides feelings of cohesion and solidity. When ego attaches to *earth,* it feels supported and secure. However, in some circumstances, *earth* may cut off the supply of air and produce a feeling of suffocation. Examples are earthquakes and landslides.

Water provides feelings of cooling and of flowing movement. Through the movement of *water,* ego is brought into contact with others. Hence *water* is the basis for sociability. If the other has been appraised as threatening, the disturbed activity of the *water* will contribute to the feeling of fear. If the presence of the other is welcomed, *water* may combine with *fire* to give feelings of pleasure or excitement. When eros is present, *water* makes its contribution to sexual feeling through the sexual fluids. Otherwise, *water* may remain calm and contribute to serenity.

Since the human body is approximately seventy percent *water,* the element of *water* may contribute to a feeling of being nurtured, particularly as thirst is slaked. It may also nurture by cooling the body when it is overheated. Under some circumstances water may drown.

Fire provides the qualities of light and heat (loaned to all by the sun). It is the basic energy of the ego itself. It is through light that the ego observes both its external and internal environments. Through its heat, *fire* contributes to a variety of feelings such as assertiveness, anger, and vanity.

Fire may have a transformative effect. For example, in the first lɛngᵃ, intense spiritual activity (tᵃpᵃs), may convert sluggishness and other forms of tᵃmᵃs into sᵃtvᵃ.

Air provides the quality of dispersion and resultant feeling of buoyancy. It also contributes to the feelings of nourishment and empowerment that we may experience from the praaN inhaled. Healing through touch derives primarily from praaN through *air*.

Air may also be a means of death—such as being swept away in a hurricane.

Aakaash is the quality of space into which the other elements may dissolve. Experiences of ego dissolution in deep meditation are based on highly refined *aakaash*.

When other elements overwhelm *aakaash* there may be feelings of being trapped with no way out, crushed, or annihilated. *Aakaash* itself can kill by means of a frightening sound that could lead to a heart attack. A message carried by sound such as "Your son just died" could have a similar effect.

The guN of t*m*s contributes to feelings of heaviness or of lethargy. R*j*s contributes to feelings of assertiveness or excitement. S*tv* contributes to feelings of purity and light.

All human feeling is derived from some combination of the elements and guN-s—the dance of eightfold nature, the dance of the quiddities. The precise pattern of the dance is influenced by the current state of the microchakras.

Emotion

Expression of an emotion takes place in the physical field, utilizing many different parts of the brain and body. Some of this expression is based on ancient patterns stored in the central channel and early brain. Other forms of expression are more dependent upon the cerebral cortex. They are strongly influenced by societal norms as well as personal idiosyncrasies.

Emotional expression may be inhibited by the practicalities of a situation. We may feel like screaming in anger (affect reaches the feeling stage) but stifle the tendency because the object of our anger has higher social status. We may scream anyway and reap subsequent praise or condemnation (or both) from others. We may express an emotion different from what we feel—an example of either tact or hypocrisy.

This discussion of affect was influenced by the views of Lazarus.[12]

Affect Formation

Ch*kr* minds constantly form and re-form affects. An affect is formed whenever an ego encounters an object. An object may be a physical object, a person, a thought, or other affects. It may also be another part of the ego's own schematic network. Personal beliefs and values are examples of the latter.

That part of the ego that makes the encounter may be above or below the threshold of awareness. Similarly, the object encountered may be above or below the threshold. Encounters involving a component that is below awareness form part of life's mystery: "I don't know what got into me," "I did not know that I could feel that way." Affects may reveal hidden aspects of ego. This revelation may be relatively simple or have ramifications that will require considerable effort and courage to accept.

The ego has the potential to draw upon all microchakras in its mind as it makes its encounters. When it is able to draw upon the sixth microchakra, feeling is informed by intuition: "I feel inspired. Why didn't I see this before?"

Modification of Affect

Modifiability of Trigger

The situational trigger of an affect can be partially or completely replaced through learning. In addition, new triggers may be added. These changes are made by the Me-maker through the methods of schema modification discussed above. For example, a young child may initially have no fear of cars. Concerned adults may then impress the danger of cars upon her. Accordingly, her schema for cars will accommodate to incorporate the affect of fear.

Miniaturization

The Me-maker may learn to reduce the magnitude of emotional expression. A father who habitually expresses flaming and uncontrollable rage toward his son may learn to express controlled disapproval instead. S. S. Tomkins calls such a process "miniaturization."[13] It is an important tool in psychospiritual development that helps us to avoid being completely dominated by an emotion.

Observation may function as a means of accomplishing miniaturization. Instead of becoming our anger, we can simply observe it—allowing it to become an object that shrinks and distances from us.

Amplification

All affects may be amplified: fear may become terror; anger may become rage; nurturance may become self-sacrifice. In chapter 9, other examples will be provided.

Opposing Affects

Sometimes one affect is used to reduce the magnitude of another. For example, courage may be used to combat fear or cheer is generated to reduce sadness.

Cause and Effect

In the flow of information through the three bodies, an affect may be either a cause or an effect. It is an effect when a trigger elicits it; then it may become a cause for the mental and/or physical acts that immediately follow. These cause and effect relationships may sometimes function completely beneath the threshold of awareness. In these cases, the affect is usually very powerful and may form part of the classical ego defense mechanisms described in the literature of psychoanalysis.

Ego-Generated Affect

Most causes of affect originate in the external environment. However, an ego may appraise itself and intentionally generate an affect: "I am so angry with myself," "I am really proud of what I have done," "I love you (while looking in the mirror)." Those who are advanced in psychospiritual practices know how to generate the affects of calmness and serenity within themselves.

Affects and Values

There is a close connection between affect and value. A natural tendency exists to value those objects that generate positive affect and devalue those that produce negative affect. However, the spiritual path sometimes demands that we alter those natural associations. Objects that elicit fear in us at times must be sought in order to conquer our fear. From the viewpoint of the spiritual evolution of the species, one purpose of natural or human-made catastrophes is to provide vast numbers of people an opportunity to serve selflessly and conquer their fear of death. Acts of courage and cowardice are retained in the central channel and influence subsequent births.

9

Affects and the Three Lenga-s

THE AFFECTS AND PSYCHOSPIRITUAL GROWTH

The "iron chains" of the first lɛngᵃ, the "silver chains" of the second lɛngᵃ, and the "golden chains" of the third lɛngᵃ are formed from both positive and negative affects and their supporting beliefs. Ego creates these chains and is bound by them. They must be weakened or shed in order to proceed along the path of psychospiritual development. In the following pages the affects listed in Table 8.2 will be examined in detail in order to explicate their important role in the functioning of the chᵃkrᵃ minds.

Some Ego-Enhancing Early Positive Affects

- ✦ Joy
- ✦ Interest
- ✦ Play
- ✦ Nurturance
- ✦ Assertiveness

JOY

Ego experiences great pleasure.

Carroll E. Izard, a researcher on emotional development, has observed:

From about the age of 4 or 5 weeks to the age of about 4 or 5 months the infant will smile at any human face that nods gently toward it from about 2 feet away. It is as though the infant has an endless supply of smiles, a virtually limitless quantity of joyful feelings to be shared with any other human being who will take the time or provide the right stimulation.

In the everyday world of mother and infant, the young infant's ability to smile prolifically has a profound effect upon its developing relationship with its mother and other caregivers. As the mother bends over the baby to minister to its needs, the baby smiles. The baby's smile tends to elicit a smile and positive vocalizations from the mother. The increased social stimulation that is purchased by the infant's easy smile is a very positive force for the baby's health and well-being. Babies who are deprived of this kind of social interaction may experience depression, withdrawal, and even a physical debilitation . . .[1]

Dance of the Elements

It is primarily the element of *fire* that enables the ego to experience joy. The uplifting quality of *air* is also drawn on, and other elements may be employed for nuance. The elemental "dance" reaches a climax upon goal attainment in a particular chᵃkrᵃ mind and may be followed by contentment. When the feeling of joy reaches the physical plane, we may literally "dance for joy."

A less intense state of joy is *happiness*. A more intense state of joy is *ecstasy*.

First-Lɛngᵃ Joy

First Chᵃkrᵃ. Joy will be triggered in the first chᵃkrᵃ when ego acquires objects that add to its security or feeling of identity. Large acquisitions, such as a house or car, will occasion great joy. The overarching philosophy of the first chᵃkrᵃ ego could be summarized as "I possess objects, therefore I am."

Second Chᵃkrᵃ. Exchange with others is the function of the second chᵃkrᵃ. Some of these exchanges—sexual, financial, and other—are particularly joyful. The most joyful are the ones that have the greatest meaning within the context of the whole schematic network that the ego has constructed around itself. Examples of second-chᵃkrᵃ joy are finding a mate, making a sale, and executing a skillful tennis shot.

Third Chᵃkrᵃ. The ego of the third chᵃkrᵃ is focused on power and competition. Hence it is winning that brings about the most joy. Building a successful company produces this joy, as does recognition for being "number one" in a field of endeavor. In politics, for instance, an election to public office will bring about joy, and the higher the office, the greater the joy.

Second-Lɛngᵃ Joy

Fourth Chᵃkrᵃ. The greatest joy for the fourth-chᵃkrᵃ ego derives from surrendering the egos of the first lɛngᵃ. This is accomplished through service to others: either to a person, a cause, or a deity.

A surgeon will feel joy after the successful completion of a long and difficult operation. A psychotherapist will be joyful after the dramatic improvement of a chronically depressed client. A devotee who, after years of worship, experiences the presence of the deity will feel boundless joy.

Fifth Chᵃkrᵃ. There are intrinsic links between joy, freedom, and creativity. Joy is an expression of freedom and freedom is a prerequisite for creativity. This dynamic is especially evident in the fifth chᵃkrᵃ due to the presence of *aakaashᵃ*, which stimulates both freedom and creativity. The natural accompaniment of this process is joy and the most potent outlet for joy is sound. "Sounds of joy" ring throughout human history.

Examples of fifth-chᵃkrᵃ joy are: finding a creative solution to a burdensome problem, composing a unique work of art, or sustaining a pure tone in singing. The highest joy is discovering the inner guru, which frees us from all elemental minds.

Third-LENGᵃ Joy

Sixth Chᵃkrᵃ. The principal goal of the sixth chᵃkrᵃ is balance: between the solar and lunar energies and among the three guNᵃ-s. When accomplished, all senses are internalized. All normal affect is then absorbed into intuition. Joy is transformed into an ecstasy that may be experienced in deep meditation.

Seventh Chᵃkrᵃ. In the sᵃmaadhE experiences of the seventh chᵃkrᵃ, joy, ecstasy and contentment combine into bliss (aanandᵃ): the eternal state of Consciousness.

INTEREST

Ego focuses attention on an object.

Izard has observed that interest is the most frequently experienced positive emotion. He summarized its pervasive function in the following way:

> The emotion of interest has played a large role in the evolution of the human being, serving adaptive functions developed over the course of humankind's existence. The nature and development of human relationships has been shaped largely by the fascination the human race holds for itself—people are more interesting to people than anything else. Interest also plays a significant part in the attainment of sexual pleasure as in the maintenance of long-term sexual relationships. Interest also assists in the development of competencies and, thus, intelligence.
>
> The emotion of interest can be invested in possibility and thus supports investigation, exploration, and constructive activity. It is a necessary support for per-

ceptual and cognitive development, and it plays a powerful role in the processes of attention, learning and memory.[2]

The affect of interest has its origin in the exploratory activity of all mammals. Some researchers classify exploration as a drive that is programmed into the early brain.[3] Its purpose is to acquire information about the objects in the animal's environment. When an object attracts the animal's attention for any reason (e.g., if the object smells good to eat), attention becomes focused and the affect of interest is triggered.

Noticing is a less intense state of interest. *Excitement* is a more intense state of interest.

Dance of the Elements
Interest may involve any or all elements.

First-LEngª Interest
First Chªkrª. Infants are interested in objects that satisfy their drives of hunger, thirst, and pain avoidance. Nipples, mash, clean diapers, and a warm blanket are examples of such objects. Newborns also show an innate interest in the human face.

The child who develops free of significant blockages will readily explore her environment and find that a number of objects are "interesting." If the child is blocked or inhibited in her exploratory activity, her capacity to find interesting objects and activities will suffer.

As the adult years approach, interests are determined by patterns of microchakra openings and blocks. For example, suppose that somebody walking in a field spots a deer grazing at a distance. If 1:1 is blocked, the spotter will wish to be carrying a rifle. If 1:1 is open, an interest in killing the deer cannot arise.

Interests based in the first chªkrª embrace farming, house building, homemaking, and exercises involving contact with the earth, such as running, jumping, and wrestling.

Musical interests include drumming, rock and roll, and hip-hop.

Second Chªkrª. Second-chªkrª interests include developing interpersonal relations (often those where we have a slight advantage). Water sports such as swimming, surfing, and canoeing utilize second-chªkrª energy, as do musical instruments that are picked or plucked with deep feeling.

Third Chªkrª. Interest in various organizations characterizes the third chªkrª. These include professional, social, musical, religious, and political organizations. Membership in such organizations may provide considerable status.

Second-Lɛngᵃ Interest

Fourth Chᵃkrᵃ. Openings in the fourth chᵃkrᵃ will stimulate an interest in following a religious path. The capacity for love expands and, if 4:5 is open, will extend to a love of sustained-tone music.

Fifth Chᵃkrᵃ. Fifth-chᵃkrᵃ interests include the quest for identity and the use of sound to facilitate this quest. There is no better tool than sooryᵃ *aakaashᵃ* for awakening the inner guru. An interest in sound can be arrived at through work with the other elements, such as in sculpting and painting.

Third-Lɛngᵃ Interest

Sixth Chᵃkrᵃ. The principal interest in the sixth chᵃkrᵃ is in balancing the three guɴᵃ-s. There is a desire to explore the varieties of *aakaashᵃ* in order to discover the still point within. Meditation is of great interest.

Seventh Chᵃkrᵃ. In the seventh chᵃkrᵃ interest settles on attaining various states of sᵃmaadhɛ. Life is lived from the Hretᵃ pᵃdmᵃ of the heart chᵃkrᵃ and utilizes non-attached action (nɪshkᵃrmyᵃ sɛddhɛ).

PLAY

Ego interacts with an object simply for joy.

The physiological psychologist Jaak Panksepp has observed:

> Although cortical processes surely add a great deal of diversity to our playful behaviors, especially as we develop, it is unlikely that the primal brain "energy" for playfulness emerges from those higher brain functions. These energies probably emerge from the same ancient executive systems that govern RAT [rough and tumble] play in other species. As those primitive playful impulses percolate through the brain, they assume new forms ranging from slapstick humour to cognitive mirth. Indeed the hallmark of PLAY circuitry in action for humans is laughter, a projectile respiratory movement with no apparent function, except perhaps to signal to others one's social mood and sense of carefree camaraderie.[4]

Dance of the Elements

Play may involve any or all elements.

An ego that is *amused* is engaged in a less intense type of play. An ego that is more intensely engaged in play may be *competitive*.

First-Leng^a Play

First Ch^akr^a. Rough and tumble play is characteristic of the first ch^akr^a. Prototypical examples of such play can be observed in the behavior of puppies and kittens. A natural vitality and exuberance is obvious. Little children engaged in rough and tumble play may exclaim that they are having "so much fun." Adults who can allow themselves to be children again may experience similar fun.

The "me-centeredness" of the first ch^akr^a may distort the carefree fun that flows from the early brain. Boys and girls may insist on a feeling of victory and subjugate their playmates. Play must now have a winner and a loser. There is often a "hit and run" quality to it where the other is not given a chance to respond before being declared the loser.

This theme of play as conquering may be carried into adulthood. It forms a support for extreme attitudes of competitiveness that may be active in the third ch^akr^a. War is the extension of this attitude to the greatest degree. War has even been regarded as the "play" of kings.

Another form of first-ch^akr^a play is gambling. The first ch^akr^a ego sometimes wants something for nothing, and is willing to take risks to get it.

Second Ch^akr^a. Play in the second ch^akr^a involves one-to-one exchange. Sexual intercourse is prototypical. Games of skill and wit—such as fencing, tennis, chess, and poker—provide other outlets for expression of second-ch^akr^a play. In these games, the opponent is given an equal opportunity for victory.

Third Ch^akr^a. Team sports such as soccer, baseball, and hockey are examples of third-ch^akr^a play. In the business arena, competition with other companies may produce aggression and a desire to be "number one." In political history, this aggressive desire has led to the colonization of nations and the arrangement of royal marriages to consolidate power.

Second-Leng^a Play

Fourth Ch^akr^a. The association between play and competitiveness that was common in the first leng^a cannot be sustained in the second leng^a. Here, awareness of the other is accompanied by a strong desire to share. Play returns to the instinctual spirit of rough and tumble; that is, to its state before being acted upon by the strong egoism of the first leng^a. The more refined ego of the second leng^a has no desire to be a "winner."

In the fourth ch^akr^a, play is focused on the fun of movement and activity. For example, in tennis the goal would simply be to keep the ball in the air for as long as possible. The emphasis is on the fun, the exercise, and the socialization, not on being declared a victor.

Fourth-ch^akr^a energy is usually focused on a deity. This comes with the awareness that the universe is a Divine game and that we are playing our part with sincerity and light-heartedness. The fourth chᵃkrᵃ is energized by faith.

Fifth Chᵃkrᵃ. In the fifth chᵃkrᵃ, the ego has become refined enough to attune to the elements. It may then become their master (tatvᵃtEEtᵃ) and use the elements to play with the feelings. This is done by chanting the tone that corresponds to the element. For example, lamenting *air* (tone F, *ma*), crying *fire* (tone E, *ga*), flowing *water* (tone D, *re*), and playing *aakaashᵃ* (tone G, *pa*).

By activating the elements in succession, they can be used as a staircase to go beyond *aakaashᵃ* into the play of the guNᵃ-s, leading to meditation.

Third-LEngᵃ Play

Sixth Chᵃkrᵃ. The three guNᵃ-s of tᵃmᵃs, rᵃjᵃs, and sᵃtvᵃ are the objects of play in the sixth chᵃkrᵃ. The sixth chᵃkrᵃ ego that has mastered them is called guNaatEEtᵃ. However, rather than intentionally influence them, a guNaatEEtᵃ is inclined to only witness their powerful effect on the lower chᵃkrᵃ minds and on nature in general.

Seventh Chᵃkrᵃ. In the seventh chᵃkrᵃ, eightfold nature has been transcended. The various states of sᵃmaadhE that are achievable here may be regarded as the play of awareness at an extremely refined level. All of the activity of ordinary life is done without personal likes or dislikes. All is simply natural law (retᵃ).

NURTURANCE

Ego aids the well-being of an object.

Human nurturing has two interrelated sources. The first was embedded long ago in the instinctive programs of the early brain, and led our mammalian ancestors to breastfeed and otherwise care for the infant, individually and collectively. This same instinct for nurturing and cooperation explains mutual grooming and group hunting practices.

Dance of the Elements

The second source of nurturing is the love energy generated by the *air* of the fourth chᵃkrᵃ. This energy may readily take the form of empathy. When this energy is flowing, those in need can easily elicit a caring response.

To *support* is to less intensely nurture. To *protect* is to more intensely nurture.

Nurturance in Attachment and Identity Formation

The search for identity begins when the newborn infant is laid upon the mother's bosom. The Me-maker of the first chᵃkrᵃ utilizes the rooting reflex to find the nipple. Success stimulates the sucking reflex and the resulting milk, combined with the comfort of resting on mother's body, may help to open the first and fourth microchakras in all chᵃkrᵃ-s. In addition, the bond between mother and infant is strengthened in the physical field, the subtle field, and the causal field. This three-field bond sustains the mother's intuitive knowledge of when her baby needs her.

Initially, the Me-maker of the baby detects no difference between itself and the mother. During this period of unity, no feelings of abandonment can arise. The longer this period lasts, the richer the second lᴇngᵃ will be. When the baby finally separates from the mother, she may show her attachment by clinging, reaching to be picked up, and objecting to separation. The Me-Maker now perceives mother as the secure base of its existence. This perception takes on a whole new importance when the baby becomes capable of crawling and walking (between 9 and 12 months). She is then presented with a choice that will recur at many points throughout life: to explore the unknown or to fear the unknown. If the attachment between mother and baby has been good, praanic pods will be vibrating with energy and the schema of mother as a reliable haven will have been established. The choice to explore will then be easy—she can always return to mother. On the other hand, if the attachment between mother and baby is weak, fear may allow only minimal exploration (or compulsive exploration).

In the above discussion, attachment is seen as a positive influence in the baby's development. In later periods of life, attachment may be a negative influence. The object of attachment (animate or inanimate) may be a barrier to psychospiritual advancement. It is for this reason that the practice of "nonattachment" or noncling-ing is advocated by many spiritual teachings.

The more unconditional love—the more care, affection, and touch—a baby is given during the right-channel age, the easier it will be for her to practice nonat-tachment later in life.

First-Lᴇngᵃ Nurturance

First Chᵃkrᵃ. The ego of the first chᵃkrᵃ is basically "me" oriented and focused on achieving a sense of bodily identity. The aggressiveness with which the healthy ego approaches this task is mitigated by the tendency toward empathy available from an opening in 1:4. When this tendency is great the result is a desire to nurture, which may even be seen in very young children as they take care of younger siblings and pets.

The nurturance affect is not exclusively directed outward, of course. The ego may direct toward itself some of the empathic energy that it has available. Caring for yourself is a dharmic response that expresses gratitude for the birth you have been given. The response may include habits of exercise, self-massage, and consumption of natural, organic food.

Second Chᵃkrᵃ. Exchange is the dominant activity of the second chᵃkrᵃ. The healthy ego is looking out for itself in these give-and-takes, and usually expects to take as much as it gives (and preferably a little more). This "even" exchange can be altered by energy from 2:4, which allows the ego to accept an exchange where *the other* benefits more; for example, helping a friend in need.

Third Chᵃkrᵃ. The ego of the third chᵃkrᵃ is focused on the acquisition of power within a community. The empathic energy of 3:4 often enables the person seeking power to be more acceptable to other community members. In a political context, it adds to the "likeability factor." Voters often choose a candidate who manifests a capacity for nurturance. They prefer a leader who is confident, strong, and protective—such as Abraham Lincoln or Mahatma Gandhi.

Second-Lɛngᵃ Nurturance

Fourth Chᵃkrᵃ. The fourth chᵃkrᵃ is the center of love from which all empathic and nurturing feelings flow. In the first lɛngᵃ, it was more appropriate to refer to the energy of the fourth microchakras as empathic and nurturing because the three chᵃkrᵃ-s of the first lɛngᵃ do not have the essential characteristic of love: surrender of the ego. In the first three chᵃkrᵃ-s the egos feel nurturing, but not unconditional love. In the fourth chᵃkrᵃ, the ego *dissolves* in love. The *air* energy of love replaces much of the *fire* of ego. The object of this love is usually a deity but may be an infant, another person, or a cause.

Fifth Chᵃkrᵃ. An opening in 5:4 is usually found only in those of advanced development. They may nurture others through a healing voice, chant, or touch.

Third-Lɛngᵃ Nurturance

In the third lɛngᵃ, selfishness returns but in a far more refined way than existed in the first lɛngᵃ. Now the ego has shed its iron and silver chains. Its only interest is to nurture itself in order to remove the golden chains and to discover the Self.

ASSERTIVENESS

Ego focuses its energy on goal attainment.

Dance of the Elements

The primary element in assertiveness is *fire*. It may be modulated by other elements, depending upon the champions and saboteurs that affect its expression.

An ego that is less intensively assertive is *assured* or *sanguine*. An ego that is more intensely assertive is *brazen* or *overbearing*.

First-Lᴇɴɢᵃ Assertiveness

First Chᵃkrᵃ. All animals must acquire food. They do it by devouring plants or preying on other animals. Both are done without any strong emotion. It is simply an assertion of their innate right to exist upon the planet. "I am! I devour!" This assertiveness is stored deep within the early brain and forms part of the ego of the first chᵃkrᵃ (1:3).

As the ego of the first chᵃkrᵃ inevitably encounters obstacles to its goals, it needs to draw upon its capacity for assertiveness. Assertiveness is the most important of all the affects. It is the means by which dhᵃrmᵃ may be followed. In the first chᵃkrᵃ, assertiveness is dedicated to meeting the goals of physical security and bodily identity.

The regulation of assertiveness in the first chᵃkrᵃ may be understood through the dynamics of the archetypes residing in it: Gᵃɴᴀsʜᵃ, Daakᴇɴᴇᴇ, and the "nibbling mouse." An uncontrolled Daakᴇɴᴇᴇ energizes the nibbling mouse that personifies gluttony—an ultimately self-destructive behavior. Those who wish to combat their gluttony and promote feelings of security and contentment can bring the mouse under control by invoking Gᵃɴᴀsʜᵃ—the remover of obstacles. He is able to lull Daakᴇɴᴇᴇ to sleep.

Similar explanations of the relationship between other affects and archetypes could be provided, but are beyond the scope of this book.

Second Chᵃkrᵃ. In the second chᵃkrᵃ, assertiveness occurs within the context of exchange with others. If 2:4 is open, a balanced ego asserts itself in sexual, business, and other exchanges in a manner that is considerate of the other person. There is a healthy give and take.

Third Chᵃkrᵃ. Assertiveness in the third chᵃkrᵃ frequently involves competition with others. This may be within sports, business, or various professions and organizations. If the assertiveness is modified by 3:4 energy, the ego will seek cooperation whenever possible. Great leaders are made of such cooperation. On the other hand, if assertiveness is influenced by patterns of severe blockage, the ego may be pathologically competitive.

Second-Lᴇɴɢᵃ Assertiveness

Fourth Chᵃkrᵃ. In the fourth chᵃkrᵃ, a major change in ego energy takes place. The blunt assertiveness through which the energy typically expresses itself becomes refined. A new awareness of the presence of love creates a desire to align with that love, and serve it. Assertiveness, therefore, becomes modified to service. Devotion to a power greater than that of the ego becomes the new paradigm. Love is associated with godliness.

Fifth Chᵃkrᵃ. In the fifth chᵃkrᵃ, the assertiveness that had modified itself to service looks for creative ways to further refine itself. This leads to the dissolution of all elements in an altered state, eventually awakening the inner guru.

Third-Lɛngᵃ Assertiveness

Sixth Chᵃkrᵃ. In the sixth chᵃkrᵃ it is not strictly correct to refer to affects. The residue of former feelings and emotions continues, but as components of intuition—the dominant form of mentation in the sixth chᵃkrᵃ. The assertive components of the sixth chᵃkrᵃ are discernment (vɛchaarᵃ) and alignment. The sixth chᵃkrᵃ ego intuits its alignment with retᵃ.

Seventh Chᵃkrᵃ. In the seventh chᵃkrᵃ, only the subtlest amount of ego persists to assert itself in various sᵃmaadhɛ-s. Finally, it leaves the body from the tenth gate to merge with the Self.

Some Ego-Contracting Early Negative Affects

+ Fear
+ Anger
+ Distress
+ Disgust

FEAR

Ego perceives an object as threatening.

Charles Darwin, in *The Expression of the Emotions in Man and Animals* gave the following description of the innate behavioral indicators of extreme fear or terror:

> . . . the eyes and mouth are widely opened, and the eyebrows raised. The frightened man at first stands like a statue motionless and breathless, or crouches down as if instinctively to escape observation.
>
> The heart beats quickly and violently, so that it palpitates or knocks against the ribs; but it is very doubtful whether it then works more efficiently than usual, so as to send a greater supply of blood to all parts of the body; for the skin instantly becomes pale, as during incipient faintness. The paleness of the surface, however,

is probably in large part, or exclusively, due to the vasomotor centre being affected in such a manner as to cause the contraction of the small arteries of the skin. That the skin is much affected under the sense of great fear, we see in the marvelous and inexplicable manner in which perspiration immediately exudes from it. This exudation is all the more remarkable as the surface is then cold, and hence the term cold sweat; whereas, the sudorific glands are properly excited into action when the surface is heated. The hairs also on the skin stand erect; and the superficial muscles shiver. In connection with the disturbed action of the heart, the breath is hurried. The salivary glands act imperfectly; the mouth becomes dry, and is often opened and shut. . . . One of the best marked symptoms is the trembling of all the muscles of the body; and this is often first seen in the lips. From this cause, and from the dryness of the mouth, the voice becomes husky or indistinct, or may altogether fail.[5]

Fear is the strongest of the iron chains of the first LEngᵃ.

Dance of the Elements

The most important element governing fear is *water*. It is *water* that recruits the various physiological components described by Darwin and programmed deep within the early brain; for example, fear's provoking of involuntary urination. If fear persists, dark *aakaashᵃ* may pervade both mind and body. This will increase the sense of loneliness and isolation, and add to the burden of fear.

A less intense state of fear is *apprehension* or *worry*. A more intense state of fear is *terror*.

First-LEngᵃ Fear

First Chᵃkrᵃ. During the developmental years of the first-chᵃkrᵃ age many situations have the potential to trigger fear: separation from parents, encounters with strangers or animals, nightmares, thunder and lightning storms, unexplained noises, deep water. Before the child is old enough to develop his own coping skills, he is dependent upon the wisdom of his parents to prevent potential triggers from becoming actual triggers. Unfortunately, in many typical child-rearing practices, this wisdom is lacking. Having infants and young children sleep alone in a dimly lit or dark room often produces a first encounter with fear—a fear that is repeated nightly. The recitation of scary bedtime stories only exacerbates the fear.

Second Chᵃkrᵃ. In the second-chᵃkrᵃ age the focus is on interpersonal relations and the emphasis is usually on the positive emotions. When fear is generated, the opposite emotions of confidence and courage are summoned to reduce or eliminate it. A common fear of the second-chᵃkrᵃ age is diffidence in social situations, leading to feelings of embarrassment. Normalcy is cherished.

Adults, particularly parents and teachers, differ significantly in the degree to which they deliberately use fear to control children during the second-chᵃkrᵃ age. For some children, the arousal of fear may be necessary for socialization; for others, socialization may be accomplished mainly through positive affect.

Third Chᵃkrᵃ. The play of the third-chᵃkrᵃ age involves establishing relations with peer groups, career training institutions, and religious establishments. Each of these groups knows how to generate fear as they shape their new recruits. The peer groups know that the greatest fear of each member is to be ostracized and so may threaten accordingly. The career training institutions organize their demands based upon the fear of failure to attain their standards in the time that they allot. Employers often base their demands upon fear of dismissal and financial loss. The religious establishments hold the trump card: they threaten with fear of dire consequences after death should a member not follow their teachings. Thus does a species still ignorant of its Divinity wallow in a sea of fear. Perhaps it is for this reason that the most frequent gesture (mudraa) of the Tantric deities indicates "Fear not" (abhayᵃ mudraa). In this gesture the deity raises the right arm at the elbow with palm facing forward and fingers pointed toward the sky.

Second-Lᴇɴgᵃ Fear

Fourth Chᵃkrᵃ. Fear is most common in the first lᴇɴgᵃ but may also occur in the other lᴇɴgᵃ-s. In the fourth chᵃkrᵃ, the imagination may prompt the belief that "my god will punish me."

Fifth Chᵃkrᵃ. In the fifth chᵃkrᵃ, fear of other people may inhibit creative expression and the voice may be timid.

Third-Lᴇɴgᵃ Fear

Sixth Chᵃkrᵃ. The unconscious fear of the extinction of the race contributes to sexual urges. It does not subside until L6:2 is open and we are released from the obligation to reproduce. In this state, second-chᵃkrᵃ energy is converted through service, devotion, prayer, creativity, and meditation.

Seventh Chᵃkrᵃ. Fear even continues into the seventh chᵃkrᵃ where it is finally mastered in L7:2 when the person is able to perform jᵃlᵃ sᵃmaadhᴇ: temporarily merging with the Self while meditating underwater.

ANGER

Ego focuses destructive fire at an object perceived to interfere with its goals.

Charles Darwin provided the following description of anger:

> Under moderate anger the action of the heart is a little increased, the colour heightened, and the eyes become bright. The respiration is likewise a little hurried; and as all the muscles serving for this function act in association, the wings of the nostrils are somewhat raised to allow of a free indraught of air; and this is a highly characteristic sign of indignation. The mouth is commonly compressed, and there is almost always a frown on the brow. Instead of the frantic gestures of extreme rage, an indignant man unconsciously throws himself into an attitude ready for attacking or striking his enemy, whom he will perhaps scan from head to foot in defiance. He carries his head erect, with his chest well expanded, and the feet planted firmly on the ground. He holds his arms in various positions, with one or both elbows squared, or with the arms rigidly suspended by the sides. With Europeans the fists are commonly clenched.[6]

Dance of the Elements

Fire is the main element of the ego and is used in a variety of ways. When anger erupts, the causal body gathers *fire* in preparation for an attack on the object that evoked the anger. The form of the attack is most gross when fire is combined with *earth* (such as throwing hot rocks on an enemy). The quality of the attack becomes subtler as the element combining with *fire* shifts from *earth,* to *water,* to *air,* to *aakaash*.

A less intense expression of anger is *annoyance*. A more intense expression of anger is *rage*.

As Panksepp noted, evolution has built anger circuits into our subcortical brain in order to increase the probability that goals will be attained.[7] Anger can marshal energies for that purpose. As the early brain becomes refined through psychospiritual practices, anger is one of the emotions that must be subjected to that refinement. Modern society recognizes this need through courses in "anger management." Both Tᵃntrᵃ and Vᴀdaantᵃ have always regarded anger (krodhᵃ) as an obstacle to spiritual progress.

First-Lᴇɴɢᵃ Anger

First Chᵃkrᵃ. An innate expression of anger may be seen in infants only a few months old when they are restrained in some way. The eyebrows are drawn, the mouth forms an open rectangle, and the eyes may become narrowed.[8] This anger may be pure, or mixed with crying and other signs of distress (see below).

The objects that the ego requires in the first chᵃkrᵃ concern survival. They are a matter of life and death, and those who interfere with their acquisition may elicit the fiercest, most murderous type of anger. The urge is to completely eradicate and bury the other. However, if the threat is perceived as less than existential, the urge may be reduced accordingly to simply push or swat the offending one out of the way.

All individuals possess a number of anger scripts in order to cope with first-chᵃkrᵃ threats in their lives. Similarly, groups of people develop scripts to contend with the existential threats posed by other groups. At the national level, enormous sums of money are spent on this effort.

The ego of the first chᵃkrᵃ frequently sees anger as having desirable qualities, leading to pride in the capacity to be angry at injustice, or at having certain people or groups as enemies. Anger may be so deliberately incorporated into a person's self-schema that a role of "avenger" may be adopted. To move past these righteous claims of anger requires considerable spiritual work.

When the ego of the first chᵃkrᵃ has been impaired by severe blockages, it may turn anger inward and direct blame for all shortcomings upon itself. The murderous tendencies of first-chᵃkrᵃ anger may then lead to suicide.

Second Chᵃkrᵃ. Each interpersonal relationship is vulnerable to episodes of anger. Even the most lovable person may do things that arouse frustration. Normal scripts allow for this and try to keep the expression of anger to a minimum. However, in those relationships that are near breaking, the second-chᵃkrᵃ ego behaves more subtly than the ego of the first chᵃkrᵃ. The distorted scripts—based on the combination of *fire* with *water*—may involve cunning and mysterious displays of anger in order to extract revenge for the damage the offender is perceived to have caused.

Fear is an important factor in constructing the script that anger will use. If the object causing anger is also feared, little overt anger may be expressed. On the other hand, if fear is completely absent, excessive force and bullying may accompany the expression of anger.

Third Chᵃkrᵃ. The ego of the third chᵃkrᵃ is the *fire* of the *fire* and seeks to maximize its power. It is the most rational of all egos and draws upon this rationality when expressing its anger. Therefore, impulsive expressions of anger are usually avoided. An exception is the authoritarian ruler of a group who may spew invective at his captive audience.

From the perspective of the first lɛngᵃ, it appears that something or another is always getting in the way and that frequent anger is inevitable. To transcend this perspective requires a deep appreciation of the law of kᵃrmᵃ. There is a reason for everything, including that flat tire on your way to work. Your anger will not fix it. When struggling, it is good to ask, "Who is getting angry?" It is always an ego and never the Self.

A basic technique of anger management is the method of disidentification, discussed in chapter 8. Allow the anger to be present. Just observe it. Do not become the anger. Do not allow it to unduly influence your thoughts. Note any other saboteurs that arise in tandem with anger. They will teach you much about your habitual relation with anger. Some people have developed a dependency upon anger as a way of defining themselves. Anger becomes part of their comfort zone.

Second-Lᴇɴɢᵃ Anger

Fourth Chᵃkrᵃ. The dominant energy in the fourth chᵃkrᵃ is love. Love is more powerful than anger. An ego full of love, while able to recognize provocation, refuses to respond in kind. It may use an abstraction to refer to the situation: "You know, when you do something like this, it makes me angry."

An exception may occur when dealing with those who are completely trapped in the first lᴇɴɢᵃ. Such people may be unable to fulfill a simple request to change a behavior unless the request is accompanied by expressions of anger—which those in the second lᴇɴɢᵃ can easily feign.

Fifth Chᵃkrᵃ. In fifth-chᵃkrᵃ awareness, provocation is recognized and immediately drowned in *aakaashᵃ*. Nothing is said. One refuses to pollute the *aakaashᵃ* with manifestations of anger.

The use of fifth-chᵃkrᵃ energy to express abusive language occurs only in the first lᴇɴɢᵃ by means of the fifth microchakras in the first three chᵃkrᵃ-s. Even then, it is an offense against dhᵃrmᵃ to use universal energy in a vulgar way.

Third-Lᴇɴɢᵃ Anger

Sixth Chᵃkrᵃ. Anger does not arise in the sixth chᵃkrᵃ as a personal emotion. However, injustices are recognized and action is taken with compassion.

DISTRESS

Ego experiences energy moving in an opposite direction to its goal.

The crying response is the first response the human being makes upon being born. The birth cry is a cry of distress. . . . It is a response of distress at the excessive level of stimulation to which the neonate is suddenly exposed at being born.

In the cry the mouth is open, the corners of the lips are pulled downwards, rather than upwards as in laughing, and vocalization and breathing are more continuous, rather than intermittent as in laughter. In addition there is an arching of the eyebrows that accompanies crying, which, if it appears without crying, gives a sad expression to the face.[9]

Dance of the Elements

The capacity to wail in distress is programmed within the early brain of most mammals. Its most basic cause is physical pain. Wailing draws upon the vocal apparatus and the element of *aakaash^a*. After a few weeks, the human infant may add weeping to its expression of distress. Weeping is expressed through the *water* element. Continued weeping may involve the *fire* element as shown by the redness of the eyes.

An ego that is less intensely distressed is said to be *annoyed*. An ego that is more intensely distressed is said to be *suffering* or *grieving*.

First-LEng^a Distress

First Ch^akr^a. In addition to physical pain, the basic wail of distress is frequently associated with the separation of an infant from a caregiver. The reason for this is not hard to find. Feelings of security, basic to a healthy first ch^akr^a, emerge from the nurturance that the caregiver gives to the helpless young. This creates a bond between nurturer and infant and, at the emotional level, an attachment. Even a temporary severance of this attachment is a cause for distress (separation distress). Panksepp describes the complex neurochemical circuitry of the brain that evidence suggests underlies attachment and separation distress.[10]

It is with wailing and tears that the infant apprises the caregiver of its feelings of separation, wet diaper, state of hunger, itchy skin, and other torments. In later years, as the socialization process proceeds, the child will learn to suppress this expression—a fact generally more true for males than for females. Although suppressed, the feeling may be as strong as ever. Under particularly severe suppression, the feeling may be buried deep in apaanic pods. It may then come to form part of a saboteur pattern that blocks psychospiritual growth. Eventually, in a healing environment, a person can learn to cry again and "let it all out" in order to free the ch^akr^a mind for further growth.

Too much *aakaash^a* may cause distress to the fragile ego of a young child by producing sensations of spaciness and disorientation. A young child should not be present during extended periods of chanting enriched with soory^a *aakaash^a*.

The goals of the first ch^akr^a involve existential security. Distress arises when there is an absence of the objects (food, clothing, housing, etc.) needed to meet those goals, or when objects that have been meeting the goals are removed. Distress may then meld with other affects, such as fear or anger.

Prolonged distress may be amplified into feelings of grief, suffering, or anguish with which the ego seems helpless to cope. In such crises, habits of attachment may be broken as the ego reaches out to higher energies in its own chᵃkrᵃ and in those above it.

Second Chᵃkrᵃ. The ego of the second chᵃkrᵃ builds the network of interpersonal relationships that are so essential to the human as a social creature. These relationships provide pleasure and joy but may also include periods of distress. When things do not go the way they "should," the ego is compelled to search for a means of alleviating the distress. The means may be found quickly or only after many years—sometimes extremely difficult years.

Praarᵃbdhᵃ kᵃrmᵃ speaks most clearly to us through the relationships that life provides. It is relatively easy to be grateful to those who nurture us. It is much less easy to be grateful to those who antagonize and distress us. Yet grateful we should be, because it is the challenging relationship that draws out our latent qualities of perseverance, patience, compassion, observation, and transcendence.

Third Chᵃkrᵃ. The ego of the third chᵃkrᵃ focuses on assertiveness and the acquisition of power. Distress may serve as an indicator of how our assertiveness is developing. If the situations that distress us are relatively trivial, then our assertiveness may require strengthening. On the other hand, if we are seldom seriously distressed we may have developed an assertiveness that is masking true feeling. In this case, the potential for callousness and indifference is high. These two spiritual saboteurs are often lurking in the background.

Second-LEngᵃ Distress

Fourth Chᵃkrᵃ. Separation distress takes on new meaning in the fourth chᵃkrᵃ. The refined ego is acutely aware of its separation from the Divine. Sometimes this awareness is accompanied by a longing for union, but oftentimes separation is accepted as inevitable and there is simply a desire to serve the Divinity. Inspiring poems of love and longing for the Supreme have been composed by saintly poets from diverse religious traditions.

Fifth Chᵃkrᵃ. In the fifth chᵃkrᵃ, forms of distress are miniaturized. There may be the simple awareness, for example, that sound (received or emitted) is not moving in the proper direction. The ego then implements subtle, corrective scripts and there is no possibility of distress being amplified into suffering and anguish.

Third-Lᴇɴɢᵃ Distress

Sixth Chᵃkrᵃ. Mentation in the sixth chᵃkrᵃ takes the form of intuition into which distress is incorporated and much reduced. Its only purpose is to provide feedback as to when meditation is not proceeding well.

Seventh Chᵃkrᵃ. Distress becomes an extremely subtle indicator that the ego has not been sufficiently released to permit sᵃmaadhᴇ.

DISGUST

Ego perceives an object as having repulsive qualities.

Izard provides the following information about disgust:

> The origins of the emotions in the evolutionary process cannot always be traced with precision and certainty. An exception may be found in the origins of disgust as a differentiated aspect of the primitive avoidance mechanism. Disgust has its evolutionary roots in the very old parts of the brain that serve the chemical sense of taste and eating behavior. A clear and specific expression of disgust can be obtained by putting a little bit of bitter substance on the tongue of the newborn infant. This is true even for infants in which the more recently evolved layers of the brain (the cerebral hemispheres) are dysfunctional due to disease or birth defect. Such disgust expressions obviously have little or no psychological component; that is they are not based upon cognitive evaluation or appraisal of the bitter substance. Thus, the disgust expression we see in young infants is primarily a function of neurochemical processes, which are independent of learning or memory.[11]

Dance of the Elements

The above paragraph indicates that the prototypical affect of disgust involves the sense of taste (distaste). This is an aspect of the *water* element.

A less intense type of disgust is *dislike,* or *antipathy.* A more intense type of disgust is *loathing* or *revulsion.*

First-Lᴇɴɢᵃ Disgust

First Chᵃkrᵃ. When disgust is generated by foul-tasting or foul-smelling food, it serves as a warning that the food is toxic; it threatens the security of the physical body and should not be eaten. If it has been eaten, it should be ejected. A disgusting object is one that one would want to "spit out" and not incorporate into the body.

The child may generalize its capacity for disgust to include foods that it simply finds unappealing. Famous examples are spinach and squash. The ego forms an opinion of these foods and symbolically designates them as disgusting or "yucky." It then refuses to have anything to do with them. The basis for experiencing disgust has then shifted from intrinsic properties of the object to opinions of it constructed by the ego as Me-maker. Opinion-based disgust plays an important role in first-lɛngᵃ functioning.

Cultural and religious differences in food preference and eating habits can be the basis of disgust. Some religions teach that the meat of the pig is "unclean," and simply the thought of eating it can make a believer want to vomit (while in other cultures pig meat is a major delicacy). The Tantric and Vedic traditions teach that all meat is tᵃmᵃs (ignorance-enhancing) and should be avoided by those seeking to develop spiritual qualities. Microchakra Psychology is generally in agreement with this view but suggests that some forms of fish and fowl may be necessary where the climate is colder. The Eskimo culture is the clearest example of this. Fish or fowl may be helpful in the treatment of some physical diseases.

The values and prejudices of parents are a fertile source for a child's acquisition of notions of disgust. The expression may be gross—the outright shunning of certain religions, races, or philosophical views—or as subtle as an upturned nose or grimace of the lips.

As the Me-maker determines what is disgusting, aesthetics can be a major factor in the choosing. Objects are more likely to be judged disgusting if they are at variance with pleasurable feeling-patterns already in our schematic network.

Second Chᵃkrᵃ. In the second chᵃkrᵃ, deficient personal hygiene is a common cause of disgust. The social disapproval of those who trigger this disgust is often considerable. Fear of becoming such a trigger helps to fuel giant cosmetic and advertising industries.

Disgust, by definition, involves personal repulsion. However, disgusting qualities that are not in the immediate environment are frequently a topic of fascination. Tabloid magazines and similar media are able to generate huge sales based on this. The minds of the first lɛngᵃ have an intrinsic interest in their own "shadow" side.

When we read reports of those who are moving along the path of spiritual devolution we are prompted to reflect on our own spiritual path. Our reflection may take many forms: it may be satisfaction with our own (perceived) moral superiority, it may be to register anger at the offender or to take pleasure in his degradation. On the other hand, it may be to observe "there but for the grace of God, go I" or to have compassion for the offender and all concerned.

Third Chᵃkrᵃ. In the third chᵃkrᵃ, personal disgust combines with group disgust. A person may even join a group to combat the seemingly disgusting qualities of another group. Often there is consensus on what constitutes a disgusting quality, and entire groups are universally condemned. Examples of such groups are price gougers, drunken drivers, and child molesters. In most cases, however, the definition of "disgusting" is in the eye of the beholder: farmers in the opinion of ranchers; conservatives in the opinion of liberals; or children in the opinion of some adults.

Blockages within the third chᵃkrᵃ and third microchakras may result in a weakening of ego. Failures that occur as a consequence of this weakness may be accompanied by feelings of self-disgust.

Second-LEngᵃ Disgust

Fourth Chᵃkrᵃ. Disgust is an affect that primarily belongs to the first lEngᵃ. In the fourth chᵃkrᵃ it is overwhelmed by love. There is a recognition that all external objects are Divine. Negative emotions either do not arise or they are given little or no weight in the functioning of the ego.

Fifth Chᵃkrᵃ. In the fifth chᵃkrᵃ, disgust is miniaturized into dislike of dissonant sound.

Third-LEngᵃ Disgust

Sixth Chᵃkrᵃ. In sixth chᵃkrᵃ awareness, there is a strong preference to direct the senses inward to experience finer, more beautiful energies. Disgust is abandoned along with other affects linked to the external world. The senior author encountered a vivid example of this way of life when he visited a holy man (saadhu) in India. This man deliberately dwelled near an open sewer that carried excrement from the village. But because his sense of smell had been internalized, he remained undisturbed by the odors of his surroundings.

Some Ego-Enhancing Later Positive Affects

- ✦ Eros
- ✦ Confidence
- ✦ Pride
- ✦ Hope

EROS

Ego experiences delectable sensations.

Dance of the Elements

The initial arousal of eros involves *fire* and *water*. Any vocal expression associated with eros utilizes *aakaashᵃ*.

A less intense experience of eros is *titillation*. A more intense experience of eros is *orgasm*.

First-LEngᵃ Eros

First Chᵃkrᵃ. Eros is a feeling derived from the sex drive of the central channel connected to the early brain. The principal object of the first chᵃkrᵃ is our own body. A positive attitude toward eros can integrate its energy into the sense of bodily well-being.

Second Chᵃkrᵃ. The second chᵃkrᵃ is the home of eros. The natural second-chᵃkrᵃ rhythms and associated hormones periodically activate eros without any external trigger. Eros is the principal affect in second-chᵃkrᵃ sexual exchanges. It may blend with other affects such as interest, play, joy, and love. Many view a successful and happy marriage as one in which this blend of affects is present.

If there is significant blockage in the second chᵃkrᵃ, eros will blend with such negative affects as guilt, shame, and hate. Then, interest in eros will be distorted or perverted.

Third Chᵃkrᵃ. The expression of eros in the third chᵃkrᵃ is very dependent upon readiness of the third-chᵃkrᵃ ego to surrender to the fourth chᵃkrᵃ. If it is far from ready, the third chᵃkrᵃ ego will utilize eros in its quest for power. This may manifest in the need for many sexual partners. Eros may also be used as a weapon to bend a partner to one's will.

Second-LEngᵃ Eros

The activity of pure erotic energy is usually limited to the first lEngᵃ. Openings in the microchakras of the fourth chᵃkrᵃ serve to naturally convert any erotic energy that rises there into love. The presence of blockages may prevent this conversion and result in a variety of erotic fantasies.

There are two main divisions of Tᵃntrᵃ: Left Tᵃntrᵃ and Right Tᵃntrᵃ. The latter is used to refine the ego and align with the higher chᵃkrᵃ-s. The former is practiced by those who merely wish to gain power over others. Both employ various erotic practices.

Couples engaged in right-Tantric sexual union bring eros to a higher quality in the heart chᵃkrᵃ. Such couples are usually—or usually become—soul mates.

CONFIDENCE

Ego judges itself competent to meet demands of a situation.

Dance of the Elements

A feeling of confidence is based primarily on the *earth* element, which is found in the first microchakra of all chᵃkrᵃ-s. Judgments of confidence are based on the state of this microchakra, combined with memories of past successes.

An ego expressing a less intense type of confidence is said to have *pluck*. An ego expressing a more intense type of confidence is said to be *brash* or *impudent*.

First-Lᴇɴɢᵃ Confidence

First Chᵃkrᵃ. Among the competencies that add to the feelings of confidence in the first-chᵃkrᵃ ego are: a) the ability to provide nutrition for the body, b) the ability to exercise the body, c) the ability to clothe the body, d) the ability to shelter the body, and e) the ability to rest the body.

Second Chᵃkrᵃ. Confidence in the second chᵃkrᵃ is based upon interpersonal skills. The more we are able to communicate with clarity and persuasiveness, be successful in business dealings, have friends, and a sound relationship with a mate, the more confident we will become.

Third Chᵃkrᵃ. Third chᵃkrᵃ confidence develops from the construction of a satisfactory relationship with one or more groups. The group may be our immediate or extended family, or a religious, sports, military, political, professional, or other group. Acceptance from the group, meeting the group's challenges, and being cheered—the louder and longer, the better—is the fuel for confidence.

Second-Lᴇɴɢᵃ Confidence

Fourth Chᵃkrᵃ. Belief in our feelings defines fourth chᵃkrᵃ confidence and a clear awareness emerges of the distinction between feeling and emotion. Feelings are closer to the subtle body (connected with the right hemisphere) than are emotions (connected with the early brain). The more confidence we have in our ability to observe and work with our feelings, the easier the path of ego refinement will be. This work with feeling may be enhanced by the mediation of left-hemisphere rationality. For example, inspirational stories of heroic deeds can strengthen feelings of faith and commitment.

Fifth Chᵃkrᵃ. Confidence in the fifth chᵃkrᵃ is defined by the surrender to *aakaashᵃ*. This surrender brings us closer to Cosmic Intelligence (Mᵃhᵃt). While it is helpful (but not essential) for the third microchakras of the lower four chᵃkrᵃ-s to be open, the surrender itself is imperative. It is the only way to rise above our ethnocentric background and morphogenetic limitations. Subtle sound and mᵃntrᵃ—which produces soorya *aakaashᵃ*—are traditional means of accomplishing the surrender.

The microchakra that must be open is the third of the fifth. If 5:3 is closed, surrender cannot occur; nor can the rate of breathing fall enough to effect true meditation, nor can we ever generate our own sooryᵃ *aakaashᵃ*. It is for this reason that, throughout history and in all cultures, the urge to open 5:3 has motivated some to use—and abuse—mind-expanding substances. Whereas these substances (sometimes called entheogens) act on the crucial third microchakra of the fifth chᵃkrᵃ, the effect is wildly undependable. Sooryᵃ *aakaashᵃ* is a much safer, more reliable, key to unlocking 5:3.

Lack of confidence in the fourth chᵃkrᵃ will severely inhibit the development of confidence in the fifth chᵃkrᵃ unless the ego of the fifth chᵃkrᵃ takes refuge in *aakaashᵃ* and allows the four chᵃkrᵃ minds below it to surrender.

Third-Lᴇɴɢᵃ Confidence

Sixth Chᵃkrᵃ. The surrender of the sixth-chᵃkrᵃ ego defines sixth-chᵃkrᵃ confidence. When this is done, a state of true meditation (4 breaths per minute or fewer) is achieved. When the third microchakra of the sixth chᵃkrᵃ is surrendered, we are allowed to witness the light above the prism (see page 83). This is a necessary prerequisite for the balancing of the guɴᵃ-s.

Seventh Chᵃkrᵃ. The surrender of the ego of the seventh chᵃkrᵃ (7:3), which enables the complete cessation of breath, defines seventh-chᵃkrᵃ confidence. (Sometimes the breath stops while daydreaming; this condition should not be confused with sᵃmaadhᴇ).

PRIDE

Ego judges itself praiseworthy for its accomplishments or possessions.

Dance of the Elements

Pride is related to the *fire* of ego. A person may be said to "shine with pride." Triggers of pride may include compliments from others or the judgment of our own ego.

A less intense attitude of pride is *satisfaction.* A more intense attitude of pride is *egotism* or *pretentiousness.*

First-Lᴇɴɢᵃ Pride

When first lᴇɴɢᵃ goals are attained, the attainment is usually accompanied by healthy pride. This feeling contributes to the smooth functioning of the first-lᴇɴɢᵃ egos and to their capacity for refinement. Excessive or unwarranted pride is called "vanity" and is discussed later in this chapter.

Second-Lᴇɴɢᵃ Pride

In the second lᴇɴɢᵃ, the caterpillar of pride is transformed into the butterfly of unconditional love. There is a deep appreciation of the truth of the Vedantic teaching that "you are not the doer" and an understanding that pride is an emotion that belongs to an earlier stage of one's development. Whereas in the first lᴇɴɢᵃ pride is a champion, in the second lᴇɴɢᵃ pride is a saboteur.

HOPE

Ego directs feeling toward possibility of goal attainment.

Dance of the Elements

In its purest form hope is associated with the energy of love and trust. Like love, hope travels on *air,* but hope also utilizes *aakaashᵃ,* which dissolves many of the saboteur thoughts that interfere with hope.

To *wish,* or to *await,* is to less intensely express hope. To *foresee* is to more intensely express hope.

First-Lᴇɴɢᵃ Hope

First Chᵃkrᵃ. In fulfilling the needs of the body, difficulties typically arise. But a healthy ego generates hope in order to stimulate effort to overcome any obstacle.

Second Chᵃkrᵃ. Second-chᵃkrᵃ activity focuses on interpersonal relationships. Hoping that these relationships will meet our expectations is part of the second-chᵃkrᵃ experience. Tact and diplomacy may be used to ensure success.

Third Chᵃkrᵃ. With respect to group activity, hope proceeds in phases. First there is the hope that one will be accepted into the group. Then there is the hope for good relationships within the group. This may be followed by hope for a leadership position in the group.

Second-Lᴇɴɢᵃ Hope

Fourth Chᵃkrᵃ. Hope is based in the fourth chᵃkrᵃ. It is the feeling that enables the ego to embrace the uncertainties of life and accept its adversities. The old question,

"What are the desires of thy heart?" asks what we hope for. Our answer reveals much about where we are on the psychospiritual path.

For those centered in the fourth chᵃkrᵃ, there may be a hope that prayers will be answered. In some faiths, there is a hope that the intensely worshipped deity will appear in the presence of the devotee.

Fifth Chᵃkrᵃ. In the fifth chᵃkrᵃ, there may be a hope that the voice will have the quality to produce enough sooryᵃ *aakaashᵃ* to lead to prᵃɴᵃvᵃ. Spiritual practices are often performed to awaken the inner guru.

Third-Lᴇɴgᵃ Hope

Sixth Chᵃkrᵃ. In the sixth chᵃkrᵃ, hope is directed at the integration of solar and lunar energies and the ability to function androgynously—neither emphasizing male nor female qualities. This happens when all three guɴᵃ-s are in balance.

Seventh Chᵃkrᵃ. The hope to attain nᴇrguɴᵃ sᵃmaadhᴇ is characteristic of the seventh chᵃkrᵃ. When this sᵃmaadhᴇ is attained and the guɴᵃ-s are in balance, there is nonaction in action (nɪshkᵃrmyᵃ sᴇddhᴇ).

Some Ego-Contracting Later Negative Affects

- ✦ Shyness
- ✦ Shame
- ✦ Guilt
- ✦ Sadness
- ✦ Envy
- ✦ Hate

The negative affects previously discussed—fear, anger, disgust, and distress—all have neurochemical circuits in the early brain and are intrinsic to every human, in or out of society. On the other hand, the affects of shyness, shame, and guilt as well as sadness, envy, and hate derive their meaning within a societal context. Without the society, these emotions cannot arise. Their existence is also dependent upon the evolutionary emergence of the cerebral cortex. Panksepp explained:

> When the mushrooming of the cortex *opened up* the relatively *closed* circuits of our old mammalian and reptilian brains, we started to entertain alternatives of our own rather than of nature's making. We can choose to enjoy fear. We can choose to make art out of our loneliness. We can even exert some degree of control over

our sexual orientations. Most other animals have no such options. Affectively, we can choose to be angels or devils, and we can construct and deconstruct ideas at will. We can choose to present ourselves in ways that are different from the ways we truly feel. We can be warm or acerbic, supportive or sarcastic at will. Animals cannot. These are options that the blossoming of the human cerebral mantle now offers for our consideration.[12]

Panksepp also noted that, "in some yet undetermined manner, these secondary, cognitive-type emotions may also be linked critically to the more primitive affective substrates . . . "[13] This, indeed, seems likely: we only have to reflect upon the fear and other primitive emotions that lie within such emotions as shame and hate.

SHYNESS

Ego feels vulnerable.

Although facial cues are minimal, and other expressive movements difficult to measure objectively, just about everyone feels confident in identifying signs of shyness. The toddler who responds to an approaching stranger by turning her head, hiding her face, and clinging to mother or father is recognized as shy. Similar types of behavior can be observed in infants as young as 3 or 4 months. . . .

The common core of the shyness experience is the feeling of vulnerability in social situations. It is the vulnerability of the self, the self-image or ego that is involved. This may make the shy individual inclined to avoid certain types of social encounters, but it does not necessarily make them unsociable. . . . The shy person may enjoy social life as much as the person who is not shy, but the conditions for social enjoyment may be different.[14]

Dance of the Elements

In shyness, the affect of assertiveness and the correlated *fire* are weaker than normal. Conversely, it is likely that the dissolving element of *aakaash*[a] has a stronger than normal influence on the ego. The shy child may feel slightly spacey, which causes uncertainty and contributes to her vulnerability.

A less intensely shy person is *meek* or *hesitant*. A more intensely shy person is *diffident* or *wary*.

First-Lᴇɴɢᵃ Shyness

Shyness is most common in toddlers or young children and fades as the child grows older and meets society's demands for assertiveness. If shyness should persist into the second- and third-chᵃkrᵃ ages, it functions as a saboteur of healthy ego functioning.

In adulthood, those who are shy may be attracted to confident people but have difficulty in establishing long-term relationships with them. It is easier to gravitate to others who are also shy.

Second-Lᴇɴɢᵃ Shyness

Should energy reach the second lᴇɴɢᵃ, any remaining shyness will dissolve. The act of surrendering the ego is what shy people really want. They much prefer a life based in the second lᴇɴɢᵃ to one in the first lᴇɴɢᵃ, where assertiveness is so important. In some cultures shyness is appreciated in women as a virtue and indicates someone who is more spiritually advanced than most.

SHAME

*Ego is partially consumed by its own fire in
response to the disapproval of self or others.*

Dance of the Elements

Awareness of the cause of shame tends to promote uncontrolled activity of *fire*. Those less susceptible to shame may reduce the scale of this tendency.

Shame is experienced less intensely when one is *embarrassed* or *teased*. Shame is experienced more intensely when one is *mortified, disgraced,* or *humiliated*.

First-Lᴇɴɢᵃ Shame

First Chᵃkrᵃ. A person's own body is the most likely trigger of shame in the first chᵃkrᵃ. It may be judged as too fat, too thin, too weak, and so forth. We may also be ashamed of speech or actions we have taken in pursuit of first-chᵃkrᵃ goals.

First-chᵃkrᵃ experiences of shame may be expressed in words as "I wished the earth would swallow me" or "I could have buried my head in the sand."

Second Chᵃkrᵃ. The genitals are the organ of action of the second chᵃkrᵃ. Shame associated with this organ may constrain a person to make love in the dark so that the partner does not see his nakedness. Some go so far as to avoid sexual partners altogether, and practice solitary masturbation.

Various attempts to promote relationships based on friendship, romance, or business may also result in actions for which shame is felt.

Sometimes we are deliberately shamed by another. Parents may punish children in front of their friends or relatives. Children with physical or mental abnormalities, or from a minority culture, are particularly vulnerable to being shamed by other children. Frequent derisive laughter can humiliate and provide long-term damage to a child.

Shame may be directed at other affects. We may be ashamed of our own greed or the greed of close friends or family members. Being ashamed of oneself for throwing a temper tantrum or otherwise "losing control" is relatively common.

Third Chªkrª. Shame administered by a group is third-chªkrª shame. It is usually derives from violation of a group code. Sports teams, student groups, religious groups, street gangs, social clubs, and others have different means for shaming their members into conformity with their codes. In some cultures, those who transgressed were forced to wear a special badge or have their heads shaved as ways of shaming them.

Sometimes we feel ashamed for lacking the skills that are expected of group members.

Episodes of shame are a normal part of human growth. Those who are "shameless" have a problem. However, when shame is administered in a vicious and traumatic manner, a life-long saboteur pattern may be established.

GUILT

Ego condemns itself for violating some value that it holds.

Dance of the Elements

Whereas shame weakens the ego, guilt does not. It is simply another (albeit difficult) fact with which the ego must cope. The ego may even be strengthened as it struggles with guilt. If, because of the pressure of guilt, a monumental job is undertaken, a large amount of energy may become available as adrenaline is released.

Feelings of guilt require some development of conscience whose source is the fourth-chªkrª capacity for empathy. Conscience entails significant openings in the ego (4:3) and intuition (4:6) of the heart (*air*) chªkrª. If these microchakras are blocked, the person will lack the necessary sensitivity to truly feel guilt (although pretense will be possible).

Self-reproach is a less intense feeling of guilt. *Remorse* is a more intense feeling of guilt.

First-Lengᵃ Guilt

First Chᵃkrᵃ. In the first chᵃkrᵃ, the ego may feel guilty for failing to adequately care for the body even though it has the capacity to do so. In some circumstances, it may feel guilty for not developing the skills necessary to adequately feed, exercise, clothe, and shelter the body.

Second Chᵃkrᵃ. Situations that might arouse guilt in the second chᵃkrᵃ include: being unfaithful to a spouse, failing to help a friend, stealing from a business partner, and ignoring a neighbor or a stranger whom we could have helped.

Third Chᵃkrᵃ. Action taken against a group may be cause for feelings of remorse or guilt. The action is often verbal: we may speak in a derogatory manner about a group or group member, only to discover later that the slander had been uncalled for. A more severe example of guilt is that of a person who has committed treason against her country. Such a person may feel guilty for as long as she lives.

Second-Lengᵃ Guilt

Fourth Chᵃkrᵃ. In the first three chᵃkrᵃ-s, guilt is tied to our relationships in the physical field. In the fourth chᵃkrᵃ, any feelings of guilt are tied to our metaphysical belief system. The concept of "sin" has been used by various religions to script guilt and fear into the relationship between the individual and the Divine. This may create more problems than it solves for those on a sincere psychospiritual quest.

SADNESS

Ego is aware of its separation from a valued object.

Dance of the Elements

In sadness, the natural gregariousness of *water* is inhibited. It may hide itself in *earth.* In deep grief, it is transformed to tears. Grief that rends the heart uses dark *aakaashᵃ* to express itself through sobs and moans.

Less intense types of sadness are *unhappiness* or *disappointment.* More intense types of sadness are *heartbreak, grief,* and *depression.*

First-Lengᵃ Sadness

First Chᵃkrᵃ. First-chᵃkrᵃ losses that may lead to sadness include loss of health, loss of money, loss of land, and loss of shelter.

Second Chᵃkrᵃ. The second chᵃkrᵃ is the source of sadness associated with interpersonal relationships: sadness at not finding a mate, sadness over a dispute with a friend or learning that a friend has encountered misfortune, sadness related to the departure of a loved one or related to the loved one's illness or death.

Third Chᵃkrᵃ. Third-chᵃkrᵃ sadness is often associated with loss of status within a group. It may also be based on a calamity undergone by a group of which the person is a member.

Second-Lᴇɴgᵃ Sadness

Fourth Chᵃkrᵃ. The prototype for sadness occurs in the fourth chᵃkrᵃ. It is based on the awareness of separation from the Source of all. This derives from the original separation of Potentiality (Mahaakuɴdᵃlᴇɴᴇᴇ) from Stasis (Pᵃrᵃmᵃ Shᴇvᵃ). An awareness of this separation is part of the unconscious motivation of all and is stored in the accumulated (sᵃmchᴇtᵃ) kᵃrmᵃ. This type of sadness may be emphasized by some religions and philosophies.

Fifth Chᵃkrᵃ. A very miniaturized feeling of sadness may occur in the fifth chᵃkrᵃ if this chᵃkrᵃ-s goals are not met; for example, if the inner guru is not awakened.

Sadness does not extend into the third lᴇɴgᵃ.

ENVY

Ego feels inferior because of another's possession,
accomplishment, or quality and desires to take it for itself.

Dance of the Elements

The *fire* of the ego is weakened by *earth* or *water* as envy attacks it. The ego feels diminished, partially buried, or drowned, and fights back by directing its remaining *fire* at the envied one.

To *hanker* for is to less intensely envy. To *begrudge* is to more intensely envy.

First-Lᴇɴgᵃ Envy

First Chᵃkrᵃ. The objects that may elicit envy in the first chᵃkrᵃ are innumerable, several examples being: physique, health, money, and material goods (house, car, clothes, jewelry).

Second Chᵃkrᵃ. In the second chᵃkrᵃ, interpersonal relationships are envied; for example, the relationship between husband and wife, or father and daughter, or employer and employee, or guru and disciple.

Third Chᵃkrᵃ. The relationship between an individual and a group is the object of envy in the third chᵃkrᵃ. Such relationships may include: membership in an exclusive club, an entertainer's popularity with an audience, or a politician's high stature with the electorate.

Second-Leng^a Envy

Envy is an affect that is usually limited to the first lɛng^a. If energy is sufficiently refined to move to the higher lɛng^a-s, it is unlikely to be captured by envy. In the rare cases when envy does occur in the higher lɛng^a-s, it is in a much-reduced form and is directed toward the spiritual accomplishments of another.

HATE

Ego wishes to seriously injure or kill.

Dance of the Elements

Hate is the arousal of the central-channel instinct to kill that was developed during the long evolutionary climb. It arranges any and all elements to serve this purpose. Sometimes hate is accompanied either by anger or by a "cold fury."

A less intense form of hate is *abhorrence*. A more intense form of hate is *psychotic loathing*.

First-Leng^a Hate

First Ch^akr^a. Hate may be directed toward anyone who is perceived as threatening the first-ch^akr^a goal of physical survival. Sometimes a pattern of saboteurs will cause hatred to be aimed at the self, with an attendant danger of suicide.

Second Ch^akr^a. In the second ch^akr^a, hate may be aimed at anyone who interferes (or threatens to interfere) with an important relationship. It may also be directed at the partner in a relationship when that relationship breaks down.

Third Ch^akr^a. In the third ch^akr^a, hate is directed at a group. An individual may hate a group or one group may hate another. In wartime, hate may be directed at the enemy. Sometimes hatred (or something close to it) is directed toward a competitive group. Common examples may be found in business or sports.

Beyond the first lɛng^a, it is not possible to arouse hatred.

Some Ego-Refining Later Positive Affects

- ✦ Love
- ✦ Gratitude
- ✦ Serenity

LOVE

Ego has heart-felt devotion to an object.

Dance of the Elements

It is the *air* of the heart chᵃkrᵃ that conveys love, whether that love be a tender touch or the adoration of a deity.

To *care for,* or to *like* is to less intensely love. To *adore* or to *venerate,* is to more intensely love.

First-Lᴇɴɢᵃ Love

First Chᵃkrᵃ. The home of love is in the fourth chᵃkrᵃ where it is found in its purest form. It descends into the first lᴇɴɢᵃ via the fourth microchakras. In the first chᵃkrᵃ, 1:4 permits the ego to love its body and thereby care for it. Healthy self-love is a foundation upon which higher forms of love may build.

Second Chᵃkrᵃ. The flow of energy in 2:4 facilitates the attainment of all goals in the play of the second chᵃkrᵃ. All human relationships, even the most casual, are enhanced by the presence of reciprocal love in some amount.

Third Chᵃkrᵃ. The purpose of love in 3:4 is to refine the ego of the third chᵃkrᵃ in preparation for its surrender to the second lᴇɴɢᵃ. Philanthropic and various service organizations tend to recruit those who have 3:4 open. Living such teachings as "Love thy neighbor as thyself" may help to open 3:4.

Second-Lᴇɴɢᵃ Love

Fourth Chᵃkrᵃ. The root of love is in the fourth chᵃkrᵃ where inspiration also resides. The beloved inspires the ego, which sees in the beloved some portion of the divine qualities of Truth, Goodness, and Beauty (sᵃtyᵃm, shᴇvᵃm, sundᵃrᵃm).

The prototype of love is the ego's love for the Divine itself. The ego may accompany this love with a feeling of gratitude for all the True, Good, and Beautiful things that it has experienced. It may also feel devotion and a desire to serve the deity, a cause, or any aspect of life itself.

Fourth-chᵃkrᵃ love is unconditional. It is based only on the ego's recognizing and valuing the qualities of the loved object—not on any action that the beloved might take vis-à-vis the lover.

Air is the dominant element in the fourth chᵃkrᵃ and forms the basis of love (as seen in chapter 3, *air* is symbolized by the leaping deer). In love, the ego has two choices: it may attempt to merge with the loved object, or maintain a distance that permits awe and devotion. These are the two perspectives of love: union and separation.

Fifth Ch^akr^a. The objects of love in the fifth ch^akr^a are *aakaash^a* and sound because they bring the ego closer to the True, the Good, and the Beautiful within us.

Third-LEng^a Love

Sixth Ch^akr^a. The sixth ch^akr^a is beyond the elements and beyond lunar/solar duality. This is symbolized by the androgynous deity Ardh^anaarEEshv^ar^a—half man and half woman. Love at this stage greatly exceeds in refinement that which originated in the fourth ch^akr^a. It is now a subtle energy circulating with the symbolically intertwined halves of Ardh^anaarEEshv^ar^a.

Seventh Ch^akr^a. In the seventh ch^akr^a, Love merges into Bliss (aanand^a) as all traces of duality fade away. Consciousness alone exists—the all-encompassing Subject.

GRATITUDE

Ego acknowledges the assistance of one or more others in fulfilling its desires.

Dance of the Elements

The manner in which *air* is used to refine the *fire* of the ego is dependent upon the thoughts that shape the particular affect. When an ego is aware of its indebtedness to another, it summons a modified form of love to express this awareness. This is gratitude.

A less intense manifestation of gratitude is *thanks*, or *appreciation*. A more intense manifestation of gratitude is *blessing*.

First-LEng^a Gratitude

First Ch^akr^a. Gratitude is a derivative of love. The ego is touched by the goodness of the other and wishes to acknowledge this feeling. In the first ch^akr^a, gratitude may be expressed for a healthy body and directed toward our parents; or, gratitude may be shown to teachers and employers who are responsible for our being able to provide for ourselves. If health has been imperiled, gratitude may go to those who restored it.

Second Ch^akr^a. The second ch^akr^a aims at achieving good relationships with others but especially those relationships that place the person at a slight advantage. Gratitude toward those who have provided comfort and pleasure in these relationships can mitigate the selfish aspect and, thereby, help to refine the ego.

Third Ch^akr^a. Gratitude in the third ch^akr^a is directed to those groups that have welcomed our participation. Such gratitude often causes intensified activity on behalf of the group and gives us an added sense of identity. Gratitude is also a means of repaying karmic debt. On a civic level, we may be so grateful to our country that we volunteer to risk our life for it.

Second-LEngᵃ Gratitude

Fourth Chᵃkrᵃ. In the first lengᵃ, the perceived source of goodness to which gratitude is offered are other people or forces in the material field. Now, in the second lengᵃ, gratitude is offered to an entity in the nonmaterial fields, usually a deity or abstract principle.

The refinement of the ego based on gratitude continues. As with the affect of love, the grateful individual may seek to merge with—or establish an awe-ful distance from—that which evokes the gratitude.

Fifth Chᵃkrᵃ. The aesthetic neck and throat area is the recipient of the fifth-chᵃkrᵃ energy, *aakaashᵃ,* and a doorway to the third lengᵃ. When refined sooryᵃ *aakaashᵃ* enters L5:6, it may awaken the inner guru. Gratitude for this awakening will be felt toward the outer guru who first provided this sooryᵃ *aakaashᵃ*.

Third-LEngᵃ Gratitude

Sixth Chᵃkrᵃ. In the sixth chᵃkrᵃ, the elements have been transcended and attention is focused on the guNᵃ-s. If gratitude appears at all, it would be focused on the spiritual tradition that enabled the aspirant to experience the sixth chᵃkrᵃ and continue on the path of Self-discovery.

Seventh Chᵃkrᵃ. Nonduality has been achieved. There is no "other" to receive gratitude.

SERENITY

Ego functions with no sense of tension or stress.

Dance of the Elements

In periods of serenity, the champion patterns are dominant and information processing proceeds smoothly. Any or all elements may be active. Breathing rate is in the range of 16 to 12 breaths per minute, and slightly lower when awareness is in the higher lengᵃ-s.

One who is less intensely serene is *placid*. One who is more intensely serene is *impassive*.

First-LEngᵃ Serenity

In the first lengᵃ the senses are directed outward. When first-lengᵃ minds are serene there is often a feeling that all is well with the (outer) world.

Second-Lᴇɴɢᵃ Serenity

In the second lᴇɴɢᵃ the senses either continue to be directed outward toward a deity who inspires serenity, or inward, toward the inner guru and a serenity derived from absorption in *aakaashᵃ*. Consequently, periods of serenity are much more frequent with a breathing rate of around eight breaths per minute.

Third-Lᴇɴɢᵃ Serenity

In the third lᴇɴɢᵃ, eightfold nature—the source of serenity's disruption—has been transcended. All activities are now done in a state of serenity.

Some Ego-Inflating Later Negative Affects

- ✦ Possessiveness
- ✦ Greed
- ✦ Vanity

POSSESSIVENESS

Ego will not share.

Dance of the Elements

At the root of possessiveness is a fear that we will lose what we have. This fear, like all others, is tied to *water*. The ferocity with which we are possessive involves the degree of *fire*. The cunning that we employ to be possessive may draw upon the creativity available from *aakaashᵃ*.

An ego that is less intensely possessive is *protective*. An ego that is more intensely possessive is *jealous*.

First-Lᴇɴɢᵃ Possessiveness

First Chᵃkrᵃ. The objects that satisfy the needs of the first chᵃkrᵃ (money, food, clothing, housing) may be the cause for feelings of possessiveness.

Second Chᵃkrᵃ. In the second chᵃkrᵃ, possessiveness causes us to restrict (or attempt to restrict) the freedom of those with whom we have relationships. The more dominant we are in the relationship, the easier it is to be possessive.

Third Chᵃkrᵃ. In the third chᵃkrᵃ, possessiveness is often focused on the sources of power. Employees may not be willing to share their "know-how" with other employees. Companies take steps to protect their trade secrets. Whereas, in the first two chᵃkrᵃ-s, possessiveness is usually an obstacle to spiritual growth, the situation in the third chᵃkrᵃ is more complex. There may be practical and, indeed, dharmic reasons for being possessive.

Possessiveness is confined to the first lɛngᵃ.

GREED

Ego has an insatiable desire for some objects.

Dance of the Elements

The prototypical greed is excessive indulgence in food. The term for this is gluttony, and is associated with digestive *fire*. Other forms of greed also make use of an insatiable consuming *fire*. It has been said that Nature can provide for all of the needs of everyone but is unable to provide for all of the wants of anyone.

An ego that is less intensely greedy is *acquisitive*. An ego that is more intensely greedy is *avaricious*.

First-Lɛngᵃ Greed

First Chᵃkrᵃ. Greed in the first chᵃkrᵃ is for material comforts.

Second Chᵃkrᵃ. In the second chᵃkrᵃ, males may be greedy for the attention of females and vice versa.

Third Chᵃkrᵃ. Greed for power is the chief greed of the third chᵃkrᵃ. It is the source of much human strife and warfare, and forms the basis of the constant conflict that characterizes the present Kᵃlɛ yugᵃ. Greed is a major factor in keeping the triangle of the third chᵃkrᵃ burning downward.

Greed seldom rises beyond the first lɛngᵃ.

VANITY

Ego exaggerates its qualities or accomplishments.

Dance of the Elements

The vain ego has the perception of itself inflated by *air*. In a sense, the person is literally "full of hot *air*." This distortion is aided by excessive direction of love (and its *air*) toward the self. The grounding effect of *earth* is minimal. The play of vanity floats upon the *water* of fear—fear of casting an image less attractive than desired. For example, vanity motivates a person to drive a car that is more expensive than can be afforded.

A less intensely vain ego is *puffed up*. A more intensely vain ego is *swaggering*.

First-Lɛŋgᵃ Vanity

First Chᵃkrᵃ. When vanity is operating in the first chᵃkrᵃ, possessions (such as body, car, clothing, jewelry, home) are perceived to be grander than most others would judge them to be.

Second Chᵃkrᵃ. In the second chᵃkrᵃ, vanity may cause a variety of difficulties in interpersonal relations. Honest exchange is not possible because the vain ego cannot present an unbiased perception of itself. Some insecure people may fantasize their desirability.

Third Chᵃkrᵃ. Just as in the second chᵃkrᵃ, honest communication is impaired. Hence it is difficult to participate in a group in a realistic way. If, despite this, some status in a group is achieved, it will be used to further feed the person's vanity. It is very difficult to be a true friend or to find one.

Vanity is usually limited to the first lɛŋgᵃ.

Some Ego-Transcending Later Positive Affects

✦ Contentment

✦ Bliss

CONTENTMENT

Ego has reached its goal. No desire remains.

Dance of the Elements

When contentment is felt, it registers in the seventh microchakra of each chᵃkrᵃ. The dance of the elements in the lower microchakras is witnessed with ease and laughter. This script holds true for all chᵃkrᵃ-s in the first two lɛŋgᵃ-s. In the sixth chᵃkrᵃ, contentment occurs when the three guɴᵃ-s are in balance. In the seventh chᵃkrᵃ, contentment is replaced by silence and bliss.

BLISS

Bliss is the natural state of Consciousness.

Bliss is the only monistic affect and, unlike the other affects, is not an experience. It is the complete surrender of the refined ego as it submerges in Consciousness. In the state of bliss, duality has evaporated.

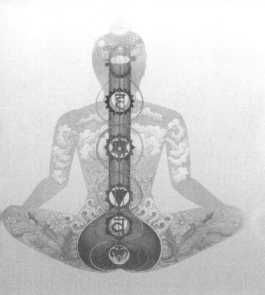

10
Integrating the Three Bodies

THE SIGNIFICANCE OF INTEGRATION

In chapter 2, it was stated that the two cerebral hemispheres evolved in order to civilize the early brain. In the early stages of this process, some Darwinian method of evolution might have occurred. Now, however, the task of evolution is with education and the need for each member of society to eventually learn how to work efficiently with their own nonmaterial energies. This chapter provides an introduction to some methods intended to be helpful in this lifelong task.

It will be recalled that the three fields in which the play of life occurs are the causal, subtle, and physical and that, in the human, these are represented by the thought body, the feeling body, and the physical body. It will also be recalled that the thought body operates at the highest rate of vibration and pervades the other two. The next fastest rate of vibration occurs in the feeling body that pervades the physical body. The physical body operates at the slowest rate of vibration and is also the one to which our awareness is most adapted.

The Three Bodies and the Tripartite Brain. The thought body, at the physical level, is based in the left hemisphere of the brain; at the subtle level it operates mainly through the first, third, and fifth chᵃkrᵃ-s—the solar chᵃkrᵃ-s.

The feeling body is based in the right hemisphere at the physical level; at the subtle level it operates primarily through the second, fourth, and sixth chᵃkrᵃ-s—the lunar chᵃkrᵃ-s.

The early brain is the seat of the intuition that first called for the emergence of the cerebral hemispheres in order to fulfill its vast potential. It operates through the sixth microchakras in the central channel and increasingly demands coordination of the tripartite brain so that all minds may harmonize their reason, feeling, and intuition; that is, act in an integrated manner. Information operating at different speeds (vibrational levels) must be drawn together in awareness.

This is done by opening the appropriate microchakras.

The methods of integration to be considered in this chapter are:

+ Synchronizing with the Cosmic Cycles
+ The Dawn Program
+ Internalizing the Senses
+ Increasing Sound Sensitivity
+ Integrative Mentation
+ Meditation
+ Witnessing
+ Three-Body Purification
+ Speech Fast
+ Regulating Desire
+ Color of the Day

SYNCHRONIZING
WITH THE COSMIC CYCLES

The emerging field of chronobiology studies the importance of the rhythmic recurrence of biological events. It distinguishes three classes of rhythms: 1) ultradian, those that occur more often than once per day, 2) circadian, those that last approximately twenty-four hours, and 3) infradian, those that occur less often than once per day. Chronobiology is discovering something known to the Tantric and Vedic traditions for centuries: namely, that optimum health and well-being is connected to living in harmony with these rhythms. Conversely, disruption of these rhythms contributes to poor functioning and poor health.

Ultradian Rhythms

The typical ultradian rhythm lasts between 90 and 120 minutes. In discussing how these rhythms may be seen as a bridge between biology and psychology, E. L. Rossi and B. M. Lippincott listed numerous ultradian rhythms that have been the subject of experimental investigation.[1] These included cycles of muscle tonicity, response latency, thermoregulation, urine flow, fantasy, and affective behavior.

Nasal Rhythms

Of particular interest to InnerTuning are the comments of Rossi and Lippincott on the nasal cycle:

In a wide ranging series of studies Werntz et. al. . . . found that subjects could voluntarily shift their nasal dominance by forced uni-nostril breathing through the closed nostril. Further, this shift in nasal dominance was associated with an accompanying shift in cerebral dominance to the contralateral hemisphere and autonomic nervous system balance throughout the body. . . . The ultradian nasal cycle is not only a marker for cerebral hemispheric activity, but it also could be used to change voluntarily the loci of activity in the highest centers of the brain and autonomic system that are involved in cybernetic loops of communication with most organ systems, tissues, and cells of the body. Some of these investigators hypothesized that this nasal-brain-mind link may be the essential path by which the ancient practice of breath regulation in yoga led to the voluntary control of many autonomic nervous systems functions for which the Eastern adepts are noted . . .[2]

The nasal cycle has indeed been used by svᵃrᵃ yogis (adepts in the science of breath) for centuries and has a basic role in InnerTuning. When the breath is moving predominantly through the left nostril (ɛdaa), the right hemisphere is more active; when it is moving predominantly through the right nostril (pɛngᵃlᵃ), the left hemisphere is more active. When the breath is moving through both nostrils equally it is in sushumnaa and hemispheric functioning is balanced.

Sushumnaa breath occurs naturally a few minutes before sunrise. It occurs again at sunset and briefly during the transition of the breath from one nostril to another. At these times it does not usually last longer than 56 seconds. However, it is a necessary condition for deep meditation, and sushumnaa breath is extended beyond 56 seconds by meditators—a point discussed in more detail below.

When the right nostril is dominant, body chemistry is predominantly acidic (the stomach secretes more gastric acid) and more body heat is produced. The temperament is more assertive.

On the other hand, when the left nostril is dominant, body chemistry is predominantly alkaline and the system is cooled. The temperament is more passive. When breath is in the sushumnaa channel, chemistry reaches a state of equilibrium.

Nasal Rhythm and Various Tasks

Some tasks are governed primarily by the right cerebral hemisphere such as drinking, working with melody, focusing on feelings, or visualizing art. If the left nostril is open at these times, the right hemisphere will be fueled with lunar energy and the tasks better performed.

A similar situation holds for tasks that are primarily governed by the left hemisphere such as eating, working with rhythm, reasoning, and speaking. Solar energy from an open right nostril enhances performance of these tasks.

When the three bodies are integrated, the left nostril is more frequently open during the day and the right nostril during the night. Yogis aspire to this phenomenon. Methods of deliberately switching nostril dominance are described in the discussion of the dawn program below.

Circadian Rhythms

In its long evolutionary development, the human body has adapted in various ways to the changing amount of light from one sunrise to the next. This solar rhythm of 24 hours forms an external clock. The internal physiological processes that are joined to this clock have been termed "circadian" rhythms (L. *circa,* approximately; *dies,* day). The cycle of waking and sleeping is the most obvious circadian cycle. R. Refinetti gave a comprehensive review of circadian physiology and the strong evidence that, in the human, the circadian pacemaker is centered in a small nucleus at the base of the brain called the *suprachiasmatic nucleus.*[3]

The Pineal Gland

Located in the center of the brain is a small gland about one centimeter long. It is called the "pineal" gland because it is shaped like a pinecone. Descartes (d. 1650) believed that it was the seat of the soul since it appeared to be undivided into left and right halves. In a later century, microscopic examination showed that it is composed of two halves.

The pineal gland is located deep in the brain behind the space between the two eyes. Some mystical traditions have called it a "third eye" and associate it with the light used in some parapsychological abilities such as clairvoyance. It is the sense organ of the sixth chªkrª and the organ of action for the seventh chªkrª.

The pineal gland helps to regulate the amount of the melatonin hormone in the system that it produces during the dark half of the diurnal cycle. Melatonin secretion by the pineal gland reaches a climax around 3:00 a.m. Melatonin serves a variety of functions including antioxidation and retinal support.

In the modern age, the greatest enemy of the pineal gland is the electric light bulb. Before this invention, people, for the most part, lived their lives in synchrony with the diurnal cycle of light and dark. They arose long before dawn and retired relatively soon after dark. With this lifestyle, melatonin production was unimpaired and balance maintained with serotonin and dopamine.

Today, few notice when the sun rises or sets. Ignoring this rhythm may cause special difficulties for night-shift workers and those who travel across time zones by jet airplane. Such people are often required to engage in the activities of the day when their circadian rhythm is set to night or vice versa. These and other challenges of modern life make it doubly important to appreciate the circadian rhythm and the benefits that can accrue from working with it rather than against it.

Practitioners of InnerTuning try to maximize their production of melatonin by using artificial light as little as possible. During the night, low wattage lights are scattered throughout the house and flashlights used when needed.

Infradian Rhythms

The infradian rhythm of most importance to InnerTuning is the lunar cycle or lunar month. This month is measured from new moon to new moon and requires an average period of 29.53 solar days. During the lunar month the moon goes through all of its phases. At the new moon, the unilluminated side of the moon is facing earth; therefore, the moon is not visible. During the next fortnight, the side facing earth gradually becomes more and more illuminated. Commonly identified phases during this period are the waxing crescent moon, the first-quarter moon, and the waxing gibbous moon. The fortnight culminates with the appearance of the full moon. The moon then enters its waning phase and passes through the stages of waning gibbous moon, last-quarter moon, and waning crescent moon. Finally, another new moon appears and the cycle repeats.

The Tantric tradition divides the lunar month into 30 equal parts, which are termed tɛthɛ-s. A tɛthɛ refers to the angle that the earth makes with the sun and the moon. During a lunar month, this angle travels through 360 degrees. Hence, each tɛthɛ is 12 degrees. The first tɛthɛ begins at the new moon and the sixteenth tɛthɛ at the full moon. The duration of a tɛthɛ varies within the approximate range of 20 to 27 hours.

Nasal Cycle and the Tɛthɛ-s

In the science of svᵃrᵃ yogᵃ, an important relationship between the nasal cycle and the tɛthɛ-s was discovered. It was found that, after the new moon, the left nostril is operating at the moment of sunrise and continues to be dominant for at least one hour. This domination of the left nostril and active right hemisphere occurs on each of the next two mornings. The reverse is true after the full moon; that is, the right nostril and left hemisphere are dominant at sunrise for three days. At other times a pattern of three left days followed by three right days (or vice versa) usually occurs.

When there is a disturbance in the natural cycle and the proper nostril does not open for an extended period of days, body chemistry becomes disturbed. Psychological and physiological difficulties may be apparent in such a period.

In order to assist students of this system to check their nasal cycle, InnerTuning publishes an annual *Prana Calendar* (at www.innertuning.com), which combines the solar and lunar calendars. For each day of the year, the *Prana Calendar* gives the time of sunrise and the nostril that should be dominant at that time. Procedures for shifting nostril dominance are discussed later in this chapter in reference to the dawn program.

Ch^a^kr^a^ Rhythms

In addition to the ultradian rhythms of the physical field, InnerTuning suggests that there is an ultradian rhythm in the subtle field. This is due to the fact that, during a twenty-four hour period, energy cycles twice through all seven ch^a^kr^a^-s. This is illustrated in Table 10.1 on pages 268–269. Entries in the chart are obtained by dividing the amount of time between sunrise and sunset by seven, and similarly dividing the time between sunset and sunrise. This ultradian rhythm in the subtle field influences those in the physical field as energy moves from subtle to gross.

The ch^a^kr^a^ energy chart shown in Table 10.1 is calculated for New York City. To use the chart, the reader should determine the time of sunrise and sunset at his or her location and adjust the times for each ch^a^kr^a^ period accordingly. It is the same every year in each city. At sunrise the petals of each ch^a^kr^a^ lotus open; at sunset, they close.

Energy drops from the seventh to the first ch^a^kr^a^ in both the AM and PM. The chart is originally derived from the fact that, at the equator, the early morning drop takes place two hours before sunrise. It was in India, near the equator, that sv^a^r^a^ yog^a^ was discovered millennia ago. The farther you are from the equator (humanity's birthplace) the more the difficulties you will experience with the first ch^a^kr^a^.

As the circadian cycle unfolds, the nested cycle of the ch^a^kr^a^-s is activated: each ch^a^kr^a^ successively becomes the most active ch^a^kr^a^. This cycle of ch^a^kr^a^ activity has major consequences for human physiology and psychology. Of particular importance is the period before sunrise when the first and second ch^a^kr^a^-s are activated.

The First-Ch^a^kr^a^ Period

Two hours before the sun rises at the equator, there is a sudden drop of energy from the seventh ch^a^kr^a^ to the first. The body squirms, trying to wake us up. Most healthy babies naturally have a bowel movement during the first-ch^a^kr^a^ hour.

When energy enters the first ch^a^kr^a^, insecurities associated with blocked energy in this ch^a^kr^a^ are aroused. A bowel movement at this time eliminates apaan^a^ and prevents the blockages from being strengthened. If the bowel movement leads to contentment (momentary opening of 1:7) feelings of insecurity are lessened. This is an opportune time to work on issues connected to those feelings.

TABLE 10.1 CHᴬKRᴬ ENERGY CHART

Chᵃkrᵃ	Jan-1	Jan-15	Feb-1	Feb-15	Mar-1	Mar-15	Apr-1	Apr-15	May-1	May-15	Jun-1	Jun-15
1	4:50	4:50	4:43	4:31	4:17	4:00	3:38	4:22	4:04	3:53	3:45	3:43
2	6:56	6:54	6:42	6:26	6:06	5:44	5:16	5:54	5:31	5:15	5:03	5:00
Sunrise	7:20	7:18	7:06	6:50	6:30	6:08	5:40	6:18	5:55	5:39	5:27	5:24
3	8:15	8:16	8:08	7:57	7:42	7:26	7:04	7:47	7:30	7:18	7:10	7:09
4	9:35	9:38	9:35	9:28	9:19	9:08	8:53	9:41	9:30	9:22	9:18	9:18
5	10:55	11:00	11:02	11:00	10:56	10:50	10:41	11:35	11:29	11:26	11:26	11:27
6	12:15	12:22	12:28	12:31	12:32	12:32	12:30	13:29	13:29	13:30	13:33	13:37
7	13:35	13:44	13:55	14:03	14:09	14:14	14:18	15:23	15:28	15:34	15:41	15:46
1	14:55	15:06	15:22	15:34	15:46	15:56	16:07	17:17	17:28	17:38	17:49	17:55
2	16:15	16:29	16:49	17:06	17:23	17:38	17:56	19:11	19:28	19:42	19:57	20:05
Sunset	16:39	16:53	17:13	17:30	17:47	18:02	18:20	19:35	19:52	20:06	20:21	20:29
3	18:20	18:32	18:48	19:00	19:12	19:21	19:33	20:42	20:54	21:03	21:15	21:21
4	20:26	20:36	20:47	20:54	21:01	21:05	21:10	22:14	22:20	22:25	22:33	22:37
5	22:32	22:39	22:46	22:48	22:50	22:49	22:47	23:46	23:46	23:47	23:51	23:54
6	0:38	0:43	0:45	0:43	0:39	0:32	0:24	1:18	1:12	1:09	1:09	1:10
7	2:44	2:46	2:44	2:37	2:28	2:16	2:01	2:50	2:38	2:31	2:27	2:27

Chᵃkrᵃ	Jul-1	Jul-15	Aug-1	Aug-15	Sep-1	Sep-15	Oct-1	Oct-15	Nov-1	Nov-15	Dec-1	Dec-15
1	3:47	3:54	4:05	4:14	4:24	4:33	4:43	4:52	4:05	4:17	4:31	4:42
2	5:04	5:13	5:28	5:42	5:58	6:12	6:28	6:43	6:02	6:18	6:36	6:49
Sunrise	5:28	5:37	5:52	6:06	6:22	6:36	6:52	7:07	6:26	6:42	7:00	7:13
3	7:13	7:20	7:30	7:40	7:50	7:59	8:08	8:18	7:31	7:43	7:57	8:08
4	9:22	9:27	9:33	9:38	9:42	9:46	9:49	9:54	9:00	9:08	9:18	9:27
5	11:31	11:34	11:36	11:36	11:35	11:33	11:30	11:29	10:30	10:33	10:39	10:47
6	13:40	13:41	13:39	13:35	13:27	13:20	13:11	13:05	11:59	11:58	12:01	12:06
7	15:49	15:48	15:42	15:33	15:20	15:07	14:52	14:40	13:29	13:23	13:22	13:26
1	17:58	17:55	17:45	17:31	17:12	16:54	16:33	16:16	14:58	14:48	14:43	14:45
2	20:07	20:02	19:48	19:30	19:05	18:41	18:14	17:52	16:28	16:14	16:05	16:05
Sunset	20:31	20:26	20:12	19:54	19:29	19:05	18:38	18:16	16:52	16:38	16:29	16:29
3	21:23	21:20	21:10	20:57	20:38	20:19	19:58	19:42	18:24	18:14	18:09	18:11
4	22:40	22:39	22:33	22:24	22:11	21:58	21:43	21:32	20:20	20:15	20:13	20:17
5	23:57	23:58	23:56	23:52	23:44	23:37	23:28	23:22	22:16	22:15	22:18	22:23
6	1:13	1:16	1:19	1:19	1:18	1:15	1:13	1:12	0:13	0:16	0:22	0:30
7	2:30	2:35	2:42	2:47	2:51	2:54	2:58	3:02	2:09	2:16	2:27	2:36

On the other hand, many people do not take advantage of this rhythm. Their insecurities cause them to cling to the comfort of their "security blanket" and they are functionally anally retentive. This pattern simply strengthens the feelings of insecurity.

Each individual has to find his or her own time of peristalsis in the first-chᵃkrᵃ period to enjoy perfect health of all three bodies.

The first-chᵃkrᵃ period is Brahmᵃ muhoortᵃ, the time of Brᵃhmaa, who is portrayed with four heads, one head looking toward each of the four cardinal points of the compass. Visualizing yourself seated and relaxed in the center of a yellow square with an awareness of the four directions will evoke archetypal feelings of security and prepare you for a spiritual journey.

The Second-Chᵃkrᵃ Period

This is a very special time in the circadian cycle. Spiritual traditions all over the world have recognized it and greeted the dawn with prayer and ritual. Even the birds recognize this unique time of day and announce it with great enthusiasm. The air is crisp and fresh. It is the optimum time for meditation and absorption of sᵃtvᵃ. In addition, rising before sunrise helps to integrate the three bodies. "Do not let the sun catch you in bed" is the advice of the guru.

Twenty-four minutes before the sunrise, energy moves to the second chᵃkrᵃ. If you are asleep, fear-laden dreams may occur and strengthen the blocks associated with the fear. On the other hand, if you are awake and in a seated posture, second-chᵃkrᵃ fear may be converted to fourth-chᵃkrᵃ unconditional love or sixth-chᵃkrᵃ transcendence. Mᵃntrᵃ is of major help in this process.

Other Chᵃkrᵃ Periods

Other chᵃkrᵃ periods are less crucial but can serve as a source of strength when needed. For instance, a problematic relationship may find improvement by communication between the parties during a fourth-chᵃkrᵃ period when energy is in the heart.

THE DAWN PROGRAM

Sleep

During the nighttime, as energy cycles through the chᵃkrᵃ minds, they continue to process information acquired during the day, modifying some schemas and scripts accordingly. During sleep, while KuNDᵃlEnEE silently ascends from the first chᵃkrᵃ to visit the seventh chᵃkrᵃ, it pauses at each chᵃkrᵃ along the way. When it finds that a mind is struggling with some concern, it may induce a dream to help resolve that concern. Interpreting such a dream may require knowledge of the symbolism that KuNDᵃlᴇNᴇᴇ uses. The return journey from the seventh chᵃkrᵃ to the first chᵃkrᵃ is always completed before awakening. KuNDᵃlᴇNᴇᴇ may use this second opportunity to again induce dreams. If needed, any chᵃkrᵃ mind can summon the KuNDᵃlᴇNᴇᴇ at any time during the night. The dreams induced by KuNDᵃlᴇNᴇᴇ are intended to aid the evolution of the jᴇᴇvᵃ.

InnerTuning practitioners usually go to sleep early in order to have sufficient rest and recuperation before greeting the sun.

Transition Styles

There are several distinct ways in which people make the transition from the tᵃmᵃs state of sleep to full wakefulness. These include:

+ Allowing maximum sleep. There is great difficulty in breaking the grip of tᵃmᵃs, therefore you succumb to it for as long as practicalities permit.

+ Up and at 'em. You jump out of bed—from tᵃmᵃs to rᵃjᵃs. This may be done before or after dawn and with or without the aid of an alarm clock. You then execute the following script: toilet, wash, dress, breakfast, (commute), job. Subscripts are sometimes introduced to aid others such as children and neighbors. The "up and at 'em" style is the usual favorite of societies that teach a work ethic.

+ Record dreams. You may make a slow transition from tᵃmᵃs to rᵃjᵃs as you recall your dreams and write them down or speak them into a voice recorder to be used later as a source for integrative mentation (see below).

+ Attend to hypnopompic. The hypnopompic state is a semiconscious state that precedes wakefulness. Tᵃmᵃs is still present but not at full strength. The information processing related to personal concerns of the chᵃkrᵃ minds (that began the previous night) continues. Consequently, attending to this state may permit helpful feelings and intuitions to emerge.

Each of the above transitional styles has some benefit and the same person may use different ones on different occasions. None, however, has the same benefits as the InnerTuning style.

InnerTuning Wake Up

The purpose of the InnerTuning wake up is to express gratitude for being given another day of life, to align energy with the nasal cycles, and to store sᵃtvᵃ for use during the day. The InnerTuning wake up balances all seven chᵃkrᵃ-s. The following paragraphs contain a list of steps in the ideal wake up. Feel content by practicing those that you can.

- ✦ Bed
  - ▪ Each person needs a different amount of sleep to be completely rested. Get that rest by going to bed early enough. If necessary, set an alarm clock to remind you when to go to bed. Avoid late night TV; if you wish to see those programs, record them automatically and view them at an earlier hour on another day.
  - ▪ Sit in bed for a minute and repeat a mᵃntrᵃ or send good thoughts to someone before sleeping.
  - ▪ The rested body will awaken naturally one half-hour before sunrise in summer and more than an hour before in winter.
  - ▪ Determine nostril dominance. When sufficiently awake, sit up slowly and quietly observe your breath. Find out which nostril is dominant (more fully open) by gently blocking each side in turn and exhaling through the other nostril. Blocking is best done by placing the thumb under the nostril. Alternatively, check the temperature of the nostrils. The cooler side is more open.
  - ▪ Kiss the palm of the hand on the same side as the dominant nostril, feeling gratitude for your uniqueness and your new day.
  - ▪ Pray or recite an appropriate mᵃntrᵃ provided by a qualified teacher.
  - ▪ Step out of bed leading with the foot on the same side as the dominant nostril. This is the most energetic side of the body.
  - ▪ Drink lots of fresh water.
- ✦ Exercise Area
  - ▪ Do some gentle stretches for a few minutes. Emphasize abdominal area.
- ✦ Bathroom
  - ▪ Defecate. This may be facilitated by first drinking some warm water with lemon juice. Taking some vitamin C before bedtime might also be helpful.
  - ▪ After using toilet paper, anus should be washed with water. Apart from being a high level of hygiene, this helps the body to retain satvic energy.
  - ▪ Repeating the first chᵃkrᵃ sound of HLL aids defecation by drawing energy to the first chᵃkrᵃ.
  - ▪ The normal position for defecation is squatting, as it aligns the muscles for evacuating the bowels. The design of a standard toilet inhibits squatting and places strain on the muscles of evacuation. (However, special

equipment that assists squatting on a standard toilet is available through various media sources dedicated to Yoga.) Squat whenever circumstances permit.

- On days when you fail to defecate at this time, you may continue with the dawn program but keep eyes open while reciting mᵃntrᵃ-s and meditating.
- Shower. Use lukewarm water.

+ Meditation Area
- Ideally the meditation area is outdoors. Otherwise, your room should have access to as much sunlight as possible and a window for fresh air.
- Wrap yourself in a meditation shawl and sit facing the rising sun.
- Chant mᵃntrᵃ for at least three minutes.
- Sit quietly until sunrise. Observe any thoughts that occur. Do not react to them.
- At sunrise, again check the nostrils. If the dominant one does not match that indicated in the *Prana Calendar,* switch it using the following procedure.

Switching Nostril Dominance

There are three methods for switching the dominance of the nostrils. These should be attempted in the order listed.

+ Lie down on the side of the dominant nostril with a pillow placed under the rib cage. This drains the mucous out of the sinus and opens the nondominant nostril. In healthy people, change occurs within one to three minutes.
+ Block the dominant nostril by placing your thumb underneath its opening. Breathe through the nondominant nostril rapidly and with force.
+ Block the dominant nostril with a small cotton plug while simultaneously distending the nondominant nostril.

Phasing In the Dawn Program

If you wish to ease into the dawn program, you may start by following it a minimum of twice a month on the crucial mornings following the first dawn after the full moon and on the first dawn after the darkest night (new moon). These days are indicated in the *Prana Calendar.*

Another possibility is to arise regularly before dawn on one or two days each week. On all other days you could do the program whenever you normally arise (without checking nostril dominance at sunrise).

The dominant nostril at sunrise may also be verified at sunset.

INTERNALIZING THE SENSES

Internalizing the senses (prᵃtyaahaarᵃ) causes them to be directed inward toward the subtle body rather than outward toward the external environment. Internalizing of all five senses—smell, taste, sight, touch and hearing—prepares us for meditation.

Internalized Hearing

For spiritual development, the most important of all five senses is hearing. In order for the sense of hearing to be internalized, it is important that our body first become sound sensitive. Most people have sensitivity to hearing, but with regular practice of appropriate listening exercises, the whole body will become sound sensitive.

As the sound sensitivity of the body increases we tend to become aware of the slightest sounds and are careful to make only the minimum sound necessary to perform such tasks as closing a door, putting a knife and fork on a plate, or speaking in a manner that is easily audible for the listener. As that sensitivity increases, we can hear the sound through the skin. This is a major achievement.

Internalized Touch

When hearing is internalized, the other senses will also gradually invert. The organ of action for the heart chᵃkrᵃ and the *air* element is the skin. As sound vibrations are heard by the body, the sense of touch also intensifies and we become very aware of the sensations of the body and the feelings that we feel in our heart chᵃkrᵃ.

The moon rules over the seventh chᵃkrᵃ and Venus rules over the heart chᵃkrᵃ. To strengthen this 7:4–4:7 connection is extremely important; with the internalizing of the sense of touch our feelings, especially of peace and contentment, become very deep. Watching the night sky and seeing the planet Venus near the moon can make us feel part of the universe. This is especially true of young lovers. The experience opens their hearts, and their feelings for one another are strengthened and felt at a higher level.

Internalized Sight

The internalization of sight may be developed through meditation (ideally at dawn; if missed, at dusk). The *fire* element in the form of light may be felt in the solar plexus that connects to the third chᵃkrᵃ. In this way the eyes, the sense organ of the third chᵃkrᵃ, experience calmness and learn to internalize. After some years the eyes become soft like those of a deer.

Internalized Taste

Internalizing of taste is gradually accomplished by placing the tongue at the base of the upper teeth. This increases sensitivity to taste and the *water* element in the body is better controlled and purified. This technique is also used to control thought.

Internalized Smell

Internalizing of smell is accomplished by means of anal contractions coupled with special breathing exercises (praaNaayaamᵃ).

One by one, all the five elemental minds gradually turn inward; when our five senses are inverted a sense of peace and quiet and the ability to see internal phenomena emerge. This does not mean the ability to see internal organs such as the liver, kidneys, and spleen—though that may happen. Instead it refers to an ability to see the subtle body and how it interfaces with the physical. The rate of breathing gradually diminishes. As it reaches the range of four to two breaths per minute, discernment among the guNᵃ-s causes us to develop more precise intuition and meditation ensues naturally.

INCREASING SOUND SENSITIVITY

A Comparison of Sight and Sound

The sense of sight is associated with the third chᵃkrᵃ and the element of *fire*. Vision is the dominant sense in most humans, which is reflected in the fact that the visual cortex covers a significantly greater area of cortex than that of any other sense. Nature (prᵃkretE) uses externally directed vision to keep us busy with first lEngᵃ pursuits.

On the other hand, free will (purushᵃ) makes most use of internally directed hearing to free us from nature and raise our energy to the higher lEngᵃ-s. Hearing occupies the second highest amount of sensory cortex. Hearing is based in the fifth chᵃkrᵃ, whose primary element is *aakaashᵃ*—the most subtle of the elements and the one into which the others will dissolve (see discussion of LEElaa model in chapter 2).

The refinement of hearing forms the pathway for the refinement of all chᵃkrᵃ minds. For spiritual growth, it is crucial that our sense of hearing be inverted. As hearing is refined to detect subtler and subtler stages of sound, free will is given the opportunity to operate at these more refined levels. The result is increasing control over our affects, thoughts, and behavior.

The ability of the body to absorb sooryᵃ *aakaashᵃ* through the pores of the skin contributes to overall sound sensitivity.

12-Tone and 22-Tone Music

As the LEElaa model shows, sound commences at the static (pᵃraa) phase, passes through the luminous (pᵃshyᵃntE) phase, and then enters the illuminated (mᵃdhyᵃmaa) phase. All these phases take place in the seventh and sixth chᵃkrᵃ-s. Finally sound reaches the audible (vɪkhᵃrEE) phase and is expressed with the voice, the organ of action for the fifth chᵃkrᵃ. What we do with our voice determines whether we bring out the Divine qualities of the sound or whether we bring out malevolent qualities.

Very beautiful arrangements of notes in 12-tone music can be made, which bring heavenly feelings down to Earth. Alternatively, the listener may be raised from the earth plane to a heavenly one. The discrete scale of 12 tones enables beautiful bouquets and other flowering arrangements to be produced by the musical community.

On the other hand, the more continuous scale of 22 tones permits one tone to blend with another and form magnificent garlands. The merging of one tone with the next may generate an altered state of awareness. The 22-tone scale permits a greater in-depth exploration of the affects. In Indian classical music, for instance, (especially Dhrupᵃdᵃ and KAraanaa styles), an octave may be deeply explored and a skilled singer may take an hour to reach its seventh note. The many creative variations of merging from one note to another is a very delicate art.

It is said that a great classical singer of this life is born as a naadᵃ yogi (adept in the science of sound) in the next life. They carry within themselves experiences of merging of one note into another. This helps them, by observing the principles of naadᵃ yogᵃ, to produce sooryᵃ *aakaashᵃ*. The skill required is no longer singing; instead, it is chanting. The difference is that singing requires breathing to occur through the mouth. Breathing with chanting to influence the first four chᵃkrᵃ-s and related diagrams may be either through the mouth or the nose. However, when the purpose is to influence diagrams that include microchakras of the fifth, sixth, or seventh chᵃkrᵃ-s, it is crucial that breathing be through the nose so that the cilia there have an opportunity to purify the inhaled praaɴᵃ. Sooryᵃ *aakaashᵃ*—which is capable of forming and maintaining the connections within the pentagon, hexagon, and septagon diagrams—can only be produced from this purified praaɴᵃ.

Right-Channel and Left-Channel Music

In the right channel, music moves energy downward toward grounding in the first chᵃkrᵃ. We feel that we belong on this earth and have the joy of being alive. In the left channel, music moves energy upward toward the higher chᵃkrᵃ-s. Both 12-tone and 22-tone music may be used for these purposes. When right-channel music is being played, the notes are struck. In contrast, left-channel music requires that the musician play the notes; in music that affects the highest chᵃkrᵃ-s, the notes are simply touched.

Chanting Mᵃntrᵃ

Mᵃntrᵃ and Archetypes

The Tantric tradition teaches that there are 330 million gods and goddesses (archetypes), of which only some are invoked in any one yugᵃ. Most mᵃntrᵃ-s are the names of archetypes and are used to invoke their energies. Some archetypes have multiple types of energy associated with them. Among others, both ShEvᵃ and VESHNu have one thousand names. The power of these names has built up in the morphogenetic field as a result of millennia of repetition. The best way to appreciate these mᵃntrᵃ-s is to repeat some of them after hearing them over and over again.

Chapter 3 listed the major archetypes associated with each chᵃkrᵃ. InnerTuning uses selected mᵃntrᵃ-s associated with these archetypes to weaken various saboteurs and strengthen champions.

Effectiveness of Mᵃntrᵃ

The effectiveness of a mᵃntrᵃ is dependent upon a number of factors:

+ Appropriateness of the mᵃntrᵃ for the issue it addresses
+ Sentiment with which the mᵃntrᵃ is chanted
+ Precision with which the mᵃntrᵃ is articulated
+ Quality of *aakaashᵃ* that accompanies recitation of the mᵃntrᵃ
+ Number of repetitions of the mᵃntrᵃ
+ Melody or meter of the mᵃntrᵃ

The Mᵃntrᵃ AUM

The initial subtle vibration (prᵃNᵃvᵃ) with which Cosmic Potentiality (MahaakuNdᵃlEnEE) separated from Stasis (Pᵃrᵃmᵃ ShEvᵃ) expands into the mᵃntrᵃ AUM.

A—brings energy down in the right channel
U—brings energy up in the left channel
M—uses activated energy to open the central channel

This mᵃntrᵃ invokes the energies of the tripartite principles. "A" represents Brᵃhmaa, the creator; "U" stands for Vᴇsʜɴu, the preserver; "M" symbolizes MahAshvarᵃ, the transformer.

Properly chanted mᵃntrᵃ-s create the finest *aakaashᵃ*. The AUM mᵃntrᵃ is the best example of this. Making the "A" (aa) sound properly with pure praaɴᵃ inhaled through the nose will ground the energy and we will feel very relaxed in an extra short time. A properly chanted "U" sound will bring the energy upward to the higher chᵃkrᵃ-s, creating an unmatched feeling of peace and unconditional love. The "M" sound brings the energy to the seventh chᵃkrᵃ where a total feeling of contentment is experienced.

Sooryᵃ *Aakaashᵃ*

Sooryᵃ *aakaashᵃ* has three main functions. The first function is as a purifier. In chapter 3, it was learned that the head is the storehouse of all *aakaashᵃ* (black, red, yellow, and so on). All other forms of *aakaashᵃ* are inferior to (more gross than) sooryᵃ *aakaashᵃ*. As an individual evolves spiritually, sooryᵃ *aakaashᵃ* gradually replaces the other forms of *aakaashᵃ* and pushes them further and further away from the head. At the time of liberation (mokshᵃ), the head is filled with golden light (sooryᵃ *aakaashᵃ*).

During three body purifications, sooryᵃ *aakaashᵃ* aids in emptying the old pods filled with early apaanic memories—in both the left and right channels. The sooryᵃ *aakaashᵃ* is produced by chanting mᵃntrᵃ according to the principles of naadᵃ yogᵃ. Normally, this *aakaashᵃ* is absorbed through the ears in silence after the chant stops. After many years of practice, some people are able to absorb it through the skin. A very few can do this naturally (they are sound sensitive; not necessarily musically sensitive) and make excellent spiritual candidates.

The second main function of sooryᵃ *aakaashᵃ* is to influence the connections within the diagrams among microchakras. It aids in both the formation and strengthening of positive diagrams. It also is an important method of weakening negative connections.

Sooryᵃ *aakaashᵃ* facilitates the experience of the Witness (saaksʜᴇᴇ) as it helps to increase the sense of distance between the Self and the empirical world. This is its third main function.

The Classical Ten Inner Sounds

Table 10.2 lists the inner sounds that have been reported through the centuries by advanced aspirants who have inverted their hearing.

TABLE 10.2. THE CLASSICAL TEN INNER SOUNDS (NAAD[a])

1	Chirping birds (uplifting)
2	Crickets (hypnotic)
3	Bell (love in heart, joy)
4	Conch (a quiet intoxicating calm)
5	Vina or tambura (cold sensations in spine, intoxicating)
6	High-pitched drum (vibrates fifth ch[a]kr[a] and top of head)
7	Flute (reveals the secrets dear to the heart of people; we feel like dancing in bliss)
8	Low-pitched drum (being in perfect rhythm; experience of hollowness inside; hearing everywhere)
9	Elephant trumpet (creates a high pitched *ni* sound; we are as light as a feather and in bliss, aanand[a])
10	Thunder roar (dissolution)

Listening to InnerTuning Sounds

The sounds of InnerTuning are intended to facilitate internalizing of the senses and to release patterns of energy in the subtle field. Recordings of these sounds are available from www.innertuning.com. They are part of a series of essentially *live* sacred sound offerings.

Prepare for listening by observing the following:

- ✦ Have a bowel movement as early in the day as possible, preferably before dawn.
- ✦ Sit facing east with spine comfortably erect.
- ✦ Devote attention fully to the sound. Do not play InnerTuning sounds for entertainment or during conversation.
- ✦ Keep eyes closed except where contraindicated.
- ✦ Hear the sounds at low volume first.
- ✦ After a few repetitions, chant along.
- ✦ Gradually raise the volume slightly.

This series of sounds is part of a remarkable archive developed by Sri Shyamji Bhatnagar working with a dedicated student for over four decades.

Adhyakshaya—for Confidence

The commanding quality that the Adhyakshaya mᵃntrᵃ evokes stimulates the *fire* element in the first chᵃkrᵃ (1:3). This enhances qualities of stability and confidence. This set contains a recording for use in the morning and an evening recording for use before sleep. The morning chant is in C natural; the evening chant is in C sharp.

Bajaranga Bali—for Courage

The dominant trait of the second chᵃkrᵃ is healthy exchange—the ability to give and receive. Coupled with the energy from the heart chᵃkrᵃ, this exchange becomes unconditionally loving. Blockages to the microchakras of the second chᵃkrᵃ are the basis of fear that restricts our ability to be generous and loving. Repetition of the mᵃntrᵃ Bajaranga Bali strengthens the connections between the second and the fourth chᵃkrᵃ-s.

Ramava—for Integrity

Ramava is an endearing name for Ram—the archetype of the third chᵃkrᵃ. He is known as the perfect man of integrity. This gives him the ability to surrender his ego to higher chᵃkrᵃ-s. Sri Shyamji's chanting of Ramava aids in refining the ego enabling it to surrender to the heart chᵃkrᵃ.

Meré Ram—for Joy in Life

The uplifting sounds of Meré Ram inspire energy to travel from the first motivational principle to the higher ones. At the same time the left (lunar) channel is filled with vibrancy encouraging our talents to flourish. Through this connectedness, we experience more joy of life.

Radhay Radhay—for Compassion

Sri Shyamji chants Radhay in this recording in a manner designed to help the egos of the first lɛngᵃ surrender to the second lɛngᵃ. The sounds of Radhay will create the space necessary for the emergence of compassion for ourselves and others.

Shree Radhay—for Heart Chᵃkrᵃ

Chanting Radhay mᵃntrᵃ helps to transform unexpressed feelings into energy available to the higher chᵃkrᵃ-s. "Ra" is the sound of the sun, light, or fire that is concentrated in the solar plexus. "Dh" is a syllable that fully expands the diaphragm to allow fresh vital praaNᵃ to come into the body. "A" is the sound of manifestation.

Santoshi Mata—for Depression

When we lose something we feel sad or even depressed. Every calamity has a negative and a positive side. Negative is the loss; positive is the new beginning. As we are enveloped in these sounds, like a caterpillar that wraps itself in a cocoon, we too can emerge transformed like the butterfly, and realize that our loss is not a sacrifice but one of growth and refinement of ego.

Sharaday Ma—for Creativity

S^{a}r^{a}sv^{a}tEE is the consort of Br^{a}hmaa, the creator, and is the goddess of fine arts and creativity. She resides in the fifth ch^{a}kr^a and all fifth microchakras. In addition to creativity, fifth-ch^{a}kr^a qualities are communication, eloquence, truthfulnesss, and inner knowledge. This beautiful recording evokes an abundance of the fifth ch^{a}kr^a element *aakaash^a* and energizes the complete fifth ch^{a}kr^a.

Sadho—for Spiritual Zeal

Kabir was one of fifteenth-century India's greatest spiritual poets who practiced the yoga of breath (sv^{a}r^a yog^a) and the yoga of sound (naad^a yog^a). In this recording, Sri Shyamji has infused the beautiful words of Kabir's poem with his own unique approach to sv^{a}r^a yog^a and to naad^a yog^a. This produces a heart-rending feeling in the listener, which kindles a zeal to connect with the Divine within.

Aum Ram—for Insomnia

This recording calms the tripartite brain (left cerebral hemisphere, right cerebral hemisphere and animal brain). Sri Shyamji chants the primal m^{a}ntr^a AUM. "A" is the sound of creation; it vibrates the left hemisphere and brings energy down the right channel. "U" is the sound of preservation and brings energy up the left channel and vibrates the right hemisphere. "M" is the sound of transformation that vibrates the central channel and the animal brain.

The chanting of the m^{a}ntr^a "RAM" facilitates the surrender of the ego of the third ch^{a}kr^a and permits the energy to rise to higher ch^{a}kr^a-s. In so doing, thoughts and feelings subside, giving rest to the physical body. In this state of relaxation you are prepared for deep sleep.

Gayatri Mantra—for Wisdom

Through recitation of this m^{a}ntr^a we evoke the balance necessary to internalize the senses and to experience stillness. In this stillness, our three bodies (physical, feeling, and thought) are integrated. The Gayatri m^{a}ntr^a leads us to an effulgent (self-luminous) light. Sri Shyamji's chanting of this m^{a}ntr^a induces a reduced rate of breathing, deeply calms the nervous system and provides a haven of peace.

INTEGRATIVE MENTATION

In chapter 8, it was explained that mentation had four components: observing, reasoning, feeling, and intuition. When any one or more of these components is focused on mental activity that facilitates the integration of the three bodies, the process is called integrative mentation. In general, integrative mentation involves striving to attain higher values and refine ego energy. It is the refined ego that makes the integration possible. An important stage in the integration of the three bodies is the reversal of the downward-pointing *fire* triangle of the third chᵃkrᵃ.

The details of integrative mentation are related to each lᴇngᵃ and the goals of each chᵃkrᵃ mind within a lᴇngᵃ.

First-Lᴇngᵃ Integrative Mentation

Basic mentation is directed at the ordinary problems of life and pertains to the goals of the first three chᵃkrᵃ minds—the first lᴇngᵃ. Common topics of concern include food, housing, health, money, sex, family, and entertainment. They also include business, professional, and social relationships. Many people go through life and mentate on nothing other than first-lᴇngᵃ issues. Their horizon simply does not extend beyond the first lᴇngᵃ.

When a saboteur (such as anxiety, anger, or compulsiveness) becomes particularly bothersome it can cause a switch from basic mentation to integrative mentation. In an attempt to root out the saboteur, you may examine memories, attitudes, and beliefs that are normally below the threshold of awareness. This effort may also require getting more deeply in touch with feelings or being more attentive to intuitions that are trying to lead you out of the difficulty. Professional help may be sought as you marshal your energies against the saboteur.

The senior author has had hundreds of clients who came to learn to meditate when they had severe mental problems; some had terminal illnesses. They later felt grateful to their maladies that brought them to the gift of InnerTuning.

Second-Lᴇngᵃ Integrative Mentation

When some energy moves to the second lᴇngᵃ a different set of priorities emerges and directs mentation. Fourth-chᵃkrᵃ energy of unconditional love plays a crucial role in the integration of the subtle and physical bodies. This love gives birth to a new form of mentation in the ego of the fourth chᵃkrᵃ. You are no longer the same person, partly because you no longer observe, think, and feel in the same way. The details of this shift are dependent upon the karmic gift that triggered the unconditional love. Perhaps it was the birth of a child, acquiring a pet, being needed by an ill neighbor, or joining an organization that meets a significant need in society. In all such cases, inspiration derives from someone or something in the physical field.

Potentially more powerful is the inspiration of unconditional love from a source in the nonmaterial fields. This may follow a seeming "miraculous" recovery from a life-threatening illness, appreciation for the gift of a special talent, or a calling to a life's work of service. Mentation is permanently altered by such events. The most powerful occurrence happens when you meet a spiritual teacher and recognize a deep relation from the beginning.

Third-LEng^a Integrative Mentation

In the sixth ch^akr^a, reasoning and feeling are absorbed into intuition. Observation and enhanced intuition are all that remain of mentation. This simplified mentation is used to continue the integration of the three bodies.

In the seventh ch^akr^a, the three bodies have been united and all mentation ceases. Energy is fully devoted to s^amaadhE.

Integrative Mentation and the Stages of Sound

The quality of mentation varies with our sensitivity to levels of audible sound (vIkh^arEE) and to the preceding stage of illuminated sound (m^adhy^amaa). Integration of the three bodies involves lowering the threshold of awareness for our thoughts, our feelings, and our intuitions. As they descend from subtle to gross, the sooner we become aware of them, the better. If we are aware of them early enough, it will be easier to exercise our free will (purush^a t^atv^a) and influence their descent. If we fail to do this, mentation is more likely to function in stereotypical patterns guided by nature (pr^akretE t^atv^a) and social conditioning. The pre-audible level of mentation has been referred to as the "microgenetic level" by U. Hentschel, G. Smith, and J. G. Draguns[4] and the level of "felt meaning" by E. T. Gendlin.[5]

In the modern world reading is an essential skill. There are two main methods of teaching this skill: sight reading and sound (phonetic) reading. Both have benefits and drawbacks. A major drawback of the phonetic method is that it conditions our thinking to operate at the level of audible sound (vIkh^arEE). This makes it very difficult to attend to the microgenetic level of mentation. Significant research will be required in order to overcome this dilemma.

MEDITATION

This section examines meditation from the viewpoints of the Bhᵃgvat GEEtaa, Advitᵃ Vᴀdaantᵃ, and the philosopher J. Krishnamurti. It then presents the approach of InnerTuning to meditation (see plate 13).

Meditation in the Bhᵃgvat GEEtaa

The Bhᵃgvat GEEtaa devotes a whole chapter to meditation, at the core of which are these beautifully clear verses of instruction:

In a clean place, having established a firm seat, neither too high nor too low, with a cloth, a deerskin and kusha grass on it

There, making the mind one-pointed, controlling the functions of the mind and the senses, let him, sitting on that seat, practice yoga for inner purification

Holding the body, the head and the neck firmly in one line and motionless, gazing on the tip of the nose, without looking around

Serene minded, free from fear, firm in the vow of celibacy, the mind restrained, let the accomplished yogi sit with Me as the Supreme

Always keeping the mind controlled, thus engaging himself with Yoga, the Yogi attains the Supreme Peace of abiding in Me, resulting in Liberation

One who eats too much, or does not eat at all, who is addicted to too much sleep, or is ever wakeful, such a one, Oh Arjuna, cannot (practice) Yoga

(But) the one, whose food and recreation are optimum, whose effort in actions is moderate, whose sleep and waking are optimum, attains Yoga, the destroyer of pain

When the subdued mind establishes in the Self only, when all desires cease, then (that person) is said to be an accomplished Yogi

As a lamp in a windless place does not flicker thus a Yogi with subdued mind is engaged in Yoga of the Self

When thought has ceased, restrained by the practice of Yoga, and when seeing the Self by the self, he is content within himself

He knows the limitless Bliss that transcends the senses and, established firmly in discrimination, he never wavers from Reality

Having attained this, he sees no acquisition beyond it, and established thus, he is not disturbed even by a great sorrow

The severance from the union with pain, know that to be termed Yoga. One must embrace this Yoga with determination and without despondence

Willing to give up all desires without exception, completely restraining the aggregate of senses with the mind

(The Yogi) should withdraw step by step, through firmly sustained discrimination, not thinking of anything else, keeping the mind in the Self

Whenever the wavering and fickle mind wanders out, he should restrain it through the control of the Self

The unsurpassed Bliss approaches such Yogi, whose mind is quiescent, when passion is subdued, who has become Brahman, the Blemishless

The Yogi, thus always practicing Yoga, free from blemishes easily reaches the Infinite Bliss of encountering Brahman

The Yogi constantly established in Yoga sees all beings residing in the Self. He sees the same (Brahman) everywhere

From him who sees Me everywhere and sees everything in Me, I will not disappear nor will he to Me.[6]

In these verses at least four fundamental components of meditation are described: 1) prepare by sitting still, 2) focus concentration inward, 3) transcend mentation, and 4) transcend ego. It is pointed out that the task is difficult and perseverance is required.

Numerous books on meditation have been written—from a variety of cultural and theoretical perspectives. They offer diverse ways to implement the four components. Some approaches simply ignore one or more of the components and offer a different definition of meditation.

Meditation in Advɪtᵃ Vᴀdaantᵃ

For Advɪtᵃ Vᴀdaantᵃ, the fourth component is obviously the most important. If the ego can be transcended with minimum time spent on the other steps, so much the better. Satchidānandendra stated:

> It has been explained how the monk who has attained through dispassion to genuine adoption of the life of wandering mendicancy must necessarily carry out the discipline of hearing the texts and pondering over them regularly and continually until he gains immediate vision of the Self. He who does not attain this immediate vision merely from *hearing*, must carry out further regular hearing, supported by *pondering* over the meaning. Weak and mediocre candidates, however, must also perform *sustained meditation* (nididhyāsana . . .) [emphases added]
>
> . . . Nididhyāsana . . . means fixing the mental gaze on the principle of reality to determine its true nature, like one examining a jewel.
>
> . . . He tries to attain direct vision of reality (here in this very world) by turning his mind away from all else . . . after the rise of knowledge nothing further remains to be done . . . its result is described . . . as right metaphysical knowledge, and from this comes immediate liberation. . . .[7]

In this quotation, the texts referred to are the foundational texts of Vᴀdaantᵃ (see appendix A). The method of *hearing* will be sufficient for those whose praarᵃbdhᵃ-s entitle them to liberation.[8] Hearing at a level of utmost profundity (an early stage in the descent of sound) such verses as "You are That" will remove the veil of ignorance and bring about recognition of the Self. More commonly, it will be necessary to *ponder* the meaning of the texts until intuition of their truth arises.

If neither hearing nor pondering bring about transcendence of the ego, then sustained meditation is recommended. Satchidānandendra further described the practice:

> . . . one concentrates one's mind on the subtle principle, Atman. At the end of this discipline, one becomes conscious of the fact that the mind itself is a superimposition on Atman. Then the mind becomes no mind, that is to say, it is realized essentially as Atman himself.[9]

It is essential to remember that Advɪtᵃ Vᴀdaantᵃ is a teaching for those whose energies are concentrated in the third lᴇngᵃ. For more on this teaching see appendix A.

Krishnamurti on Meditation

J. Krishnamurti is one of the few philosophers whose views clearly give central importance to the third lEng[a]. His writings concerning meditation both converge with and diverge from the teachings of InnerTuning. In either case, they are worthy of consideration.

It has been noted above that meditation requires the transcendence of thought. Krishnamurti's condemnation of thought is sweeping:

> Why are we influenced? In politics, as you know, it is the job of the politician to influence us; and every book, every teacher, every guru—the more powerful, the more eloquent, the better we like it—imposes his thought, his way of life, his manner of conduct upon us. So life is a battle of ideas, a battle of influences, and your mind is the field of battle. The politician wants your mind; the guru wants your mind; the saint says, do this and not that, and he also wants your mind; and every tradition, every form of habit or custom, influences, shapes, guides, controls your mind. I think that is fairly obvious. It would be absurd to deny it.
>
> We are saying that a mind that is influenced, shaped, authority-bound, obviously can never be free; and whatever it thinks, however lofty its ideals, however subtle and deep, it is still conditioned. I think it is very important to understand that the mind, through time, through experience, through the many thousands of yesterdays, is shaped and conditioned, and that thought is not the way out. Which does not mean that you must be thoughtless, on the contrary. When you are capable of understanding very profoundly, very deeply, extensively, widely, subtly, then only will you fully recognize how petty thinking is, how small thought is. Then there is a breaking down of that wall of conditioning.[10]

Elsewhere he applies this perspective specifically to meditation:

> To find out what a religious mind is, one must totally negate all rituals and symbols invented by thought. If you deny, negate, that which is false, then you find what is true. You negate all the systems of meditation because you yourself see that these systems are invented by thought. They are put together by man.[11]

Krishnamurti makes an important distinction between concentration and attention and explains a key concept of "choiceless awareness."

> Concentration is another invention of thought. In school you are told to concentrate on the book. You learn to concentrate, trying to exclude other thoughts,

trying to prevent yourself from looking out of the window. In concentration there is resistance, narrowing down the enormous energy of life to a certain point. Whereas in attention, which is a form of awareness in which there is no choice, a choiceless awareness, all your energy is there. When you have such attention there is no center from which you are attending, whereas in concentration there is always a center from which you are attending.[12]

The state of meditation is described in the following passage:

Meditation is the sense of total comprehension of the whole of life, and from that there is right action. Meditation is absolute silence of the mind. Not relative silence or the silence that thought has projected and structured, but the silence of order, which is freedom. Only in that total, complete, unadulterated silence is that which is truth, which is from everlasting to everlasting.

    This is meditation.[13]

It may be suggested that the "sense of total comprehension" to which Krishnamurti refers is sixth chᵃkrᵃ intuition and the "right action" that automatically flows from it is what the Tantric and Vedic traditions call retᵃ.

Krishnamurti discusses the relation between observation and meditation:

To understand oneself there must be observation, and that observation can only take place *now*. And it is not the movement of the past observing the now. When I observe the now from my past conclusions, prejudices, hopes, fears, that is an observation of the present from the past. I think I am observing the now, but the observation of the now can take place only when there is no observer who is the past. Observation of the now is extraordinarily important. The movement of the past meeting the present must end there; that is the now. But if you allow it to go on, then the now becomes the future, or the past, but never the actual now. Observation can only take place in the very doing of it—when you are angry, when you are greedy, to observe it as it is. Which means not to condemn it, not to judge it, but to watch it and let it flower and disappear. Do you understand the beauty of it?

    . . . Allow observation in which there is no choice: just observe your greed, your envy, your jealousy, whatever it may be, and in the very observation of it, it flowers and undergoes a radical change. The very observation without the background brings about a change.

    . . . In doing that, obviously, authority has no place. There is no intermediary between your observation and truth. In doing that, one becomes a light to oneself. Then you don't ask anybody at any time how to do something. In the very doing, which is the observing, there is the act, there is the change. Go at it!

So freedom to observe, and therefore no authority of any kind, is essential.[14]

Krishnamurti correctly describes the role of observation in transcending thought. In the next section, it will be explained that awareness of the way in which observation changes with the lɛngᵃ will deepen our understanding of it. It will also be indicated that wise instruction can be helpful in learning to meditate though, indeed, at the level of the third lɛngᵃ, it is uncalled for.

InnerTuning Meditation
Observation and Meditation

In everyday speech, the term "observation" is usually employed within the context of the first lɛngᵃ. In this case, it refers to a perceptual relationship between the ego and any object in the empirical world. This relationship is often accompanied by judging of some type on a scale of opposites. The food is observed to be too hot or too cold. The clerk is observed to be fawning or aggressive. The clothes are observed to be too gaudy or too drab. It is a normal part of first lɛngᵃ functioning. At this level, such judgments may be necessary in order for the ego to make decisions and act. However, if we rise above this level of egoistic judging we are able to integrate the subtle and causal fields with the physical.

As observation moves from the first to the second and third lɛngᵃ-s, it becomes increasingly nonjudgmental. Events are perceived in an increasingly objective way. The start of this objectivity begins near the top of the first lɛngᵃ in 3:6. Significant opening of this microchakra is a prerequisite for additional openings in the higher lɛngᵃ-s. The energy of 3:6 opens the ego of the first lɛngᵃ to some awareness of a world beyond simple sensory gratification. In the second lɛngᵃ, the ego gradually becomes refined and judgments become less intense. Observation becomes purer and simple recognition of "what is" becomes stronger. However, the elements are still at play; feelings, particularly of devotion, are strong, and attachment to them prevents pure objectivity.

When energy is concentrated in the sixth chᵃkrᵃ, the three guɴᵃ-s replace the five elements as the source of chᵃkrᵃ functioning. There is now an emphasis of the more abstract qualities of tᵃmᵃs, rᵃjᵃs, and sᵃtvᵃ over the concrete world of objects based on the elements. For example, the appeal of a beautiful dish of food may be eradicated if the sixth chᵃkrᵃ detects the energy of tᵃmᵃs associated with it. The sense of discernment among the guN^a-s, which first appears in the sixth ch^akr^a, is a prelude to the ultimate discernment (vEchaar^a) between ego and Self. When energy is concentrated in the sixth ch^akr^a, it is easier to achieve pure objective observation (saakshEE).

In order for energy to move to the sixth ch^akr^a, issues that tie the ego to the first lEng^a must be resolved. If they are not, these issues will demand attention and function as saboteurs of observation. Many of these issues focus on authority. Krishnamurti recommended rejecting all authority and following our own path. This is very difficult to do. Instead, InnerTuning recommends systematic working through of authority issues.

In addition to authority issues, the common fear of loss of individuality must be overcome. This fear can prevent the larger cosmic perspective of the sixth ch^akr^a from arising.

Preparation for Meditation

The main objective of all preparation is to purify each of the three bodies as much as possible. This will permit satvic energy to flow in them and soory^a *aakaash^a* will be retained.

The term "meditation" is in widespread use and covers a variety of practices and objectives unrelated to those discussed above. Some of these, such as relaxation and prayer, may be quite beneficial. They also may not require much preparation. However, it is folly to attempt to activate the sixth and seventh ch^akr^a-s (the focal area of meditation) without careful preparation. Apaan^a may rise unchecked and produce disturbing experiences ranging from mild headaches to psychosis.

Without proper preparation, there can be an increase in such negative affects as anger, hostility, fear, and lethargy. In addition, the grip of ego identification with the first lEng^a may be strengthened rather than lessened. These negative effects that may accompany inadequately prepared meditation might be the reason why some people reject meditation altogether. Unfortunately, in our times, many systems that teach meditation do not also teach preparatory purification. InnerTuning emphasizes that, if preparation cannot be adequate to prevent toxic energy from invading the higher ch^akr^a-s, it is better to not attempt meditation; instead prayer is advised.

Long-term preparation for meditation requires that you lead a lifestyle in conformity with dh^arm^a and keep the guN^a-s in balance. You must identify with the role of spiritual aspirant in order to play the cosmic game in which meditation is one of the highest components. To attempt meditation from an adharmic perspective is to pursue devolution.

Medium-term preparation for meditation involves adhering to the dawn program (described above) as much as possible. This increases the amount of s^a^tv^a^ in the system.

Short-term preparation for meditation requires an early bowel movement on the day of the meditation. If this is not possible, you should meditate with eyes open so as to prevent the rise of apaan^a^.

You can increase the amount of *aakaash^a^* in your system by listening to sounds of InnerTuning before commencing meditation.

The Meditative State

Whereas integrative mentation aims at refining any and all ch^a^kr^a^ minds, meditation aims at transcending all mentation, balancing the three guN^a^-s, and permitting your Vibrancy (Sh^a^ktE t^a^tv^a^) to merge with Stillness (ShEv^a^ t^a^tv^a^). For very advanced aspirants, continuation of meditation may lead to temporary merging with the Self (s^a^maadhE).

Meditation occurs when the following conditions have been met.

+ The body is in a stable posture with spine perpendicular to the earth. Several methods may be used to attain this. The classical one is seated with both legs folded, right over left. This is the lotus posture (p^a^dmaasan^a^) and is the one that permits maximum rotation of the ch^a^kr^a^-s.
+ The senses have been directed inward.
+ Breathing is even through both nostrils (sushumnaa breath).
+ Breathing is at the rate of four breaths per minute or fewer.
+ Energy is concentrated in the sixth or seventh ch^a^kr^a^.

None of these conditions can be forced. They must occur naturally as a result of adequate preparation and may take a long period of time. When these conditions are met and energy is concentrated in the sixth ch^a^kr^a^, observation can be held steady and unwavering. Then the guN^a^-s are in balance and the observer is outside spacetime, close to the Witness. No value judgment is placed on anything that happens. There is little ego with which to do so.

If possible, this true meditative state should be maintained for at least nine minutes.

Proximate Meditation

It may take years of practice and spiritual work (saadh^a^naa) before the meditative state described above can be regularly attained. In the meantime, the states that are attainable may be called "proximate" meditation. The saboteurs that attack during proximate meditation (such as bodily discomforts and distracting thoughts) can be identified and later weakened by means of physical exercises and integrative mentation.

Intruding thoughts, feelings, and sensations should be acknowledged (not suppressed) and observed until they gradually recede. They may become something like a ticking clock in the background while one is absorbed in reading an interesting novel.

As you simply observe thoughts you create distance. At some point a tiny space appears between thoughts. Focusing on that empty space can increase its size; then that increased space attracts soory^a *aakaash^a* produced by m^{a}ntr^a.

Soory^a *aakaash^a* is produced by hearing InnerTuning sounds, by chanting yourself, or by pure silence. When all minds are absorbed by the soory^a *aakaash^a*, meditation happens naturally. Some people have reported out-of-body experiences (fifth ch^{a}kr^a) before entering a deep meditative state (sixth ch^{a}kr^a).

Consecration of the Meditation Mat

It is a helpful practice to maintain your own meditation mat. Whenever you approach it, do your personal m^{a}ntr^a and allow the vibrations from it to leave through your fingertips. Then touch the place where you are going to sit and bring your fingertips to your forehead. By doing that, you are more conscious of your sitting and your connection in the universe becomes more secure. It is not just an empty ritual. When 4:1 opens up, planetary identity becomes more stable. When it is blocked you live without feeling that you are a citizen of the world.

WITNESSING

There are three "windows" where an ego is capable of contacting the Witness (saak-shEE). The first window is between the first and second lEng^a-s. From this window, self-observation of the first lEng^a is particularly clear. It is easier to take a good look at yourself and work through personal problems. A therapist may help to open this window.

A second window for contacting the Witness appears between the second and third lEng^a-s (fifth and sixth ch^{a}kr^a-s). This window may be available when inferior *aakaash^a* is expelled from the seventh ch^{a}kr^a and golden (soory^a) *aakaash^a* replaces it. A panoramic view of the universe may then be obtained. Sometimes, this is followed by a meditative state. The utilization of the second window may be helped by a guru.

In both instances, the Witness provides a peek at the cosmic game of hide and seek.

At the end of the game (liberation), a third window opens fully as you realize that you are Consciousness. For this window to open, there is no help. You are on your own.

VAdaantᵃ explains this with the following story: A guru points to a bird sitting on a tree. Exactly behind the bird is a star. A rare aspirant will see the star.

THREE-BODY PURIFICATION

Bodily toxicity, unnatural lifestyles, negative thinking, emotional shocks, and daily wear and tear disturb the elements of all three bodies. Elements and combinations of elements play an essential role in the quality of our feelings and mentation. For example, when *earth* is in abundance, we feel solid and grounded. Our confidence is strong. When *air* is plentiful, we may feel buoyant and more loving.

Under conditions of stress and toxicity, the elements lose some of their purity and potency. They may then have a negative effect on our physical functioning, feelings, and mentation. A dispersed *earth* may make us feel weak and sluggish. Polluted *air* can cause us to feel uncaring.

InnerTuning has had over four decades of experience in helping people to purify the elements and integrate the three bodies. As a consequence, thousands of people have had the personal experience of strengthening themselves.

This experience has centered on a five-day retreat. Except where contraindicated, participants in the purification group do not eat solid food throughout the five days. They are provided with high-quality herbs and husks, teas, vitamin C, special tonics, and protein drinks. This diet is intended to cleanse the intestinal and urinary tracts, among other organs. It takes two days to purify the physical body.

On the third day, emphasis shifts to the subtle body and feelings that may have been buried under the threshold of awareness. Sometimes old memories from early childhood emerge. This is part of the purification process. Since all participants are there for the same purpose, they provide an unusually supportive environment for each other. Amazing psychological resolutions are made.

As the InnerTuning sounds and mᵃntrᵃ-s are chanted they act deeply on the subtle body. This supports the purification process and helps to increase sensitivity to sound. On the third day, the subtle body begins to respond to the sounds more deeply.

On the fourth day, purified energies of the physical and subtle bodies permit all three bodies to compact. The process of mentation may begin to feel clearer. Special sounds that produce golden (soory^a) *aakaash^a* are chanted. This highly refined *aakaash^a* pushes more dense and toxic *aakaash^a* out of the causal body. Consequently, the breathing rate drops and participants improve their meditation.

The fifth day is devoted to consolidating the gains of the previous days and preparing to preserve them after the retreat ends.

SPEECH FAST

The vocal cords are the organ of action for the fifth ch^{a}kr^a whose primary element is *aakaash^a*. When this organ is at rest, the amount of *aakaash^a* in the three bodies increases and their integration is facilitated. On the other hand, negative thinking and use of foul language pollutes *aakaash^a* in the head and further separates the three bodies.

Some people require considerable loudness and activity in their vocal cords in order to be aware of their thoughts. Others are able to think more silently. In general, feeling requires more silence than reasoning, and intuition more silence than feeling.

M^{a}ntr^a acquires more potency as it is first practiced aloud, then in silent repetition, and finally by simple intention. In this way m^{a}ntr^a follows a principle of homeopathy: "less is more." Reasoning and feeling similarly benefit from as much silence as possible, and deep thinking occurs in silence. To maintain and deepen silence is a skill. Many cultural forces move us in the opposite direction, such as the hypnotic effect of television and the demand for gossip.

One method for reducing the amount of chatter in our minds is to keep the tongue parked at the base of our upper front teeth when not speaking. The gentle touch of the tongue in this area vibrates the subtle nerves (naaDEE-s) within it. The tongue is an organ of the second ch^{a}kr^a; parking it helps to reduce or even suspend thoughts.

Parking the tongue at the base of the upper front teeth also helps to hold *aakaash^a* in the head, its natural home. This leads to dissolution of the first five elemental minds, which allows the Witness (saakshEE) to emerge.

Many spiritual traditions have recognized the importance of silence. Some advanced aspirants are advised to do speech fasts (mown^a) for an extended period of time. Speech fasts are an integral part of the purifications discussed above. Prolonged speech fasts lasting weeks or even months are particularly beneficial. Some saints remain silent for decades.

It is important to keep the *aakaash^a* as pure as possible during a speech fast. The lower elements of *earth, water, fire,* and *air* more readily dissolve into *aakaash^a*

during a speech fast. This makes it easier to transcend the lower minds that are associated with them. Attention may then be focused on balancing the guṆᵃ-s and moving toward Stillness (SHᴇvᵃ tᵃtvᵃ).

Another benefit of speech fasts is that integrative mentation is facilitated. The threshold of awareness is generally lowered and important suppressed memories become more available for the psychological issues to be resolved.

REGULATING DESIRE

Tradition teaches several techniques that help to integrate the three bodies by regulating our desires.

+ Daily duties. You should care for your body, your home, and your relationships on a daily basis.
+ Mental control. Under most conditions, it is better to direct the chᵃkrᵃ minds rather than allow the chᵃkrᵃ minds to direct you. This is facilitated by maintaining focus on a short-term task until it is completed. Directing the mind helps to overcome the guᴎᵃ of tᵃmᵃs.
+ Action without personal desire. Performing actions simply because they are part of your dhᵃrmᵃ without becoming emotionally involved in the action strengthens the effectiveness of the causal body. For example, a soldier may kill the enemy on orders of his commanding officer without any feeling of hatred. On the other hand, he may work himself up to a fury of hatred for the enemy. In the latter case, the distance between his three bodies is increased.
+ Sense of nondoership. The more you attach to your actions and expect reward, the more you increase the guᴎᵃ of rᵃjᵃs. To overcome this guᴎᵃ, it helps to develop the awareness that all action is done by eightfold nature. This permits the three bodies to draw closer together, a necessary prerequisite for a life of dhᵃrmᵃ.
+ Nonreaction. Abstinence from reacting to a situation (mentally or physically) helps to overcome the guᴎᵃ of sᵃtvᵃ. This is a requirement for liberation (mokshᵃ).

COLOR OF THE DAY

Energy from the spectrum of colors is mostly absorbed by the eyes, some by ingestion and some by the skin. Each day of the week is influenced by a different heavenly body. Wearing something that matches its associated color helps you to absorb its energy and benefit your chᵃkrᵃ-s. The item worn may be clothing or jewelry. You can also eat foods of that color.

TABLE 10.3. COLOR OF THE DAY

Day	Color	Heavenly Body
Monday	Light Blue; Silver	Moon
Tuesday	Orange; Pink; Red	Mars
Wednesday	Green	Mercury
Thursday	Yellow	Jupiter
Friday	White; Multicolor	Venus
Saturday	Black; Navy Blue	Saturn
Sunday	Gold	Sun

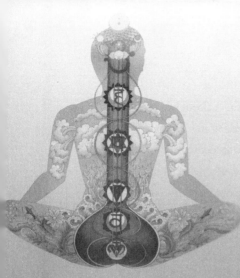

11
Subjective Science

The preceding chapters have set forth the theory of Microchakra Psychology and the practices of InnerTuning. This final chapter seeks to put them within the context of Western science as it has been developing since the sixteenth century and as it has recently been changed by quantum physics. It also seeks to suggest a path for their future development.

THE RISE OF MODERN OBJECTIVE SCIENCE

Astronomy and the Birth of Science

The formative years of objective science were marked by a clash between the geocentric and heliocentric theories of the universe. The former taught that the Earth was at the center of the universe. It had been proposed by Aristotle in the fourth century B.C.E. and, in conjunction with Biblical interpretation, was maintained as an official doctrine of the Catholic Church in the sixteenth century. In direct contradiction, the heliocentric theory held that the sun was at the center of the universe and the Earth circled around it.

The advancement of the heliocentric theory required the development of several distinct conceptual and physical tools. These served as prototypes for the major components of science in its subsequent growth:

+ The authority of nature. Questions about the sky were put directly to the sky rather than consulting scriptural authority. This is an example of what came to be called "naturalistic observation."
+ Model building. A model of the universe with the sun at its center was first proposed by Copernicus who died in 1543—the year that it was published. Prior to this, other models had been advanced in an attempt to explain the varied phenomena observed in the sky.

+ Data Collection. A significant step in astronomy was taken by Tyco Brahe (1546–1601), who was given a small island with an observatory by the King of Denmark. Brahe designed and built the most accurate pre-telescopic instruments for tracking heavenly bodies. For over twenty years, he patiently and accurately recorded their movement. Before his death, he passed this invaluable information on to Johannes Kepler.

+ Mathematical laws. Kepler was a mathematician who, in carefully studying the data he had been given on the motion of Mars, was able to discover three basic laws of motion. These laws were later shown to apply not only to Mars, but to all other bodies in astronomical orbit.

+ Technological advance. In 1608, Hans Lippershey—a Dutch lensmaker— made his design for a telescope publicly available. Its magnification power was three times that of the eye alone.

The tools just listed were assembled by Galileo Galilei (1564–1642), who became the most prominent advocate for the heliocentric theory. Having heard of Lippershey's invention, Galileo proceeded to develop his own models, soon achieving magnification of twenty times. With this telescope he was able to detect the brightest four moons of Saturn in 1610. Since they were orbiting a body other than the earth, he regarded this as evidence against the geocentric theory. Galileo's promotion of the heliocentric theory brought him into open conflict with the Church, which eventually tried and condemned him for heresy, forced him to recant under threat of torture, placed him under house arrest, and banned the publication of his books. Hence, at the beginning of the scientific adventure, a split was established between science and religion.

Galileo made many other contributions to science and is often regarded as the father of modern science.

In succeeding centuries, science advanced rapidly to build our modern world. A major part of this advance involved the construction of machines. The analogy of the machine permeated the thinking of many scientists. Newton envisioned the universe as a gigantic clock whose parts moved with mathematical precision according to laws that he had discovered. Descartes, having viewed human-like statues move their limbs by means of hydraulic pressure, concluded that human anatomy could similarly be regarded as machine-like. Today, the successors of Descartes struggle to support the analogy of the brain and the computer. The numerous successes of mechanism have helped to keep science tied to the material field alone.

The Doctrine of Materialism

In general, the scientific advances of the early nineteenth century engendered widespread optimism. Scientific theory was demonstrating ever more astonishing explanatory and predictive capacities. The technical applications of science in agriculture, industry, public health, and medicine came increasingly to drive substantial improvements in prosperity, comfort, and health. These were far more visible and impressive than a variety of concomitant, arguably detrimental developments such as industrial pollution and increasingly lethal weaponry. In sum, science—increasingly being viewed as a single body of knowledge—came to be seen as the embodiment of human progress and the power of human reason made manifest.[1]

The success of science brought hubris with it:

In 1845 . . . four young, enthusiastic and idealistic physiologists, all pupils of the great Johannes Müller, all later to be very famous, met together and formed a pact. . . . They were, in order of age, Carl Ludwig, who was then twenty-nine. Emil du Bois-Reymond, Ernst Brücke, and Hermann von Helmholtz, then twenty-four. They were joining forces to fight vitalism, the view that life involves forces other than those found in the interaction of inorganic bodies. The great Johannes Müller was a vitalist, but these men were of the next generation. Du Bois and Brücke even pledged between them a solemn oath that they would establish and compel the acceptance of this truth: "No other forces than common physical chemical ones are active within the organism."[2]

The same intolerance that the Church had shown toward Galileo was now brought into science with this religious doctrine of materialism. It is a doctrine that restricts science to the physical field and has inhibited the study of the nonmaterial fields until recent decades. For many it continues as an inhibitor to direction of the senses inward.

LANGUAGE IN OBJECTIVE AND SUBJECTIVE SCIENCE

In the first half of the twentieth century, a number of scientists, philosophers, and mathematicians addressed the issue of the relationship between language and science. Though they varied in the details of their positions, collectively their views have been referred to as Logical Positivism or Logical Empiricism.

Logical Positivism

Schlick expressed a positivistic view of the meaning of language:

> It is the first step in every kind of philosophizing, and the basis of all reflection, to realize that it is absolutely impossible to give the meaning of any claim save by describing the state-of-affairs that must obtain if the claim is true. If it does not obtain, then the claim is false. The meaning of a proposition obviously consists in this alone, that it expresses a particular state of affairs. This state-of-affairs must actually be pointed out, in order to give the meaning of the proposition.[3]

The possibility of being able to point to something in the physical field as being the meaning of a word reflects its denotative meaning. For example, the word *table* may denote a wooden object four feet wide, six feet long, and three feet high. The connotative meanings of table (something to eat on, to write on, purchased at a bargain price, and so on) are irrelevant to the positivistic task of constructing a scientific language through denotation.

The basic propositions of science are expressed in terms of logically structured statements that express the relationships existing between the denoting terms—hence, logical positivism.

Language that did not meet the criteria of logical positivism was regarded as incomprehensible and meaningless from the standpoint of science. Most of the vocabulary of religion and metaphysics fell into this category. This consequence is understandable when we remember that much of this vocabulary refers to nonmaterial fields and requires the exercise of feeling or intuition in order to provide the meaning. For example, the term "suffering soul" has no denotative meaning. Its meaning is attained only through empathy or intuition and an interpretive framework not bound by strict empiricism.

Operationism

In 1927, the physicist Percy W. Bridgman wrote a book entitled *The Logic of Modern Physics*. In it he described a procedure that others later called "operationism." The procedure is intended to assure that denotative meaning is assigned to concepts admitted into physics.

> In general, we mean by any concept nothing more than a set of operations; *the concept is synonymous with the corresponding set of operations.*[4]

As an example, Bridgman discussed the concept of "length."

Our task is to find the operations by which we measure the length of any concrete physical object. We begin with objects of our commonest experience, such as a house or house lot. What we do is sufficiently indicated by the following rough description. We start with a measuring rod, lay it on the object so that one of its ends coincides with one end of the object, mark on the object the position of the other end of the rod, then move the rod along in a straight line extension of its previous position until the first end coincides with the previous position of the second end, repeat this process as often as we can, and call the length the total number of times the rod was applied. This procedure, apparently so simple, is in practice exceedingly complicated, and doubtless a full description of all the precautions that must be taken would fill a large treatise. We must, for example, be sure that the temperature of the rod is the standard temperature at which length is defined, or else we must make a correction for it; or we must correct for the gravitational distortion of the rod if we measure a vertical length; or we must be sure that the rod is not a magnet or is not subject to electrical forces. All these precautions would occur to every physicist. . . . In *principle* the operations by which length is measured should be *uniquely* specified. If we have more than one set of operations, we have more than one concept, and strictly there should be a separate name to correspond to each different set of operations.[5]

During the 1930s, 1940s, and 1950s, those psychologists who were attempting to make psychology a science "just like physics" seized upon operationism as a tool to accomplish this goal. They attempted to abolish terms that could not be given operational definition such as "mind," "self," or "will." The excess connotative meaning of other terms was sheared off with the operational scissors. Hence, the famous "Intelligence is what the intelligence tests measure." All of this led Bridgman, twenty-seven years after his proposal was first published, to declare:

I feel as if I have created a Frankenstein, which has certainly gotten away from me. I abhor the word *operationalism* or *operationism* which seems to imply a dogma, or at least a thesis of some kind. The thing I have envisaged is too simple to be dignified by so pretentious a name.[6]

Of the current status of positivism, the philosopher Passman declared in 1967:

Logical positivism, then, is dead or as dead as a
philosophical movement ever becomes.
But it has left a legacy behind.[7]

Positivism and operationism have indeed left a legacy, particularly in psychology. They have encouraged overly simple thinking about the relationship between language and mind by limiting discussion to the physical field. Language pervades all three fields; it helps to form thought and generate feeling. The language of mᵃntrᵃ taps into the most profound levels of manifestation in order to bring about change.

Microgenesis

It will be recalled from the discussion of the LEElaa model in chapter 2 that sound proceeds through four stages as it manifests the universe: static sound, luminous sound, illuminated sound, and audible sound. Within the transition from illuminated sound to audible sound, there is an area that may be called the microgenetic level.

Microgenesis refers to the gradual change from vague to specific. This change may take various periods of time, ranging from less than a second to several days or longer. An appreciation of this microgenetic level is essential in order to understand human information processing. Some experimentation done at this level is reported in Hentschel, Smith, and Draguns.[8] Felt meaning is an example of activity at the microgenetic level.

Felt Meaning

The work of Eugene Gendlin cogently developed the relationship between language and the subtle field. His technique of "focusing" is a practical application of this relationship.

> What, then, is this "concrete" or "preconceptual" experiencing? We cannot talk about it without the use of symbols. . . .
>
> It is something so simple, so easily available to every person, that at first its very simplicity makes it hard to point to. Another term for it is "felt meaning," or "feeling." However, "feeling" is a word usually used for specific contents—for this or that feeling, emotion, or tone, for feeling good, or bad, or blue, or pretty fair. But regardless of the many changes in *what* we feel—that is to say, really, *how* we feel—there always is the concretely present flow of feeling. At any moment we can individually and privately direct our attention inward, and when we do that, there it is. Of course, we have this or that specific idea, wish, emotion, perception, word, or thought, but we *always* have concrete feeling, an inward sensing whose nature is broader. It is a concrete mass in the sense that it is "there" for us. It is not at all vague in its being there. It may be vague only in that we may not know what it is. We can put only a few aspects of it into words. The mass itself is always something

there, no matter what we say "it is." Our definitions, our knowing "what it is," are symbols that specify aspects of it, "parts of it," as we say. Whether we name it, divide it, or not, there it is.[9]

Indeed, as Gendlin states, the felt meaning is a "mass" that is always there and it is "vague" in the sense that it must be explicated by the application of a matching symbol that "feels right."

From the viewpoint of Microchakra Psychology, felt meaning is the product of the openings and blocks in the microchakras. Chᵃkrᵃ minds process feelings emanating from openings and blocks. Each chᵃkrᵃ mind generates feelings regarding closeness to its goals and obstacles to its goals.

THE CALL
FOR A SUBJECTIVE SCIENCE

Objective science was built on the assumption that an objective world existed independently of anyone who observed it. It also assumed that a good scientist was essentially neutral or impartial in collecting and interpreting data. In the past several decades, these assumptions have been increasingly challenged.

As we reported in chapter 1, interpretations of quantum mechanics have called into question the assumption of a solid physical reality. In its place are probability waves, one of which is brought into manifestation through the intentional measurement of an observer. The mind of the scientist is now recognized as central to the enterprise of science. The scientist, like everyone else, is woven into the universe and cannot step outside in order to observe.

This situation has been recognized by Amit Goswami who has integrated quantum physics, ancient Indian metaphysics, and psychology.[10] Danah Zohar has developed another compelling combination of quantum physics and psychology.[11]

Apart from quantum physics, there are other reasons for focusing on the subjective nature of science. Robert G. Jahn and Brenda J. Dunne call attention to some:

Inclusion of subjective information within the framework of science clearly constitutes a huge analytical challenge. Many contend that it should not even be attempted—that subjectivity should be categorically excluded from any of the "exact" sciences. Others feel equally keenly that in a world progressively more driven by individual and collective emotional resonances, orchestrated consumer reactions, media-manipulated politics, and delicate interpersonal expectations, for science to deny its immense intellectual power and cultural influence to this entire hemisphere of common human experience and expression would not only be irresponsible, it could be dangerously self-constraining.[12]

B. Alan Wallace in his book *The Taboo of Subjectivity* details the history through which scientists gradually came to exclude subjectivity from their domain of activity. He contends that now is the time to end this taboo.[13]

To the degree that the theory and practices presented in the previous chapters resonate with truth, it too suggests that the time to expand science has come.

A COMPARISON OF OBJECTIVE AND SUBJECTIVE SCIENCE

The following paragraphs compare and contrast objective science (OS) with subjective science (SS) on a number of dimensions. Together these dimensions delineate most of what constitutes a science as distinct from other forms of knowledge such as religion, philosophy, and art. Microchakra Psychology is given as an example of subjective science.

Purpose
The purposes referred to here may also be seen as values. This is in agreement with those who contend that there is no such thing as a "value free" science.

> **OS:** To describe phenomena found in the physical field (empirical world) and, when possible, to predict or control their behavior.
>
> **SS:** To refine egos so that they may observe and influence more and more phenomena of the subtle field. In so doing, to work with all three fields and gradually integrate the three bodies.

The refinement of ego is based on the refinement of schemas and scripts that provide the structures for more subtle energies to influence. For example, self-images that contain more altruism, more creativity, and more stillness support the flow of subtler energies.

Mentation
A phenomenon is any segment of the universe selected for study.

> **OS:** Emphasizes observing and reasoning about empirical phenomena located in the physical field only. Limits reference to feeling and intuition to a few instances of scientific discovery.

SS: In addition to observing and reasoning about the empirical world, senses may also be internalized to observe phenomena that can only be felt or intuited.

Causality

OS: All physical and chemical phenomena have physical and chemical causes. There are no nonmaterial causes. In addition, causality is due to preexisting conditions (physical determinism, mechanism) and proceeds independently of the observer. There is no room for purpose (teleology).

SS: Microchakra Psychology emphasizes the causal role of the ego in each chᵃkrᵃ mind. It is the fire of the third microchakra in each chᵃkrᵃ that directs its mentation. Of course, behind each ego lies the causal field, and Supreme Intelligence (Mᵃhᵃt). Ultimately, the Vedantic teaching that, "You are not the doer" applies. Teleology is built into the system as each chᵃkrᵃ mind has its own goals. Subjective science includes all three fields; hence, in addition to physical and chemical causes, feelings and intuitions also have causal status.

Hypothetical Constructs

OS: Hypothetical constructs are structures that are assumed to exist in the physical world and influence its functioning. Specifics of the functioning are predicted from the assumed details of the construct. The most famous example, in modern times, is the use of various models of the atom as hypothetical constructs before atoms could be seen.

SS: Hypothetical constructs play a similar role to those in objective science. However, the structures that they describe are in the subtle or causal field. They are used to make predictions about the way energy will flow in these fields. The chᵃkrᵃ-s, microchakras, and memory pods are examples of such constructs.

Validation of Hypothetical Constructs

OS: Hypothetical constructs are validated based upon their capacity to make successful predictions. Most commonly, these predictions are tested by means of carefully designed experiments.

SS: In subjective science, hypothetical constructs become the tools of one or more egos. Validation is based on their capacity to aid an ego in releasing positive and more subtle energies. The presence of these emergent energies must be felt or intuited. Hence, constructs are validated by the user community over time. Those passed on by the Tantric and Vedic traditions have centuries of validation behind them. This does not mean that a subjective science may not eventually modify or replace some of them.

LENGᵃ Dominance

OS: Objective science is limited to the first LENGᵃ, more specifically the third chᵃkrᵃ. The goal is to have a rational (left hemispheric) understanding of phenomena and, if possible, to predict and control them.

SS: In addition to the methods of objective science, subjective science internalizes the senses in order to feel and intuit phenomena. Hence it utilizes all three LENGᵃ-s and the complete tripartite brain. Right-hemispheric feeling must be developed to at least the same degree of strength as left-hemispheric reasoning.

Experimental Relationships

The experimental relationship may be symbolized by the IV-O-DV model.

The independent variable (IV) is applied by the experimenter. It is completely under the experimenter's control and independent of anything that the object (or subject) does.

Any object (O) or subject to which the independent variable is applied may contain one or more hypothetical constructs (e.g., atoms) that are assumed to be influenced by the independent variable.

The DV (dependent variable) is the resultant effect of the action of the independent variable (IV) upon the object (O).

OS: Objective science conducts all experiments under the influence of the materialistic doctrine. All independent variables, dependent variables, and hypothetical constructs are based in the physical field only.

SS: All variables and hypothetical constructs may be drawn from any of the three fields. The independent variable may frequently be a releaser. An example is, a mᵃntrᵃ that acts upon a chᵃkrᵃ to yield a dependent variable measured by the report of a feeling or pattern of feelings.

Interobserver Agreement

OS: For a phenomenon to qualify as objective it must be observable by more than one observer under comparable conditions.

SS: Phenomena in subjective science are known by more than one person through the use of understanding and empathy. The latter is a quality of the fourth chᵃkrᵃ that plays a central role in a subjective science, just as the third-chᵃkrᵃ plays a central role in objective science.

MICROCHAKRA PSYCHOLOGY AND
THE FOUR FUNCTIONS OF THEORY

Rychlak proposed that personality theory could be described in terms of its four main functions. He described these as a) descriptive, b) delimiting, c) integrative, and d) generative.[14] Microchakra Psychology is now examined in terms of these four functions.

Descriptive Function of Microchakra Psychology

Descriptive terms delineate the phenomena that are the focus of a theory. These phenomena may be observed by extraverting the senses or by inverting them. In the latter case, considerable training may be required before the phenomena may be sensed, felt, or intuited.

Microchakra Psychology describes the esoteric anatomy of the subtle field. Inverting the senses for a long period may be required before significant perception of this anatomy arises in awareness. In the meantime, the components of this anatomy are treated as hypothetical constructs. The value of each construct may be understood in terms of its contribution to the whole system of Microchakra Psychology.

All terms used in Microchakra Psychology, including those whose referents are parts of subtle anatomy, are intended to permit the awareness of the aspirant to work with more and more subtle energies. Conversely, it may be said that gross energies are peeled away for what seems like endless layers. Even then, in moments of weakness, they may recur at any time. To permanently eradicate them requires tremendous development.

Delimiting Function of Microchakra Psychology

The delimiting function of a theory sets boundaries between phenomena with which the theory is directly concerned and those with which is it is not concerned. The phenomena that are of most concern to Microchakra Psychology are those that influence the integration of the three bodies and the upward flow of refined energy. The theoretical aspects of these phenomena have been discussed in the first nine chapters of this book and the practical aspects in the tenth chapter.

Spirituality and Religion. Microchakra Psychology makes a sharp distinction between spirituality and religion. Spirituality refers to the refinement of human energy until it eventually reaches the Self (Consciousness). Religions are complex organizations with many diverse practices. Some of these practices aid spiritual development and some inhibit it.

Integrative Function of Microchakra Psychology

The integrative function of a theory refers to its capacity to show relationships among its constructs. It also refers to the capacity of the theory to show relationships with facts and theories outside its immediate domain.

The hybrid LEElaa model integrated ancient information on the stages of sound and the principles of creation with some knowledge of microchakra functioning. It integrates the three fields—causal, subtle, and gross—by indicating how manifestation descends from one to the other. Portions of the LEElaa model might eventually be integrated with findings from quantum physics.

The microchakra model itself integrates many facts of psychology, spirituality, and metaphysics. More integration will occur as the model is advanced in the future.

Generative Function of Microchakra Psychology

Data is the lifeblood of any science. It strengthens the science either by supporting its current assumptions or calling them into question and prompting revision. Future research and data collection under the aegis of Microchakra Psychology will include the following areas:

- ◆ Assessment of openings and blocks
  - ▪ Development of various psychometric procedures for assessing saboteur and champion patterns
- ◆ Sensory inversion
  - ▪ Development of new methods for facilitating the inversion of the senses
- ◆ Sensitivity to *aakaash*[a]
  - ▪ Research on factors influencing sensitivity to *aakaash*[a] (This is the "missing link" required to expand science beyond the physical field)
- ◆ Articulation of m[a]ntr[a]
  - ▪ Development of new methods for teaching correct pronunciation of m[a]ntr[a]
- ◆ Chanting and the saboteurs
  - ▪ Research on types of chanting and their influence on saboteur patterns
- ◆ Integrative mentation
  - ▪ Research on the various aspects of integrative mentation
- ◆ Community
  - ▪ Development of methods to serve the community of those interested in Microchakra Psychology and InnerTuning

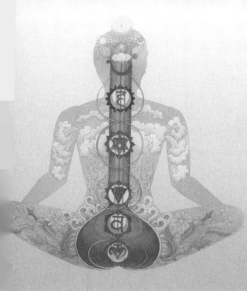

Advitᵃ Vᴀdaantᵃ: A Third-Lᴇngᵃ Viewpoint

The ancient land of India was known as Aryᵃ Vrᵃtᵃ (the land of the Aryans). The inhabitants were inspired by four major texts that are known as the Vᴀdᵃ-s (means of knowledge). The way of life based on these texts is called the Vedic tradition. Among the followers of this tradition, some went more deeply inward than others. Their approach is called Vᴀdaantᵃ. As noted in chapter 1, there are several versions of Vᴀdaantᵃ. It is the nondual (advitᵃ) version that most clearly reflects the operation of the third lᴇngᵃ.

The goal of Vᴀdaantᵃ is to remove ignorance (avᴇdyaa). This is the ignorance of who we truly are—the Self (Aatmaa).

Pure Śaṅkara Vᴀdaantᵃ

The unsurpassed proponent of Advitᵃ Vᴀdaantᵃ (Advaita Vedānta) was Sri Śaṅkarāchārya who lived around 500 BCE.* He wrote commentaries on the three foundational texts of Vᴀdaantᵃ: the ten principal UpᵃnᴇsHᵃd-s, the Bhᵃgvat Gᴇᴇtaa, and the Bhrᵃmᵃ sutra. Through the brilliance of these commentaries, he established the preeminence of his interpretation.

Recently, Sri Satchidānandendra has published a comprehensive and authoritative examination of pure Śaṅkarā Vᴀdaantᵃ.[1] His disciple Sri Ātmanandendra has shared this wisdom with the senior author and his students. Microchakra Psychology sees this teaching as representing the third lᴇngᵃ. Some of the fundamental teachings of Advitᵃ Vᴀdaantᵃ are:

- ✦ Consciousness is one without a second (nondual). It is the substratum of all that is.
- ✦ Only that which never changes is ultimately real. Anything subject to change

---

*Not all scholars agree with this dating. Many place Śaṅkarā in the eighth century C.E.

is ultimately unreal. In Vᴀdaantᵃ, the unchangeable is called Brᵃhmᵃn and the changeable refers to the world of the senses, the empirical world.

✦ Consciousness is unchangeable and real. Awareness is changeable and ultimately unreal.

✦ The ego (ahᵃmkaarᵃ) is changeable and ultimately unreal. The Self is changeless and ever real. Liberation (mokshᵃ) culminates from the complete realization and actualization of this distinction.

✦ Discernment (vᴇchaarᵃ) is the practice in which we gradually perceive the difference between our apparent identity and the sublime Self.

In his magnum opus, *The Method of the Vedanta,* Sri Satchidānandendra, explains why the various interpretations of Sri Śaṅkarāchārya's commentaries are so different. He notes that many scholars failed to discriminate Śaṅkara's statements regarding transcendental Reality (Brᵃhmᵃn) from those regarding empirical reality. This produced considerable confusion. It is imperative that this confusion be avoided by any future attempts to approach the topic of Consciousness.[2]

SELF AND EGO

Changeless Self and Changeable Ego

> *Two birds, together, companions, depend on the same tree (the body).*
> *One eats the sweet fruit, the other looks on.*
>
> Muṇḍaka Upaniṣad 3.1.1 (Ātmanandendra trans.)

This little parable has significance for understanding ourselves and our relationship to Brᵃhmᵃn. The first bird stands for the ego that is absorbed in activity; the second bird represents the (transcendental) Self that is Brᵃhmᵃn. The Upᵃnᴇsʜᵃd-s describe Brᵃhmᵃn as the self-effulgent light.

Sri Śaṅkarā gave the following commentary on this parable:

Of these two occupying the tree, one is the Knower of the Field . . . as associated with the apparent conditioning adjunct of the subtle body. Failing to discriminate the true Self from the subtle body, he resorts to the tree and eats the berries in the form of experience of the pleasures and pains arising as the "fruit" of his previous deeds. It is called "sweet" (not in the sense of being invariably pleasurable but) in the sense of being rich with a variety of gradations of feeling. The other does not eat. He who does not eat is the Lord, ever pure, conscious and liberated by nature, omniscient, having all creatures for his apparent conditioning adjunct. For he is the prompter both of the experiencer and the experienced, simply by existing as the eternal Witness. He is the other who looks on, not eating. He only observes.[3]

Moving beyond the parable of the two birds, the Upᵃnᴇsʜᵃd-s teach that the Self (Aatmaa) is ever real and the ego (ahᵃmkaarᵃ) is ultimately unreal. The ego is bound to spacetime, undergoes many changes, and eventually dissolves. On the other hand, the Self is independent of spacetime and forever changeless.

In a simplified manner, the distinction between ego and Self can be illustrated in the following example: A three year old may say "I am hungry." This same statement may be repeated when the person is a vigorous twenty-five year old and again when bent over and frail at ninety-eight. Does the "I" in each case refer to the body?—clearly not. At twenty-five, the body of the three year old is not recognizable; nor are the younger bodies at ninety-eight. The "I" refers to the Self that has not changed at all during this period of ninety-eight years.

The Undeniable Self

Sri Ātmanandendra provides the following definition of Reality: "That alone is Real the absence of which we cannot conceive."[4] It is the Self alone whose absence cannot be conceived. It is impossible to deny our Self—for who would assert the denial? It is this undeniable Self that is the substratum of all experience. The Self is also referred to as the Witness (saakshᴇᴇ). It is the same in all beings. Apparent differences among beings belong to the realm of the ego.

IGNORANCE

Our inability to discriminate between the Self and the ego is called ignorance (avᴇdyaa). It is part of the usual human condition and is also referred to as "uncaused" or "beginningless" (anaadᴇ) ignorance.

From the standpoint of the highest truth, our Self is unborn, nondual pure Consciousness by nature, eternally raised above all change. But from the worldly standpoint based on metaphysical Ignorance, it appears to be divided into knower, knowledge and known, into actor, act, instruments and results, into experiencer, experience and experienced. This is beginningless Ignorance. You cannot ask for a cause of it [since the very asking is done in Ignorance].

For it is the very nature of Ignorance that it should set up the appearance of the existence of things that do not really exist. [emphasis added][5]

The Rope and the Snake

Elsewhere, Sri Satchidānandendra, explained the consequences of failure to discriminate the Self from the ego.

> For it is a clear fact of experience that when the true nature of anything is not discerned, various false notions about it arise. So it is the Self, the real metaphysical principle, that is imagined under various names and forms when its true nature is not discerned. On this a great authority [Śaṅkarā] has said: "As a rope imperfectly perceived in the dark is variously imagined as a snake or stream of water or in other ways, so is the Self wrongly imagined as this and that."[6]

In other words, the rope stands for Consciousness as the substratum. Ignorance is represented by the darkness. This ignorance is reflected in the innumerable false notions of the Self that the ego formulates. Thus multiplicity is born out of beginningless ignorance and the One appears as many.

Mutual Superimposition

Advit[a] Vadaant[a] teaches that ignorance is the mutual superimposition of the Self onto the ego and of the ego onto the Self. Therefore, the continuous discernment (vEchaar[a]) between the Self and the ego has to become second nature to us in order for liberation to occur.

The S[a]mskret[a] word for superimposition is adhyaas[a], which literally means "to sit facing." Sri Ātmanandendra states that

> . . . we may understand adhyaas[a] as something that pops up if we face it, if we become aware of it, or if the identification with the ego begins. All this, again, is only after adhyaas[a] has become operative, which means that if we accept it, it can come up and if we do the vEchaar[a] and get rid of the ego, there can also be no adhyaas[a] or anything incidental to that. Ultimately, we accept it, it is there; we don't, it is nowhere.[7]

The usual condition is to fully accept the empirical world. Sri Satchidānandendra cited Śaṅkarā:

> (And from that there results) this natural worldly experience, based on wrong knowledge and involving a synthesis of the real with the false, which expresses itself as "I am this" and "This is mine."[8]

The True Method of VAdaant^a

Satchidānandendra has described the method of VAdaant^a as follows:

> . . . the concern of the Upanishads is to communicate to sincere enquirers direct experience of the supreme reality as their own Self—that supreme reality which is nondual, has no particular features, and is beyond the range of speech and mind.
>
> They know that, to this end, the texts begin by falsely ascribing to this entity various attributes that it does not really possess. They know that the texts refer to it by such terms as "Being," "the Absolute," "the Self," and so on, and speak of it as knowable, as being of the nature of Consciousness and Bliss . . .
>
> But these attributes are only imagined in this way for purposes of instruction. These same upanishadic texts mean to ward off any suspicion that the superimposed attributes belong to the supreme reality. So at the end of various passages of teaching they clearly retract what they had said earlier.[9]

This method of attribution (adhyaarop^a) and subsequent retraction (apavaad^a) of attributes is called "the method of VAdaant^a." Approximate ideas are used to direct the mind in the direction of the unknowable, then they are removed and their inadequacy recognized with the statement of the Up^anESH^ad-s "neither this nor that" (nAtE, nAtE). In this way the inquiring mind is brought closer to the truth of the Self.

Superimposition and Personality

Among the false ideas that flow from ignorance are the usual beliefs that we are agents of activity and enjoyers of the fruits of that activity. It is only through discernment (vEchaar^a) that we can come to see that these beliefs are false. In the meantime, the ego—through fear (as a result of ignorance)—builds a network of attitudes and beliefs based on attraction and repulsion. The Tantric and Vedic traditions contain a list of six major psychological tendencies that result from this attraction-repulsion dichotomy: 1) desire, 2) anger, 3) greed, 4) lack of discernment, 5) arrogance, and 6) envy.[10] These are sometimes called "the six afflictions." They must be transcended.

THE THREE STATES

As an aid for discovering the Ultimate Reality, Advit^a VAdaant^a advocates a careful examination of the three states (av^asthaatr^ay^a): waking (jaagret^a av^asthaa), dream (svapn^a av^asthaa), and deep sleep (sushuptE avasthaa). All of these states occur in the context of ignorance.

The natural inclination both of the individual and of society is to attach most importance to the waking state. When the other two states are examined, it is usually to see how they serve the waking state. However, if the states are to be used to help in the discovery of Ultimate Reality, equal value must be given to each state.

In the waking state we experience spacetime and causality. To perceive the waking world we are dependent upon secondary illumination such as the sun or electric light. The waking world exists in the waking state (not the reverse) since nobody experiences it except in the waking state.

Upon entering the dream state, the waking state laws of spacetime and causality do not apply. There is not the slightest awareness of the waking state. The source of illumination for dreams emanates from within. It is the inner light (pr^akaash^a). The same Witness, the undeniable "I," which had observed the waking world now observes the dream world.

In deep sleep all experience of duality vanishes. The Chaandogya Up^anESH^ad (6.8.1) says:

> When this Spirit sleeps . . . then, my dear one, he is merged . . . in pure Being, he
> has become one with his own Self. . . . That is why they say of him "he sleeps". . .
> for he has become one with his true Self. . . .[11]

In deep sleep we are in our true nature—the Self. The unreal worlds of waking and dream are shed. It is largely for this reason that so many look forward to sleep. Upon return to the waking state, one may say, "I slept soundly." In this way one accounts for the undeniable "I," the eternal Witness, even though in deep sleep there was no awareness of anything at all!

Sri Ātmanandendra summarizes the three states as follows: Where Consciousness illumines the duality, we experience either waking or dream state; where Consciousness illumines the absence of duality, that is the deep sleep state. The method of examining the three states opens one to the intuition of the underlying reality behind each state. In fact, it takes us to the view of Sri Ātmanandendra that the highest intuition *is* Reality.[12]

Satchidānandendra cited Gauḍapāda (the guru of Śaṅkarā) on transcendence of the three states:

> When the individual soul, asleep under a beginningless illusion, finally awakens,
> he awakens to a knowledge of the unborn, sleepless, dreamless, nondual reality.[13]

Liberation (Moksh^a)

Vedantins refer to a liberated person as a gyaanEE (one who knows). However, in this state, one cannot know that one knows. It is no more possible to say "I am enlightened" than for a sleeping person to say "I am asleep." At this time, the three fields become maximally contracted and integrated with each other. Consequently, the aggregate of thoughts, feelings, and physical body simply flow together automatically in a pattern uninfluenced by ego, guided only by ret^a. Superimposition, then, goes only one way: Self onto ego. There is no ego to be superimposed onto the Self.

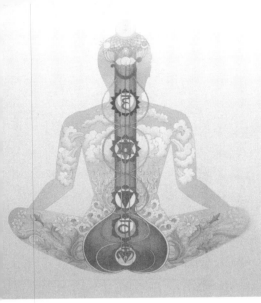

APPENDIX B

Glossary of
Sᵃmskretᵃ Terms

Meanings given are for the contexts used in the text
🪔 = Basic Term

🪔 aagyaa आज्ञा
Commander. Discerner. The name of the sixth chᵃkrᵃ.

🪔 aakaashᵃ आकाश
Nontranslatable. Common approximations are "ether" and "space." The concept refers to a subtle experience produced by sound and is learned by repeatedly listening to the mᵃntrᵃ-s and sounds of InnerTuning. *Aakaashᵃ* is the purest of the five elements and has gradations of hue.

🪔 aanandᵃ आनन्द
Bliss. Contentment in the seventh microchakra of the seventh chᵃkrᵃ brings bliss (aananndᵃ). Other seventh microchakras simply provide contentment.

aapah tᵃtvᵃ आप: तत्व
Water element.

🪔 aasanᵃ आसन
Seat. Any seated posture that is intended to facilitate meditation.

🪔 Aatmaa आत्मा
Self. It is the Self implied by the teaching "You are That" of the Upᵃnᴇsнᵃd-s and that gives meaning to the practice of discernment between Self and not-Self (vᴇchaarᵃ).

abhayᵃ अभय
Fearless.

adhyaaropᵃ अध्यारोप
Attribution. The first part of the method of Vᴀdaantᵃ.

adhyaasᵃ अध्यास
Superimposition.

🪔 adhyaatmᵃ yogᵃ अध्यात्म योग
Supreme yoga of Bhᵃgvat Gᴇᴇtaa in which Self is united with Consciousness.

🪔 advɪtᵃ अद्वैत
Nondual. Derived from the teaching of the Upᵃnᴇsнᵃd-s that Consciousness (Tᵃt) is an undivided (nondual) whole.

agnᴇ tᵃtvᵃ आग्नि तत्व
Fire element.

ah^amkaar^a अंहकार

Me-maker. Ego. The sense of oneself as distinct from others. One of the four aspects of the psychic organ (antaahk^ar^an^a).

☙ **a-k^a-th^a** अ–क–थ

The a-k^a-th^a triangle is located within the KaamAshv^arEE ch^akr^a, which is part of the som^a ch^akr^a network. The a-k^a-th^a triangle is called the "womb of the universe" (j^ag^adyonEE) and is the source of the petal sounds for the ch^akr^a-s beneath it.

amret^a अमृत

Nectar.

anaadE अनादि

Beginningless. Uncaused. That which is eternal. Consciousness is anaadE.

anaah^at^a अनहत

Unstruck. Refers to sound that is not caused by striking two objects together, which emanates from Supreme Intelligence (M^ah^at): naad^a and rechaa. Anaah^at^a is also the name of the fourth ch^akr^a, where naad^a is first heard.

andh^akoop^a अन्धकूप

Blind cave. The top third of the "cave of Br^ah-maa" located in the hollow space between the cerebral hemispheres.

antah^ak^ar^aN^a अन्तःकरण

The psychic organ. It contains four aspects: sensory mind (m^an^as^a), intellect (buddhE), awareness/memory (chEtt^a), and ego (ah^amkaar^a).

anubh^av^a अनुभव

Our own experience (in the first two lEng^a-s) or intuition (in the third lEng^a).

☙ **apaan^a** अपान

A form of praaN^a that is needed to regulate the flow of energy in the first and second ch^akr^a-s. Whenever the fumes arising from apaan^a move above the second ch^akr^a, the effect is deleterious.

apavaad^a अपवाद

Retraction of a previous assertion. The second part of the method of VAdaant^a.

☙ **Ardh^anaarEEshv^ar^a** अर्धनारीश्वर

Symbol of solar-lunar balance. The deity Ardh^anaarEEshv^ar^a is portrayed with its left side as female (lunar) and its right side as male (solar). Ardh^anaarEEshv^ar^a rules over the sixth ch^akr^a, indicating that polarity has ended.

asht^adhaa अष्टधा

Eightfold. For example: asht^adhaa pr^akretE (eightfold nature).

☙ **aumkaar^a** ओम्कार

Repetition of the m^antr^a AUM.

av^asthaatr^ay^a अवस्थात्रय

The three states: waking, dream, and deep sleep.

av^adhoot^a अवधूत

A holy person with no dwelling, whose roof is the sky and bed is the earth.

avEdyaa अविद्या

Ignorance. According to VAdaant^a, the inability to discern between ego and Self.

Baal^a Br^ahmaa बाल ब्रह्मा

The child Br^ahmaa. Archetype of Divinity as a toddler.

BaaN^a lEng^a बाण लिंग

Arrow lEng^a. The second lEng^a.

🕉 **bEEjᵃ mᵃntrᵃ**   बीज मंत्र

Seed sound. A sound that germinates with repetition.

bEndu   बिंदु

Point. Dot.

Bhᵃgvat GEEtaa   भगवत् गीता

Lord's Song. A dialogue between the Supreme (as Lord Krishna) and Arjuna (as the best in humanity) in the midst of a great battle. It illuminates the most fundamental issues of life with a wisdom that has been acclaimed by people from many diverse cultures.

bhᵃktᵃ   भक्त

A devotee. One who has unconditional love for the Divine.

bhᵃktE   भक्ति

Devotion.

Bhrᵃmrᵃ guhaa   भ्रमर गुहा

Cave of the bumblebee. The lower third of Brᵃhmᵃrᵃndhrᵃ, the hollow space between the cerebral hemispheres.

Brᵃhmaa   ब्रह्मा

A manifestation of ShᵃktE in charge of creation. The other two manifestations of the trinity are VEShNu (preservation) and MahAshvarᵃ (transformation).

Brᵃhmaakaashᵃ   ब्रह्माकाश

Yellow *aakaashᵃ*.

Brᵃhmᵃdvaar   ब्रह्मद्वार

The door of Brᵃhmaa. The entrance to the right channel in the first chᵃkrᵃ.

🕉 **Brᵃhmᵃ muhoortᵃ**   ब्रह्म मुहूर्त

The time of the gods. The period of approximately 1.5 hours before sunrise when energy

is most pure and therefore spiritual work is maximally beneficial.

Brᵃhmᵃn   ब्रह्मन्

A synonym for Tᵃt, Consciousness—the substratum of all that is. Not to be confused with the deity Brᵃhmaa.

🕉 **Brᵃhmᵃrᵃndhrᵃ**   ब्रह्मरन्ध्र

The hollow space (pool of *aakaashᵃ*) between the two hemispheres of the cerebral cortex leading to the tenth gate. Synonymous with "cave of Brᵃhmaa."

buddhE   बुद्धि

Intellect. One of the four aspects of antahᵃkᵃrᵃNᵃ.

🕉 **chᵃkrᵃ**   चक्र

Wheel. A vortex of spinning energy in the subtle field. There are seven major chᵃkrᵃ-s.

chEddaakaashᵃ   चिदाकाश

A special *aakaashᵃ* available in R7:4 that aids in attaining bhᵃktE sᵃmaadhE.

chEtrENEE   चित्रिणी

The left channel of sushumnaa naaDEE.

chEttᵃ   चित

Memory.

dᵃmᵃroo   डमरु

A two-sided drum of ShEvᵃ.

DaakEnEE   डाकिनी

A sister power of KunDᵃlEnEE that resides in the first chᵃkrᵃ.

darshᵃnᵃ   दर्शन

Viewing. Indian classical philosophy contains six different viewpoints (darshᵃnᵃ-s). The term also means to sit quietly in the presence of a holy person in order to absorb their energy.

dAvª देव

A male deity.

dAvªdªttª देवदत्त

One of the ten praaɴª-s. Facilitates yawning.

DAvªnaagªrEE देवनागरी

The language of the gods. It is the most widely used script for the Sªmskretª language. It is also used for Hindi.

DAvEE देवी

A female deity.

dhªnªnjªyª धनंचय

One of the ten praaɴª-s. Facilitates swelling in a corpse and is the last praaɴª to leave the body at death.

dhªrmª धर्म

Laws that support the universe. Spiritual evolution requires that we follow our own unique path in a righteous, dutiful (dharmic) manner in all aspects of life.

dhyaanª ध्यान

Meditation.

dukhª दुःख

Suffering.

dvaarªpaalª द्वारपाल

Doorkeeper. In both the right and left channels there are three doorkeepers that block the fumes of apaanª.

Echhaa इच्छा

Desire or will. This is one of the three basic powers that lie dormant in the female principle (MªhaakuɴdªlɛɴEE) while the universe is in a cycle of rest. Together with the other two powers, knowledge (gyaanª) and action (kreyaa), it

initiates the next cycle of manifestation. Similarly, individual KuɴdªlɛɴEE causes rebirth due to unfulfilled desires.

Edaa इडा

Breathing channel that begins in the first chªkrª, criss-crosses the first six chªkrª-s, and terminates in the left nostril.

EEshaanª Shɛvª ईशान शिव

Manifestation of Shɛvª dwelling in the fourth chªkrª.

EEshª ईश

Abbreviation for EEshaanª Shɛvª.

EEshvªrª ईश्वर

Lord.

Etªrª lɛngª इतर लिंग

Other lɛngª. Other worldly—not pertaining to the world of the five senses (empirical world).

☉ Gªɴashª गणेश

The son of Shɛvª and his representative in the first chªkrª. With a pot belly and the head of an elephant, he is ever happy. Gªɴashª also stands for security and memory. Known to overcome obstacles.

Gªngaa गँगा

The river Ganges. Symbolizes the left channel.

☉ guɴª गुण

A part of eightfold nature that is subtler than the elements. There are three guɴª-s: tªmªs (inertia, darkness), rªjªs (transformative energy), and sªtvª (purity, light).

guNaatEEtª गुणातीत

Master of the three qualities (guɴª-s), who has the capacity to control the guɴª-s rather than be controlled by them.

⊚ guru गुरु
Remover of ignorance. A teacher of spiritual wisdom.

gyaan^a ज्ञान
Knowledge.

gyaanAndrEy^a ज्ञानेन्द्रिय
Sense organs.

gyaanEE ज्ञानी
One who knows. The reference is to metaphysical wisdom. A gyaanEE is one who has attained moksh^a.

HaakEnEE हाकिनी
A sister power of KuNd^alEnEE that resides in the sixth ch^akr^a.

H^anumaan^a हनुमान
A representative of ShEv^a whose m^antr^a removes fear in the second ch^akr^a. He is the only deity in the Tantric pantheon who is celibate. H^anumaan^a is a model of unconditional love through his devotion to the Divine couple SEEtaa and Raam^a.

Hret^a p^adm^a हृत पद्म
The lotus of the heart. A small lunar ch^akr^a that is situated within the fourth ch^akr^a between the fifth and seventh microchakras.

j^ag^adyonEE जगद्योनी
Womb of the universe. Used to refer to the a-k^a-th^a triangle and the basic sounds from which the universe was created.

j^aD^a जड़
Root.

j^al^a जल
Water.

j^ap^a जप
Repetition (usually of a m^antr^a).

jaagret^a av^asthaa जागृत अवस्था
Waking state. One of the three states—the others are dream and deep sleep.

⊚ jEEv^a जीव
The entity that evolves through countless cycles of birth-death-rebirth in the material world. In the human birth it has the potential to realize that it is Aatmaa.

k^apaal^a कपाल
Skull.

⊚ k^arm^a कर्म
Action in any form: physical, verbal, or mental.

k^armAndrEy^a कर्मेन्दिय
Organs of action.

KaakEnEE काकिनी
A sister power of KuNd^alEnEE that resides in the fourth ch^akr^a.

kaam^a काम
Desire. Usually sensual/sexual desire. It is a subdivision of EchhAA.

Kaam^adhAnu कामधेनु
A mythical cow that is located above the som^a ch^akr^a and feeds nectar into it from its udders.

KaamAshv^ar^a कामेश्वर
The lord of desire. He is the representative of ShEv^a in the a-k^a-th^a triangle.

KaamAshv^arEE कामेश्वरी
The goddess of desire. She is the representative of Sh^aktE in the a-k^a-th^a triangle.

kaarᵃNᵃshᵃrEErᵃ कारण शरीर

The causal field. It is the locus of both Supreme Intelligence (Mᵃhᵃt) and of the thought bodies in humans. Anything that occurs in the physical field has its origin in the causal field.

☙ **khᵃndᵃ** खंड

An area within the first chᵃkrᵃ shaped like a downward-pointing triangle. All subtle nerves (naaDEE-s) originate here.

koormᵃ कूर्म

One of the ten praaNᵃ-s. Facilitates movement of eyelids.

krekᵃlᵃ कृकल

One of the ten praaNᵃ-s. Facilitates sneezing.

kreyaa क्रिया

Action. One of the three eternal powers of ShᵃktE: will, knowledge, action (Echhaa, gyaanᵃ, kreyaa).

krodhᵃ क्रोध

Anger.

kuNdᵃlᵃ कुण्डल

A curl.

☙ **KuNdᵃlEnEE** कुण्डलिनी

Potential energy.

LaakEnEE लाकिनी

A sister power of KuNdᵃlEnEE that resides in the third chᵃkrᵃ.

☙ **lEElaa** लीला

Play. By means of eightfold nature and transcendent awareness, ShᵃktE conducts the play of the universe.

☙ **lEngᵃ** लिंग

Mark. An egg shaped icon. Arguably, humanity's most ancient object of worship. A symbol of ShEvᵃ.

lokᵃ लोक

Plane of existence.

mᵃdhyᵃmaa मध्यमा

Intermediate. Middle. One of the four stages of sound.

mᵃhaa महा

Great.

MᵃhaakuNdᵃlEnEE महाकुण्डलिनी

The great potential of dynamic energy. When the universe is in a cycle of rest, MᵃhaakuNdᵃlEnEE lies in the embrace of Pᵃrᵃmᵃ ShEvᵃ (Stasis).

MᵃhaashᵃktE महाशक्ति

The great dynamic energy.

MahAshvarᵃ महेश्वर

Great Lord. A name of ShEvᵃ as ruler of the early brain.

Mᵃhᵃt महत्

Supreme Intelligence. The finest aspect of ShᵃktE (a contraction of Mᵃhaa tᵃtvᵃ).

mᵃnᵃsᵃ मनस

Sensory mind.

mᵃNEpurᵃ मणिपुर

Jewel of fire. The name of the third chᵃkrᵃ.

☙ **mᵃntrᵃ** मंत्र

Mind expander. A sonic releaser of innate patterns of energy in the subtle field.

maalaa माला

Rosary.

maayaa माया
Illusion.

☼ **moksh^a** मोक्ष
Liberation from the cycle of birth, death, and rebirth.

moolaadhaar^a मूलाधार
Root support. The name of the first ch^akr^a.

☼ **mown^a** मौन
Silence.

mudraa मुद्रा
A gesture.

☼ **naad^a** नाद
An internal sound. Audible to one who has internalized the sense of hearing.

☼ **naad^a yog^a** नाद योग
Ten classical sounds (naad^a-s) are heard by a naad^a yogi. After the naad^a-s have been heard by the yogi, the capacity to produce pr^aN^av^a emerges.

☼ **naaDEE** नाड़ी
Subtle nerve. There are 72,000 naaDEE-s in the feeling body, according to the most commonly cited estimate. The three principal ones are Edaa, pEng^al^a, and sushumnaa.

naag^a नाग
One of the ten praaN^a-s. It facilitates coughing, belching, and vomiting.

naam^a नाम
Name.

nAtE नेति
Not this. The saying "nAtE, nAtE" (Not this! Not this!) is used to implement retraction of previous assertions in the method of VAdaant^a.

nErguN^a निर्गुण
Without quality—formless.

nErjh^ar^a guha निर्झर गुहा
Ripple-free cave. Calm cave. Middle third of the hollow cave (Br^ahm^ar^andhr^a) between the two cerebral hemispheres.

nIshk^army^a नैष्कर्म्य
Action that has become nonaction. Occurs only in advanced aspirants. Acts that normally have karmic consequences have none because they are done with neither desire nor attachment.

oj^as ओजस
Life force of a higher vibration.

p^admaasan^a पद्मासन
Lotus posture with right leg over left. Classical seated posture for meditation.

p^akhaav^aj^a पखावज
Royal drum of ancient India.

p^anch^a k^anchuka-s पंचकंचुका
Five limitations. The means of implementing illusion and hiding Consciousness from mortals.

    kaal^a काल
    Time.
    k^alaa कला
    Division. Fractionation.
    vEdyaa विद्या
    Knowledge.
    raag^a राग
    Desire. Attachment.
    nEy^atE नियति
    Karmic laws of cause and effect.

P^anch^av^aktr^a पंचवक्त्र
ShEv^a with five heads. Resides in fifth ch^akr^a.

ⓖ pᵃraa परा
Beyond. Beyond the three fields.

paapᵃ पाप
A blemished act.

pᵃrᵃm परम्
Absolute. Supreme.

Pᵃrᵃmaatmaa परमात्मा
Supreme Consciousness (Advɪtᵃ Vᴀdaantᵃ).

Pᵃrᵃmᵃ Shᴇvᵃ परमशिव
Supreme Shᴇvᵃ. Consciousness. Stasis.

pᵃshyᵃntᴇ पश्यन्ति
The second stage of the four stages of sound: pᵃraa, pᵃshyᵃntᴇ, mᵃdhyᵃmaa, and vɪkhᵃrᴇᴇ.

pᴇngᵃlᵃ पिंगल
Breathing channel that begins in the first chᵃkrᵃ, criss-crosses the first six chᵃkrᵃ-s, and terminates in the right nostril.

pᵃrkaashᵃ प्रकाश
Effulgent light. The light in the nonmaterial fields. Illuminates dreams.

pᵃrkretᴇ प्रकृति
Nature. Usually contrasted with spirit (purushᵃ). Eightfold nature (ashtᵃdhaa pᵃrkretᴇ) contains the five elements and three guɴᵃ-s.

ⓖ prᵃɴᵃvᵃ प्रणव
Subtlest sound frequency heard internally.

prᵃpᵃnchᵃ प्रपंच
For the five (senses). The empirical world is referred to as prᵃpᵃnchᵃ. Continuous involvement with the senses must cease in order to intuit Reality.

prᵃtyaahaarᵃ प्रत्याहार
Internalizing the senses. Normally, the senses are directed toward the external environment. With practice, they may be directed inward.

ⓖ praaɴᵃ प्राण
Vitality. The vital energy that pervades the universe.

praaɴaayaamᵃ प्राणायाम
Breathing exercises that enhances vitality.

ⓖ praarᵃbdhᵃ प्रारब्ध
That portion of the accumulated karmᵃ that determines the current birth.

prethvᴇᴇ tᵃtvᵃ पृथ्वी तत्व
Earth element. The most dense of the five elements.

purushᵃ पुरुष
Awareness of individuality. Awareness that spirit is distinct from matter (prᵃkretᴇ). Will.

ⓖ rᵃjᵃs रजस्
Transformative energy. One of the three guɴᵃ-s.

raagᵃ राग
Attraction. Attachment.

Raakᴇnᴇᴇ राकिनी
A sister power of Kuɴdᵃlᴇnᴇᴇ who resides in the second chᵃkrᵃ.

Raamᵃ राम
An incarnation of Vᴇshɴu. He and his wife Sᴇᴇtaa ruled during the Trᴀtaa yugᵃ. He is revered as the ideal man of integrity.

rechaa ऋचा
The creative wisdom immanent in the causal field.

reSHE ऋषि

An unusually gifted person who was able to hear the eternal wisdom omnipresent in the universe. The wisdom received by the reSHE-s was later written and known as the VAdª-s.

☬ retª ऋत

Natural law. That which is automatically obeyed. Examples are planetary movement and the autonomic nervous system.

roopª रूप

Form.

Rudrª रुद्र

Representative of SHEVª in the third chªkrª. Rudrª in meditation indicates that the ego is in a state of surrender to the second lEngª.

rudraakshª maalaa रूद्राध माला

Rosary of rudraakshª beads, which symbolize the eyes (akshª) of SHEVª. The beads are made from the seeds of the blue-marble tree (*Elaeocarpus ganitrus*).

sªguNª सगुण

With quality or form.

sªhªsraarª सहस्रार

Thousand. The name of the seventh chªkrª lotus.

☬ sªmaadhE समाधि

A state of the seventh chªkrª wherein ego temporarily merges with the Self while in meditation and breathing ceases.

sªmaanª समान

Name of praaNª in the third chªkrª.

sªmchEtª kªrmª संचित कर्म

Accumulated kªrmª. Accumulation accrues across all the lives of the jEEVª.

sªmsaarª संसार

That which moves naturally. Refers to our universe in which the cycle of birth, death, and rebirth occurs.

sªmskaarª संस्कार

The memory trace that results from any experience. It is formed simultaneously in all three fields: physical, subtle, and causal.

☬ sªnaatanª dhªrmª सनातन धर्म

Eternal laws of the universe.

SªrªsvªtEE सरस्वती

Goddess of fine arts and creativity.

☬ Sªt सत्

Being. Truth. Usually used to refer to Consciousness.

☬ sªtvª सत्व

The guNª of light and purity. Satvic thoughts, feelings, and acts refine the chªkrª minds.

sªtyªm, shEVªm, sundªrªm
सत्यम् शिवम् सुन्दरम्

Truth, Goodness, Beauty.

saadhªkª साधक

Aspirant. A practitioner of the higher spiritual laws.

saadhªnaa साधना

Practices that aid spiritual growth.

saadhu साधु

Advanced saadhªkª.

SaakEnEE साकिनी

A sister power of KuNdªlEnEE that resides in the fifth chªkrª.

ⓢ **saakshEE** साक्षी
Witness. Leads to Consciousness.

Saamkhyᵃ सांख्य
The oldest philosophical system of India.

ⓢ **Sᵃmskretᵃ** संस्कृत
Well refined. Perfected language.

SEddhE सिद्धि
A power. A parapsychological ability.

SEEtaa सीता
Wife of Raamᵃ. Born of earth.

ⓢ **ShᵃktE** शक्ति
Vibrancy. The dynamic and creative force of the universe. The Supreme Intelligence.

ⓢ **ShEvᵃ** शिव
Auspicious. Stasis.

ShEvᵃdvaarᵃ शिवद्वार
The door of ShEvᵃ. Located in the first chᵃkrᵃ at the entrance to the central channel.

ⓢ **shrutE** श्रुति
Basic sound frequencies of the universe. Also refers to sacred scriptures.

shuddhᵃ शुद्ध
Pure.

shunyᵃ शून्य
Void.

somᵃ सोम
A minor chᵃkrᵃ between the sixth and seventh chᵃkrᵃ-s.

sookshmᵃ shᵃrEErᵃ सूक्ष्म शरीर
The subtle body that contains the chᵃkrᵃ-s.

sooryᵃ सूर्य
Sun.

ⓢ **sooryᵃ aakaashᵃ** सूर्य आकाश
Solar (golden) *aakaashᵃ*. Finest of all *aakaashᵃ*-s. It is stored in the seventh chᵃkrᵃ and utilized in the seventh microchakras.

sthoolᵃ shᵃrEErᵃ स्थूल शरीर
The gross field of physical matter; the empirical world.

sukhᵃ सुख
Happiness.

ⓢ **sushumnaa** सुषुम्ना
Cluster of three channels: vᵃjrENEE, chEtrENEE, and ShEvᵃ naaDEE.

sushuptE avasthaa सुशुप्ती अवस्था
Deep sleep state.

svᵃbhavᵃ स्वभाव
Our true nature (Consciousness).

ⓢ **svᵃrᵃ** स्वर
Tone in a musical scale. Also, sound of breath in either nostril as examined in svᵃrᵃ yogᵃ.

svᵃtᵃntryᵃ स्वतन्त्रय
Established in Self. One who has attained liberation.

svᵃdhEshтHaanᵃ स्वधिष्ठान
Self-supported. Name of the second chᵃkrᵃ.

Svᵃyambhoo lEngᵃ स्वयंभू लिंग
Self-born (one of the thousand names of ShEvᵃ). The name of the first lEngᵃ.

svapnᵃ avᵃsthaa स्वप्न अवस्था
Dream state.

ॐ tᵃmᵃs तमस्
Inertia. Ignorance. Darkness. Most dense of the three guNᵃ-s.

tᵃnmaatraa तन्मात्रा
Subtle sensations that are precursors to the elements.

ॐ Tᵃntrᵃ तंत्र
Methods for expanding awareness of body and mind, which protect the aspirant from domination by the empirical world. The two chief methods are mᵃntrᵃ and yᵃntrᵃ.

tᵃpᵃs तपस्
Performance of spiritual practices to increase light.

Tᵃt तत्
That. Refers to Consciousness.

ॐ tᵃtvᵃ तत्व
Element (*earth, water, fire, air, aakaashᵃ*). A principle.

tᵃtvaatEEtᵃ तत्वातीत
Master of the elements. Liberated from the five elemental minds.

TEthE तिथि
A lunar day.

udaanᵃ उदान
Name of praaNᵃ in the fifth chᵃkrᵃ.

upaasᵃnaa उपासना
Worship.

Upᵃ nESHᵃd उपनिषद्
Ten principal Upᵃ nESHᵃd-s are the foundational scriptures of Advᵻtᵃ VAdaantᵃ.

vᵃjrENEE वज्रिणी
The right channel of sushumnaa naaDEE.

vᵃrᵃ mudraa वर मुद्रा
Blessing gesture.

Vaagᵃ dAvEE वागदेवी
Goddess of speech, a form of SᵃrᵃsvᵃtEE.

Vaak वाक्
Speech.

vaayu tᵃtvᵃ वायु तत्व
Air element.

ॐ VAdᵃ वेद
Sacred knowledge. Ancient scriptures originally heard by the reSHE-s. They are the foundation of the Vedic tradition.

ॐ VAdaantᵃ वेदान्त
End of the VAdᵃ-s. Culmination of Vedic wisdom.

vEchaarᵃ विचार
Discernment. The practice of discerning between ego and Self.

vEdyaa mudraa विद्या मुद्रा
A gesture symbolizing the bestowal of knowledge.

VESHNu विष्णु
The Preserver.

VESHNudvaarᵃ विष्णुद्वार
The door of VESHNu. The entrance to the left channel in the first chᵃkrᵃ.

vEshuddhᵃ विशुद्ध
Ultra pure. The name of the fifth chᵃkrᵃ.

vEsphoTᵃ विस्फोट
An explosive sound.

vɪkhᵃrEE वैखरी

Audible. The grossest of the four stages of sound.

vrettE वृत्ति

A thought wave.

vyaanᵃ व्यान

One of the five major praaNᵃ-s. It pervades the whole body.

vyᵃvᵃhaarᵃ व्यवहार

Apparent reality, constructed when the five senses are directed outward. The empirical world.

☙ **yᵃntrᵃ** यंत्र

A geometrical pattern used in contemplation and meditation. As mᵃntrᵃ calms the left hemisphere, yᵃntrᵃ calms the right hemisphere.

☙ **yoga** योग

Union.

☙ **yugᵃ** युग

A cosmic age. Four yugᵃ-s form a major subcycle within larger cycles:

    Sᵃtyᵃ सत्य
      (1,728,000 years)
    TrAtaa त्रेता
      (1,296,000 years)
    Dvaaprᵃ द्वापर
      (864,000 years)
    ☙**KᵃlE** कलि
      (432,000 years)

Human awareness of inner Divinity decreases as the cycle proceeds from Satyᵃ yugᵃ to KᵃlE yugᵃ.

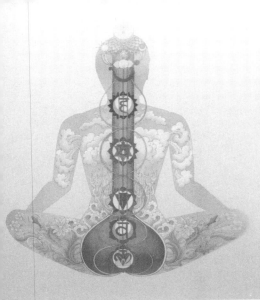

Notes

Chapter 1. Preparation for the InnerTuning Adventure

1. Trans. Sri Ātmanandendra.

2. Sri Swami Satchidānandendra, *The Method of the Vedanta: A Critical Account of the Advaita Tradition*, trans. A. J. Alston (London and New York: Kegan Paul, 1989), 89.

3. trans. Sri Ātmanandendra.

4. Sri Ātmanandendra, personal communication.

5. Gerard J. Larson, and Ram S. Bhattacharya, eds., *Sāṃkhya: A Dualist Tradition in Indian Philosophy* (Princeton, N.J.: Princeton University Press, 1987).

6. Robert Nadeau and Menos Kafatos, *The Non-Local Universe: The New Physics and Matters of the Mind* (New York: Oxford University Press, 1999), 2.

7. Evan J. Squires, cited in K. A. Choquette, *The Holonomic Paradigm: Biophysics, Consciousness, and Parapsychology* (www.Xlibris.com, 2001), 143.

8. Robert G. Jahn and Brenda J. Dunne, *Science of the Subjective* (Princeton, N. J.: Princeton Engineering Anomalies Research, School of Engineering and Applied Science, Princeton University, 1997).

9. B. Alan Wallace, *The Taboo of Subjectivity: Toward a New Science of Consciousness* (New York: Oxford University Press, 2000).

Chapter 2. The Cosmic Play

1. This interview was conducted in the early 1980s by Placido P. D'Souza and was retrieved August 13, 2002, from www.rediff.com/news/jan/29sagan.htm.

2. For additional discussion of yugᵃ-s see, for example, Arthur L. Basham, *The Wonder That Was India: A Survey of the Culture of the Indian Sub-Continent Before the Coming of the Muslims* (1954; reprint, New York: Grove, 1969), 320 ff.

3. Swāmi Pratyāgātmānanda, *Japasūtram: The Science of Creative Sound* (Madras, India: Ganesh & Co, 1971), 10–11.

4. http://dictionary.reference.com

5. Paul D. MacLean, *The Triune Brain in Evolution: Role in Paleocerebral Functions* (New York: Plenum Press, 1990).

6. Sri Ātmanandendra, personal communication.

Chapter 3. The Subtle Field

1. Most of the material in this chapter is based on classical sources.

2. Shyam S. Goswami, *Laya Yoga: An Advanced Method of Concentration* (London: Routledge & Kegan Paul, 1980).

3. Gopi Krishna, *Kundalini: The Evolutionary Energy in Man* (Berkeley, Calif.: Shambhala, 1971).

4. Robert E. Hume, trans., *The Thirteen Principal Upanishads* (1921; reprint, Madras: Oxford University Press, 1949).

5. Harish Johari, *Chakras: Energy Centers of Transformation* (Rochester, Vt.: Destiny Books, 1987), 14.

6. Swāmi Pratyāgātmānanda, *Japasūtram: The Science of Creative Sound*, 33.

7. Goswami, *Laya Yoga: An Advanced Method of Concentration*.

8. Rupert Sheldrake, *A New Science of Life: The Hypothesis of Formative Causation* (London: Blond & Briggs, 1981).

9. Masaru Emoto, *The Hidden Messages in Water*, trans. D. A. Thayne (Hillsboro, Ore.: Beyond Words Publishing, 2004).

10. Sir John G. Woodroffe, *The Serpent Power: Being the Sat Cakra Nirupana and Paduka Pancaka: Two Works on Laya-Yoga, Translated from the Sanskrit, with Introduction and Commentary*, 11th ed. (Madras, India: Ganesh, 1978).

11. Johari, *Chakras: Energy Centers of Transformation*, 141.

Chapter 4. Basic Microchakra Dynamics

1. Bhᵃgvat GEEtaa, 9:26, trans. Sri Shyamji Bhatnagar.

2. Bhᵃgvat GEEtaa, 9:34, trans. Sri Ātmanandendra.

3. Bhᵃgvat GEEtaa, 7:21, trans. Sri Ātmanandendra.

4. Deut. 6:5 New Revised Standard Version.

5. Col. 3:14–16 New Revised Standard Version.

6. David B. Chamberlain. Retrieved December 28, 2002, from www.birthpsychology.com/life before/fetalsense.html.

7. Ibid.

8. Barbara Harper, *Gentle Birth Choices*. Rochester, Vt.: Healing Arts Press, 1994.

9. Ibid., 33.

10. Ibid., 43.

11. Frederick Leboyer, *Birth without Violence* (New York: Knopf, 1975), 4 f.

12. Retrieved January 4, 2003, from www.birthpsychology.com/violence/chamberlain1.html.

13. Susan L. Diamond, *Hard Labor* (New York: Tom Doherty Associates, Forge, 1998).

14. Henci Goer, *The Thinking Woman's Guide to Better Birth* (New York: Penguin Putnam, Perigee, 1999).

15. D. Jackson, *Three in a Bed: The Benefits of Sleeping with Your Baby* (1989; reprint, New York: Bloomsbury, 1999), 22.

16. Abraham H. Maslow, *Toward a Psychology of Being* (Princeton, N.J.: Van Nostrand, 1962).

Chapter 5. Openings and Blocks in the First Lᴇɴɢᵃ

1. Lord Acton, British historian (1834–1902).

Chapter 6. Openings and Blocks in the Second Lᴇɴɢᵃ

1. Bhᵃgvat Gᴇᴇtaa, 18:23–24, trans. Ātmanandendra.

Chapter 8. Advanced Microchakra Dynamics

1. Carl G. Jung, *The Portable Jung*, ed. J. Campbell, trans. R. F. C. Hull (New York: Viking Penguin, 1971).
2. Sheldrake, *A New Science of Life: The Hypothesis of Formative Causation* (London: Blond & Briggs, 1981).
3. William James, *Principles of Psychology*, vol. 1 (1890; reprint, New York: Dover Publications, 1950), 121.
4. Sri Swami Satchidānandendra, *Intuition of Reality,* 2nd ed. (Karnātaka, India: Adhyātma Prakāsha Kāryālaya, 1995).
5. Eugene T. Gendlin, *Focusing,* 2nd rev. ed (New York: Bantam, 1982).
6. Susan Goldberg, *Attachment and Development* (London and New York: Oxford University Press, 2000), 14.
7. Andrew N. Meltzoff and Jean Decety, "What Imitation Tells Us about Social Cognition: A Rapprochement Between Developmental Psychology and Cognitive Neuroscience," *Phil. Trans. R. Soc.* London B, 2003, 358, 491–500. Published online 14 February 2003.
8. Roberto Assagioli, *Psychosynthesis: A Manual of Principles and Techniques* (New York: Hobbs, Dorman, 1965), 22.
9. Jaak Panksepp, *Affective Neuroscience: The Foundations of Human and Animal Emotions* (New York: Oxford University Press, 1998), 337.
10. Candace B. Pert, *Molecules of Emotion: Why You Feel The Way You Feel* (New York: Scribner, 1997), 257.
11. Richard S. Lazarus, *Emotion and Adaptation* (New York: Oxford University Press, 1991), 191.
12. Ibid.
13. Silvan S. Tomkins, *Affect, Imagery, Consciousness,* vol. I. (New York: Springer, 1962), 183.

Chapter 9. Affects and the Three Lᴇɴɢᵃ-s

1. Carroll E. Izard, *The Psychology of Emotions* (New York: Plenum, 1991), 132 f.
2. Ibid., 128.
3. Panksepp, *Affective Neuroscience: The Foundations of Human and Animal Emotions,* 296.
4. Ibid., 287.
5. Charles Darwin, "The Expression of the Emotions in Man and Animals," edited by Francis Darwin (1872; reprint in *The Works of Charles Darwin*, vol. 23, edited by P. H. Barrett, and R. B. Freeman (New York: New York University Press, 1989), 226 ff.
6. Charles Darwin, *The Works of Charles Darwin,* vol. 23, 187 f.
7. Panksepp, *Affective Neuroscience: The Foundations of Human and Animal Emotions,* 189 f.

8. Manfred Holodynski and Wolfgang Friedlmeier, *Development of Emotions and Emotion Regulation,* trans. J. Harrow. (New York: Springer, 2006), 106.

9. Tomkins, *Affect, Imagery, Consciousness,* vol. II, 3.

10. Panksepp, *Affective Neuroscience: The Foundations of Human and Animal Emotions,* 261 ff.

11. Izard, *The Psychology of Emotions,* 257.

12. Panksepp, *Affective Neuroscience: The Foundations of Human and Animal Emotions,* 301.

13. Ibid.

14. Izard, *The Psychology of Emotions,* 314 f.

Chapter 10. Integrating the Three Bodies

1. Ernst L. Rossi, and B. M. Lippincott, "The Wave Nature of Being: Ultradian Rhythms and Mind-Body Communication," in D. Lloyd and E. L. Ross, eds., *Ultradian Rhythms in Life Processes: An Inquiry into Fundamental Principles of Chronobiology and Psychobiology* (London and New York: Springer-Verlag, 1992).

2. Ibid.

3. Roberto Refinetti, *Circadian Physiology* (London: Taylor & Francis, CRC Press, 2000).

4. Uwe Hentschel, Gudmund Smith, and Juris G. Draguns, eds., *The Roots of Perception: Individual Differences in Information Processing within and Beyond Awareness* (Amsterdam and New York: Elsevier, 1986).

5. Gendlin, *Focusing.*

6. Bhᵃgvat GEEtaa, 6:11–30, trans. Sri Ātmanandendra.

7. Sri Swami Satchidānandendra, *The Method of the Vedanta: A Critical Account of the Advaita Tradition,* trans. A. J. Alston. (London and New York: Kegan Paul, 1989), 146 f.

8. Sri Swami Satchidānandendra, *Introductions (to Vedānta texts),* (Karnātaka, India: Adhyātma Prakāsha Kāryālaya, 1996), 21.

9. Sri Swami Satchidānandendra, *The Method of the Vedanta,* 83.

10. Jiddu Krishnamurti, *Reflections on the Self,* ed. R. Martin (Chicago: Open Court, 1997), 184.

11. Jiddu Krishnamurti, *This Light in Oneself: True Meditation* (Boston and London: Shambhala, 1999), 31.

12. Ibid., 33.

13. Ibid., 35.

14. Ibid., 113 f.

Chapter 11. Subjective Science

1. Michael Singer, *The Legacy of Positivism* (London and New York: MacMillan, Palgrave, 2005), 9.

2. Edwin G. Boring, *A History of Experimental Psychology,* 2nd ed. (New York: Appleton-Century-Crofts, 1957), 708.

3. Montz Schlick, "Positivism and Realism," trans. P. Heath, in S. Sarkar, ed., *Logical Empiricism at its Peak* (1932; reprint, New York and London: Garland, 1996), 37 f.

4. Percy W. Bridgman, *The Logic of Modern Physics* (New York: Macmillan, 1927), 5.

5. Ibid., 9 f.

6. Percy W. Bridgman, "The Present State of Operationalism," in *The Validation of Scientific Theories*, edited by P. G. Frank. (New York: Collier, 1961), 76.

7. Charles W. Tolman, ed., *Positivism in Psychology: Historical and Contemporary Problems* (New York: Springer-Verlag, 1992), 1.

8. Hentschel, Smith, and Draguns, eds., *The Roots of Perception: Individual Differences in Information Processing within and Beyond Awareness.*

9. Gendlin, *Focusing,* 11.

10. Such as Amit Goswami, R. E. Reed, and M. Goswami, *The Self-Aware Universe: How Consciousness Creates the Material World* (New York: Jeremy Tarcher, Putnam, 1995).

11. Dana Zohar and I. N. Marshall, *The Quantum Self: Human Nature and Consciousness Defined by the New Physics* (New York: William Morrow, 1990).

12. Jahn and Dunne, *Science of the Subjective.*

13. Wallace, *The Taboo of Subjectivity: Toward a New Science of Consciousness.*

14. Joseph F. Rychlak, *A Philosophy of Science for Personality Theory* (Boston: Houghton Mifflin, 1968).

Appendix A. Advitᵃ Vadaantᵃ

1. Sri Swami Satchidānanandendra, *The Method of the Vedanta: A Critical Account of the Advaita Tradition,* trans. A. J. Alston (London and New York: Kegan Paul, 1989).

2. Ibid.

3. Ibid., 101.

4. Sri Ātmanandendra, personal communication.

5. Sri Swami Satchidānanandendra, *The Method of the Vedanta: A Critical Account of the Advaita Tradition,* 425.

6. Ibid., 48.

7. Sri Ātmanandendra, personal communication.

8. Sri Swami Satchidānanandendra, *The Method of the Vedanta: A Critical Account of the Advaita Tradition,* 51.

9. Ibid., 1 f.

10. Woodroffe, *The Serpent Power: Being the Sat Cakra Nirupana and Paduka Pancaka: Two Works on Laya-Yoga, Translated from the Sanskrit, with Introduction and Commentary,* 11th ed.

11. Sri Swami Satchidānanandendra, *The Method of the Vedanta: A Critical Account of the Advaita Tradition,* 95 f.

12. Sri Ātmanandendra, personal communication.

13. Sri Swami Satchidānanandendra, *The Method of the Vedanta: A Critical Account of the Advaita Tradition,* 106.

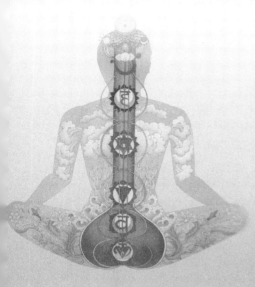

Bibliography

Assagioli, Roberto. *Psychosynthesis: A Manual of Principles and Techniques.* New York: Hobbs, Dorman, 1965.

Basham, Arthur L. *The Wonder That Was India: A Survey of the Culture of the Indian Sub-Continent Before the Coming of the Muslims.* 1954. Reprint, New York: Grove, 1969.

Boring, Edwin G. *A History of Experimental Psychology.* 2nd ed. New York: Appleton-Century-Crofts, 1957.

Bridgman, Percy W. *The Logic of Modern Physics.* New York: Macmillan, 1927.

———. "The Present State of Operationalism." In *The Validation of Scientific Theories.* Edited by P. G. Frank. New York: Collier, 1961.

Choquette, Keith A. *The Holonomic Paradigm: Biophysics, Consciousness, and Parapsychology.* www.Xlibris.com, 2001.

Darwin, Charles. "The Expression of the Emotions in Man and Animals." Edited by Francis Darwin. 1872. Reprint in *The Works of Charles Darwin,* vol. 23. Edited by P. H. Barrett, and R. B. Freeman. New York: New York University Press, 1989.

Diamond, Susan L. *Hard Labor.* 1996. Reprint, New York: Tom Doherty Associates, Forge, 1998.

Emoto, Masaru. *The Hidden Messages in Water.* Trans. D. A. Thayne. Hillsboro, Ore.: Beyond Words Publishing, 2004.

Gendlin, Eugene T. *Experiencing and the Creation of Meaning: A Philosophical and Psychological Approach to the Subjective.* Glencoe: Macmillan, The Free Press, 1962.

———. *Focusing.* 2nd rev. ed. New York: Bantam, 1982.

Goer, Henci. *The Thinking Woman's Guide to Better Birth.* New York: Penguin Putnam, Perigee, 1999.

Goldberg, Susan. *Attachment and Development.* London and New York: Oxford University Press, 2000.

Goswami, Amit, R. E. Reed, and M. Goswami. *The Self-Aware Universe: How Consciousness Creates the Material World.* New York: Jeremy Tarcher, Putnam, 1995.

Goswami, Shyam S. *Laya Yoga: An Advanced Method of Concentration.* London: Routledge & Kegan Paul, 1980.

Harper, Barbara. *Gentle Birth Choices*. Rochester, Vt.: Healing Arts Press, 1994.

Hentschel, Uwe, Gudmund Smith, and Juris G. Draguns, eds. *The Roots of Perception: Individual Differences in Information Processing within and Beyond Awareness*. Amsterdam and New York: Elsevier, 1986.

Holodynski, Manfred, and Wolfgang Friedlmeier. *Development of Emotions and Emotion Regulation*. Trans. J. Harrow. New York: Springer, 2006.

Hume, Robert E., trans. *The Thirteen Principal Upanishads*. 1921. Reprint, Madras: Oxford University Press, 1949.

Izard, Carroll E. *The Psychology of Emotions*. New York: Plenum, 1991.

Jackson, D. *Three in a Bed: The Benefits of Sleeping with Your Baby*. 1989. Reprint, New York: Bloomsbury, 1999.

Jahn, Robert G., and Brenda J. Dunne. *Science of the Subjective*. Princeton, N.J.: Princeton Engineering Anomalies Research, School of Engineering and Applied Science, Princeton University, 1997.

James, William. *Principles of Psychology,* vol. 1. 1890. Reprint, New York: Dover Publications, 1950.

Johari, Harish. *Chakras: Energy Centers of Transformation*. 2nd rev. ed. Rochester, Vt.: Destiny Books, 2000.

Jung, Carl G. *The Portable Jung*. Ed. J. Campbell. Trans. R. F. C. Hull. New York: Viking Penguin, 1971.

Krishna, Gopi. *Kundalini: The Evolutionary Energy in Man*. Berkeley, Calif.: Shambala, 1971.

Krishnamurti, Jiddu. *Reflections on the Self*. Ed. R. Martin. Chicago: Open Court, 1997.

———. *This Light in Oneself: True Meditation*. Boston and London: Shambhala, 1999.

Larson, Gerald J., and Ram S. Bhattacharya, eds. *Sāṃkhya: A Dualist Tradition in Indian Philosophy*. Princeton, N.J.: Princeton University Press, 1987.

Lazarus, Richard S. *Emotion and Adaptation*. New York: Oxford University Press, 1991.

Leboyer, Frederick. *Birth without Violence*. New York: Knopf, 1975.

MacLean, Paul D. *The Triune Brain in Evolution: Role in Paleocerebral Functions*. New York: Plenum Press, 1990.

Maslow, Abraham H. *Toward a Psychology of Being*. Princeton, N.J.: Van Nostrand, 1962.

Meltzoff, Andrew N., and Jean Decety. "What Imitation Tells Us about Social Cognition: A Rapprochement Between Developmental Psychology and Cognitive Neuroscience." *Phil. Trans. R. Soc.* London B, 2003. 358, 491–500. Published online 14 February 2003.

Nadeau, Robert, and Menas Kafatos. *The Non-Local Universe: The New Physics and Matters of the Mind*. New York: Oxford University Press, 1999.

Panksepp, Jaak. *Affective Neuroscience: The Foundations of Human and Animal Emotions*. New York: Oxford University Press, 1998.

Pert, Candace B. *Molecules of Emotion: Why You Feel The Way You Feel*. New York: Scribner, 1997.

Pratyāgātmānanda, Swāmi. *Japasūtram: The Science of Creative Sound*. Madras, India: Ganesh & Co, 1971.

Refinetti, Roberto. *Circadian Physiology*. London: Taylor & Francis, CRC Press, 2000.

Rossi, Ernst L., and B. M. Lippincott. "The Wave Nature of Being: Ultradian Rhythms and Mind-Body Communication." In D. Lloyd and E. L. Rossi, eds. *Ultradian Rhythms in Life Processes: An Inquiry into Fundamental Principles of Chronobiology and Psychobiology.* London and New York: Springer-Verlag, 1992.

Rychlak, Joseph F. *A Philosophy of Science for Personality Theory.* Boston: Houghton Mifflin, 1968.

Satchidānandendra, Sri Swami. *The Method of the Vedanta: A Critical Account of the Advaita Tradition.* Trans. A. J. Alston. London and New York: Kegan Paul, 1989.

———. *Intuition of Reality.* 2nd ed. Karnātaka, India: Adhyātma Prakāsha Kāryālaya, 1995.

———. *How to Recognize the Method of Vedānta.* 2nd ed. Karnātaka, India: Adhyātma Prakāsha Kāryālaya, 1995.

———. *Introductions (To Vedānta texts).* Karnātaka, India: Adhyātma Prakāsha Kāryālaya, 1996.

Schlick, Moritz. "Positivism and Realism." Trans. P. Heath. In S. Sarkar, ed. *Logical Empiricism at its Peak.* 1932. Reprint, New York and London: Garland, 1996.

Sheldrake, Rupert. *A New Science of Life: The Hypothesis of Formative Causation.* London: Blond & Briggs, 1981.

Singer, Michael. *The Legacy of Positivism.* London and New York: MacMillan, Palgrave, 2005.

Tolman, Charles W., ed. *Positivism in Psychology: Historical and Contemporary Problems.* New York: Springer-Verlag, 1992.

Tomkins, Silvan S. *Affect, Imagery, Consciousness,* vol. II. New York: Springer, 1962.

———. "Script Theory." In J. Aronoff, A. I. Rabin, and R. A. Zucker, eds. *The Emergence of Personality.* New York: Springer, 1987.

Wallace, B. Alan. *The Taboo of Subjectivity: Toward a New Science of Consciousness.* New York: Oxford University Press, 2000.

Woodroffe, John G, Sir. *The Serpent Power: Being the Sat Cakra Nirupana and Paduka Pancaka: Two Works on Laya-Yoga, Translated from the Sanskrit, with Introduction and Commentary.* 11th ed. Madras, India: Ganesh, 1978.

Zohar, Danah, and I. N. Marshall. *The Quantum Self: Human Nature and Consciousness Defined by the New Physics.* New York: William Morrow, 1990.

FOR MORE INFORMATION
ABOUT INNERTUNING

For more information on InnerTuning classes, work-
shops, retreats, and chᵃkrᵃ consultations or to purchase
CDs of sacred sound, please visit our website:

www.innertuning.com

Index

BOOKS OF RELATED INTEREST

Chakras
Energy Centers of Transformation
by Harish Johari

The Yoga of Truth
Jnana: The Ancient Path of Silent Knowledge
by Peter Marchand

**Yoga: Mastering the Secrets
of Matter and the Universe**
by Alain Daniélou

Secret Power of Tantrik Breathing
Techniques for Attaining Health,
Harmony, and Liberation
by Swami Sivapriyananda

Layayoga
The Definitive Guide to the Chakras
and Kundalini
by Shyam Sundar Goswami

The Yoga-Sūtra of Patañjali
A New Translation and Commentary
by Georg Feuerstein, Ph.D.

The Yoga of Spiritual Devotion
A Modern Translation
of the Narada Bhakti Sutras
by Prem Prakash

The Chakras in Shamanic Practice
Eight Stages of Healing and Transformation
by Susan J. Wright

Inner Traditions • Bear & Company
P.O. Box 388
Rochester, VT 05767
1-800-246-8648
www.InnerTraditions.com

Or contact your local bookseller

HOW TO USE THE
ENCLOSED CD OF SACRED SOUND

The CD included with this book is a recording of the SHREE RADHAY mantra, which helps to open the heart chᵃkrᵃ.

Meaning of the Mantra

The heart chᵃkrᵃ (our feeling center) is in constant communion with the thymus gland (the healer within). The heart chᵃkrᵃ is filled with unconditional love, devotion, kindness, and forgiveness. An open heart chᵃkrᵃ leads to radiant skin and/or the power of healing hands.

Chanting the RADHAY mantra helps to transform unexpressed feelings into energy that is available to the higher chakras. "Ra" is the sound of the sun, light, or fire that is concentrated in the solar plexus. "Dh" is a syllable that fully expands the diaphragm to allow fresh vital energy (prana) to come into the body. "A" is the sound of manifestation.

To Achieve the Optimum Effects of the Mantra

InnerTuning sounds are subtle yet powerful. Adhering to the following prerequisites will ensure the best results.

- Before working with the mantra, have a bowel movement as early as possible (best before dawn) and follow with a shower.
- Wearing clean loose clothing, sit facing east.
- Play the CD at a low volume with the eyes closed.*
- Listen to the CD for forty consecutive days. After forty days of learning the mantra, chant along.
- While chanting, breathe through the nose only. This will supply the purest prana to the mantra and enhance its effectiveness.
- After the recording finishes, continue sitting quietly for a few minutes.

These sounds are intended for internalizing the senses and should not be played for entertainment.

---

*Until the full protocol can be met, listen to this CD when your stomach is empty. Keep your eyes open and fixed downward at a single point.